God of the City
Thou art with thy people
In tenement and crowded street;
In surging, groping throngs
With leaded feet.
Behold thy people,
All gathered here, fenced-in,
Trapped by jagged, concrete walls;
Tied by ropes of steel, imprisoned.
Hear thy people.
They cry for Life and Liberation,
The entertainer says — "here"
In trumpet blast and misty light,
In the smell of smoke and wine
come and dine.
In dope and dance, here and there
In mistrust and fear.
What build we here a garden or a tomb?
O Divine Architect, make gates in the city;
Build windows of hope.
Lift the ceiling that we may behold the stars.
Help us to create the city beautiful,
By endowing it with a soul to care for thy people.
Thou hast said — Love thy neighbor.
Thou hast spoken the liberating Word.

> *Rt. Rev. Richard B. Martin*
> *Suffragan Bishop*
> *Diocese of Long Island*
> *1966—1974*

Dominion In the Sea

History of the Diocese of Long Island

John W. Davis
G. T. S. '45

By
The Reverend Canon John W. Davis
Historiographer
Diocese of Long Island

The Georgin Foundation
Hempstead, New York

Designed and Edited By

Kenneth J. Cynar and Donna M. DeStasio

Printed in the United States of America by
    Sentinel Printing Company
    Division of Hempstead Sentinel, Inc.
    Hempstead, New York

Dedicated to

my wife, Bette

and my son, Jed

who lived through every minute of this history.

FOREWORD

Dominion in the Sea surveys the first one hundred and ten years of the Diocese of Long Island. Its author, the Historiographer of the Diocese since 1966, is a priest and scholar educated and ordained on Long Island, and this labor of love is the fruit of years of diligent research. The interweaving of diocesan events and personalities with the salient features of local and national life gives the work expanded value and significance. It will serve as a mine of useful information to current readers as well as to later historians. It deserves a high place among diocesan histories as a commentary on the Church in society.

I congratulate Canon Davis on his achievement and I commend *Dominion in the Sea* to the joyful study of all Episcopalians in Long Island and to the public at large.

> Jonathan G. Sherman
> Bishop of Long Island

Author's Preface

Dominion in the Sea is a labor of love. Having been actively engaged in diocesan work for almost twenty years, as Director of Youth, College, and Camp DeWolfe, I had the wonderful opportunity to visit in and work with nearly every church in the Diocese. As I travelled from as far west as Brooklyn Heights and as far east as Greenport and Easthampton, I came to know the clergy and the devoted parishes; I shared in many of the trials and triumphs that each had as it met its community and ministered to its population. I came to see the intrinsic value of cooperative work as done by each Archdeaconry and as coordinated in the diocesan structure. Being an historian, I turned to the beginnings, and became involved in finding out how each parish and mission began, how they fit into the Diocese, and how the Diocese began and the way in which it worked. For eight years I followed the quest of understanding the Diocese and its constituent churches. I gathered as much information as I could find, sorted and classified the various elements, and attempted to put them in some kind of framework of reference that would make sense and that would be most easily comprehended by the average reader. The result of my research and my writing you have before you. For better or for worse it is a loving attempt to put into words the story of people of Long Island, the countless men and women, priests and lay persons who tried to make known their message to all who wanted to hear. It is simply the story of an island, the dominion in the sea, and the way in which this part of God's mission, the Diocese of Long Island ministered to it.

The history of the Diocese of Long Island has as its primary basis the *Journals* published annually by the Diocese. All one hundred and eight of them were used. Besides the proceedings of the Diocesan Conventions, they contain a great deal of other information. There are reports by commissions, committees, departments, together with financial and statistical data. Full use was made of all of these. The material culled from the *Journals* was verified and amplified by other sources, published and unpublished, many of which can be found in the Diocesan Archives. To better understand the community to which the Diocese ministered, I used all the accepted local histories together with many parish histories. Newspaper clippings and magazine articles helped round out the story.

Since so much in the Episcopal Church depends on the office of the Bishop, I have used as the general framework of reference the episcopates in the Diocese. There are five major divisions beginning with Bishop Littlejohn and ending with the election of Bishop Witcher. An examination of Long Island in 1868, the beginnings of the Episcopal Church in Colonial times, and the major expansion of the churches on Long Island is made as prelude to the establishment of the Diocese in 1868. Within the framework of the five episcopates three major themes are carried out: missionary extension, charitable works, and education. Other important emphases are woven into the fabric: the building of the Cathedral center, the advance of the city on the Island, the wars, the major social problems, and the political and financial pressures. With so much material available it is impossible to include everything the Diocese did. However, the major work of the Diocese is here. It is hoped that they may whet the appetite of many to seek further.

I want to take this opportunity to thank all those who have given me so much help and encouragement. Without them this history never would have become a reality. First and foremost I am indebted to Kenneth and Donna Cynar whose devotion and help made possible the minutia of long hours of conferences, reading, re-reading, correcting, editing and general layout and format. I appreciate the time given by Dr. Myron Luke and Dr. Milton W. Hopkins, and Bishop MacLean who was most helpful on the Melish case. Thanks to Jeannette Bennett who proofread all of the copy. I want to especially thank Jeannine Broomhall who typed the original manuscript and Norma Gallagher who retyped so much of the material. I also owe a debt of thanks to Ruth Hauggard, Joyce O'Connor, Valerie Hansen, Debra Csajko, Natalie Post, Marjorie Holm, Cindy Reid and Louise Schwarzchild who helped in this project. Last and certainly not least I am deeply appreciative of Howard C. Ris, my dear friend, who donated all the p-per for this first edition. It took the devoted effort of so many to make this *Dominion in the Sea* a reality. To all of them I can simply say thank you.

Writing the history of the Diocese of Long Island has given me much pleasure. My only hope is that you will enjoy reading it as much as I did writing it. And, that you too, like myself, will come to love and respect that portion of God's work known as the Diocese of Long Island, the Dominion in the Sea.

TABLE OF CONTENTS

Bishop's Foreward *4*

Preface *5*

Section I   The Setting: Long Island in 1868 . . . . *8*
  Chapter 1   The Two Long Islands *10*

Section II   A Golden Church for a Gilded Age, 1868-1901 . . . . . *20*
  Chapter 2   Land of the Pilgrims' Pride *22*
  Chapter 3   A Giant Awakens *34*
  Chapter 4   It Takes a While To Get Started *42*
  Chapter 5   The World, the Work, and Mrs. Stewart *56*
  Chapter 6   A Tale of Two Cities *72*
  Chapter 7   Ending is Beginning *91*

Section III   Alabaster Cities and Fruited Plains, 1901-1925 . . . . *98*
  Chapter 8   The Second Bishop *100*
  Chapter 9   The Quest for Social Justice *107*

Chapter 10   Between Two Worlds *121*

Chapter 11   Booze, Boom, and Blasphemy *136*

Section IV   Between Two Wars, 1925-1942 . . . . *148*

Chapter 12   A City Rector for a Country Constituency *150*

Chapter 13   Boom, Bust and Backtrack *156*

Chapter 14   Recovery and Retirement *163*

Section V   The Times They Are A'Changin, 1942-1966 . . . .*166*

Chapter 15   A Yet More Glorious Day *168*

Chapter 16   The Golden Evening *181*

Section VI   New World A'Comin, 1966- *194*

Chapter 17   A Time of Troubled Water *196*

Postword *221*

Bibliography *222*

Church of the Holy Trinity, Brooklyn. Mid-nineteenth century.

Section One

The Setting
Long Island in 1868

I WILL SET HIS DOMINION IN THE SEA.

Chapter One

The Two Long Islands

In 1868, Long Island wore two faces. It was a point between two divergent forces that were changing the American nation. Post-Civil War Long Island was emerging modern America. A tension existed between the old simple agrarian way of life and the modern urban and industrial order. The effects of modern industry, huge metropolitan cities and immense material progress were just beginning to be felt. Rural Long Island was becoming urban Long Island.

Long Island, a 125 mile stretch of land projecting from the mainland into the Atlantic Ocean, offered an interesting variety of settings. Wooded regions, sheltered caves, and sandy beaches edged the central open plains and scrub-oak barrens. Surrounded on four sides by water, the island's containment did not mean unity but rather a limited arena for a diffusion of life and work. In 1868, it was on the one hand the populous City of Brooklyn, huddled close to the tip of Manhattan Island, and on the other, small villages and hamlets spread throughout its length, pocketed in the fertile farmland or green woodland that extended from the city to Montauk Point.

DISTANT AND SET APART

Brooklyn, incorporated as an autonomous municipality for four short years, boasted a population of over 350,000 people confined within the small area of twenty-five square miles. Outside the city limits the rest of the 1,348 square miles amassed only a total population of a little over 100,000 who lived in virtual isolation from the growing city and from each other. One town in Queens County (which then included Nassau) came nearest to the population density of the city. Jamaica, a thriving crossroad town of 3,000, had as its chief attribute a long main street dotted with stores and taverns on which countless farmers and travelers went their way, but never stayed. The immediate outskirts of the Brooklyn City itself were still rural and bucolic. Flatbush, Gravesend and New Utrecht had farmlands with small towns and all aspects of country life. Queens presented much the same picture. Small villages dotted the vast expanse of farm and pastureland fringed with infant industry on its East River shores. Suffolk continued the agricultural nature of the island, interspersed with wooded areas where villages and hamlets hugged closely the sheltering coastline. Suffolk was cut by the sandy bushy plains and pine barrens that spread like a wall between its north and south shores.

A feeling of isolation and a sense of disunity were accentuated by the lack of adequate transportation and communication. Although greatly improved, means of transit still insulated the various parts of the island from friendly intercourse or prosperous business contact. Three main roads fanned out from the busy and attractive community of Brooklyn—North Country Road, or Northern Boulevard; Middle Country Road, or Jericho Turnpike; and South Country Road, or Montauk Highway. These afforded the chief lateral routes of transit to and from the metropolitan area for the market-bound farmer or the pleasure rider, on horse or in stagecoach. Laid out in the eighteenth century, they had not much improved. Plank roads, a fad that swept New York State in the 1850's as the accepted means of street paving, mingled with plain dirt concourses to make travel difficult, costly and bothersome. Construction and maintenance rested almost entirely either in the hands of local road commissioners or with the local farmer who had neither the money nor the competence to build all-weather roads. Farmers usually paid their road taxes by personal and team labor on the highways. Toll booths set up at regular intervals were not able to sufficiently provide for proper maintenance. Because of these conditions, roads were left to deteriorate.

Cross-island traffic presented even a worse picture. Although local turnpikes were built to connect some of the larger communities, these too were run down and most times abandoned. In complete disrepair, they were left to the ravages of weather and the despair of the traveler.

The Long Island Railroad had by 1868 well advanced into the hinterlands of the island. Product of the railroad boom that hit the United States in the middle of the nineteenth century, the one track line was part of a grandiose scheme to afford quick and easy transit between New York and Boston. The route of least resistance chosen was through the center of the island, most of the way cutting through the Nassau grass plains and the Suffolk scrub oak barren regions. The plan of the "Boston through" route was to use the railroad train to Greenport where connections could be made with the Stonington ferry's steamboat. From Stonington, passengers would take the Old Colony Railroad to Boston. In four years of carrying freight and passengers between the two cities, little thought was given to the island region through which the train passed. Depots or whistlestops, where the train could stop for fuel and water, were established along the line. One accommodation train ran every day, one day to get to the city, the next to leave the city, for the convenience of the neighboring territory. As the railroad ignored the surrounding regions, the islanders resented the unwelcomed addition to their domain. Antagonism was increased by the old woodburning iron horse, which did damage to the area. Live sparks emitted by the engines started serious fires causing great loss to the cordwood industry, and destroyed homes, game and wildlife. The failure of the line in 1848 forced it to look to the surrounding country for support and business. At the same time, the local inhabitants began to see in the railroad the possibilities of quick transit to the city markets. By 1868, the Long Island Railroad was accepted by the people of the island, and several branch lines had been laid. It had reached Glen Cove by spur from Mineola; Hempstead by spur from Mineola; Northport by spur from Hicksville; and Sag Harbor by spur from Riverhead.

Two independent railroads had been in operation for many years, serving the north and south shores. The Southside Railroad was running more or less regularly between Jamaica and Patchogue with stations at Amityville, Babylon and Wellwood. The Flushing and Northside Railroad serviced the Flushing area as far as Great Neck.

All three lines ran as many as five trains a day at the breakneck speed of twelve to fifteen miles an hour. Travel on the lines was tedious and nerve-wracking, with many parts of the island still without adequate transportation. In Suffolk County, the railroad depots, converted into stations, were so far from the concentration of population that much trade was lost and the residents had to look for other means of quick passage. It had only one advantage, it sped-up mail delivery to the far regions of the island.

Because of remoteness of the railroad, poor roads, and irregular schedules, many island residents still depended to a great degree on the natural waterways for easy transit. Reliance upon the water for an easier and faster means of travel was more feasible in Eastern Queens and Suffolk Counties in order to reach other parts of the island or Connecticut, or to transport produce and products to market in the New York area. A familiar sight on the North River (Long Island Sound) was the sloop or two masted schooner, manned by a crew of hired hands of progressive and enterprising farmers in the winter. They transported cordwood for the fires of city homes, hay and grain for the thriving horses of the metropolitan area, sometimes oysters, charcoal or other needs of the city. They would return with a load of lumber, brick, or coal from New Haven, Haverstraw or New York.

Commercial steamboats of differing size mingled with the homemade sloops to assist the traveler and the producer and to furnish competition with the railroad. Side wheel steamboats plied a course between various points on the north and south shores and the New York region or Connecticut. Steamships on Long Island Sound remained formidable competition for railroad. Businessmen, journeying between New York and Boston, preferred the overnight steamers since they could spend a full day in either city and reach their destination the next morning without experiencing the discomforts of a poorly ventilated sleeping car. An increasing number of summer residents and resort travelers in the 1860's used this means of reaching their spacious country seats or the large hotels that were springing up all along the eastern shores. Port Washington, Islip, Glen Cove and Flushing were favorite resort areas.

Natural wooded areas and undeveloped lands made overland travel difficult and tedious. The familiar stagecoach with its galloping horses and rocking carriages served as an important means of transit between island communities and to and from the City of Brooklyn. Areas near Brooklyn had stagecoach lines which ran regularly and connected with the city. But as one left the populated area the stagecoach became an intermediary between the railroad and the town. Stages ran regularly between Flushing through Newtown to Brooklyn. Jamaica was an important center for stagecoach travel. If one wished to brave the danger and dust of the road, horseback was used. Truck farmers in their familiar wagons laden with produce took the long trip to market. The horse and carriage provided the family its means of travel, and if energetic, a traveler could accomplish the same on foot.

THE FACE OF BROOKLYN

The center of Kings County was the City of Brooklyn, fourth largest city in the United States. The recently incorporated area of Brooklyn Heights, South Brooklyn, Williamsburg and Greenpoint was a thriving, busy suburban community dependent on its New York neighbor for livelihood. A large group of Brooklyn salaried people, wage earners, bankers, brokers and businessmen spent their daylight hours in New York. Leaders in commerce and finance who found the short trip across the river easier than exploration in the rocky vastness of upper Manhattan selected Brooklyn Heights as their place of residence.

Thirteen ferries plied their course between Brooklyn and Manhattan, day and night. The dashing commuter rode for a penny in gaily decorated steam ferries which vied in conveniences and accommodations to afford passengers a place of pleasure as well as a means of transport. From the ferry slips the huge floating castles rushed madly across the East River at headlong speed competing with each other for time and customers and many times inviting frightful collisions. A familiar sight was the dashing commuters hustling each other to be the first ashore.

Twenty-five miles of horsedrawn railroads radiated out from the ferry slips making the outskirt areas within easy reach of the city. The slow moving vehicles drawn by horses wandered along its two-rail track. Conveniences included hard seats and straw covered floors. The Brooklyn City Railroad had an added attraction of a small stove which warmed passengers in the winter months.

The city center of population was the Brooklyn Heights section. Here, shipowners and traders of the 1820's had established their homes so as to be in constant view of their ships as they moved in and out of the harbor. By mid-nineteenth century their ranks had been swelled by the financiers, bankers, and commercial barons of New York. It was the first modern suburb in a real sense, a haven of genteel secularism and refined culture. No mansion in New York City could compete with those on the Heights. It was not until 1872, when A. T. Stewart built his Fifth Avenue palace, that the Heights received any kind of competition. By 1868, the elite section of the Heights, replete with imposing brownstones, had expanded to include South Brooklyn, a little less fashionable but just as desirable section, and Williamsburgh, where the homes bespoke the prosperity of Civil War investment. Park Slope had joined the ranks of fine and sought after living areas with the most ideal location on the top of the Slope. Prospect Park and Eastern Parkway had been already laid out as Brooklyn began to develop its natural beauty. The northern section of the city, Greenpoint, the former province of East Indian shippers whose street names showed the oriental connection, was composed of small wooden imitations of the brownstones. Hunters Point, the western extremity of the Long Island and Flushing and Northside Railroads, just beyond Greenpoint, was a thriving, bustling and crowded depot. Brownsville, named for the farmer who subdivided his land for city lots in 1865, was beginning to attract residents. Bedford, the most ancient and charming section of the city, together with New Brooklyn had been passed over for the more popular sections of development. They were sparsely settled and offered a good area for speculation or growth.

The closely settled, crowded city center had mushroomed in all directions. The fastest growing section of the outlying Kings County was the township of New Lots. The white collar worker, the businessman, and the tradesman were settling in East New York, focal point of expansion. Laid out in city blocks as early as 1835, East New York did not attract interest and dwellers until after the Civil War. The horse-drawn railroad had connected this farthest point of the county with the thriving city center and the ferries. In a few short years, the population of the flat and extended tract of land had jumped from 5,009 in 1865 to almost 8,000 in 1868. Modest homes predominated with a sprinkling of more elaborate residences. Apart from East New York's expansion, the other bordering townships had shown some population influx, but not its magnitude or rapidity. Flatbush, once the center of the county, had with the removal of the county seat to the faster growing ferry area in 1834, lost its preeminence. It had a small village with some elegant dwellings. Its chief attributes were Erasmus Hall Academy, the Kings County Almshouse, Nursery and Lunatic Asylum, and the public parade grounds. Its 2,778 residences had almost doubled by 1868. South of Flatbush was the farming community of Flatlands. It had less than 2,000 residents, scattered throughout the area or compacted in the hamlets of Parkville and Canarsie. Transients passed through enjoying the rural scenery and fresh air, but never stayed. The chief attraction was its most southerly portion, the popular Coney Island, offering ocean breezes and bathing. West of Flatbush was the remaining township, New Utrecht. The region had shown a small decline in its population. Three small villages dotted its expanse. Bay Ridge was a suburban community, New Utrecht itself a compact village, and Fort Hamilton, near the United States military grounds, was an attractive but thinly settled commuter district. The township was still very much the oasis of the city's summer houses.

Front, Dock and James Streets, downtown Brooklyn, circa 1870.

A Nice Place to Live —

The City of Brooklyn had in 1868, all the advantages and conveniences of modern living. Paved streets afforded easy passage for the hurrying carriage or the ambling streetcar. The five hundred miles of streets were thoroughly lighted with gas. Home life, so pronounced, had the advantage of gas illumination. Sanitary conditions were continually being improved by the installation of underground water and sewers. The city was a community of homes, with few hotels to accommodate the visitor. Homes, ranging from the ornate mansions on the Heights to simple dwellings in the outer areas were tastefully decorated. Rich vermillion and gold could be found in the more advanced and wealthier homes. Mauve and deep green predominated the array of fussy, overly decorated Victorian furnishings. Parlors were cluttered with much paraphernalia. There were richly carved rosewood or black walnut sofas and chairs covered with brocades, silk, satin or green velour. Bookcases and tables vied with the parlor organ or piano as the center of an evening's entertainment. Iron fireplace radiators or air heating furnaces were located in the fireplace whose marble mantel contained innumerable objects. And every home was not a home without the fancy hat stand in the hallway. Modern conveniences and an attractive community meant higher standards which affected all the residences.

The Brooklyn resident had many opportunities for leisure time pleasure and enjoyment, all within easy reach of his home. In the warm summer months, escape from the heat could be found in the luxury of sea bathing and ocean air at Rockaway Beach or Coney Island. A steamer ferry or the Bath and Coney Island Railroad made them readily available. At the beach, a familiar sight was the gaily colored portable tents dotting the sand, or the portable bath-houses on wheels rolled directly into the water for privacy. The more affluent escaped summer by resorting to their summer homes as far out on the island as Babylon. For those who could not afford the time or money, a novel experience awaited the city-bound. In 1868, a Salt Water Swimming Bath opened in the heart of Brooklyn. The forty by seventy foot pool, filled with salt water from the East River, had regular hours for men and for women, and never the two should meet. A favorite pastime for the more prosperous was to drive to Prospect Park or a more extended trip on the Shore Road to Fort Hamilton. For the baseball fan, Brooklyn had its favorite teams. Avid and emotional support encouraged the Atlantics of Brooklyn, the Excelsiors of Brooklyn, and the Eckfords of Greenpoint. The big game of 1868 was the match between the team of the Atlantic Club with that of the Athletic Club of Philadelphia.

In the winter, a galaxy of entertainment spots offered pleasure to the city dweller. Brooklyn, in spite of its Puritanical veneer had many public theaters, lecture halls, and itinerant shows. One could attend the theater and hear such personalities as Mrs. Siddons-Smith or frequent the innumerable lectures, readings, and public appearances of well-known personalities. Subjects ranged from astronomy to character building. Lecturers included the national figure, James G. Blaine, British author, and the hometown favorite, Henry Ward Beecher. More inviting were the gay and carefree circuses, minstrel shows, and burlesques, featuring performers such as "Joe" Emmett or General and Mrs. Tom Thumb.

Most popular, either in winter or summer, were the corner saloons. They were the "poor workingman's club" which more than likely was the only escape he had for entertainment or diversion. The saloon keeper was a respected man in town; his establishment far out numbered the churches in the city.

However, at all times, and for most people, the few hours of the day left after travel and work were spent in the home. When not involved in some phase of family life, the Brooklynite resorted to reading and relaxing. Prominent in every home was the family Bible which had its honored place on table or bookstand. No home of substance was without its shelf of well-known authors, or periodicals. Accepted reading were the works of Washington Irving or Charles Dickens, or of the new authors, Bret Harte or Mark Twain. Newspapers were also in abundance. Seventeen newspapers, prominent among which was the *Brooklyn Daily Eagle*, gave local and national information to the reader.

Brooklyn had an expanded superior educational program. In 1868, free public education was an accepted fact. By an act of state legislation in 1843 the local Board of Education had been established with control of the public school system in the whole city. There were forty tax supported schools with 554 teachers and 31,160 pupils. There was no strict demarcation between elementary, secondary and college levels. although the trend was to define the various levels of grades. Elementary school had six grades with divisions of primary, male and female. In 1866, the course of study had been standardized with uniform textbooks. Free textbooks was an issue that had not been resolved. One school in the city had given free textbooks as part of the pupil's fee. Boys' schools were strongly classical, preparing students for business or the professions. Girls' schools concentrated on cultural and artistic subjects with the purpose of adequately training girls for their domestic duties.

College preparation was largely in the hands of the privately owned and operated academies. In the city there were 200 private educational institutions with 628 teachers and over 25,000 students. Church sponsored schools predominated with a growing number of secular institutions. The Roman Catholic Schools, rapidly increasing in number, offered a comparable education. The parochial schools served as sources of homeland and ethnic culture in addition to teaching rudimentary schooling. Among the more prominent secular institutions were the Brooklyn Female Academy; Brooklyn Polytechnic Institute where the new scientific learning was being taught; and Adelphi Academy, all preparing the student for college. Public high schools were rare. Schools were completely segregated. One out of thirteen of the public schools was given to Blacks. And, although opportunity for public education existed, a small portion of the school population took advantage of it. Less than fifty percent of the potential 130,000 children between the ages of five and twenty-one received any formal instruction. The rest were either working at jobs or left to their own devices.

Education was still characterized in a control by the white Protestant Puritan. The Protestant version of the Bible, hymns and prayers from denominational sources, and in some places, the use of textbooks detrimental or offensive to other religious bodies were in current use. However, a growing secularism was beginning to corrode secular public education. The Board of Education, trained largely under such influences, wanted a completely unified course of study, organized and controlled by the state, in which common secular ideals would be inculcated. Teacher training in this objective was more and more gaining support.

Cultural interest centered in the libraries and other community projects. The Brooklyn City Library, a privately sponsored institution, had in 1868 occupied its new and enlarged facilities. The Brooklyn Institute circulated books, conducted classes in drawing, and secured an annual address for Washington's Birthday. The Long Island Historical Society, formed in May 1863, had attracted widespread support with plans for the erection of a permanent building. Art had been fostered by the Brooklyn Sketch Club.

A City of Churches —

The city of Brooklyn had been from its inception, the eminent domain of the white Anglo-Saxon Protestant. Settled and guided by the English, the Dutch and the Scottish-Irish, the city had taken as its framework of reference the ethos and mores of the founding fathers. By the middle of the nineteenth century it had become the very fiber of the city. From the Heights and the Hill emanated the Brooklyn ethos, a peculiar mixture of individualism, economic prosperity, social superiority and complacency, overlaid with a veneer of the Protestant Puritan precept. The acme of the Brooklyn genteel secularists were the Abiel A. Lows and the Pierreponts, who considered Brooklyn their own special private province and field.

But the city had experienced a change in the mid-fifties and sixties that altered its complexion and makeup. Since 1847, there had been a steady infiltration of foreign born to soil the pure country of the Puritan. By 1868, 251,381 were native born, 144,718 foreign born. Many of the foreign immigrants, instead of passing through, stayed and took up permanent residence. Most of the new comers were Irish and German, who lived in mixed neighborhoods of rented homes or flats, or gravitated to centers of common language and customs, Shantytown and Dutchtown. Other ethnic groups had come to lessen the firm grip of the dominant class. The Jews, in Brooklyn as early as the Revolutionary War, were less than 1,000 families. A smaller group of foreigners were the Scandanavians. Dock workers formed their own little society during the winter living on the barges in the Gowanus Canal. The non-white population of the city remained only a little over 4,000, even with the arrival of free Southern Blacks. Brooklyn always had its "colored folks" and because of their small number did not present a threat to the natives' existence. The Blacks had their two schools, and their own churches. All groups began to experience the effect of the American melting pot. They themselves changed as the character of the city changed. Most evident was in the religious life of the city.

A favorite appellation, cherished by every Brooklynite was the name "City of Churches." Coined in 1829, the term carried with it a certain high moral tone, a sense of well-being and superiority. Even with the relaxation of a strict and narrow code of ethics, the name persisted and as Brooklyn expanded so did the conviction that Brooklyn was a true churchly city.

To the casual observer, Brooklyn did seem like a "City of Churches." Church going was the rule rather than the exception, being very much a social and family affair. Sunday after Sunday, the affluent church goers would stuff themselves into their rented pews to hear the latest pronouncement or the first prediction. Each church had its women's sewing circle, its Bible classes, its missionary society and Sunday school. An outstanding demonstration of Brooklyn churches was "St. Children's Day," the Annual Sunday School Parade. Begun in 1861, it attracted thousands of marchers, primly dressed and properly organized parading through the city streets.

The dominant note of all Protestant sects was the power of the pulpit and preaching. The chief high priest of the sermon was Henry Ward Beecher who packed them in at Plymouth Church. His reputation was so widely known that additional ferry boats had to be used on Sundays to accommodate the overflow crowds that came from New York to hear his sonorous semantics. Beecher expounded on a large assortment of subjects, ranging from the "Excise Tax" to "How to Be Happy." Most Sunday orators performed the same task. Sermon topics centered on character building, thrift and industry, and effulgent attempts to elicit a better life. More moralistic than theological, sermons were meant to bolster not change. Beecher had his pulpit rivals, for in Brooklyn there were other men of equal rank. They numbered among them C. Dewitt Talmadge, G. Richard Storrs and Abram N. Littlejohn.

Huge temples of worship had been erected by all the major sects. Most imposing were the liturgically-oriented Episcopal Churches who had a preponderance of modified Norman and Neo-Gothic structures. The jewel of the crown was the Church of the Holy Trinity on Brooklyn Heights, a monument to money, whim and the Gothic obsession of architect LeFevre. Close rivals in size were Plymouth Church and the Church of the Pilgrims. New England in flavor, they resembed large auditoriums or meeting halls. Holy places rose in close proximity to each other. Within a few short blocks, three Episcopal churches opened their doors, seating 600 to 1,200 each.

By 1868, there was good evidence of a growing religious pluralism, engendered by the multiplication of churches and sects. The two progenitors of church life, the Dutch and the English, had welcomed into their ranks the Methodist, Presbyterians, Baptists and Congregationalists, together with several other minor sects.

The Protestant churches had themselves been multiplying. There were 172 houses of worship. The most numerous, the wealthiest, and the most influential were the Methodist and the Protestant Episcopal, the former numbering thirty-eight, the latter thirty-five. The Presbyterians and Baptists followed closely with twenty-seven churches each. There were seven Lutheran churches ministering to the new German element and two Quaker Friends Societies. Religion was segregated with seven churches for the Blacks.

The Protestant monopoly over the religious life of Brooklyn had been lessened by the establishment of Roman Catholic Churches. Once established, these Non-Protestant congregations began to grow rapidly, mostly fed by the influx of the foreign born. In 1868, the Roman churches numbered twenty-six locations with appendages of parochial schools, hospitals and orphanages. As a witness to the dynamics of this church, the cornerstone of a new Roman Cathedral was laid on June 21, 1868.

The Jewish population, small in relative number, had been organized into two synagogues. In 1862, Congregation Beth Israel was founded in Williamsburgh and a synagogue erected. A few years later, a second congregation was formed. Called Congregation Beth Elolhim, they purchased an abandoned Episcopal church for their building.

In the growing threat of religious pluralism, the Protestant churches recognized the need for closer, more harmonious co-operation in areas where single ventures had proven ineffective. The Brooklyn City Mission and Tract Society, founded in the 1830's was a co-operative undertaking on the part of the Protestant churches to establish new work by systematic visitation and tract distribution. Non-denominational, supported by gifts from all churches, it employed fourteen missionaries, and had founded a large number of Protestant churches throughout the city. A new inter-denominational agency, founded in 1866, indicated the tension of church fear. The Brooklyn Liberal Christian Union had been formed "to unite all Christian denominations in the work of mutual improvement and practical benevolence." Its efforts were directed to the implementation of social projects and charitable works.

No effort on the part of the dominant Protestant churches could stop the deep-rooted change in moral and religious life of the city. In 1868, most churches were beginning to recognize and bitterly resent the infiltration of ideas contrary to their point of view. Their strict and narrow puritanism, the core of all city life, had been infringed upon by a growing liberal attitude on the part of some enlightened clergy and by the incipient thriving Roman Catholic Church. In the years before the Civil War, a deep feeling of religious animosity pervaded the city. Resentment towards the new and foreign Irish and German Roman Catholics grew out of the fear of popery and Romishness. The pulpit furnished the chief means where religious intolerance was enkindled and enflamed. The strange attitudes of the aliens, the peculiar religious customs and above all the large number of Roman Catholics added fuel to the fire. Whenever a Protestant church was bought by the Roman Church a renewed campaign of bitterness and hatred flared openly. Although the heat of animosity died down during the Civil War, the fear remained. The Roman Catholic Church presented a formidable force that threatened not only their control but their very existence. Freedom of religion, the Protestants loudly advocated, but it was freedom for their own clique.

Signs were appearing that the puritannical control of the Protestants over city life was weakening. In 1857, street cars were allowed to run on Sunday. By 1868, a controversy centered on the keeping of the Sabbath had appeared with a conflict of two opposing views, the strict Calvinistic interpretation and the freer more relaxed view of the immigrant. Protestants still held the upper hand shown in several incidents: condemnation of the opening of the National Academy on Sunday in New York, forbidding the use of play swings in Prospect Park on Sunday and the condemnation of Barnum's prize baby show.

Some of the local Brooklyn clergy had been active in various reform movements. They had assisted in the underground slavery movement and had openly assisted the Black in his fight for emancipation. The Civil War had increased the nation's drinking habit and a vehement crusade of temperance advocates was on the rampage against the use of alcohol. The lamentable spread of divorce together with a post war growth of religious indifferentism and genteel secularism heralded even more strongly the quickening movement of change. Liberalism, advocated by some of the more advanced of the Protestant ministers, hastened the imminent change. The "City of Churches" would grow in the number of buildings, in a growth of congregations and the amassing of wealth. But they had to reckon with far-reaching changes of great moral and religious scope which were just beginning in the year 1868.

Clouds on the Horizon —

The Brooklyn resident, involved in his day to day routine, was unaware of any change in his city or in his life. As he enjoyed his country living with modern conveniences, he would have been dismayed or shocked at any thought of alteration. Yet, as he went about in 1868, two momentous forces were unleashed that would change completely the face of Brooklyn and all Long Island.

In 1868, Andrew H. Green made a lengthy report to the Board of New York. In it he called attention to "the important subject of bringing the City of New York and Kings County, a part of Westchester and part of Queens and Richmond, including the various suburbs of the city within a certain radial distance from the center, under one common municipal government to be arranged in departments under a single executive head." "Green's hobby" as it was jokingly called did not receive immediate support, but thirty years later it did bear fruit, in the consolidation of Greater New York.

Another plan, having a more definite and deeper meaning for Brooklyn took final shape. Colonel Julius W. Adams, an eminent engineer residing in Brooklyn, matured the plan to span the East River. He interested William C. Kingsley, a contractor, who together with him, persuaded Justice Alexander McCue and Henry C. Murphy, both politically influential, to sponsor a bill. Drawn up by Murphy, the bill passed the State Legislature and became law in 1867. The project gained the support of the Common Councils of New York and Brooklyn. John A. Roebling was appointed Chief Engineer. His plans approved and soundings for permanent footings were made in 1868. The Brooklyn Bridge was under way.

A PLAIN AND OPEN FACE

An observant traveler unacquainted with Long Island, would have been struck by a drastic change on leaving the city environs. The busy, bustling dynamic life disappeared quickly as he progressed out on the island, giving way to an open, quiet pastoral scene of Queens and Suffolk Counties. From the city to the Queens border was a relatively short trip, but long in terms of outlook and life.

COUNTRY COUSIN

Queens County embraced all that portion of land beginning at the Gowanus Canal and ending at the Suffolk County line. The county had been divided into six townships: Newtown, Flushing, Jamaica, Hempstead, North Hempstead, and Oyster Bay. Most of the area was farmland dotted with small villages of varying size, with a concentration of population in the western end. The township of Newtown was more heavily populated, being near the urban center of New York. North Hempstead had a lesser number of residents. Between Brooklyn and Long Island stood Jamaica, a thriving commercial and business center of over 3,000 inhabitants, the link between east and west.

Jamaica was the hub of island activity. To Jamaica came the farmer with his loaded wagon, meeting other farmers from other areas, before starting the long trek to the Brooklyn markets. Here trains of sometimes thirty or forty wagons were assembled to drive the plank road that led to the distant city markets. The village was one long street closely lined with trees, nothing more than a turnpike, on which the only visible residence was the home of ex-Governor John A. King and his family. Every other house was either a store or a tavern, catering to the transient marketer or salesman. Jamaica was still remote from the rapidly developing New York and Brooklyn to which cities it had for many years the slow transportation of a horse-car line. The Brooklyn-Jamaica Railroad connected with East New York where the horse-car took its passengers into the city. The Southside Railroad and the Long Island Railroad had terminal connections with Hempstead. The outlying towns were not as yet in railroad connection with the Brooklyn ferries.

North Village Avenue, Rockville Centre, late nineteenth century.

Jamacia's surrounding area, although largely farmland, was beginning to feel a small real estate development. The Lefferts farm, just north of the Jamaica plank road, had been laid out in city lots. Richmond Hill, as the development was called, had just begun its life as a small ideal community. A New York broker, Albon P. Man, had purchased the farmland with the intention of creating a garden spot for the workers of congested Manhattan, antedating by several years the purchase and plan of A. T. Stewart on the Hempstead plains. Nearby Woodhaven, organized in 1850, had a small population which centered around the agateware factory.

The greatest growth and concentration of population was in the western township of Newtown. Hunters Point, the busy freight terminus of the Long Island Railroad, had several ferry connections to New York. Ravenswood was small as was the village of Newtown, a market gardening community where several prospering New York merchants had their residences. Woodside, adjacent to Long Island City, was a thriving village built up by mechanics of all trade. Winfield, close to Newtown, had almost 4,000 residents with local industries of coffin-making, foundry and die-casting. Long Island City and Astoria accounted for most of the 20,000 residents, being near the urban center and the ideal location for city commuters.

The township of Flushing was outgrowing itself. Almost 14,000 people lived in the area that included West Flushing, College Point, Whitestone and Bayside. The center was the village of Flushing where stage and railroad connections to the city made living more commodious. All the aspects of modern living were being introduced. Gas lines provided this most important utility. Several large boarding schools, a town hall, churches and newspapers added to village life with an Insane Asylum and a brick, coal and lumber industry to offer work. West Flushing, or Corona, a developing village, had some local industry. College Point was the fastest growing community in the township. Named for the short-lived Episcopal church and seminary, College Point had many large residences, gas and sewer pipes, curbed and guttered streets, and rapidly growing industries. Whitestone, Bayside and Douglas Manor were small communities clinging to shoreline. The United States Army had established a federal military reservation at Willets Point, where a corps of engineers guarded the New York harbor.

Between Jamaica and its eastern neighbor, Hempstead, stretched the Hempstead plains, a prairie-like land, flat and bare of trees. The township of Hempstead had a population of 14,000. The village of Hempstead, its center, had a settlement of only 2,000 people. Hempstead, or Clamtown, had the aspects of a bustling community with several academies, horsedrawn railroads, a system of public schools and busy townfolk. Around the village were smaller distant communities: Rockville Centre, settled in 1854 had a few houses; Pearsalls (Lynbrook) was the site of the Brooklyn Water Works; and Freeport or Raynorsville, boasted a few comfortable homes.

Between Hempstead and its northern neighbor, the township of North Hempstead, stretched the open plains, broken by small hamlets at Floral Park and Fosters Meadow. Mineola, midway between the north and south shores, was a scattered village having as its attraction the site of the County Courthouse, the Queens Agricultural Society fairgrounds and the junction of the Long Island and Hempstead Branch Railroads. On the sound were some isolated communities: Great Neck, the end of the Flushing Northside Railroad; Manhasset, a small village with a few elegant mansions and small ugly tenements; Roslyn, the home of William Cullen Bryant, with only a handful of people; Sea Cliff, a summer excursion resort with steamboat connections to the city; and Glen Cove, an organized city, whose industries were expanding and whose community was growing. Nearest to Suffolk, and least populated of all the towns was Oyster Bay. Hicksville, "that place of vanquished greatness," had in 1836, been the prospect of a real estate development. Lots were laid out and sold at exorbitant prices in the midst of abundant speculation. But the "miserable abortion" never fully materialized, even though the Long Island Railroad put a station there in 1842. Some Germans had settled there in 1852, but its hopes were never fulfilled. Hicksville remained a large unoccupied town with a tavern, a few pig-pens and a very few scattered houses with little enclosures. North of Hicksville was the village of Jericho, the stamping grounds of the Quaker, Elias Hicks, and some stiff-necked farmers.

Oyster Bay on the sound was small with some summer residences, among which was the home of Theodore Roosevelt's grandfather to which "Teddy" came in the summer months. Farmingdale, called "Hardscrabble" was the place of that "popular specimen of humanity which good old Long Island produces. Farmingdale rears its towers in the midst of the brush and is one of the numerous offspring of the railroad, deriving no considerable portion of its importance from the fact that the trains stop here for the passengers to get pie, coffee and sandwiches."

THE LAND OF THE CLAM DIGGER

Between Farmingdale and the forked tongue of the island spread the land of the "true Long Islander," the County of Suffolk. Isolated from the west end of the island, its easy and friendly connection with New England made Suffolk more New England Yankee than New York Cosmopolitan, more staid, conservative and Protestant. Suffolk's townships had been settled largely by emigrants from New England, or religious refugees from England. By the middle of the nineteenth century it still retained its Yankee flavor, haunted by the memories of Puritans, pirates, Indians, and the revered exploits of 1776 and 1812. Suffolk depended more than any other county on the water for its means of transit. The Long Island Railroad had a line to Greenpoint but it was too remote from the Suffolk communities to be used to any extent.

The first generation of settlers came to Southold and Southampton in 1640, establishing small footholds in

Babylon, viewed from Great South Bay.

the deserted and distant land. They founded other settlements in Easthampton in 1648, Shelter Island in 1652, Huntington and Smithtown in 1653, and Brookhaven in 1655. From small settlements, in the seventeenth century, Suffolk grew to be the largest populated island county in the eighteenth century. New communities grew up, mostly settled by emigrants from the Puritan communities, but also mixed with some adventurous men from the western end of the island and by hardy English settlers who could withstand the hostility exhibited by the founding fathers. By the nineteenth century Suffolk had reached its greatest growth and began to wane as the western end of the island gained.

Suffolk County's population of 42,869 in the years immediately following the Civil War showed no great increase. Where Queens County had grown by over 10,000 residents, Suffolk's increase could only be accounted under 4,000. Most of its ten townships, apart from Huntington (which included Babylon in 1868), had very little growth. The Town of Brookhaven remained the same in these years; Southampton lost some people; only Huntington showed any real noticeable gain.

Huntington township which stretched from Long Island Sound to Great South Bay, had two centers of settled towns; Huntington and Babylon. Two and one half miles from the railroad station, Huntington had a community of 2,433 with churches, a union school, a printing press, and small factories. Babylon, smaller in resident numbers, was a favorite place for fishing parties. Ketchum's Tavern, famous for George Washington's visit, provided local historical interest.

Smithtown and the Branch, having a population of 2,085, consisted of scattered homes and small hamlets. In 1868, its novel aspect was St. Johnsland, a branch of St. Luke's Hospital, an Episcopal institution of fifteen buildings and seventy-five inmates where useful labor by the aged, honest and industrious poor, was manifest. Smithtown also had a trotting course near the small village of Saint James.

Islip's major attractions were Bay Shore and Islip, small towns with fishing and hunting as a prominent aspect and a few summer residences. Between the two was The Olympic Club, organized by the Volunteer Firemen of New York City as a pleasure resort. Nearby Brentwood's distinction was its sensational origin, founded by a group of free thinkers known as "Modern Times" in which free love and freedom were practiced and finally abandoned as impractical. A touch of international flavor was added to Suffolk by the settlement of Hussites at Bohemia. In

1853, the "foreign folk" built a small community keeping much to themselves, providing a labor supply for the nearby farmers. Sayville had a scattered village of under 1,200 people with four churches and a school.

The Town of Brookhaven had Setauket, Port Jefferson and Patchogue as its major villages. Port Jefferson had a good harbor not much used at this time and a limited number of manufacturing plants. Setauket, a small sleepy village, could not compete with its southern neighbor, Patchogue, which in being the terminus of the South Side Railroad, had a busy bustling town atmosphere. Largest village in the township, Patchogue had four churches, a union school and several factories. The communities of Fire-Place, Yaphank, the Moriches and South Haven were collections of houses, at the most fifty in number. The other hamlets on the north shore and in the middle pine barrens had very little, if any, town or industry.

Riverhead, the Suffolk County Seat, was just that—a courthouse, county buildings, some churches and a seminary. Featuring a population of 1,200, most life in Riverhead was transient. Court business, county records or law trials drew visitors to the village for a short stay living at the two local hotels.

The two forks of the island jutting out from Riverhead were populated by the Long Island farmer and mariner, quiet little towns or hamlets, far removed from any great concourse with New York or Brooklyn. Southold on the north fork was largely agricultural with Greenport, incorporated in April 1868, the site of several oil factories. The Hamptons on the south fork had scattered villages, some of historical importance, but none really engaged in any pursuit other than fishing or farming. Sag Harbor, once the dynamic port of the whaling industry, had declined, still retaining its separate district of customs and its right as a port of entry, but doing less and less trade year by year. The town of Shelter Island was purely agricultural, with grain raising and sheep husbandry its chief pursuits.

Simple rural life in Queens and Suffolk was confining, time-consuming and hard, affording little time for anything but work and household duties. The rural countryside did not share the same enthusiasm for education as Brooklyn or the more developed sections of Queens. Although there was a sprinkling of large union schools and college preparatory academies in the more developed towns, education in the surrounding areas was not pursued with the same interest as in the City of Brooklyn. Schools varied in size, construction, and in curriculum. The small one room school house predominated. In the small communities, education was under the direction of a local committee which many times was one person. School budgets for facilities included every conceivable building used: log, framed, brick or stone school houses and outhouses, school sites, fences and repairs. Some schools had the older system of a circle of benches around a board painted black; or in newer fashion, rows of seats, facing the teacher who had a more modern desk in front of the room. Schools closed and opened at odd times and for various reasons. Sometimes the winters were so severe that a necessary winter recess was called; sometimes schools were open in the summer. Because of irregular school times, and the fact that some students had work on the farms at certain seasons, it often took a long time for a student to reach the "fifth reader." Teachers who were not too well-trained were apt to be chosen. Education for the country areas was sporadic, disorganized and very much a local community matter.

THAT OLD TIME RELIGION

The religious life of Queens and Suffolk in many respects, reflected the stern and unbending fiber of the Long Islander. The country was the stamping grounds of the New England Protestant. Religion was simple, austere, rigid and confining. Narrow Puritanism held a firm grip upon the inhabitants, unrelenting in its drive to approve any new or liberal ideas or traditions.

After the Civil War, the Methodist Church had become the largest single denomination in all of the rural area. Sixty-seven Methodist churches ministered to the once-predominent independent and separatist brethren. The forty-three congregational and forty-eight Presbyterian churches of the early Puritan settlers were firmly entrenched in most of the settled areas of the island, retaining still their place of leadership and their stronghold of authority. Only a sprinkling of Episcopal churches carried on the Anglican traditions, and only in the larger settled areas. In Queens, nineteen, and in Suffolk, only seven, Episcopal churches managed to survive and grow amid the incipient hostility of the cold and unbending Protestant residents. Roman Catholics experienced an even more hostile attitude. Roman Catholics were thinly settled in Suffolk where only two churches were built. In Queens, nearer to the city, ten Roman churches were established and were in a flourishing state.

Religion, apart from the regular Sunday attendance at services, permeated the life of the community. In some ways, religion and politics were intimately bound up in the church and the town meeting. Founded as religious societies, most of the island communities retained their stiff and rigid mosaic code, forcing it upon the life and tenor of town life. "Blue laws" retained their standing, and no new or novel liberal ideas could penetrate or change the closed community atmosphere.

Nevertheless, some newcomers did settle and add a new dimension to life. But they could not in any way change the fundamental character of the island village. They were submerged in the rigid pattern of life and abided by the overbearing attitude and terse acceptance of themselves as strangers and aliens. Religious intolerance, an inheritance from the past, remained and colored the law-oriented village, hamlet or town. In 1868, Eastern Long Island was a part of New England, in religious and moral character, in social customs, and above all, in an intolerance for anything that had not been around for one hundred years or more.

19

Bishop Abram N. Littlejohn. First Bishop, Diocese of Long Island.

Section Two
A Golden Church for A Gilded Age
(1868 - 1901)

I WILL SET HIS DOMINION IN THE SEA.

Chapter Two

Land of the Pilgrims' Pride

A latecomer to Long Island, the Episcopal Church experienced great difficulty in establishing churches and in expanding its work. In the seventeenth and eighteenth centuries it played many roles: alien church; favored church; enemy church; and finally in the early nineteenth century, dormant church. In spite of all the opposition and discouragement, it did sink its roots deep into Long Island life.

Religious life on Long Island in the Colonial Period, so intimately bound up with the political life, was predominantly of a radical Protestant variety. Settlers from the Dutch Lowlands and refugees from England brought with them a Puritan ethic and a strict Calvinist theology which permeated their lives and tempered their communities. The Puritans, including various interpretations of pilgrim, separatist and independent, regarded the Church of England, from which they migrated to the new world, as being insufficiently purged of the errors of Rome. They came to the new land to avoid conformity to the corruptions which they believed existed in the Anglican liturgy and in the government. The entire group of refugees from England or settlers from New England, except for the Dutch section of western settlement, eventually came under the control of men who belonged to one phase or another of the Puritan movement which grew out of the more radical sections of the reform party in England. Although theoretical differences existed between separatists and independents, both groups found congregationalism a congenial form of government and Calvinism a common theology.

These radical Protestants came to America, not to establish a haven of religious freedom where every man could practice "freedom of conscience," but to establish a spiritual commonwealth in which they could practice and enforce their own ideas. The New Israel which they intended to found comprised settlements in which the theocratic concept of the state was paramount. In it the state acted for the church; the legal and moral code was the law of the Old Testament; and each member abided by stringent religious and moral precepts. These communities, refuges from intolerance, became in their own development strongholds of intolerance. Each community became a law unto itself and raised barriers which no stranger could overcome. The free non-conformist had become extremely conformist with more deadly seriousness and more intense passion.

ALIEN CHURCH

Occasional settlers of the English Church persuasion had attempted to live on Long Island among these stern and unbending new Israelites, but were either shunned or forced out. Prior to 1664, some English made sporadic attempts to conduct Prayer Book services and to establish Anglican life, but their efforts proved futile. A lack of sufficient numbers, a deficit of funds, and the intense antagonism of the local residents created an atmosphere within which the traditional church suffocated.

With the restoration of the House of Stuart to the English throne in 1660, a determined attempt was made to reduce the New England colonies and the Province of New York to political and ecclesiastical obedience. King Charles II gave to his kinsman, James, Duke of York, the patent to the lands occupied by the Dutch and English settlers in the middle and northern colonies. When New Amsterdam became New York in 1664, the initial organization and establishment of the Anglican Church on the Island began.

One of the first acts of the newly-appointed royal governor was the calling of an assembly to formulate new laws for colonial government. The "Duke's Laws Convention" met in 1665 in the small hamlet of Hempstead. Two delegates from each town were summoned to be informed of the new mode of political institution and church regulation. The decrees were the first code of the state's colonial law. The stipulations in regard to church life were simple: each town was to erect a building to be used solely for church purposes; to provide a house for a clergyman; and to levy a tax to raise monies for the clergyman's salary. No minister was allowed to officiate who had not received ordination, either from some Protestant bishop or from some minister within His Majesty's domain or within the dominion of some prince of the Reformed religion. Two overseers were to be chosen to make the rate of assessment for the support of the church and clergyman.

The war between England and Holland in 1672 brought New York and the eastern towns of Long Island under Dutch rule for the brief space of one year. But after the declaration of peace, a new governor for New York was appointed by Duke James. The governor's administration was marked by the calling of the first representative body in the province. In this general assembly there were eighteen freeholders who divided Yorkshire, or Long Island, into three counties, Kings, Queens and Suffolk.

When James II became King, the General Assembly of the Province was abolished and James proclaimed Sovereign of the Province. At this time, there were Church of England people in Jamaica, Newtown and Flushing, but not enough to constitute a church. The province came under the direction of the Committee on Foreign Plantations, an arm of royal rule. By royal authority, new instructions were issued to the royal governor to bring the Church of England into an established position and to give it the same position it held in the mother country.

The policy of James II was affirmed in the sovereignty of William and Mary, who, after the Glorious Revolution of 1688, continued the policy of church establishment. In New York this purpose was expressed by the first governor sent out by the government. An attempt to get a bill introduced in the General Assembly for settling a regular ministry in the Province failed for lack of support. Church life had become so lax throughout the colonies that the royal governor took steps to correct the unhealthy situation. A new governor, Colonel Caleb Heathcote, arrived in the colony in 1692 and found it "the most rude and heathenish country I ever saw in my life. For a territory that pretended to be Christian, New York somehow managed to be without the least marks or footsteps of Religion of any sort."

In 1693 another royal governor, Fletcher, a staunch partisan of the Anglican Church, compelled the Provincial Assembly to adopt an act "for settling the ministry." The Act, forwarded by the governor and obediently passed by the Assembly, ruled that there should be a "settled ministry" with a "good, sufficient Protestant minister" to officiate and have the care of souls in Queens County. One was required for Jamaica and its adjacent towns and farms and one for Hempstead with its adjacent towns and farms. The ruling also provided for a yearly meeting for all freeholders to choose two wardens and ten vestrymen and ordered a "reasonable" tax be levied for the maintenance of the minister and the poor.

Similar provisions were made for Manhattan, Staten Island, and Westchester. Obviously, the main objectives on Long Island were Queens (and Nassau). Kings County was not mentioned because of its large Dutch settlement; and Suffolk was much too Puritan to even demand attention.

An ambiguity in the terms and the concision of the phrasing left the bill open for interpretation. The assembly which passed the bill was largely Dutch and Protestant. For them, the bill merely affirmed their "freedom of conscience" and enabled them to continue their congregational policy with government subscription. The prospect of government "induction" of new clergy into their churches did not seem likely or immediate. Moreover, the Dutch members of the assembly were on cordial terms with the Anglicans, as they were with all the Protestant sects, and so cared little who was chosen to minister to them. For the Governor and other Anglicans, the bill meant something entirely different. The term "sufficient minister" meant only one thing to them—an Anglican divine. The terms warden and vestryman were familiar terms to the Anglican, having for many years denoted the lay officials of the English Church parochial organization. Governor Fletcher's bigotry manifested itself in the "exclusive interest of the Episcopal Church, a step in the program consummated in 1695 to make the Church of England the Church in the colonies." The imposition of a general tax on all freeholders, "irrespective of their religious affiliation was perpetrated for the public support of the Episcopal clergy." The lack of provision for Suffolk County was interpreted as meaning the definite sanction of the Anglican Church in Queens and Nassau. Because of the bill, great bitterness was engendered between the Anglicans and the Dissenters, Quakers and Independents, a bitterness which hindered the progress of the Episcopal Church.

As an immediate reaction to the bill, several communities began to collect taxes to establish churches. But it was the Protestants who began first: Dissenters in Jamaica undertook to establish their own specific formularies; Flushing engaged in its Quaker pursuits and Newtown in its independent form; and Hempstead was involved in a joint operation of all three. The west end of the island, predominantly Dutch, continued to expand the Dutch Calvinist denomination, with three churches at Breuklen, Flatbush and Flatlands.

The east end of the island, beyond Oyster Bay, felt no effect of the bill. The settlers who came from New England and Connecticut owed their loyalty to New Haven and Hartford. By the Treaty of Hartford in 1650, all towns had placed themselves under the protection of the Connecticut colony. Some inhabitants had migrated from Massachusetts, but they considered themselves a part of the Hartford Covenant. They lived as they did before, fearful of God and of men.

Except for a few scattered attempts, English churchmen on the island made little or no effort to take advantage of the 1693 Bill. Unable to settle in large numbers in any community held firmly by the radical Protestants, they constituted less than ten per cent of the population—a distinct, but highly influential, minority. The number of Anglican churchmen did not increase appreciably with English rule, and ascendancy was gained only by imposition of royal order. Official favor and social prestige made the Anglican Church the "class church" of government officials, rich merchants, and wealthy landholders. An Anglican Church, when established, was not so much representative of the population of the land, but rather of its government subsidy and royal imprimatur. The aristocratic minority, most of them churchmen, differed in both numbers and interests from the middle class and farmers who comprised the bulk of the population. Farming families were self-sufficient, living simple and grim lives. The aristocrats preferred town life, where all was pleasant, convenient, and cavalier. They disdained the dissenting middle class, not only because of the hard memories of the English Civil War and Cromwell, but also because of a distaste for the Yankee "levelling" ideas. Likewise, the Dissenters harbored an intense antagonism to the churchmen because of what they represented: the Established Church, conformity to doctrinal beliefs, and subservience to the Crown.

The Dissenters who most opposed the English Church were the Presbyterians, by and large the majority on the island. They refused to accept any Anglican divine who they felt was superimposed upon them by a repugnant central government. In turn, Royal Governors vented official wrath at Dissenter opposition by using their power to obstruct activities and to turn down requests for Presbyterian Churches. Friction between Anglican and Dissenter often came to open conflict. A crisis in 1699 at Jamaica brought out all hidden animosities. Using the Ministry Act of 1693 as their excuse, a few Anglican residents claimed the town church building for their exclusive use. The Dissenters staunchly opposed them and won the battle, but only for the time being. The Anglican minority had to capitulate. However, their resentment deepened, and more and more friction between the two opposing forces developed as the eighteenth century progressed.

St. George's Church,
Hempstead, founded 1702.
(below) The Seal of the Society
of the Propagation of the Gospel
in Foreign Parts.

FAVORED CHURCH

The most significant event in the furtherance of the Episcopal Church on Long Island occurred not on the island itself, but in the study of a distant prelate. During a visit to the colonies, Thomas Bray, Commissioner for Maryland, became convinced of the need to disseminate Christian knowledge and to propagate the Gospel in the new world. Returning to England, he began his efforts to create a permanent base for the supply and support of missionaries overseas. Confiding in the Archbishop of Canterbury, the Bishop of London, and his friends at a meeting of the newly formed Society for the Propagation of Christian Knowledge, he caused the matter to be brought up in the Lower House of the Convocation of Canterbury. A committee was appointed to investigate the matter, and a petition was sent to the King in March, 1701. By June 16, 1701, a royal charter had been issued with the first official meeting of the Society for the Propagation of the Gospel in Foreign Parts, or the S.P.G., being held on June 21, 1701, in the residence of the Archbishop of Canterbury. There, prelates, ecclesiastical dignitaries, and laymen representing the official church made plans to secure men to serve as missionaries and funds for their work.

At the time of the formation of the Venerable Society, there were in North America 43,800 members of the Church of England, with 50 clergy to minister to them. In the Province of New York, there were 30,000, of whom 1,200 attended church and 450 were communicants. At its meeting in September, 1701, the Society heard of the dire state of religion in the Colonies of New York, New Jersey and Pennsylvania. Appeals from the colonies for the missionaries were received, and the Society felt obligated to investigate the need and answer the call. It therefore sent a "mission of observance" to discover and study the state of religion in the colonies and to report where missionaries could be sent and churches established. Since the Southern Colonies were largely Episcopal, the main objective of penetration was the Middle Colonies, New York and New England.

Two missionaries were procured by the Society and approved by the Bishop of London, whose jurisdiction was the American colonies. They were the Rev. George Keith and the Rev. Patrick Gordon. Keith was to survey the various communities in the area, and Gordon had a definite assignment to the church at Jamaica. The Rev. John Talbot, Chaplain to the British ship *Centurion*, on which the missionaries made their voyage, was so impressed by the mission that he received from the S.P.G. the approval to accompany Keith on his survey. Keith and Talbot made an extended trip from Boston to Charleston under the express instructions "to preach in meeting houses whenever opportunity might offer and where possible to win them back to the church." On his way to Jamaica, Gordon stayed with the Rector of Trinity Church in New York. There he came in contact with the yellow fever, which was in epidemic proportions at the time. He left New York in June, but unfortunately contracted the fever and died on July 28, 1702, before he was able to conduct his first service in Jamaica.

The Rev. George Keith, a converted Scottish Quaker, possessed all the brashness and fortitude needed for his work. Feeling the need for something more than the Inner Light, he had come into the Church of England and took Holy Orders. In his journey throughout the colonies, he waxed bold and bright to accomplish his mission. "Wherever he went, he made a great impression. He preached at Hempstead on September 27, 1702, when the church building could not contain the people. He said they greatly desired an Episcopal minister." At the request of some of the inhabitants, he preached at Oyster Bay. In his report to the Society, written in Philadelphia on April 3, 1703, he said:

> The main thing of importance that I have at present to write to you is to tell you of the
> extreme desire that people have in several parts where I have travelled to have the Church of
> England Ministers sent to them, particularly . . . at Oyster Bay and at Hempstead.

In the company of Talbot and the Rev. William Vesey, Rector of Trinity Church, New York, Keith spoke at Flushing, a quiet hamlet of farmers belonging to the Society of Friends, "announcing himself as a minister and missionary of the Church of England." His invective caused the people to forcibly eject him from the Old Quaker Meeting House where he had previously spoken as a convinced Quaker. Again in December he returned, and again he received the same treatment.

An auspicious occasion for the advancement of the Anglican Church was the arrival of a new Royal Governor, Lord Cornbury. His arrival in May of 1702 was regarded by the clergy of the Church "as a great deliverance." Called "Father of our Church and Province," "a true nursing father to our infant church," and "true son of the Church" by the Anglican clergy, he earned the titles well by his untiring and profligate advocacy of the English Church. But his personal character little matched his church adherence.

Lord Cornbury's administration began with high hopes and good auguries; it closed in disgrace. He was a vain and imperious man who disgusted the people of New York with his unseemly behavior. A pervert, his greatest pleasure was to prance publicly in woman's dress to beguile his latest amour, to the detriment of conducting public business. His freakishness was matched by his egomania and his flights of fancy. His treatment of the local clergy who were not of his own church persuasion was brusk and unfair. At the slightest whim he would cause untold anguish for some of the Protestant ministers who aroused his anger and ruffled his feathers. He threw a Presbyterian minister into prison for preaching in a private home without his permission. He insisted on his gubernatorial license for teachers and pastors of the numerous Dutch churches and made them submit or be thrown into jail. Even the clergy of his own church were not above his personal tyranny. On occasion he abused and imprisoned some of the missionaries of the Church of England because they did not agree with him in principle or in fact. He became for all, and especially for the Dissenters, a living example of the corruption and evil of the Church of England.

In the early days of his governorship, fifty churchmen in the town of Jamaica petitioned Cornbury to fill the vacancy left by the death of the missionary Gordon. The Governor directed the Rector of Trinity Church in New York to find a temporary incumbent until the S.P.G. could appoint a permanent man. In order to escape the yellow fever epidemic which raged on Manhattan Island, Cornbury had taken up residence in the manse at Jamaica which had been kindly offered to him by the inhabitants. On leaving Jamaica, Cornbury, in his haughty and perfunctory manner, turned the keys over to the Anglican supply priest, who at his own expense had offered to take services in Jamaica. Then occurred one of those dramatic incidents which vividly pointed up the high degree of animosity that existed between the various adherents of the different churches.

The supply priest, the Rev. James Bartow, prepared for Sunday service. The Presbyterian minister, who had been in Boston, had returned and prepared for Sunday service. The bell rang on Sunday morning for services. Bartow entered the church and, much to his surprise, the service was in progress with the Presbyterian officiating. Bartow waited for a moment to take over the service, and when it appeared that he was not to do so, he went to the front pew and sat. In the afternoon Bartow, upstaging the Presbyterian, began service a little earlier than usual. The Presbyterian entered the church, started back in surprise and anger, and then went outside to an orchard next to the church. Word was passed around that he would conduct services in the orchard. An uneasiness settled on the assembled congregation. Some began to whisper; others stood up and left at once; others were caught in that moment of hesitation and indecision as to whether to go or to stay. The service was interrupted by the loud entrance of some who had gone out and had come back for their seats. In shameful disorder they tugged at the seats, hauled them out and returned for more, turning the existing confusion into utter chaos. Finally the roar subsided, and the service resumed with only half of the congregation left. At the end of the service the

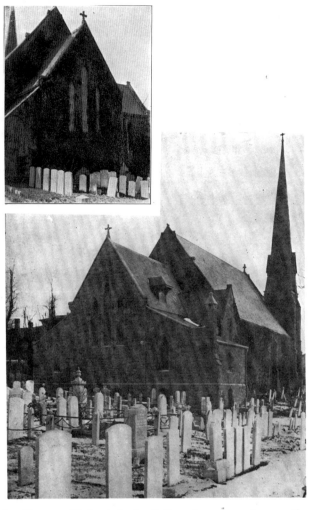

(left) Sanctuary and churchyard of Grace Church, Jamaica.
(below) St. George's Church, Flushing, founded 1702.

Anglican officient locked the church and gave the keys to the sheriff. A sequel to cap the incident occurred a few hours later. Demanding the key to the church so they could put back their seats, the Dissenters, not receiving it, went to the church, broke a window, and let in a small boy to open the door. They put back their seats but kept their cushions, loudly proclaiming that they would keep them for their own minister. As a result of the incident, Cornbury forbade the Presbyterian minister to preach again and threatened him with disturbing the peace. He acquiesced. The Anglicans had won the dispute, but a deep bitterness abided longer than the memory of the incident.

Both to fill the vacancy at Jamaica and to answer the need of Hempstead, the Venerable Society sent in 1704, two missionaries, the Rev. William Urquhart and the Rev. John Thomas. The S.P.G. missionaries faced no easy prospect in their work among the Long Islanders. Confronted by innumerable obstacles, they were continually harassed, checked, shunned, and sometimes violently opposed by the local Protestants to whom they were sent and who did not want them. Representing a very small minority of the population, they were hampered by aspersions on their character, by the questioning of their real purpose, and most of all by the fear of what they represented. All of these forces made their labors tedious, hard, and trying.

The missionaries sent by the S.P.G. were on the whole men of learning and piety. Some of the church missionaries previously sent to the new world had been worldly men interested in their own welfare, adventurers, and exploiters. The preconceived image of the Anglican clergy haunted the new missionaries. Yet Colonel Heathcote, in his 1705 report to the Society, could state "that a better clergy were never in any place, there being not among them [one] that has the least stain or blemish as to his life or conversation . . . both friends and enemies of the church agree as to the character of the gentlemen, and that they use their best endeavors to gain over the people."

In spite of public commendation, the personal characters of the missionaries were questioned many times. The Rev. James Honyman, Chaplain in the Royal Navy, had left his post to take up the work at Jamaica. Before he could take up his residence, a slander on his character created the necessity for some kind of defense. In his report to the S.P.G., Honyman made clear the reasons for such a character assassination:

> After enquiry [was] made, I found [that] the reason why my encouragement was not like to prove suitable to my expectation was founded upon a malicious story raised by one while in England . . . a criminal indicted for felony, who upon her trial asserted that I had been too intimate with her mistress at whose house I lodged some of the time, when I belonged to the ship of war that then waited on this Province.

The accused never officiated at Jamaica. He was transferred by the Society to Rhode Island.

Not only aspersions on personal character but also doubt as to effectiveness of purpose often confused and clouded their work. Time and time again the question was raised as to why they were sent to Christian communities within which were churches and regular services. Even as late as 1768 in a letter to the Lord Bishop of Landaff, New York's prominent citizen William Livingston protested the invasion of Anglican missionaries:

> What infidels have [been] converted? The immense sums expended by the Venerable Society are not laid out in missions among the native pagans... They are squandered, ridiculously squandered on missions to places where the gospel was preached, and more faithfully preached before... People at home were mendicated and sermonized out of their money.

It was felt that the real heathens were Indians and Blacks who needed ministration more than those who were already Christianized.

However, it was primarily two ancient fears that haunted the local communities and both were vested in the missionaries: the fear of episcopacy and the fear of popery. The missionary brought with him the image of the bishop. For the Long Island Protestant, the Anglican bishop represented the spector of fear, hate, and tyranny. They remembered that the bishop was more than the spiritual overseer; he was a great power in Parliament and government. Congregationalists, Presbyterians, and Quakers in varying degrees harked back to the awful, bloody persecutions they had to suffer for the sake of "freedom of conscience." The S.P.G. missionary, when he came, brought with him all that threatened to extinguish their inherent religious rights.

For the Protestants, the Anglican divines seemed to imperil the very core of colonial life. They could see in the settling of the Anglican ministry the eventual loss of democratic life, town charters, and restrictions on their freedom. They feared the imposition of more and more taxes to support not only the local clergy but worse, the establishment of an Anglo-American Episcopate. When the bishop came, they envisioned a complete halt to local freedom and enforced conformity to church dogma, rule and authority. For this reason, they erected walls of opposition, making the life of the local incumbent untenable and sorrowful.

The S.P.G. missionary could look to only a small group for any kind of moral support. Notation after notation confirmed the preponderant Protestant nature of Long Island and the feeble attempt at church establishment. Lord Cornbury himself had to admit that: "in the Country, especially on Long Island, most of the English are dissenters, being for the most part people who have removed from New England and Connecticut."

Old St. James' Church, erected 1733.

Overcoming initial opposition, the permanent establishment of the Episcopal Church on Long Island began with the arrival of the two assigned S.P.G. missionaries. The Rev. William Urquhart took up his duties at Jamaica with the responsibility of Flushing and Newtown (Elmhurst). The Rev. John Thomas was "inducted rector of Hamstead [sic] on Nassau Island in the Province of New York on the 27th day of December in the year of 1704." The Hempstead missionary wrote in his diary entry of June 27, 1705: "I have two distinct churches, fifteen miles asunder, where I preach by turns." The two churches were in the far distant places of Hempstead and Oyster Bay. Hempstead proved less trying than Jamaica. Thomas at first reported that his path was "very thorny" and "all my steps are narrowly watched." But in the succeeding years he had made his ministry among the "stiff Dissenters" so that within ten years he could cheerfully report that "All is well in my parish in general, and a happy continuance of mutual accord and affection between me and my parishioners [transpires]." The Jamaica rector experienced no such peace of mind in his work. He had to overcome tremendous opposition and never did fully gain the town's confidence or backing.

It was not until 1729 that a permanent ministry was started in Suffolk. At Setauket the Rev. Alexander Campbell held services, and under his leadership the present church building was begun. At first called Christ Church, Brookhaven, its name was changed in 1730 to Caroline Church of Brookhaven in honor of Queen Wilhelmina-Karoline, Consort of George II, who gave the silver communion ware and the altar cloths. In 1733, the S.P.G. sent the Rev. Isaac Browne, who began the long line of pastorates. It was during this time that a dispute over the church building arose between the Dissenters and the Anglicans. Once the dispute had been settled, Caroline Church prospered and grew.

A second Anglican Church in Suffolk grew out of pastoral work by a Queens County church. St. John's Church in Huntington was planted in 1745 by the missionary efforts of the S.P.G. missionaries at Hempstead. The first missionary at Hempstead to make frequent visits and great efforts to build a church and gather a congregation was the Rev. Samuel Seabury, father of the renowned Bishop Seabury. He travelled long distances to visit and to minister to the small group of interested persons. In addition to his duties at Hempstead, Seabury baptized and officiated at Huntington. In 1748, Seabury requested the S.P.G. to appoint his son, Samuel, Jr., as catechist, with a small allowance. The Society designated him to act in this capacity under the direction of his father and allowed him a salary of ten pounds a year. The elder Seabury recorded: "The Church at Huntington is also rendered very commodious and a congregation of fifty or sixty persons and sometimes more, constantly attend Divine Service there, who behave very devoutly and perform their part in Divine Worship very decently."

*(right) Caroline Church, Setauket, founded 1729.
(below) Old St. John's Church, Oakdale, first permanent church built in Islip Town, restored 1962.*

In 1762, the people were able to purchase a valuable house and "Glebe" worth 200 pounds. It was not until 1767 that a resident clergyman was procured.

Only one other Anglican Church was established in Suffolk County before the coming of the American Revolution. The first permanent church to be built in the Town of Islip was St. John's Church at Oakdale, in 1769. Built on the Nicoll land at the family's expense, it was used only occasionally for church services. It was a chapel of ease, a family chapel for the Nicolls, who were staunch Anglicans.

By the middle of the eighteenth century, the Episcopal Church on Long Island had taken firm roots. Recognized by the inhabitants as a stable and lasting institution, the Church gained the respect of the communities and the support of its growing constituency. Three churches in the Township of Jamaica were thriving concerns. All three had received a Royal Charter from the Crown in 1761. They shared the same rector who ministered not only to Jamaica but also to Newtown and Flushing. Previously, St. George's Church at Hempstead had received its Royal Charter in 1735. It and its north shore counterpart, Christ Church, Oyster Bay, prospered and grew. In comparison, the three churches in Suffolk County seemed small. Yet each of them had deep roots and continued to weather Puritan opposition and hostility. St. John's, Huntington, Caroline Church of Brookhaven, and St. John's at Oakdale each took care of the Anglicans who had settled in small numbers and attracted many of the staunch island Protestants by the warmth of its welcome and its life.

ENEMY CHURCH

In Lexington, on April 19, 1775, the shot was fired shortly after dawn. Before it was heard 'round the world, it echoed in the Episcopal Church, splintering its fiber and deadening its vitality. No other single event in the life of the nation had such a devastating effect upon the Church, leaving it structureless and impoverished.

Long Islanders, caught in the mesh of conflicting forces and ideologies, split into two groups: those who were intensely loyal to the King and Parliament, and those who desired patriotic self-determination. Loyalist and patriot fought with each other to preserve or to change the national identity. Some Islanders responded to the call of the patriots and formed local militia and Committees of Safety. After the disbanding of the Provincial Assembly in May 1775, matters grew more intense, and since the rebels controlled New York and Long Island, the loyalist cause suffered. Late in June 1776, however, the British ships appeared off Far Rockaway "with so many masts coming over the horizon that one observer said it looked like a forest rising from the sea." The local patriotic militia and the Continental Forces under General Washington prepared for the landing of the fleet with a scorched earth policy, burning grain and driving cattle eastward. The British landed in Brooklyn, and on August 27, 1776, they not only won the Battle of Long Island but also gained permanent control of the area. The victorious army camped at the strategic points of Flushing and Hellgate, with headquarters at Newtown.

For the duration of the war, Long Island served the British as a troop depot station, with a concentration of encampments in Kings County and the western section of Queens that dwindled off to a few scattered control stations in northeastern Queens and Suffolk. The island virtually became one camp as the number of troops was swelled by soldiers returned during the winter for rest and recreation after the summer campaigns.

The British army needed large quantities of wood, fodder and other supplies which were readily taken at prices set by the army or confiscated without any recompense being made to the owner. There was much theft by soldiers and marauders, as well as wanton destruction. The island not only fell prey to the entrenched forces but also paid a stiff toll to the whaleboatmen, who in the beginning of the war served as an effective arm of the Continental Forces, but who in time attracted a lawless element which robbed and murdered.

The western towns remained quiet and secure, profiting from British control. Jamaica had its soldier encampment, as did Flushing. A regiment of Hessians had winter quarters at Flushing. Newtown was filled with army officials. Hempstead, farther out, was the scene of constant strife between loyalists and patriots. Early in 1775, when a Tory-controlled town meeting voted to send no deputies to the Continental Congress, residents of the northern part of the township, whose sympathies lay with the patriots' cause, sent their own delegates. The split widened until September of 1775 when the north consisting of Great Neck, Manhasset, Port Washington and the Northern Neck, voted to secede and appointed its own militia officers and committees. The division remained throughout the war until 1784, when it was officially recognized. From 1776 to 1783, the Tories had the upper hand, oppressing and harassing the patriots. The British established troop watch stations on the eastern end of the island. Sag Harbor was seized, as was the Manor of St. George (Manorville). Although no major engagement was fought on Long Island, it suffered greatly from guerrilla warfare, intense hatred, and civil strife both on land and on water.

Although the Anglican Church was split in its allegiances, some Anglicans became leaders of the rebel movement. One patriot of note was Francis Lewis, active layman and church warden of St. George's Church in Flushing, who attended the Continental Congress and signed the Declaration of Independence as a delegate from New York. However, by and large the Anglicans on Long Island, both clergy and laity, were staunch loyalists. Being part of the Establishment, the clergy vehemently defended the royal cause. The Rev. Joshua Bloomer, Rector of the three parishes of Jamaica, Flushing and Newtown, refused to omit prayers for the King. The Rev. Leonard Cutting, Rector of St. George's Church, Hempstead, and Christ Church, Oyster Bay, was a violent and outspoken supporter of the government, and during the war a huge price was put on his head by the patriots.

Cutting became the leader of the loyalists, and when it was noised about the island mad rabble besieged Hempstead several times, driving out his supporters. Unsuccessful attempts were made to capture the loyalists in Hempstead.

During the brief period of patriot control, the Anglican Churches were besieged by the rebels. One Sunday, after the Declaration of Independence, several armed men stood guard at the doors of St. George's Church. All worshippers were to return to their homes, forbidding prayers for the King. One member of the Continental Army described the situation: "We converted the Episcopal Church into a storehouse, forbade the parson to pray for [the] King and Royal Family and made use of the communion table as a convenience for Yankees to eat upon." In Newtown the Rev. Joshua Bloomer closed his churches rather than omit prayers for the King. When principal members of his congregation at Jamaica refused to obey decrees of Congress, he wrote to the S.P.G.: "I administer the Sacraments at Newtown where I have but four or five male communicants. The others are driven off or carried away prisoners. I was forbidden to read the Prayers for the King and Royal Family. On consulting my Vestry, rather than omit any portion of the Liturgy, we shut the church five Sundays."

Royal control of the western section assured the church of safety and security. The brief period of patriot harassment gave way to a longer period in which the church profited by the prolonged occupation. The parish towns of Jamaica and Flushing were swelled by army personnel and their families. Jamaica was able to hold a successful lottery, raising 800 pounds to buy church land. In Newtown, services were resumed immediately after the occupation, and the Rector reported by 1777 that he had sixty-six communicants and had baptized twenty-four infants and two adults. St. James (Newtown) was especially fortunate in having among its worshippers a brilliant array of England's high officers: Howe, Earl Cornwallis and Prince William, who later became William IV of England.

Heavily in favor of the royal cause, the Anglican Churches remained unharmed in most cases and were left to function with regular services. In Newtown a group of young loyalists attacked the Presbyterian Church, tore down the tower, and burned the building to the ground. The Dutch Church was used as an ammunition depot and stable. The Episcopal Churches on the eastern end of the island did not fare as well. When British troops occupied Hempstead, it seemed to the loyalist Anglicans a blessing. But, as in the strange fortunes of war, instead of finding protection in the King's men, the parish was plundered and suffered insult and abuse. Services were interrupted; the parish school house was used as a guard room; and the Rector's personal land and house were abused. Christ Church in Oyster Bay was used as a barracks by the British and Hessian troops quartered there. As a result, the building soon began to decay, and eventually the communicants scattered and the church records were lost. The church in Huntington had also been used as a troop barracks, greatly damaging it. Since there had been no resident clergyman since 1774, services were held, in spite of local opposition, for the decreased number of families and refugees from Connecticut. Caroline Church was used as a hospital depot during the brief skirmish of 1777, the Battle of Setauket.

One Episcopal Church could attribute its initiation to the War for Independence. Not until the Revolution were church services regularly maintained in the little settlement that grew up around Brooklyn Ferry. From 1778 until the end of the war, the Rev. James Sayers, an expatriated royalist driven away from his parish at Fredericksburg in Dutchess County, Pennsylvania, was given sanctuary in New York. He was given permission to preach in Brooklyn. Brooklyn had a population of about 2,000, largely Dutch, and was under Dutch control. In March 1771, a lottery was proposed to build a church in Brooklyn, but the Revolution intervened. The few Anglicans in residence could easily get to Trinity Church by ferry. With the influx of British troops, the Rev. Mr. Sayers began preaching in the Dutch Church three Sundays out of four. In the Spring of 1784, services were held in two rooms in a house donated by the Rapelye family and then later in an old British barracks. In 1785, a church building was erected and consecrated as "The Episcopal Church of Brooklyn." In 1795, the name was changed to St. Ann's.

A severe blow to the Episcopal Church came when many Church of England adherents chose to leave the island. The exodus began early for Suffolk residents. The adoption of the Declaration of Independence had caused a considerable number of British sympathizers to leave at once to establish new homes beyond the states. Greater numbers began to emigrate during the final stages of the war, and for several years thereafter great numbers of Tory families chose to migrate to Canada and the West Indies or to return to the mother country. Although there was a general peace in April of 1783, it was not until November that the 7,000 to 8,000 troops, most of whom were in barracks in the parishes of Jamaica, Hempstead, Newtown and Flushing, evacuated Long Island. That year some 3,000 Tory refugees left from the County of Queens in one fleet of twenty square-rigged ships. Two thousand additional refugees sailed from Huntington Harbor for the City of St. John in Nova Scotia. Some of Hempstead's finest families had left for Nova Scotia and other places under British rule. These refugees never returned but permanently settled in their new homes. The effect of the exodus was to decimate the Long Island Episcopal Churches, taking some of the great leaders and supporters.

After the war, Long Island was especially bitter toward the loyalists. The Committee of Safety compelled non-conforming clergymen of the Church of England to close or leave their churches if they would not omit the prayers for the King and Royal Family. The Rev. Joshua Bloomer, Rector of the three Jamaica parishes, conformed and remained until his death in 1790. A copy of his Prayer Book, with the prayers for the President pasted in, can be seen in the Flushing church. Bloomer was very active in the preliminaries that organized the

American Church. In October, 1784, there was "a voluntary meeting of sundry members of the Corporation for the Relief of Widows and Orphans." After the business of this important charity was finished, the meeting resolved itself into an assembly of "several members of the Episcopal Church, both of the clergy and laity from the States of New York, New Jersey and Pennsylvania." A Committee of Correspondence was appointed "for the purpose of forming a continental representation of the Episcopal Church, and for the better management of the concerns of said Church." Bloomer was an active member of this primary convention and was appointed to the Committee of Correspondence. Bloomer and three laymen were active at a subsequent convention held in New York, which determined to appoint a committee of three clergymen "to wait upon the clergy of Correspondence for the purpose of soliciting their concurrence in such measures as may be conducive to the union and prosperity of the church." Bloomer served on this committee. The mission successful, Connecticut sent delegates to the General Convention in 1785. Bloomer remained active in the General Convention until his death. His counterpart, Leonard Cutting of Hempstead, did not stay. Because of his intense antagonism to the patriotic cause and the hatred for him, he left mysteriously and served in other churches.

The Rev. Thomas L. Moore, who became Rector of St. George's Church, Hempstead, in 1785, was present at a meeting held in New Brunswick, consisting of nine clergymen, from which came the first effective measures to have the Episcopal Churches unite themselves in convention. Out of this meeting grew the recommendation for clergymen and laymen of the state to meet in the City of New York on June 22, 1785, and to organize the first convention of the Episcopal Church in the State of New York.

The steadfast loyalists had to suffer the fortunes of war. Those who were found aiding British officers and soldiers or denouncing the patriots were arrested and exiled. Reprisal reached its crest in the confiscation of their property. Some were fined; punishment was severe and neighbors hostile. Property rights were not recognized for some years.

Hardest hit was the Anglican Church. If the war threatened the life of the Church, the post-war years wrought havoc, producing new struggles for existence. To begin with, the very name "Anglican" was a discredit in the new order of society, so much so that even prominent churchmen such as George Washington could not stem the hostility. Sadly missed, too, was the support of the British Army which had been stationed for so long on the island and had firmly supported the established church. The Long Island economy, hit by the devastation of war, took a long time to recover. Illicit trade, under the guise of patriotic duty, appeared in its true light of piracy, highway robbery, and murder. But above all, the underlying hatred between loyalist and patriot took as one of its chief subjects of dissension the Anglican Church.

The devastation of war not only caused a decrease in the ranks of the Episcopal Church but also resulted in the churches' falling into a state of great disrepair. The members of the parishes, impoverished and discouraged, could do nothing to ease the situation. The churches had been dependent upon royal control and support. When the War for Independence had been declared, the Venerable Society was sending to each missionary an average of £40 sterling a year. During the war, most areas, save New York, were cut off from their source of money. As a result, the two Long Island Rectors were able to receive their allotment for the duration of the war. With the termination of the war, the Society made its last grant of £30 on February 20, 1784. The churches, cut loose from financial support, had to struggle on their own. Their paths were made more difficult by the fact that they were without tax support, without the supervision of a bishop, without the protection of the Crown, and without many parishioners. After taking great strides forward, the Episcopal Church had been left stranded and desolate at the end of the war. Regular services were conducted, but few repairs to the buildings could be made. In 1790 Grace Church in Jamaica had only 21 communicants; St. James, Elmhurst, had 27 and Flushing only 13. St. George's, Hempstead, suffered less than had been expected. Services were continued by the clerk of the vestry until the church was able to call a new Rector in 1785. No services were held at Oyster Bay or in Suffolk County.

Only one church in the New York area was able to withstand the ravages of war and to it the Long Island churches appealed for financial assistance. Through the kind intervention of Mr. Rufus King of Jamaica, Trinity Church, New York, came to their aid, making grants of money and land. Besides securities, city lots which yielded valuable rentals were given to Grace Church, Jamaica; St. George's, Flushing; and St. James, Elmhurst. The churches, no longer able to depend on overseas support, were forced to become self-reliant. Episcopalians had to learn to support their churches with money from their own pockets. The current expenses were provided for by subscriptions, and the so-called "penny collections" on Sunday. Pew holders were assessed one dollar. It was a struggle for the decimated churches, and much that was needed in the way of building repairs and maintenance was left undone. Yet in spite of all the hardships, the Episcopal Church survived, less affluent and less influential, but able to continue its ministry to the islanders.

DORMANT CHURCH

The turn of the century marked a low point in the history of the Episcopal Church. The Revolutionary War had been long and costly, and political and social changes had been rapid. Wrangling politicians with opposing views engaged the attention of men. The establishment of an independent nation with its own political structure was tedious, time consuming and hostile. Manners began to change. Old customs and old prejudices were laid aside. Economic insecurity gained with social turmoil. Small pox devastated New England, while yellow fever

*(above) Right Rev. Samuel Seabury,
first American Bishop.
(left) St. George's Rectory, Hempstead, built in 1793.*

threatened to depopulate Philadelphia and New York. Selfishness, fear, and speculation demoralized the populace. Periodic Indian attacks continued. Drunkenness threatened to debauch the nation. French manners and French ideas inflamed the people. It was the age of Tom Paine and the attempt to create an "Age of Reason." The Church struggled desperately for its existence, sinking into a state of feebleness and apathy. "The devastation of war, the fury of political strife, the revived animosity to England and all things English, the unsettling of fixed habits, the loosening of creeds, and the weakening of reverence all wrought against her growth."

The establishment of a national church engaged the attention of churchmen throughout the new nation, and after a period of indecision and insecurity the Protestant Episcopal Church of the United States of America was founded in 1789. After the fervor of union, however, the American Church, like its English counterpart, sank to a low level of incompetence, utter abandonment and low spiritual life, becoming entirely indifferent to doctrine. The Church Fathers who had organized it were on the whole content to relapse into the church as they knew it. The clergy hardly took their office seriously, and the laity feared "enthusiasm" so much that they were content with less than earnestness. The Church, able to exist on parochial support, settled back into parish life.

For a brief period in the life of the Church, it seemed as if success had been achieved. Churchmen witnessed a huge number of confirmations. On Long Island, the Bishop of New York confirmed a class of 97 in Flushing and one of 30 in Jamaica. But the greatest witness to the Church was made at St. George's, Hempstead, where, in October of 1787, 155 persons were confirmed, "the accumulated candidates of many years." But after a few visitations the Bishop settled into his old routine, unwilling to make any effort at supervision or visitation. Diocesan conventions met irregularly, and parish life sank to a new low. Churches on Long Island felt the effects of the apathy, even though they were very involved in their own struggles for existence. Old religious hatreds and animosities still colored their attempts at founding secure parish life. Parishes in western Queens went through a series of adjustments, hoping to achieve some kind of stability. In 1797, after constant bickering, the union of the three parishes was broken by mutual consent. In a wrangle over financial matters, Flushing and Elmhurst withdrew, calling their own priest. A disagreement over the Jamaica church's solicitation of funds in Flushing set off the controversy that eventually resulted in Grace Church having its own rector. Flushing and Elmhurst continued under the new arrangement until 1810.

The Episcopal Church that showed the most notable progress was St. George's in Hempstead. The Church grew with the population and was able to make outstanding strides forward. A new parsonage was built in 1793, and the old church was replaced in 1822. On the death of the Rev. Thomas Lambert Moore in 1799, the Church called the Rev. John Henry Hobart as its Rector. The future bishop accepted the call on June 1, 1800, but lasted only six months. An inviting call from Trinity Parish in New York could not be ignored, so Hobart left to take up his duties as Assistant at Trinity Parish. It seemed as if history had repeated itself. William Vesey, a Lay Reader who had officiated in Hempstead in 1696 before the coming of its first rector in 1704, had left also to become Rector at the same parish.

In the early nineteenth century three events awoke the Episcopal Church to its mission: the election of Bishop Hobart, the election of Bishop Griswold, and the War of 1812. After the 1812 War, the United States entered a new era of peace, expansion, and prosperity. New and vigorous leaders came to the fore, representing all walks of life and all shades of opinion. Industry began to develop on a larger scale, and the population increased and shifted. As the chaotic conditions following the War of Independence subsided, a new vigor and a new spirit appeared in American life.

No institution reflected this change more than the Episcopal Church. New conditions fostered new ideas and found new leaders. The Right Reverend Alexander Viet Griswold brought a quickening spirit to all of the northern New England states, with the exception of Connecticut. The particularistic policy of the Church, in which each diocese was its own ecclesiastical empire and no central authority was recognized, became overlaid with a new emphasis. The Right Reverend John Henry Hobart, Bishop of New York, stressed ecclesiastical authority and sound structure. He emphasized the catholicity of the Church, reaffirming the historic episcopate. Bishop Griswold, in a different manner, accented the evangelical tradition, akin to the "Great Awakening" and the Methodist movement. Each contributed in his own way, one for the high church tradition, the other for the evangelical; and from the two came the tension that held the Church united, that created an atmosphere within which the Church could work effectively and could develop Sunday schools, colleges and seminaries.

The War of 1812 finally incorporated the Episcopalians into the American tradition. Churchmen, looked upon as aliens and enemies, gained a new place by fighting side by side against a common foe. Fellow countrymen recognized them as comrades of good will and men of equal patriotic fervor. By 1820 the Episcopal Church stood united and in a flourishing state. For Long Island it took a little longer, it not being caught up in the forward drive until the 1830's.

Between 1789 and 1830 only two new Episcopal churches developed on Long Island, while the others continued to fight for their place among the churches. In 1802, a new church appeared in the northeastern section of Queens County. For many years the inhabitants of Cow Neck (Manhasset) had to travel a long and hard journey to attend services at the parish church in Hempstead. The journey was made over muddy roads where light carriages were a luxury. The trip, of three hours' duration, was usually accomplished in a commonplace vehicle—a farm wagon with no springs, filled with chairs for the adults and with clean straw on the floor for the children. Many came on foot, and those who did carried their shoes and stockings until they reached the edge of the village, where they washed their feet in a pond and spruced up for the divine service. Winter months made the trip treacherous, with snow impeding the journey. In the spring and summer the coarse black sand of the Hempstead plains became muddy and dangerous. The residents of Cow Neck finally decided they could endure the long, hard journey to St. George's no longer, and they petitioned the parish vestry, which gave them permission to build a church. The building was completed in 1803 and consecrated as Christ Church, North Hempstead, at which time a class of fifty was presented for confirmation. The Rector of St. George's preached on alternate Sundays, but without a full-time clergyman the small parish had hard times. A donation from Trinity Parish, New York, helped the pledges of the parish provide for an assistant minister to take full charge of the congregation. By 1819, an academy had been established, a clergyman, Eli Wheeler of Little Neck, hired, and the church separated from St. George's Church to become an incorporated parish.

The other church to be established in this interim period was St. John's, Brooklyn. In 1826, Brooklyn was still a village. The old Dutch settlement, feeling the impetus of trade and commerce, the influx of shipowners and merchants, and the development of a prospering economy, spread in fan-fashion from the populous Brooklyn Ferry district to more suburban undeveloped areas, as far as Borough Park. Rich farmlands were still spread over Brooklyn Heights and Bedford, tilled by the thrifty, industrious Dutch. Flatbush, a thriving village and the center of the county, began to feel the competition of the western sections. The question that became more and more prominent was which would eventually be the Brooklyn center. In the midst of these developments, churchmen around Brooklyn Ferry felt the need of another church in addition to St. Ann's. They decided to go far out of the business center to build a church and so in 1826 established St. John's Church on the corner of Washington and John Streets, adjacent to Borough Hall Park. The building was finished the next year and was consecrated by Bishop Hobart. The church prospered and became one of the fashionable churches in the City of Brooklyn, only to be relocated in 1869 at its present location on St. John's Place.

By 1830 the Episcopal Church on Long Island could claim little of dynamic proportions. St. Ann's and St. John's ministered to the Brooklyn Community. The three churches in western Queens strove to hold their own. The three churches in eastern Queens, of which St. George's in Hempstead was the foremost, cared for their small flocks among small surroundings. Suffolk rated little if no lively interest. St. John's in Huntington began to show some life but none to compare with the other island churches. Caroline Church in Setauket and St. John's in Oakdale, the only other island outposts, struggled to maintain their places. It seemed as if the Church could not match the development of America or the progress of the Episcopal Church elsewhere. But Long Island's turn was to come. In another two decades life would spring up for the Episcopal Church, and churchmen would look with admiration upon the evolving entity known as the Diocese of Long Island.

Chapter Three

A Giant Awakens

As the Episcopal Church fought for its survival, rapid changes were taking place in the world and on Long Island. In July 1830, the second revolution had taken place. The rise of European liberalism and the Oxford Movement had just begun. In the United States both natives and immigrants were moving west on foot and in wagon. In the crowded cities the wheels of the new industrial age were beginning to hum. The great Hayne-Webster debate in Congress on state and federal rights astounded and confounded the nation's leaders. There was an accelerated growth of America. The population in 1830 was 12,866,000. In 1840, it had increased to 17,069,453.

In 1830, Kings County was the smallest of the three Long Island districts. There were 20,535 people, of which 12,302 lived in the Brooklyn village, compared to 22,276 in Queens and to 26,780 in Suffolk. By 1840, Brooklyn had grown to be the largest district, numbering 36,233, of which 25,671 dwelt within the limits of the old village and 11,380 in the district outside the Brooklyn area; only 30,324 people lived in Queens and 32,649 in Suffolk. The fast-moving Brooklyn village had become in 1834 the Incorporated City of Brooklyn, including five old village districts and four new adjacent wards. It covered about twelve square miles and was bounded by the town lines of Williamsburgh, Flatbush, New Utrecht, and East New York. Municipal government had outgrown its Apprentice Lyceum and moved to the new City Hall, whose cornerstone had been laid in 1836. It was not completed until 1848.

Signs of growth were everywhere. Marshes were filled, creeks and inlets dredged; factories and warehouses crowded the shores; and dozens of ships from the seven seas lay at their wharves. The Mayor and Alderman had plans for the new-born city with the "go-ahead" principle of America. In 1833, oil lamps flickered on sixteen streets; seven years later there were thirty-five miles of lighted streets. Elegant stage-coaches were seen going daily to nearer villages and three times a week to eastern Long Island. But somewhat more advanced than the stages was the Brooklyn-Jamaica Railroad, completed in April 1835 to Jamaica. Two years later steam engines were pulling strings of stage-coaches as far as Hicksville at the speed of twelve miles an hour. Greater speed, it was said, was bad for the heart.

Social conditions were improving. Social service took a step forward with the opening of the free dispensary in 1830, the appointment of a poor relief committee and health wardens, and the institution of the city poor house at Flatbush in 1832. Although slavery ended in New York State on July 4, 1827, there were still many indentured apprentices. In 1837, 538 almshouse children were working on Long Island farms. Widely discussed were the subjects of temperance and poor relief, and a spirited campaign was fought over tavern licenses. A growing hostility toward the foreign-born alien was becoming more and more evident.

Education and religion prospered under the leadership of the leading Protestant churches. There were only three public schools in 1831; private schools were more numerous. Brooklyn had seven Protestant denominations and eighteen churches. Their influence was great, and the temptation to join them was considerable. Ministers became fanatically interested in temperance and abolition. Attendance at church and Sunday school was general; it was sinful to enjoy Sunday; and there was no observance of Christmas.

It was in this period that the Episcopal Church began to establish parishes and expand its membership and influence. Within ten years, the Church had doubled its number of parishes. Six major parishes were established within the boundaries of Kings County and five in the island countryside.

The third church to be founded in Brooklyn and the fourteenth in the diocese was St. John's Church in the small suburban community of Fort Hamilton. A fashionable health and pleasure resort and the location of an important army installation, Fort Hamilton had many churchmen who found the distance to downtown Brooklyn too far for regular attendance at another church. The church was organized on September 29, 1834; seven months later a church was erected; and on July 16, 1835, it was consecrated by the Bishop of New York. St. John's soon became the focal point for activity in the small community, and among its parishioners were numbered General Robert E. Lee, who served as a Vestryman while stationed at the fort, and Stonewall Jackson, who was baptized there. The "Church of the Generals" experienced many difficulties in its early years. The near evacuation of the fort in the Mexican War; the burning of Hamilton House, many of whose guests attended regularly and donated liberally; the establishment of Christ Church, Bay Ridge, which drew many parishioners away; the yellow fever epidemic to which many of the members succumbed; and the Civil War which took away many fine Episcopal families of the South, limited the growth of the little parish to fifty-three communicants.

In 1834, when Brooklyn became a city, there were two ferries to New York, the Fulton Street and Catherine Street lines, both of which stopped running at midnight. After that hour it was impossible to get from New York, except by row boat. Two years before, the first horse-car railroad had begun service on Fifth Avenue in New York City. The first city mayor, George Hall, a reformer, insisted on closing all unlicensed saloons and banishing hogs from the streets. In 1835, there were seventeen places of public worship: one Baptist, two Roman Catholic, two Dutch Reformed, nine Methodist and three Protestant Episcopal—St. Ann's, St. John's, Brooklyn, and St. John's, Fort Hamilton.

Two churches were added to make the number of Episcopal parishes five. On May 18, 1835, Christ Church in South Brooklyn came into existence, and about the same time St. Mary's Church was formally organized. Interesting was the controversial name given the latter parish. The Oxford Movement had already captured some of the American clergy, and one of them was the Rector of St. John's Church who sent his assistant to begin services in the new area. Eighty families combined to form St. Mary's Church as one of the free churches open to all. Its early years were filled with setbacks, yet despite all the church did prosper.

In the summer of 1836, a small group of Episcopalians, attracted by the village aspect of Flatbush, lived on friendly terms with their neighbors, descendants of the Dutch settlers, and even attended the Dutch Reformed Church. Under the leadership of the Rector of St. Ann's Church on the Heights, the churchmen began to form their own parish. Availing themselves of the offered Reformed Consistory room for their meetings, they elected a vestry, collected sufficient funds so that on August 13, 1836, the cornerstone of St. Paul's Church was laid, and soon initiated services in the completed building.

(above) St. John's Church, Cold Spring Harbor.
(left) St. George's Church, Astoria, built 1828.

In 1827, Astoria had grown to large proportions, and a large nucleus of churchmen resided there. As a result, a church was organized as St. George's Parish. Ravenswood nearby had also experienced a similar growth, and St. Thomas' Church was settled there in 1839.

Three churches in the outlying rural areas were established as far out as Cold Spring Harbor on the Suffolk County line and as close as Little Neck, near Flushing. In 1813, Wynant Van Zandt, a wealthy New York merchant and a devoted churchman, had a country home on the peninsula known as Little Neck. He first established regular Sunday services in the East parlor of his home and later added an octagonal structure with two wings to serve as a chapel. Donating the present site of Zion Church, Van Zandt built a small church with his own money. Enlisting his neighbors in the building of the church, he accomplished his hope, for in 1830 the church was open and formally dedicated. In 1835, the land passed to the Douglas family, who maintained the church at their own expense. The church grew to have 105 communicants by 1868. St. John's, Cold Spring Harbor, started in 1825, only became a parish in 1837. During the early years of the nineteenth century, Glen Cove attracted many New Yorkers as a convenient place of residence or as a resort for recreation in the summer. Steamer connections on Long Island Sound with New York made travel easy. Some churchmen had held services in the community as early as 1820. Before that time, those who wished to attend services made the long journey to St. George's in Hempstead. In the same year that Moscheto Cove became Glen Cove in 1834, St. Paul's Church was erected and began its life as an outpost of the Episcopal Church.

In the mid-nineteenth century the United States was entering a period of unprecedented expansion. In the decade beginning 1840 the nation's population increased from 17,069,453 to 23,191,876. Great folk migrations began from the East to the West coast. The Oregon Territory, Texas, and the Mexican cession added more than one-third of the present United States area. A network of railroads was being laid east of the Mississippi. Another epoch of travel opened when the 234 foot side wheeler *Great Western*, two weeks out of Liverpool, docked in New York on April 24, 1848. The country was still 90% agricultural, but in 1849 manufactured goods amounted to over one billion dollars worth. Orators were loudly proclaiming the "manifest destiny" of the country.

European poverty, crop failure and political disturbances were causing a large migration on crowded ships to the American shores and especially to the New York harbor. In the decade following 1841, there came to the United States 1,713,251 immigrants, of whom nearly 46% were Irish and 26% German. Many of the immigrants remained in the New York area and began to settle in the outlying areas of Brooklyn and Long Island.

BUSTING OUT ALL OVER

In this decade of great expansion and changing population, the Episcopal Church on Long Island experienced one of its greatest growths. Between 1840 and 1850, Brooklyn's population tripled. In the City of Brooklyn, the residence census soared from 42,622 in 1840 to 131,357. Queens' and Suffolk's growth seemed insignificant in comparison. Suffolk grew from 32,469 in 1840 to 36,922 by 1850; Queens from 30,324 to 36,833. Long Island was growing fast, but it was Brooklyn, that center of island life, which emerged as dominant. In these years, the Episcopal Church almost doubled its number of churches and congregations. Fifteen new churches were added, nine of which were in Kings County and Brooklyn City.

The spread of population along Fulton Street and upward from the ferry led to the establishment of Trinity Church on Clinton Street; after six years it was dissolved and became the nucleus of St. Luke's Church which was founded in December 1841. Christ Church on Harrison Street, established in 1835, had erected its Gothic structure, designed by Richard Upjohns. At this time the only Episcopal Church on the Heights was Emmanuel, which occupied a building on Sidney Place. Due to a change in neighborhood, it was sold to the Roman Catholic Church, and the congregation was reorganized as Grace Church. Grace Church, formally organized on May 3, 1847, grew rapidly and a year later, in 1848, Richard Upjohns built the imposing structure on Grace Court.

The growth of the City necessitated the establishment of more Episcopal churches, so that by 1848 congregations had been formally organized, including the forementioned St. Luke's in 1841; St. Michael's in 1847 and St. Peter's in 1848; and St. Paul's Church, Clinton and Carroll Streets.

Three churches outside the immediate city environs were organized: in 1846, Church of the Ascension in Greenpoint and Christ Church, Bedford Avenue; and in 1849, Calvary, Eastern District. Christ Church was started as a splinter group, product of the "high" and "low" controversy that was so involving the Church at this time. St. Mark's in Williamsburgh was agitated by the two extremes of ecclesiastical convictions and ceremonial practice. The Rev. Samuel M. Haskins, Rector of St. Mark's, was one of the leading exponents of the Oxford revival. A small group of parishioners adverse to the "high church" practices withdrew and formed their own congregation. On December 30, 1845, they met to organize, and in January 1846, the first services were held in the Dutch Reformed consistory rooms.

In Queens and Suffolk, four new churches were added. The two Suffolk churches were the first to be organized since the establishments of the colonial period. St. Mark's Church at Islip and Christ Church in Sag Harbor were small but a beginning. In Queens, it was on the south shore of what is now Nassau that an opportunity to enlarge the Church's work presented itself. Trinity Chapel in Rockaway (Hewlett) had been started in 1836 as a parochial chapel of St. George's, Hempstead. Trinity Chapel continued under the Hempstead church until February 1844, when it was incorporated as a parish. In Massapequa, Grace Church, South Oyster Bay was

Grace Church, Brooklyn Heights.

located in a largely farming community with a few scattered estates. It was the only church to serve the community for many years.

Between 1850 and 1868, Episcopal parishes were organized in rapid succession. In the seventeen years; twenty churches began in Kings County and six in Queens and Suffolk. Three more churches were added to the Suffolk farming community. St. Paul's, Patchoque, organized in 1844, had by 1854, a small church, due to the efforts of a leading citizen, Brewster Woodhull. St. James Church in Smithtown began its corporate life in 1853. A post-Civil War product, St. Ann's Church in Sayville, known as St. Barnabas' Chapel, began to attract a congregation as part of the work of St. John's Church, Oakdale.

Three widely scattered congregations were formed in western Queens County. Grace Church in Whitestone, a part of the Flushing parish until 1855, began by holding services in an inter-denominational chapel donated by a local resident. Permission to form a separate parish was given by Flushing, and on September 6, 1858, Grace Church in Whitestone was formed. A new church was opened in 1860.

Astoria's population had been growing rapidly in this period. A second Episcopal church in Astoria was initiated by seventeen ardent communicants who in 1866, were holding services in a store. Through their perseverance, Church of the Redeemer was established and a church erected in 1868. A near neighbor, Long Island City, was also expanding rapidly with a need for Episcopal ministrations. In 1865, the need was answered by the founding of St. John's Church.

Nevertheless, it was in Kings County, and especially in the City of Brooklyn, that the sleeping giant, the Episcopal Church, awoke and began to stretch in every direction. Twenty churches, alive and active, had been founded. Beginning in 1851, with the establishment of both the Church of the Holy Trinity and the Church Charity Foundation, to the latter part of 1867 with the founding of the Church of the Evangelists, the Episcopal Church had begun to touch every area where people and life had mushroomed.

In the forties and fifties Brooklyn Heights was beginning to fill up rapidly into what was destined to be for many years the most desirable section of Brooklyn. In 1844, a small Episcopal chapel was built on Clinton and Montague Streets. Services were held here until 1847 when they were transferred to a new church structure. Under the influence of Edgar J. Bartow, a huge Gothic structure was envisaged. The foundation of the church was begun in 1844, and it was opened for worship on April 25, 1847. In the beginning, Holy Trinity was the personal enterprise of its founder. He secured the services of its first Rector, who brought with him many of his parishioners from Calvary Church. Bartow had also engaged the architect, Minard LeFevre, a relative, and William J. Bolton, a designer of stained glass windows. Called "the Cathedral of Brooklyn", the church was not completed until 1856 when the Bishop of New York consecrated it. During the time of construction, the church existed for four years until November 1851, as an independent personal project; then it was organized as a parish and its first vestry elected. In 1860, the parish called as its Rector the Reverend Abram N. Littlejohn.

The Church Charity Foundation had its beginnings in this period. A group of interested women headed by Mrs. Henry E. Pierrepont, rented a small house on Love Lane where three infirm and aged women were cared for. Weekly services were held there by a student of General Theological Seminary. In January 1851, the originators of the project met with some Brooklyn clergy and Mr. Conklin Bush, Mayor of the city. On February 6, 1851, steps were taken to incorporate the Foundation for the purpose of caring for the aged and orphans. All Episcopal clergy in Kings County were made members of the Board of Managers. The work of the Foundation found permanent results in the building of an orphans' home in 1858 and the opening of the charitable institution in 1861; these orphans began to receive an industrial education, for in that year a small hand printing press was donated by an interested patron for the amusement and instruction of the homeless children.

Churches in Brooklyn multiplied rapidly. Parishes began other parishes, and soon every important area was served by an Episcopal Church. The bulk of strength was in the urban area. In 1868 Christ Church had 527 communicants; Grace, 553; Holy Trinity, 555; St. Ann's, 400; St. John's, 451; St. Mary's, 461; St. Peter's, 550; and St. Luke's, 327. All were in the immediate area of Brooklyn Heights. Out-of-town parishes that could match in some way their size were the three colonial parishes: St. George's in Flushing with 350 communicants; St. George's, Hempstead, with 218; and Grace Church, Jamaica, with 190. In 1868, the numerical communicant strength of all the 35 parishes in Brooklyn was 6,917. Queens County, with its eighteen parishes, had only 1,854 communicants. Suffolk, with twelve parishes, had only 243. Brooklyn again led all the other areas in capital assets. Of the $204,720.63 invested in churches, $157,589.88 was Brooklyn's share; $41,989.73, Queen's; and $5,141.04, Suffolk's. It was natural and a foregone conclusion that Brooklyn had made the Episcopal Church on Long Island a formidable force; and that by Brooklyn and in Brooklyn was the initiating force and drive that launched the new Diocese of Long Island.

DAWNING OF A DIOCESE

The leap forward to prosperity and greatness after the Civil War could not fail to show its effects upon that portion of Brooklyn life which has given it one of its most distinctive titles, "the City of Churches." The Episcopal churches on Long Island profited most from the new prosperity, and as a part of the growth and development of Long Island after the Civil War the Diocese of Long Island was "erected."

The question of a separate diocese for the Long Island area was not new. As early as 1861 the division of the

St. Peter's Church,
State Street,
Brooklyn.

38

immense Diocese of New York, of which Long Island was an integral part, had been considered. But the Diocesan Bishop, Horatio Potter, voiced his opposition to small dioceses. However, at the 1861 New York Convention he appointed a committee to consider possible division. After repeated consultations and laborious investigation that committee reported to the Convention of 1862 that a large majority was of the opinion that no present division of the Diocese ought to take place. "I cannot feel myself warranted", said Bishop Potter, "in bringing forward at this time any proposition for the immediate division of the Diocese." The matter, however, did not die but was postponed by the intervening four-year civil conflict. Again in 1866 the suggestion of division was brought before the New York Convention. Bishop Potter reminded the Convention that the division would affect not only Long Island but also the Northern area (Albany), since the wealth of the City sustained this less fortunate part of the Diocese. Thus, an important question involved in the possible separation was raised. He also stated:

> One of the chief objections to the separation of Long Island from the Diocese of New York
> arises from the fact that the city of New York and the city of Brooklyn are virtually one city,
> the same people residing in one city and doing business in the other . . .

The question, simply put, was the problem of two bishops with two overlapping jurisdictions. Another consideration was the problem of whether the county of Staten Island would consent to union with Long Island. or wish to remain with the Diocese of New York. To investigate the situation further, the Convention appointed a committee of eight clergymen and seven laymen, headed by the Honorable Hamilton Fish, who were to report their findings to the next Convention.

At the 1867 Convention the Committee made its lengthy report. After comment was made on the unfortunate death of one of its key members from Long Island, the Honorable John A. King of Grace Church, Jamaica, former Governor of New York, the question of constitutionality was presented. The form of ascertaining the mind of the two sections of the Diocese intimately involved in the separation was a questionnaire sent to the clergy and vestries of both localities. On Long Island, 53 out of 60 clergy replied, 49 expressed themselves in favor of the erection of Long Island into a separate diocese and four were opposed. It was learned from the questionnaire that 9/10's of the clergy and 5/6's of the churchmen on the Island favored a separate diocese. The Committee did not send any circulars to the clergy on Staten Island because they found that a very large proportion of the clergy and vestries on Long Island were opposed to the union of the two areas in the proposed new diocese. The fact that there was no way of access to Staten Island from Long Island without passing through New York seemed to make it most desirable that it should remain connected with the Diocese of New York.

The Committee clearly stated that if Long Island was erected into a separate diocese, it would at once take its place among the first in point of size in the whole Church. It would rank tenth in number of clergy (70), seventh in communicant strength (8,000), and fifth in annual contributions.

The question of the Episcopal Fund and the possibility of its division between the old and the proposed new dioceses engaged the thoughtful consideration of the Committee. The final outcome of the deliberation was a recommendation that no part of the Episcopal Fund be used for the endowment of the proposed episcopate. The same stipulation held for the Fund for Aged and Infirm Clergy. The matter of a name was left entirely to the discretion of the new body.

The General Convention of the Episcopal Church that assembled in New York in October 1868, was a unique group. It was the first time that the whole Church had sat together since the days before the Civil War; in fact since 1859, which was the last convention at which delegates from the Southern states were present. The Diocese of New York was well represented by a delegation of clergy and laity, headed by the Reverend Dr. Abram Littlejohn of the Church of the Holy Trinity, Brooklyn. The lay delegates included the outstanding churchman from New York, the Hon. Hamilton Fish, and from the city of Brooklyn, the well-known Henry Pierrepont. Important to the Diocese of New York was the consent given to the erection of two new dioceses to be known as the Diocese of Northern New York and the Diocese of Long Island. On November 15, 1868, Bishop Potter of New York issued the call for a special convention to form a new diocese which would comprise the counties of Kings, Queens, and Suffolk, commonly known together as Long Island.

On November 18, 1868, the Diocese of Long Island was formed. A cold and rainy day did not stop the members, both clerical and lay, from assembling at the Church of the Holy Trinity in Brooklyn to begin a "pure branch of the one, holy and apostolic church." *The New York Times* reported:

> The Church of the Holy Trinity, corner of Pierrepont and Clinton Streets, Brooklyn, was the
> centre of greatest interest in that city yesterday, the occasion being that of organizing the new
> Protestant Episcopal Diocese of Long Island. The inclemency of the weather presented no
> obstacle to the attendance of either clergy or laity. There was a large congregation of ladies in
> the side seats and in the galleries.

The Brooklyn delegates mingled freely with country church representatives who traveled so far by horse, stagecoach, train or steamboat to be present at this momentous occasion. The thirty-two parishes of Brooklyn, the seventeen from Queens and the five from Suffolk joined together to formulate one body out of many smaller bodies.

At 10:30 A.M. the clergy, in black cassocks and white surplices, entered the church where the delegates from the various parishes were seated. The Service of Morning Prayer and Holy Communion was officiated over by the Bishop of New York, who preached and challenged the assemblage:

> And on this most interesting day, the dawning of a new era for you my dear brethren, when we begin to put together the framework and to erect the proper structure of a new diocese, we say overall the words, devotion, earnest prayer . . . [and we] . . . proclaim one only Rock . . . this now to be organized diocese, this definite and independent portion of our branch of the One, Holy, Catholic Church. The Church . . . [is] . . . a divine institution, duly organized, its faith, its ministry, its sacraments . . . a holy society, a spiritual body—a living body . . . which call for positive thinking and positive work.

Following the service the Primary Convention was called to order, and it was offered and requested that the Bishop of New York act as the presiding officer. The committee appointed to request the Bishop, headed by Governor Jones and General Crooke, reported that the Bishop had graciously accepted; and he was escorted in by the chosen delegates. The entire assemblage arose to their feet as the venerable Bishop entered and remained standing since the formalities of taking the chair were brief. The congregation next turned its attention to choosing its officers. The Reverend Jacob W. Diller of St. Luke's, Brooklyn, was chosen President; the Reverend T. Stafford Drowne of St. Paul's Church, Brooklyn, was elected Secretary. After dispensing with the formalities of considering parishes who wished to be in union with the Diocese and appointing the Committee on Nominations, the following resolution was offered by the Honorable William Ludlow of St. John's, Islip (Oakdale): "Resolved that the new Diocese created in the present Diocese of New York and consisting of the counties of Kings, Queens and Suffolk be known as the Diocese of Long Island." The resolution, temporarily referred to committee, was adopted in the afternoon session. The Convention also pondered the matter of membership in the Convention. A suggestion was make that three-months' attendance at divine service be a condition for membership, instead of one year. Two additional suggestions were make: that there be a six-month requirement or that there be none at all. A vote was taken which decided that six months would constitute the necessary attendance requirement. This resolution would be more important as will be seen later. The question of episcopal support was also raised, and the final decision of the Convention was that a committee to raise the Episcopal Fund be established and that the Bishop's salary be $6,000 per year.

At the morning session on November 19th, the Convention considered the report of the committee of twenty who were appointed by the Diocese of New York to consider the appropriation of an adequate endowment for the Episcopate of the new Diocese. The Bishop of New York and the Convention had stipulated the minimum sum of $60,000 as being fair and equitable. The appointed committee met on December 10, 1867, to consider how the endowment could be raised. They took immediate steps to appropriate the amount among the parishes on Long Island and to ask for a definite commitment on their part. The response was that,

> . . . not withstanding the depression which has prevailed throughout [the] continental community[,] $50,109.75 was pledged and paid, $36,076.24 came from the numerous and well-to-do parishes in Brooklyn, $8,257.00 from the scattered parishes in Queens and $976.50 from isolated Suffolk. The total amount collected was one-penny less than pledged.

Although the amount raised did not meet the minimum required for the endowment of the episcopate stated by New York, it was felt to be sufficient to warrant the election of a bishop with the hope that the new diocese as it grew could add and increase the endowment fund.

The afternoon session of the Convention on November 19th proceeded to the election of a bishop for the Diocese of Long Island. After appropriate collects, prayers and silent prayers, and a hymn, the nominations for the office were made. Prominent among the nine names nominated for the office were the Reverend Dr. Abram Newkirk Littlejohn, Rector of the Church of the Holy Trinity, Brooklyn; the Reverend Alexander H. Vinton; the Reverend Alexander Burgess and the Reverend Eugene A. Hoffman. On the third ballot Dr. Littlejohn was elected. The results were that out of a total clerical vote of 67, he had received the necessary 34; and out of the laity vote of 54, he had received 34—although only 28 were needed for election. On the reading of the results of the third ballot, the Convention declared Dr. Littlejohn duly elected the first Bishop of Long Island.

That Dr. Littlejohn would be a bishop there was no doubt. The question was where and when. The selection of the church leaders in Brooklyn affirmed the convictions of the Diocese of Central New York; for on November 11, 1868, eight days previous to the Long Island convention, it had elected him the bishop of that diocese. That he preferred Long Island to Central New York was not immediately known. The *Brooklyn Daily Eagle*, on August 4, 1904, retrospectively commented: " . . . he was first elected to Central New York. He neither accepted or declined until by very close ingenious and skillful canvassing he was elected the first Bishop of Long Island. To doubly confirm that Dr. Littlejohn was episcopal material, had he not been elected to Long Island, it was decided to make him Bishop of Albany."

The Bishop-elect had been recognized, not only at a local level but also in the national Church, as a leader of outstanding ability. He was born in Florida in 1824. Graduated from Union College, New York in 1845, he studied privately for the Episcopal ministry. Ordained a deacon at Auburn, New York, he moved soon after to the Diocese of Connecticut where in 1849, he was ordained to the priesthood. He served several parishes, two in

Connecticut, Meriden and Springfield, and one in New York, Amsterdam. Recognizing his outstanding academic ability, Hobart College offered him the presidency in 1858, which he declined. He came to Brooklyn in 1860 to serve as the Rector of Holy Trinity Church, where his accomplishments as pastor and money-raiser made him well known in the New York area. He was one of the ablest preachers in the Episcopal pulpit. "As a preacher and pastor the new bishop [had] few equals among the Episcopal clergy with whom preaching is not the specialty that it is with some other demoninations. His church [was] always crowded." While a Brooklyn Rector, he served as a New York delegate to the General Convention, actively participating in the proceedings and serving as chairman of several important committees. His personal characteristics matched his leadership ability. He was a fine looking man, well-formed and stately. His manner was impressive. Although naturally a reserved person, he was an agreeable conversationalist who never lost sight of his reverent character.

The most interesting fact about his selection as Bishop of Long Island was that many felt his election to be a compromise between the two factions that had split the Episcopal Church in the mid-nineteenth century. The Episcopal Church was rent by a conflict between the "high" and "low" church parties and aggravated by the growth of a third faction called "The Broad Church Party". The Oxford Movement, begun by a small group of university dons in 1833, had reached the Church in America. The men at Oxford assessed the Church as lacking its Catholic nature, which emphasized Christian tradition, especially as it was practiced in the Middle Ages, and the historic Episcopate. By these emphases they came to be called the Anglo-Catholic Party. The old high churchmen of the 1830's emphasized theological principles, while the Anglo-Catholics stressed ceremonial usage. After the Civil War, the two groups had merged. The evangelical movement, growing out of the Great Awakening, centered on a searching presentation of what they regarded as the fundamental truth of the Gospel as revealed in Jesus Christ. As a reaction against both schools of thought, men in touch with the new knowledge and discoveries of science were equally repelled by the static theology of the Evangelists as well as the traditional statements of Catholicism. They in turn formed the Broad Church Party.

The outbreak of the Civil War arrested party strife which loomed large over the use of the ritual. Matters drifted until 1868 when the Rev. Stephen H. Tyng, Jr., was brought to trial by the Bishop of New York for violating the Canon that stated no minister could officiate in another's cure without the express permission of the incumbent. The Rev. Mr. Tyng had officiated in a Methodist church in New Jersey. The trial had widespread coverage of the press. He was found guilty and was publicly admonished by Bishop Potter of New York. At the General Convention of 1868 the delegates grappled with the problem. It was referred to the Committee on Canons which brought back a majority and minority report. To ease the tension that the discussion had engendered, Dr. Littlejohn skillfully submitted a resolution which placated both parties. The matter seemed to be settled amicably.

It was against such a background that the choice of Bishop Littlejohn appeared to be a compromise between the various factions in the Church. The *Brooklyn Daily Eagle*, on November 20th, 1868, commented that "if we understand the affairs of the Diocese correctly, neither the high church party nor the low church party have a majority of the churches or the clergy while there is a small party of moderately conservative men." The critical point was the choice of a bishop. Dr. Eugene A. Hoffman of Grace Church was the candidate of the high church faction; Alexander H. Vinton, the low church. Dr. Littlejohn had advocates in both parties. "The result is the choice of a candidate who does not represent either of any defined party but fairly stands for the policy of the National Convention, which after warmly discussing the questions which agitate the church, postponed them."

A special committee, appointed by the Presiding officer of the Primary Convention to wait on the Bishop-elect, conducted him to the Chair where he addressed the assembled delegates:

> In humility the position in which your suffrages have placed me this day fills me with such profound emotion, and my decision will of necessity be embarrassed by complications which the will of divine providence has chosen at this time to throw around me ... and if after mature and prayerful consideration it shall appear to be my duty to accept the Bishopric of Long Island to which you have elected me it will be my endeavor with God's help to prove not unworthy of your confidence and your hope.

The election and presentation of the new Bishop was completed; the work of the Diocese had begun. The first committee which met at the close of the Convention to take the necessary steps of receiving the Bishop's acceptance and of planning for his consecration, ironically enough had to face as its first order of business the questioning of the legality of the most important official act of the brand new diocese—the election of its first bishop. Doubts about a proper election had been expressed to the committee. The Presiding Officer of the Convention had stopped the Rev. Alva Guion on a technicality from voting on the third ballot without any reference of such an action to the Convention. Since Bishop Littlejohn had been elected by a majority of one vote, it was claimed that if the Rev. Mr. Guion had voted, the necessary majority to elect would have had to be more than Dr. Littlejohn had received. The whole matter was referred to three lawyers, "gentlemen learned in canonical law." On December 14, 1868, after examining the case carefully and presenting their lengthy briefs, all three concurred that Bishop Littlejohn had been legally elected and could be consecrated as The Bishop of Long Island. This affirmation of the legality of Bishop Littlejohn's election symbolized the sure assertion of the Diocese's identity as a separate entity and the certain imprint that this man was to leave in shaping the course of the new diocese.

Chapter Four

It Takes a While to Get Started

DULY CONSECRATED

It was a fine winter day, bright and crisply cold. The majestic Church of the Holy Trinity on Brooklyn Heights stood out clearly as the many carriages added numbers to the already pressing crowds of handsomely dressed men in cutaway and top hat and women in crinolines or modish bustle dresses. Lines had to wait patiently at the church door as many ahead were seated. "Hundreds of ladies and gentlemen sought to enter the church but they had to submit to disappointment there not being even standing room left a few moments after the opening of the doors." It was January 27, 1869, the day of the consecration of the first Bishop of Long Island.

The interior of the large and beautiful church had been especially prepared for the solemn but joyous occasion. "The communion table was covered by white satin cloths and on the table a floral cross, of massive proportions and splendid workmanship, on either side a very large bouquet and in front a wreath of japanecis, all of white." As the procession of clergy, a mixture of black Geneva gown or white Oxford surplice, entered "every voice was hushed, and then the full organ, choir, ministers, and congregation joined in the song of praise."

Towards the end of the procession, attended by two deacons of honor, and just ahead of the consecrators, walked the Bishop-elect, proud and stately, exhibiting those combined qualities of quiet aloofness and benign geniality which were to become his signature.

The preacher of the day, the Bishop of New Jersey, gave his charge to the Bishop-elect: "The church of Christ in this land and age needs for her Bishops men of love and men of nerve: Those whose heart and imagination are large enough to take in all varieties of men and tones of thought, which the Catholic character of the church legitimately and avowedly tolerates; and whose will and conscience are resolute enough to exercise the canonical discipline of the church upon disloyal offenders be the consequences what they may."

After this exhortative address, the formal proceedings of making a Bishop continued. The Bishop-elect in his black rochet was presented by the Bishops of Western New York and Nebraska to the Bishop of New York sitting in his chair near the altar. After the reading of the testimonial and the oath of conformity, the attending presbyters vested him with the rest of the episcopal habit. After the laying on of hands, the Presiding Bishop delivered the Bible to the newly consecrated Bishop who took his place among the other Bishops during the singing of the offertory anthem.

The ceremony was followed by the administration of Holy Communion which lasted well into the afternoon. As a token of unity and a symbol of origin, the communion ware used at the service were the chalices and patens presented by Queen Anne in 1706 to parish churches in Jamaica and Hempstead. At the completion of the service, an appropriate letter of consecration embossed upon parchment, was signed and officially executed by the consecrating Bishop and his assistants. The Diocese of Long Island now had its own first Bishop.

The joyous music ended; the intended act had been well done; the clergy and the church members dispersed to their own communities to take up their pastoral duties and continue their own individual work. The erection of the Diocese and the consecration of the Bishop had been dispatched in good order. The initial act seemed well done; but the job was only begun.

NO PLACE TO LAY HIS HEAD

An immediate and pressing need the Diocese had to face and solve was an adequate episcopal residence. At the primary convention measures were initiated to provide a suitable dwelling for the new Bishop. There was a firm stipulation in the election of the executive that he was not to serve as the rector of a parish in addition to being the Bishop. He was to give his full time and energy to diocesan works and not divide his attention making the Diocese, as so often had happened, a secondary interest. Since Abram Littlejohn had been the Rector of Holy Trinity, he was forced to vacate the church rectory when the Rev. Charles H. Hall came to occupy that place as Rector in May 1869. The Bishop rented a home for a few months and then found lodgings in one of the local hotels.

The committee on the episcopal residence reported to the 1869 Convention that their first thought was that the Diocese should not buy a home for the Bishop, but they should give him a yearly allowance of $3,000 and the responsibility of finding his own home. An appeal for funds was made to all the churches in the Diocese; only two responded. Private solicitation by the chairman of the committee, Seymour L. Husted, of St. Mary's Church, Brooklyn, who had donated $1,000 himself, had brought two large pledges from Grace Church and Holy Trinity in Brooklyn. Since the Diocese was reluctant to contribute to a house allowance, the whole matter of a permanent residence was reconsidered. The committee agreed that:

> It is not seemly and right, in this great and growing city, the third city in the Union, the seat of our favoured See, with its many churches, its great wealth, and known munificence, that we should leave our Bishop, whom we have called from a noble and commodious Rectory, literally without a home "wherein to lay his head", compelled to dwell in "his own hired house", as is now the case, to be the occupant of lodgings for himself and his family in a hotel.

Their decision was to purchase a residence so as to afford a good home for the Bishop, to relieve him of the necessity of constant moves, and perhaps most important, to have a sound financial investment. The committee, unable to report in 1870, did in 1871, state that a spacious, thoroughly built, and conveniently located episcopal residence at 170 Remsen Street, had been purchased. The actual cost of the property was $39,007.04 with an extra $5,997.92 to refurbish and repair the three-story brownstone. The Bishop had received, in addition, a gift of $3,000 to furnish his new home. The matter was completed satisfactorily to both the committee and the Bishop. In his convention address of 1871, the Bishop voiced his apparent approval:

> It is with great pleasure that I inform you of the successful completion by the committee of fifteen laymen, appointed by the convention of September 1869, of the important work assigned to them. They have purchased and raised the means to pay for an Episcopal Residence which is eminently satisfactory to your Bishop, and so far as he knows, to the whole Diocese. They hand over to the Trustees of the Episcopal Fund this very valuable property without a farthing of debt.

MONEY, MONEY, MONEY.

Harder to solve and longer to persist was the question of diocesan support. Amid the lush surroundings of the wealthy and affluent Church of the Holy Trinity on Brooklyn Heights, a diocese had been organized, its executive head elected and consecrated. The component churches had gladly deliberated and voted; but when asked, they exhibited a reluctance to contribute to the support of that added touch of decor that would give dignity and grace to an already luxuriant scene. Satisfaction that if a church needed to be consecrated, a class confirmed, or a commemorative exercise held, all the splendor of ecclesiastical purple was readily available, did not elicit a willingness to contribute for the material necessities of the Bishop nor a motivation to support a diocesan program.

Inadequacy of parish support for the episcopate became immediately evident. In 1869, the Committee on the Salary of the Bishop had to admit that contributions had fallen far short of expectation so that $1,217.02 was still owed the Bishop on his annual salary. An improvement was noted by 1871 when an added increment for upkeep and repairs of the episcopal residence had been allotted. In 1872, the committee observed that contributions by parishes were "just barely sufficient to meet the payments". In 1873, a more hopeful sign was that assessments were generally acquiesced to and paid with very creditable promptness. The danger, however, persisted. The margin between parish payment and needed episcopal support did not enhance a feeling of security which the committee hoped to achieve.

The firm stipulation of the establishment of an adequate Episcopal Endowment Fund, as a prerequisite for diocesan establishment on Long Island, had brought payments and pledges from most of the island parishes. At the Primary Convention there was the assurance of a fund amounting to $45,309.74 with a pledge of $4,800 more, making a total of $50,109.75. Parishes paid by note, bond, or by promise. An abiding problem showed itself in an inability of parishes to meet their promises and in an insufficiency of large gifts to enlarge the endowment fund. Since actual donation fell far short of expectation, a committee was appointed to pursue "the apportionment of the charitable or other funds of the late undivided diocese of New York," hoping to share in the fund to which many Long Island parishes had contributed without ever having enjoyed any benefit from these contributions. The amount that Long Island "justly" claimed varied from $25,272.09 to $21,000. The committee had frustrating experiences in negotiating with the mother diocese. New York turned a deaf ear to their query, refusing to divide the New York Episcopal Fund, although they did forward a small amount to the Long Island Aged and Infirm Clergy Fund. Despair at rejection of the Island's fund claims and an already precarious situation spurred their efforts to secure money from any sources whatsoever. The immediacy of action was precipitated by the poor local support for all diocesan ventures.

The same lack of parish motivation and maintenance was evident in the contribution to the Diocesan Fund, which took care of all the necessary paraphernalia of the three day convention, including travel allowances for delegates living at a far distance. A balance of $4.74 after a year's experience made the situation crucial. After much exhortation, both episcopal and clerical, the fund did show a small balance in 1871 and 1872. By 1873, the fund was in trouble again with expenses for the year $325.37 more than receipts. An assessment of 1% on the

Rector's salary for the fund had to be raised to 1½% in order to make up the protracted deficit.

Constant pleas, emotional, theoretical, or statistical, issued forth from the Missionary Committee for sufficient funds to do their work. Although missionary giving had increased 350%, it was still only enough to underwrite existing programs and gave little room for aggressive expansion. Support had increased from a little over $1,000 in 1869 to $4,381.24 in 1871, but it was still only enough to meet contracted payments and leave a small balance for the working account. Although receipts had risen in 1872 to $5,663.08; with all expenses paid, only $677.40 or about one third the previous year's balance remained, "with which to meet the payments of the coming quarter [and] insufficient to pay the stipends of the Missionaries."

> Forty-five (45) of the Parishes and Mission Stations in the Diocese have contributed to Diocesan Missions, through your Committee, during the last twelve months, leaving nearly as many which have not signified, in this canonical and natural manner, their interest in the work. Of the churches contributing, twenty-three are in Kings County, thirteen in Queens, and nine in Suffolk. And the twenty-three in Kings County have given $3,676.89; the thirteen in Queens, $875.90; the nine in Suffolk, $1,010.29.

A slight improvement exhibited itself in 1873 with an increase of $551.14 over the previous year, yet with a decreased number of churches reporting. Missionary giving was a fluid substance; sometimes inadequate, sometimes disproportionate, but all times unpredictable.

Financial problems and much-sought solvency occupied greatly the attention and thought of the Diocese and its component members. Inability to contribute stemmed from the overburdened and debt-ridden conditions of many of the Island churches. Some churches,

> . . . stimulated by the great prosperity of the city and by a landmark ambition to attract people by fine edifices and generous appointments [had] discounted the resources of the future beyond the limits of sound judgement, and laboring under a burden which not only embarrassed themselves [made] them unable to do for the Diocesan objects what their apparent strength would lead [one] to expect.

The experience of St. John's Church, Brooklyn, when they had incurred a debt of $45,000, which although slightly reduced, still caused a heavy burden, was duplicated to a greater or lesser degree in many of the local churches. Few parishes could have stated, as did Christ Church, Manhasset, that their entire indebtedness had been cancelled.

Local support was in the process of change. The chief means of procuring money for parish finances were large contributions and pew-renting. In the years before the Civil War, a movement sprang up in the Episcopal Church to make churches free for all. The first "free church" in the Church had been founded by The Rev. William Muhlenberg. The movement spread more rapidly after the war and gained some support from the National Church. On Long Island the free church movement had taken hold and by 1869 there were ten free churches and as many free chapels making up 30% of the total number of churches. The alternative to family ownership of church seatings as an income-getter was a free weekly offering on the part of the congregation. The envelope system, either pledged or not, was becoming more and more popular. Church of the Ascension, Brooklyn, introduced the envelope system; while Emmanuel Church, "deriving its means of support from the weekly free-will offerings of the congregation, humbly presented and prayed upon the Holy Table", found the system most successful after a year's experiment. Church of the Reformation, Brooklyn, "adopted the more excellent way of Sunday offerings" with the fond hope that all "fairs, raffles, grab-bags, etc. may hereafter be dispensed with." St. Paul's, E.D., Brooklyn, elatedly stated that through the envelope system offerings had been doubled. St. Stephen's, Brooklyn, was a free church with an unpledged offertory.

The free church movement had many overtones, none of which the Bishop overlooked in his rational endorsement of the whole idea. He declared it "a most efficient, if not indispensable help in the aggressive missionary work of the church," adding that,

> This free system moreover, emancipates the churches from the small tyranny of individual ownerships, and assures to them a freer control over the common property, whether with a view to changes of interior arrangements, or to local improvements, or to multiplied services.

The renting of pews or the free-will offering did not provide all the needed funds. Extraordinary means were resorted to for parish maintenance and diocesan support. Lectures, sometimes in conjunction with musicals or concerts, brought occasional income. Ladies' fairs, often of a week's duration, and "calico balls", as well as raffles and special offerings, were popular as money-raising ventures.

The indisposition to subscribe diocesan projects or parish plans effectively did not reflect any lack of monetary resources or propensity to expend wealth of dollars in other areas of life. Long Island in general, and Brooklyn in particular, had experienced a great period of prosperity. Huge sums were spent on all phases of luxury and comforts for the good life. The source of wealth was there; it was the tapping of that source that presented the problem. The Missionary Committee ably summed up the disparity. Begging for support, they succinctly and graphically pictured the contrast:

(above) Christ Church, Manhasset, founded 1802.
(right) Diocese House, Remsen Street, Brooklyn.

There are sad incongruities in our outward exhibitions of our Christianity. Apparently the world before heaven; self above God. Ample residences for ourselves, ceiled in cedar, painted with vermillion, gleaming with gold, and God's temples, straitened, unadorned, unattractive. The appointments of our establishments marked by costliness, elegance and luxury, of God's institutions, by narrowness, cheapness and discomfort. Costly fabrics and elegant jewelry and dashing equipages for our gratification, for God's honor, cheap furnishings, meagre appliances and unkempt surroundings. Hundreds for our personal adornment and attractiveness, while fingers flashing with diamonds are outstretched forth to drop dimmed rays into God's treasury . . . There is a serious responsibility then, in the matter of the occupancy of God's temporal possessions. A just proportion is a matter of debt, and as such is to be paid.

THE HEART OF THE MATTER.

Parochial reluctance to become fully involved in the life of the Diocese was symptomatic of a deeper and far more serious tension. Continued disappointments, unwise outlay of strength, and obstruction to diocesan growth arose from "the somewhat selfish and narrow corporate individualism of parishes" that did not see the work of the Diocese as their work, nor did they see, reciprocally, that their growth was healthy only if it ministered to that of the Diocese. For many years, parishes had had little if any foresight. Since Long Island was only a small section of the larger Diocese of New York, parishes did not feel the necessity to become intimately involved. Except for occasional confirmations or visitations, local units conducted their affairs in the best style of a congregational church, feeling no compunction to engage actively or support passively another level of work. Episcopacy and the diocesan organism had only been initiated after the Island churches had developed their own self-interest and self-centered parochialism. The result of this was disorderly and random lines of development without any healthy organic life and without any vital principle of cohesion. Clergy and laity went on in a blind way, organizing parishes and building churches without any preconceived or accepted scheme of expansion, but simply as taste, caprice or personal convenience dictated. Hugh parish debts were created in a spirit of recklessness and extravagance which continued as a sore spot in church life.

The failure of a right relationship between the diocese and the parish grew out of a state of mind which was unwilling to accept the diocese, not the parish, as the true ecclesiastical unit. The duplicity of outlook and the inconsistency of the principle of congregationalism showed itself in all phases of the new Diocese. None was more evident than in the matter of diocesan support; in this area parishes objected to an assessment as a direct tax. The tension between parish and diocese appeared immediately upon the initiation of a diocesan program. It continued to prove an embarrassment to the Bishop and an harassment to diocesan expansion. The problem was not easily solved; the tension remained an unwanted undercurrent.

LEAD THE FOLLOWERS

In spite of the difficulties which beset the Diocese in becoming a separate and working financial organism and in instilling in its component parishes a sense of involvement in its work, the Diocese was fortunate in having a man who was not deterred by the new emerging difficulties. He was assisted in his task of establishing the new diocese by the dedicated clergy who surrounded him and who served as the nucleus and tentacles of the diocesan organism.

Abraham Littlejohn was forty-four years old, in the prime of life and no stranger to the Diocese. Serving for eight years as Rector of Holy Trinity, he had become thoroughly familiar with the problems, conditions and possibilities of his new field. An outstanding leader in the Diocese of New York, a national figure of pre-eminence, chairing many of the important committees of the General Convention, he had the ability and the perceptiveness to understand his position and the aggressiveness to pursue his course. As chief pastor and nominal head of the churches that stretched out from the busy, dynamic City of Brooklyn to the barren and isolated wilds of Suffolk, he had not only to inspire but also to coordinate the local parishes' share in strengthening the work of the larger unit. It was an immense task, requiring constant surveillance and astute judgment, one in which he had to rely on others for help and advice.

The Inner Corps —

Surrounding the Bishop, a small group of clergy and laity, recruited largely from the wealthiest sections of Brooklyn Heights and South Brooklyn, dominated the Diocese. Thirteen top key men decided policy and monopolized the one hundred and twenty-three elective or appointive diocesan positions. Nine clergymen, chief of whom was the newcomer, the Rev. Charles H. Hall, Rector of Holy Trinity; the Rev. Noah H. Schenck, Rector of St. Ann's Church; the Rev. Benjamin H. Paddock, Rector of Grace Church; the Rev. T. Stafford Drowne, Rector of St. Paul's Church; together with the Rev. Daniel V. M. Johnson, Rector of St. Mary's Church, held 42 or two-thirds of the 66 clergy posts. Two clergy outside the small ring, but intimately bound up in it and permitted to share in the control, were the Rector of St. George's Church, Hempstead, and the Rector of St. George's Church, Flushing. The chosen laity formed an even tighter power circle. Four laymen, Henry E. Pierrepont and Alexander V. Blake of Grace Church, Charles R. Marvin of Christ Church, Clinton Street, and John A. King of Little Neck, controlled one-third of all the sixty-six lay positions. The elite corps of clergy and laity were members of the powerful Standing Committee, Missionary Committee and the Diocesan Delegation to the General Convention.

The Outer Circle —

Neither as affluent, nor as influential as the elite group, were the other eighty-six clergy who filled the lesser diocesan positions and carried on the church's work in parishes smaller in number and more limited in scope. The clergy attended the yearly meetings, fulfilled their responsibilities on committees, and for the most part were in attendance as the group came to watch, listen and vote.

On the whole they were an active, well-equipped group, attempting, as well as they knew how, to bring the church's ministrations to their own congregations and to comfort the friendless, the needy, and the unchurched. Mostly educated at General Theological Seminary, these men had a moderate Victorian view of church and a propensity to move from parish to parish, frequently remaining in a parish no longer than two to three years.

Stipends for the clergy were thoroughly inadequate. Except for the more blessed parishes in Brooklyn Heights and its adjacent areas, the clergy's subsistence level was low, due to poor salaries gleaned from small cures. The Bishop's salary which was $6,000 a year was on a level with the more prosperous rectors of the larger city parishes. The Rector of Grace Church received one-third that, having an annual stipend of $2,000. Less populated and less popular churches descended the wage scale to sometimes a little over $500 per annum. Salaries were not equal to those earned by ordinary mechanics, some being below even that paid to unskilled laborers who worked on the farm or in the factory.

A shortage of clergy due to the obvious inequality of economic opportunity made the existing clergy overworked. Because of their continuous activity they were not able to keep up with their reading. Lack of books and lack of time produced an unscholarly attitude and an uncultivated sense of professional deficiency. The most obvious by-product was preaching which lacked freshness, variety and power.

Another problem was that provisions for health and welfare of the clergy were meagre and insufficient. Inherited from the New York Diocese was an Aged and Infirmed Clergy Fund, but it was totally inadequate to provide for the sick or the disabled clergyman. Assistance given, pitifully small, was more for act of charity than provision for dignity. Constant appeals in the Diocese did not enhance the fund nor the material support of the older clergy. Life insurance was advocated by the Bishop as a means to provide for families of deceased clergy. A policy of $2,500 worth was suggested, but the practical difficulty was to provide for a necessary annual premium. Clerical salaries were on the whole inadequaate to provide for this, so it devolved upon the vestries, congregations, or upon individual laymen. In 1871, General Convention authorized the formation of a General Fund to assist in the relief of widows and orphans of deceased and disabled clergymen. The principle was carried over into the Diocese with the expansion of coverage in the Aged and Infirmed Clergy Fund, to take care of widows and orphans.

In matters of churchmanship, by and large the clergy of the Diocese were conservative and monochromatic. There were a few who championed the principles of the Anglo-Catholic revival and their leanings were made obvious in their churches and their work. The Rev. Samuel M. Haskins, Rector of St. Mark's, Brooklyn, and the Rev. Daniel V. M. Johnson, were among the first of the American clergy to welcome the Oxford Revival, and they became leaders of the small island group. Never extremists, they exhibited "sane Catholicity" and deep theological thought. The tension between high and low church had reached its climax in the years after the Civil War. The attempts of the General Convention of 1868 to arbitrate the two opposing factions had proved ineffective. In 1871, the General Convention was presented with the proposal of a canon to list forbidden ritual practices which included many things from incense to vested choirs and choral services. The proposal failed to pass, but the heat generated in the fray had thrown farther apart the two camps. A natural outcome of the turmoil for the new diocese was the establishment of a permanent court for the trial of ecclesiastical offenses.

> Such a Court is no new experiment. It has been fully tested in a sister Diocese . . . it will secure two things most desirable in the discipline of the church: — 1. A body of triers trained to the experience of judicial functions, and duly informed of the provisions and bearings of ecclesiastical law. 2. A court the very method of whose appointment will relieve it of all just suspicion of partiality or prejudice. . . .

The court was not used. The tenor of the Diocese continued irenic, more involved in other things, by-passing opportunity to bicker or haggle. Every clergyman labored quietly in his own field, having little time for the noisy antagonisms of party strife. As men of intellect, they, of course, differed in their opinions, yet maintained their differences in an "atmosphere of large and friendly tolerism, uncongenial to the growth of any roots of bitterness."

National ferment did not find as comfortable a solution. Verbal controversy boiled over into active conflict with an eventual schism by a small group of radical evangelicals. The Rt. Rev. George D. Cummins, Assistant Bishop of Kentucky, a consistent and hard-headed evangelical, preached and received communion on October 12, 1873, in a non-Episcopal church. Censured, he left the Episcopal Church in November and on December 2, 1873, a number of evangelicals met with him in New York City to form the Reformed Episcopal Church. The "almost universal sentiment" of the Diocese was one of grief and shock at the "rash and unwise proceedings of those who have gone out from us, to add another to the already melancholy list of sects." The Diocese had no propensity for extremists in either direction. The moderate middle-of-the-road diocesan character was reflected in the words of Bishop Littlejohn:

> The soil of Long Island is not congenial to reformers of the Church's faith and order, not to discoverers and experimenters in ritualistic novelties and extravagences.

MOUTHPIECES OF THE CHURCH

The clergy were joined by active church laymen in giving leadership on a parish rather than a diocesan level, mainly by serving as wardens and vestrymen. The local elected vestry, a churchly board of directors, dealt in things temporal. They controlled and sometimes dictated budgetary expenditures, inspected church property, and kept up the physical plant's fabric to insure a proper atmosphere for the conduct of church services. A few laymen, wishing to be more actively involved in the missionary outreach, served as lay readers. This minor office, sometimes a stepping stone to the church ministry, was utilized primarily in the establishment of parochial or diocesan missions or as an appendage to a missionary program in several areas, assisting the clergy by reading the offices or visiting in the area.

The need to incorporate men more fruitfully into the active work of the church became clear to many local parishes. Some parishes had a well-conceived and well-organized men's organization known under the accepted formulary of the Brotherhood. Singly, or as a group, the Brotherhood accepted the responsibility for parish mission stations, conducting services, organizing parish groups and "teaching the rudiments of religion and the usages of our Church."

In addition to extending religious knowledge and carrying out missionary operations, the Brotherhood offered charitable relief to the aged, infirm, orphaned and destitute; organized libraries of religious books; and in some few cases assisted in the education of young men for the church ministry. A most active Brotherhood was the local group at St. George's, Flushing, organized in 1871. They capably took charge of Sunday School and Mission work at the Town Poor Farm; assisted at the mission in College Point; took over the mission work at Queens

Village when the diocesan missionary left; and established a mission at Bayside.

A regional group that encompassed both laymen and clergymen was the Brotherhood of the Protestant Episcopal Church of Brooklyn. Organized as early as 1853, the Brotherhood was primarily more charitable than missionary, more self-help than others-help. Its membership consisted of clergy able to do their duties and laymen over eighteen years of age, capable of earning a livelihood; and all members were required to be residents of the city. The objects of the society were the mutual care and relief of its members in time of sickness or accident, the burial of its deceased, the succor of their widows and orphans, the promotion of Christian fellowship and love, and also the aid of distressed members of the church generally.

A novel experiment in harnessing the power of the laity was the Parish Guild, organized at St. Stephen's Church in Brooklyn. Started in 1871, the guild was "open for membership to the Parish generally, without distinction of sex [as a] method of calling out the interest of the Laity in Church enterprises within the Parish."

Woman's Work Never Done —

Women had always been actively engaged in the work of the community and in the church. They were fund-raisers, making money through fairs, bazaars, sewing circles, musicales, and lectures. After the Civil War, women became more emancipated from the drudgery and routine of homelife and household duties and had more time to devote to themselves or to some worthwhile endeavors. The war services of women, the increasing number of women in the professions, and the use of women's clubs highlighted the aspiration of women to partake more in the life about them.

To thousands of women the club movement opened new vistas of activity and usefulness. These women, busy during the war with innumerable new tasks, could not go back to the sheltered idleness of the fifties. At first the clubs were conservative in aim, emphasizing study and cultural pursuits, but they soon annexed large provinces of civic, philanthropic and church activity.

In the Episcopal Church on Long Island, women's organizations had a multitude of names and a diversity of purposes. Called the Ladies Association, Parish Aid Society, Dorcas Society, Missionary Aid Society, or the Parish Aid Guild, they undertook to support missions at home to the Blacks or Indians, or missions abroad; to underwrite parish programs of improvements or building; and to engage in charitable work among the neighborhood poor and destitute, focusing special attention upon the wayward girl and the underprivileged orphan.

No regional or diocesan organization for women existed prior to 1871. At the General Convention of that year a new branch of the Board of Missions was created by a resolution offered by Bishop Littlejohn. Following up the convention's recommendation, on November 26, 1872, fifteen women met at St. Peter's Church in Brooklyn to form The Woman's Missionary Association of the Diocese of Long Island. By December 10th, a set of by-laws and constitution had been written and presented for approval to the fifty-one women and thirty-four clergy who came to participate in the Association's foundation. After a lengthy address by the diocesan bishop, the Association began its work, and its first contributions went towards purchasing a cow for the Bishop Whipple Hospital in Minnesota and a pair of Texas ponies for a Bishop Garrett.

A favored project of the Bishop which received much attention was the organized work of Christian women. In 1871, a special committee was appointed to study the possibility of a female parochial diaconate and sisterhoods. The subject of organized women's work had agitated the General Convention since 1850. They looked towards the formulation of some plan by which, "consistent with the principles of our Reformed Communion, the services of intelligent and pious women might be secured to the church . . . in the education of the young, the relief of the sick and the destitute, the care of orphans and the friendless, and the reformation of the vicious." In 1856, the matter was enlarged upon, discussed in emphatic terms at an ensuing convention and actually realized in several dioceses. There were in 1871, three sisterhoods in New York, two in Maryland, one in Massachusetts; and a Training School in Philadelphia for mission women and hospital nurses. The General Convention of 1871 discussed the subject, and the Pastoral Letter of the House of Bishops warmly advocated it. Bishop Littlejohn, sensing an affirmation of his own ideas, translated his opinion into fact. On February 11, 1872, in St. Mary's Church, Brooklyn, he publicly admitted six women to the office of Deaconess; and on March 15th, another in Emmanuel Church. The seven deaconesses were assigned to their tasks: two were employed at the Church Charity Foundation; one went to the Public Institution of Kings County; and four were engaged in parish work. This method of organizing the services of women was adopted because it furnished the simplest, safest and easiest way to accomplish its purpose. Apparent public confusion required the Bishop to clarify the form of admission, explaining that service was not an ordination but an admission to a sacred office with a limited tenure of ten years. A Deaconess House, to provide for communal living of deaconesses and a training center for probationers, was provided by the gift of a house, complete with furnishings, worth $20,000, given by a Charles Deake as a memorial for his dead wife. The Sisters of St. John the Evangelist had begun.

"FIRST THE BLADE, THEN THE EAR . . . "

The means by which the Bishop and his lieutenants chartered the course of the loosely knit structure known as the Diocese of Long Island was an annual meeting, the Diocesan Convention. The Convention transacted all necessary business, planned for the diocesan program, elected delegates and officers, and provided financial sustenance. Or as the Bishop himself aptly summed it up:

> We are here indeed for business, here to inspect and where needed to mend, and to keep in motion the proper machinery of Diocesan work, here to make and to alter laws as circumstances may require, here to discuss ways and means, and to establish a wise economy in the administration of all our resources.

The annual meeting was held for three days, first in the fall, and then in 1870 shifted to the spring and was composed of clerical and lay delegates from all the Island churches in union with the Diocese. The meeting was chaired by the Bishop and headed by two diocesan officers, the Secretary and the Treasurer. A series of disconnected committees, either appointed by the chair or elected by the convention, attempted to plan and execute a program in the area assigned to them. Besides the central, elected Standing Committee, there was a long list of committees, of which second in importance was the Missionary Committee. Each committee worked with its own budget, raised by itself, and with its own program, attempting to answer pressing needs as they arose in the foundation of diocesan work. There came about a conglomeration of individual working groups, each fostering at best its own aims, and each pleading for funds to underwrite what little program it could effect. The final and, in most cases, the only onus of liability rested upon the Bishop, who, through force of personality or by adamant exhortation, accrued the means and backing to extend diocesan ventures.

The mechanics of operating a new diocese occupied a great deal of time and energy in the first few conventions. Of primary importance was a local set of Canons for the Diocese which were largely adaptations of those of New York. Each new diocesan act required a proper agency or a suitable vehicle. The beginning of the Episcopal Fund made the incorporation of The Trustees for the Management and Care of the Property for the Support of the Episcopate of the Diocese of Long Island an accomplished necessity in 1869. In 1870, The Aged and Infirm Clergy Fund required a corporate body to receive and hold funds. A Diocesan Fund to care for the operation of the convention such as printing, travel allowance, etc. had to be immediately organized. And in 1871, because of an offer of land, The Trustees of the Estate of the Diocese of Long Island was incorporated according to state law.

The newly launched diocese did not easily forget its place of origin. Over and over again the Long Island Diocese made known its deep gratitude to its fostering body, the Diocese of New York. With flowery sentiment, the new diocese reaffirmed that, "the joint counsels, the united labors, and the brotherly fellowship of years gone by, when we were one Diocese, are fresh and pleasant in the memory." Yet as the new diocese labored to firmly found its own diocese, a movement was set afoot that would reunite the dioceses again. The General Convention of 1868 had stipulated that where a large diocese had been subdivided, there should be brought into being a means whereby the smaller dioceses could and should follow some kind of co-operative action. At the establishment of the Long Island Diocese and another northern diocese of Albany, the first move was made to set up some kind of federate council or provincial body. A special committee to study and recommend the project was appointed, reporting to the conventions of 1869, 1870, and 1871. One item in all the discussions became increasingly clear. The various dioceses of New York State could and should join together. The burning question was for what purpose and with what aim in view. The question remained unanswered.

THREE-PRONGED OFFENSIVE

The Diocese, following the lead of the Bishop, concentrated its ministry in three major areas of concern. At the 1869 Convention, in his primary address, Bishop Littlejohn laid down the pattern of diocesan work by which the immediate and pressing needs of the island could be met. Assessing the evolving complexity of Long Island's growth, he firmly emphasized the need for an expansion of charitable works; he openly clarified the diocesan offensive in education; and he hopefully advocated an aggressive missionary policy in all aspects of the Island community. Of the three, missionary work received the first and foremost consideration.

Here a Church: There a Church —
The immediate task took the form of providing clergy and church buildings to minister to the growing communities springing up all over the island. Previous attempts at church extension had been haphazard, temporary and fragmentary. No pre-arranged and acknowledged plan of expansion had been undertaken. Prior to diocesan foundation, clergy and laity went on in a blind way, organizing parishes and building churches as simply their own idea, or taste, or neighborhood convenience dictated. When the Diocese was formed, it assumed them as a part of its charge and duty.

> With its territory it received Mission Stations which were generally organized Parishes (nominally at least) and the Rector of the Parish was the missionary in charge of the station . . . But this plan of beginning where the completion should be, and creating a mission station by organizing a parish and appointing its Rector [left] defunct parishes as way-marks of waste and fruitless effort.

Grace Church, Riverhead.

Parochial organizations had been incorporated and church buildings built sometimes as the personal project of one individual or group of individuals. Holy Trinity on the Heights was the personal property of its originator, Edgar J. Bartow, until financial embarrassment forced him to turn it over to a Vestry. Guion Church (St. Thomas) was the child of one clergyman who canvassed an area, bought property and erected a church. Christ Church, Bay Ridge, was a joint project of several individuals who bought land and erected a church. Once established, the problem was one of keeping it going, forcing the founder to beg, borrow or sell his pet project. No thought was given to locating churches strategically. As a result, there was a constant shift of churches; sometimes they were moving to other more suitable locations; sometimes, being sold to another church, Episcopal or non-Episcopal; sometimes, sold at a loss; and sometimes, abandoned and reoccupied in a few years by a new group of Episcopalians. Holy Trinity had three different locations before settling finally on the Heights. A Trinity Church was organized, a church built, and services begun only to be discontinued in a few years and then reopened as St. Luke's Church. The first Church of the Reformation had the life span of one year; its Rector became a Presbyterian. St. Mark's Church was a joint effort of several Brooklyn churches, which moved from one location to another and finally occupied a church formerly occupied by the Church of the Messiah. Shifting churches complicated church extension and made any attempt at coordination difficult and at most expedient.

To better coordinate the expansion of the churches on Long Island, the Missionary Committee adopted an explicit set of by-laws and rules which, when presented to the Convention, received approval. In addition to stated meetings and required reports, the by-laws set the ground rules for mission church establishment. The second rule stated:

> No Missionary Station shall be established, and no Missionary appointed, except on nomination of the Bishop, in writing, and by vote of the Committee, . . . No appropriation shall be made to any organized Parish except on written application . . . of the said Parish, with the written consent and approval of the Minister, if there be one.

Church expansion followed the population movement of the Island. The improvement of transportation, roads and the opening of new lines of the railroad caused a shift of population to which the church had to respond. The Diocese realized three distinct, and in some sort peculiar, classes of mission fields. It had "the old towns and villages, of New England, themselves stationary and sometimes lifeless, their people unchanging, often full of inherited prejudices, and depleted every year by loss of young and warm blood." In contrast, "the great city and its suburban villages, growing like the mighty West, and almost defying — while at the same time splendidly challenging — the Church's effort to keep pace with its great strides and onward march to wealth and power" presented a different opportunity for the Diocese. The third field was "the haunts of sin, sorrow, crime, poverty, suffering and shame which, by an inflexible law of social life, aggregated about great and intensely active cities."

The first field work was largely in the eastern end of the Island. Its peculiar nature was aggravated by a multiplicity of denominations which made the establishment of another church body unfeasible and destined to failure. The only solution for the church was to establish an Associate Mission, with an itinerant minister living at Riverhead, which would work more effectively and less expensively than providing settled ministries in the many scattered hamlets and homesteads that dotted the rural portions of the Island. In 1872, the Rev. Thomas Cook, for some time a missionary in Queens, took up his duties at Riverhead and, in the year of his tenure, reached many neglected regions and established six wayside missionary stations. With a decline in ultra-Protestant influence and with an influx of some population, largely from the city, the Episcopal churches began to increase in number and in growth. In 1873, Suffolk County, which accounted for two-thirds of the Island area and 12% of her population, had five self-supporting parishes and 24 mission churches. The work in Suffolk was still the feeblest and still demanded the utmost effort on the part of the Diocese. More concentrated effort and greater expanding of funds for Suffolk would only come when a "normal ecclesiastical relation between the city and the country, and the mutual obligations which grow out if it, are more clearly developed and strongly felt."

Queens, part rural, part suburban, had on the whole, parishes of varying degrees in strength, activity, and membership. Missionary work was under the control of local parishes with few diocesan mission stations. Christ Church on the North Shore, held occasional services at Great Neck and Port Washington, and operated a Sunday School at Lake Success. Trinity Church in Roslyn was struggling; and Oyster Bay, Glen Cove, and Cold Spring Harbor showed no progress at all. St. George's, Hempstead, had begun a new work in Mineola. In Jamaica, Grace Church had taken under its guidance the small church in the new development, Richmond Hill. St. James Church, Newtown, had one mission at Woodside, while St. George's, Flushing, had three different areas in which work was continued; College Point, Queens Village, and the Flushing Town Poor Farm. No church had grown to match the size or strength of the colonial churches. Some, like St. George's Church in Astoria, were barely holding their own. The Whitestone Church did not keep pace with its growing population.

The Episcopal Church had its most noticeable growth in the swelling, dynamic city of Brooklyn and its suburban communities. There were forty-four prosperous churches in Kings County with membership ranging as high as 779 communicants, with seven of the strongest parishes having growing mission churches.

Most of the Brooklyn parishes were prospering, going beyond anything in former years. Within a few years after the Civil War, the rising strength of the parishes, the transition from decay to vigor and prosperity, had become one of the most remarkable features of diocesan history. An influx of population into the city and an expansion of suburban communities had swelled the ranks of the churches and had injected new life into old congregations. Even churches in the sparsely populated sections of the city were experiencing the needed tonic. In 1872, the Rector of All Saints' reported that one hundred new homes had been built and that construction of a new street railroad brought the parish twenty minutes nearer to New York. Some parishes, like St. Ann's Church, were undertaking new work. In 1872, St. Ann's accepted the old Columbia Street Union Mission, had the venerable Baptist clergyman, "who had been connected with this mission for fifteen years, confirmed", and put the work under the lay agency of the Brotherhood. Some churches were still experiencing difficulties. Aside from financial considerations, parishes had to contend with changing neighborhoods or with new construction that made relocation imperative. The Church of the Mediator, "in view of the encroachments of the East River Bridge and business and the removal of the principal supporters," was forced to relocate.

One aspect of missionary development was greatly advanced by the Diocese in 1873. L. Bradford Prince, New York Senator, later Chief Justice of New Mexico and its first governor, presented to the Diocese, in the form of a letter, the rationale for the purchase of suitable sites for eventual development:

> Everywhere on the half of the island nearest New York, farms are being cut up and embryo villages established, which naturally will in time be centers of population... Long Island is rapidly filling up with a population which is destined to increase, and before many years even the waste places of the island will be so thickly settled as to require numerous churches .... [It seemed wise to acquire] a suitable lot or plot for a future church edifice, that in days to come, when population should have accumulated requiring regular service, it would not only be an encouragement to build but... as by that time suitable property would have largely increased in price, and the best lots be unattainable.

Senator Prince, as a token of his faith, offered plots of land in Bay Side and South Brentwood, and the recently incorporated Trustees of the Estate of the Diocese of Long Island, composed of the Bishop and the Standing Committee, with authority to acquire and hold land in Queens and Suffolk, not to exceed one hundred acres, accepted the offer together with land given in Sayville, Yaphank and Brookhaven.

By 1873, the missionary expansion of the Diocese was in a "prosperous state," demanding a more liberal support. The first duty of the diocese was to itself:

> It is a poor following of the mind of Scripture and of the missionary genius of the Church, to encourage leaness and barrenness at our own door in order that we may hear of fatness and fertility thousands of miles away.

In addition to the diocesan concern for ministering to the spiritual needs of its people, was the concern expressed by the Bishop in his address to the 1869 Convention to establish a diocesan pattern for social action in the community. It followed the acceptable mode of charitable paternalism. Aware of the growing problem of city slums and the multiplication of resultant ills, idealistic energy was released in a solicitude for the poor, the defective, and the defenseless. Poverty, public health, sweatshop abuses and child labor encouraged the churches to enter such a field where public remedial or relief institutions were few and where vice, liquor, and prostitution were publicly condoned. Altruistic as the interest was, efforts were still considered good vehicles for conversion and evangelism. Alleviation meant return to the fold; amendment meant acceptance of the donor's creed and standard of conduct; Noblesse oblige, an accompanying virtue of the upper class, extended to the care of the poor unfortunate and lower common people.

Diocesan social efforts centered expressly in the expansion of the Church Charity Foundation. Since its inception, the Church Charity Foundation had moved several times, from its first location on the Heights, finally to its own property at Albany Avenue and Herkimer Street. The Home for the Aged had grown to include not only female clients but also elderly males and married couples. The orphan asylum had also increased its numbers, so that when a permanent building was erected on Herkimer Street, it included not only furnished private apartments for the aged but also new quarters for the orphans. An investment of $100,000 by the Foundation developed the two departments, accommodating seventy inmates, with a well-appointed chapel for daily services and a regularly officiating chaplain. In 1870, the Foundation established, under a separate roof, a Home for Aged Women, Aged Married Couples and Aged Men. The first building was turned to the exclusive use of the orphanage, accommodating up to 200 children.

The Church Charity Foundation was begun as a Brooklyn project. It was to be at once "a home, a church, an asylum, a house of rest, a hospital, a school, an orphanage, and a mission, thus filling out the complete illustration of the Gospel of Jesus, put into practice." But when the Diocese was formed, the need for a broadening concept of the work was explicitly advanced. The diocesan nature of the work was again and again stressed. It was not a Brooklyn institution but one "purely diocesan in character". Every churchman from Greenport to Hunters Point had an equal moral investment in this charity and was entitled to its regular dividends. To enhance its diocesan character, in addition to its Board of Managers which at first included all the Rectors in Brooklyn, and then a few elected ones, the Diocese established its Standing Committee on the Church Charity Foundation which broadened its base of operation and invested it with more of a diocesan character.

The care of the Foundation, at first under a small group of women, had been given to a larger group of workers that included first interested women, then some hired help, some teachers, and finally it was given to the deaconesses who had charge and control of the many aspects of the various departments.

After the Civil War, pauper children had become an increasing problem to the city. Made parentless by the recurring typhoid, small pox and cholera epidemics; or born in the public poor houses, where they suffered from debasing physical and spiritual contacts; or allowed to roam the streets to be pressed into indentured service, the orphan had become an object of much needed interest. The Foundation had begun on a small scale an orphans' home and had provided for their welfare. Quarters for them had been included in the permanent Foundation home but had accommodated only fifty children of the thousands who needed help. In the orphanage it had been found almost impossible to retain boys after they became twelve years of age, or if retained, to provide them with some vocational training. In 1868, a small printing press was donated to the orphanage and industrial instruction began. In February 1869, the orphans printed the first issue of *The Helping Hand* which became the diocesan vehicle of communication.

> It must ere long be recognized as the one most efficient medium of inter-communication in the Long Island Church. Here we should have the Episcopal appointments and the Episcopal acts, statements month after month of the operation in the Missionary districts, and such of the *res gesta* of the parishes generally as may serve to promote the aggregate interests of the Church. Here we should have monthly announcements of the work and wants of all our charities, and the acknowledgment of benefactions. Here, moreover, should be published a line of advertisements, selected without discrimination, and giving such business information as would be most useful to vestries, church families and the mangers of Church institutions.

By means of the printing press the boys could be held until they were sixteen to eighteen years of age and then sent forth carrying with them "a somewhat matured Christian character, and such adequate knowledge of a skilled industry as shall ensure to them, if rightly exercised, a usefull and happy career."

The Diocese began on December 1, 1870, another form of ministration to the poor by the establishment of a free public dispensary. Assisted by free services of interested doctors, the dispensary opened in a nearby store and so grew that a whole building was rented accommodating twenty-five in-patients as well as providing for the clinic work. A pressing need for a permanent hospital building made the Diocese undertake plans for such a facility. In December 1873, the new hospital building was begun and completed in 1874. The new building, added to the cluster of Foundation buildings, had twenty-five beds for regular care and several rooms for paying patrons. The Diocese also supported an active work among the public institutions, the hospitals, jails, almshouses, and asylums. "No city in the Union probably presents a wider field than the city of Brooklyn in the spiritual destitution, and the sins and sufferings and sorrows peculiar to large cities."

The church was brought to these "festering places of sin and sorrow" by two women workers, a Mrs. Fellows and Miss Eliza Coakley. Church services were supplied by the local clergy, the Rector of St. Peter's in the city of Brooklyn; and the Rector of St. Paul's, Flatbush, at the county institutions. The two women visited the city institutions, distributing literature and arranging for services. They were involved in providing clothing for released prisoners, jobs for some, burial for others, and in meeting the innumerable problems that arose as they worked with their charges.

It was a discouraging work through which it was not possible to meet all the demands of the unfortunates. At the County Asylum, the work was particularly discouraging since little could be done for the mentally ill. Visits and counselling were confined to assisting the nursing service. At the penitentiary the workers came in contact with prisoners who were hired out for thirty cents a day, which went to their board. At the local jail, the alcoholics and vagrant women required more attention than just visiting. Need for follow-up for employment and need for an alcoholics' hospital was expressed again and again.

Parish ministration to the poor and destitute had a complexity of services. Some parishes had an Employment Society to give money to poor women for work on garments which were distributed to hospitals; some had a Relief Association which gave clothing, paid the rent and bought food for the poor. Others had an Association for the Relief of the Industrious Poor which cut out and distributed material to women to do sewing for which they were paid. Sewing Schools were popular agencies which gave material out and provided instruction in sewing to poor girls. Dorcas Societies offered friendship and religious service to poor women. Mothers' Meetings attempted to ease the burden of the sweatshop woman worker.

The chief object of parochial benevolent charity was the wayward girl and the poor child. Industrial Schools provided for the street urchin who did not attend school regularly or for the young girls who were in trouble or soon to be in trouble. In these schools, the children received a simple elementary course of instruction and "a good moral and religious training, comfortable clothing for the most needy, and a daily dinner." Daily parish schools or infant care schools accommodated as many as 214 or as few as 43 pupils. Girls were given, with regular instruction, domestic training and serving lessons. The industrial schools not only kept the girls occupied but also had the added value of training them for jobs in the sweatshops where they could earn four to ten cents an hour for a ninety hour week.

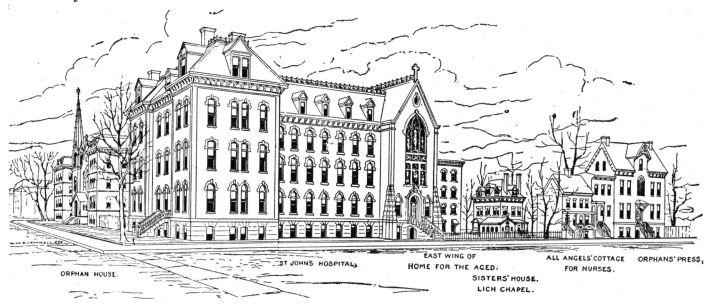

ORPHAN HOUSE.   ST JOHNS HOSPITAL.   EAST WING OF HOME FOR THE AGED: SISTERS' HOUSE. LICH CHAPEL.   ALL ANGELS' COTTAGE FOR NURSES.   ORPHANS' PRESS.

The Helping Hand

A Monthly Journal Published by

The Church Charity Foundation of Long Island

ALBANY AND ATLANTIC AVENUES

Entered at the Post Office at Brooklyn, N. Y., Nov. 14, 1879, as Second Class of Mail Matter, under the Act of March 3, 1879.

(above) Church Charity Foundation facilities.
(left) Masthead of Helping Hand printed by Orphans' Press.

Social service activity centered in the larger parishes which stood in a diversified community of very rich and very poor. Fulfilling their Puritannical imperative to assist the poor and destitute, they had not only a sense of helping but also of being helped by the good feeling of benevolent condescension.

Education is the Best Policy —

The final area of concern and perhaps the most pressing need of the Diocese, expressed again and again, was the church's total involvement in the educational system of the day. Public education had become more an accepted method of training youth than the private schools and academies, which were decreasing in influence and members yearly. Loss of control by the Protestant-oriented schools had shown an increasing counterpart in the effective dissemination of secular ideas and values. The change had alarmed church leaders who felt that with decreasing Christian standards of conduct, the youth of the community would be lost to the church.

New forces were at work in the nation and in the local community that threatened the existence of church schools and promised the separation of religious values from intellectual achievement. Symptomatic of the new ideas being forcibly advanced was the appearance at Harvard University of John Fiske, who in his two year lectureship staunchly held as the truth Charles Darwin's theory of evolution. Fiske published his lectures in 1874 as *Outline of Cosmic Philosophy*. Equally effective was the founding of the American Museum of Natural History in New York City. Both manifested the dangerous inclination of "the materialistic Gospel of perverted physical science, which accounts an unclassified bone of more value than the Cross of Jesus, and under the assumed reign of law, empties the universe of its god. . . . " Liberals of the day, among whom were counted many Protestant clergymen, had shown the inclination to subscribe to a generalization of religion "subscribing to all creeds, and ready to minister for all religions from fetishism to Christianity; holding all doctrines as they manifest religious intuitions; affirming the supernatural to be impossible . . . and revelation to be no special act but something continuous, progressive, and universal . . . . " Not to be outdone, Henry Ward Beecher, a blooming liberal, fought for the exclusion of prayer and Bible reading from the public schools. No less a force was the growing humanitarianism of the day, beginning to advocate reform "which sees all possible glories and perfection in the yet undeveloped capabilities of man, and promises to end all evils by the shifting expedient of special reforms in the industrial, domestic, and social arrangement of the world."

Controversy, added and abetted by a desire for change, centered in the popular public-supported schools. To conciliate the Roman Church which had for many years objected to the teaching of the Protestant religion in the schools and to deter the free thinkers and secularists who were involved in the public school system, a movement had developed to completely free the system from all aspects of religious teaching or practice. The retention of Bible reading was offered as an arbitrary means of at once placating the Romans and quieting the Protestant churches. Bishop Littlejohn had strong views about the public system. He viewed the situation as being the result of "the real issue . . . more Religion in the schools or none at all." For him there was no alternative but to teach the Apostles Creed, the Ten Commandments and the Lord's Prayer:

> An intelligent and virtuous citizenship is the supreme power of the State — all other ends
> being merged in this . . . To secure such a citizenship, the State, if it assume the great task at
> all, must educate the Conscience as well as the intellect of the people.

But to accomplish this task, the Christian religion presented the best accepted creed. As an answer to the disruptive influence of secular education, and as a means to train young people spiritually as well as intellectually, the church school offered the only likely and feasible solution.

The Episcopal Church had always been involved to a varying degree in education, from the early colonial days when Episcopal clergy tutored young men for college entrance to the establishment of formal training, with school buildings, teachers and curricula. In 1869, a number of church schools had come into existence, the enterprise of private individuals or the joint action of several clergymen. There were three parochial schools, Trinity Classical and English School, St. Stephen's School in the City, and St. Mark's School in Islip. Five church-related schools existed, but their connection with the Episcopal Church was tenuous. Three girls schools in Brooklyn and one in Glen Cove trained young women; The Hempstead Collegiate School and the Private Church School at Jamaica prepared young men for college studies.

To implement an expansion of church education, a Standing Committee on Christian Education was appointed. Several avenues of procedure were investigated. The Diocese could assume responsibility for one church school in operation or initiate a new school in the City of Brooklyn. An offer of $5,000 to $20,000 for a new school and a promise of a large piece of real estate for the purpose did not hasten the diocesan entrance into education. There were too many problems and too many obstacles to overcome.

No greater obstacle impeded the full participation in the field of education than apathy or disinterest on the part of parents. Of the over twelve thousand children in the diocese, only 250 of both sexes were attending schools subject to Episcopal influence or amenable to church authority. No steady or generous patronage of the already church-related school was made. Parents were governed by the whims and preference of their child; or by the partiality for particular backers; by local convenience; or by prestige and status interests of their neighborhood. The greatest difficulty stemmed from poor buildings and inadequate finance. As a result, most of the church schools were struggling for subsistence, deficient in their religious teaching, insufficient in accommodations, destitute of equipment, and lacking in a permanent teaching staff.

In spite of discouragement, the Diocese felt so strongly the necessity of proper Christian education that a plan was formulated to establish in the City of Brooklyn a boys' school and a girls' school and somewhere in Queens or Suffolk two boarding schools. The first objective was to establish two endowed schools in the City of Brooklyn, one for the boys and the other for girls. They were to have complete diocesan backing or else the schools, for lack of sufficient financial backing, were doomed to failure, as most of the other schools of the Protestant sects. The schools had to be heavily endowed and well-built in order to avoid "all possible embarrassment of incompetent and insufficient instruction and equipment, of ill-proportioned or unseemly rooms . . . so that Christian parents no longer have the excuse for conscientious conflict as to the school which should receive their patronage and moral support." A committee of five was appointed to cooperate with the Trustees of the existing Trinity School to see if the school could become a diocesan institution. Another committee of five was appointed to take "the necessary steps for procuring an Act of Incorporation of an Institution for the Education of Girls", under the direction of the Diocese. The committees, appointed in 1871, accomplished very little. The number of church-related schools had dwindled to five; three in Brooklyn and two outside the city. The Diocese still waited for the opportune moment to invest in this demanding field of concern.

While attempts were made to encourage the foundation of church day schools, the weekly occurrence, known as the Sunday School, continued to grow in teacher staff and in pupils. This answer to the "irreligiousness of education in our public schools", took on a new dimension for training character, moulding faith, worship and morals. The Sunday School's purpose was not alone to "stock the young mind with the elements of Divine Grace, but to do this always in subordination to the higher purposes of forming in the souls the habits and graces and aspiration of the Divine life."

The Sunday Schools had grown from 11,509 pupils and 1,462 teachers in 1869 to 13,191 pupils and 1,456 teachers by 1874. Although the increase appeared gratifying, there were many problems involved in running the schools. Too often the rector was too involved in other things to take a personal interest and active part in the children's school. Little attention was given to proper teaching, adequate textbooks and necessary library books. A peculiar development had made the school reform a matter that needed immediate attention. Religious education of children, which had been the prerogative and sphere of the parents, was being shifted by the family to the Sunday School.

To equip teachers and clergy better for their responsible part in the education on Sundays, the Diocese had sponsored convocations throughout the year. Several had been held in 1871, 1872 and 1873 at which there were represented over forty parishes and missions, with clergy, superintendents and teachers in attendance. The Sunday School had grown so in importance that it was taken from the direction of the Committee on Christian Education and given to a Standing Committee on Sunday Schools. Several concrete suggestions for the further development of the Sunday School were made:

1. Every Pastor to put himself in a more living and habitual connection with his school.
2. Teachers to be more carefully selected . . . and . . . better trained.
3. So far as practicable, a graded and uniform system of instruction to be established throughout the Diocese.
4. The Sunday School to be . . . (the) chief means . . . to ratify and confirm . . . what was promised . . . in Baptism.
5. Public worship.
6. Frequent catechising openly before the congregation.
7. Better classrooms, libraries, apparatus.

As was so often the case, diocesan influence in parochial training schools varied. In some, where the parish clergy were cooperative, a good relationship existed. But the Diocese had a long way to go in order to make its mark felt in this important field.

ASSESSMENT AND ADVANCEMENT

At the end of the first five years of the Diocese, the picture appeared brighter than at its beginning. Overcoming initial difficulties, facing immediate problems and creating necessary diocesan machinery, had occupied great expenditures of time and labor. By 1873, the Diocese had increased its membership from 9,837 to 11,098; its parishes from 65 to 88 and its contributions from $285,363.61 to $493,692.31. There was still work to be done, unfinished projects to accomplish, and more souls to win. But the Diocese echoed the sentiment of Bishop Littlejohn when he evaluted the first attempts at diocesan life:

> It will be seen from what has been said that the Diocese is making solid if not brilliant progress along the whole line, and that if we leave out a point here and there, the outlook is one of great promise. Certainly the change for the better in the last few years has been most remarkable, and justifies the most sanguine hope for the future.

Chapter Five

The World, The Work, and Mrs. Stewart

The slow but steady progress of the Diocese as it reached out to achieve its identity embodied disheartening trials that shaped and determined its pattern. Emerging diocesan life could not help but be affected by changing social mores and fluctuating economics that affected all of Long Island. In 1874, it seemed as if the Episcopal Church had stood still for many years. Numerically and otherwise, it stood in the same relationship to its greater community as it did in 1835. In forty years, with many more churches, the Diocese had no more communicants than those few churches had previously encompassed. It was forced by circumstances to rethink and modify its attitudes, objectives, and organization, according to its changing community.

A few years brought an imperceptible change. After 1879, the strong aspects of stable finances, energetic accomplishments, and aggressive policy manifested itself in the expanding diocesan educational and charitable institutions. A landmark appeared in the beginning of the Garden City Cathedral, but more significant and more pertinent was a growing deep-rooted awareness of the Church's task in missionary activity. Facing squarely the large urban dynamic at its west end, the Diocese realized that here was the proper forces for its energies. The city street rather than the country lane presented itself before the Diocese for help. By 1884, awareness had grown to action; the city became the focus of all diocesan energy.

GLOOM TIMES TO BOOM TIMES

The failure of the prestigious Jay Cooke and Company accompanied by the failure of large business concerns in the winter of 1873 precipitated an unprecedented economic depression that lasted for five years and five months. Hard times brought more hard times, resulting in the eventual failure of over ten thousand business firms by the end of 1878. More excruciating was the protracted effect on the factory worker, the sweat shop toiler, and the small bank depositor. Starvation and breadlines, intensifed by unemployment unrest, forced the ill-clad, ill-fed poor to demonstrate, to risk, and to break the law—only to have the law break them. Tightened purse strings and reduced consumption made wages drop and prices rise. It was not until 1878 that the eventual real estate depression, a lasting corollary of the general economic depression, struck the city. In 1878,

> the clouds that were forbidding continued to darken under the accumulated storm, prominent business concerns of thirty and fifty years — not mere speculative and insecure ventures, but houses surrounded with all the security that industry, prudence, experience and wealth can give, [had been] obliged to succumb.

Adverse economic conditions had a kaleidoscopic effect upon the financial stability of the Diocese and the churches. The depression affected in varying degrees and at varying times all sides of Church life. Some parts of the Diocese were hard hit; some fared lightly. Many churches were immediate victims but recovered early. Others seemed to prosper in the early stages of the depression, but in the last year finally succumbed. In particular, Grace Church and Holy Trinity Church, both in Brooklyn Heights and both receptacles of invested money and real estate wealth, survived until 1878 when they suffered drastic reverses. City parishes felt the depression more than country churches because rural finances were not built upon the vacillating current of monetary investment. Unfortunately, a great many parishes never regained their former financial stability. For those that did, it was not until 1880 that a stable economic foundation was assured.

Some local units, like All Saints Church, Brooklyn, had hard financial times:

> There were mortgages on the corner lots and on the new chapel and a second mortgage held . . . Interest payments could not be met. Clergy salary was frequently unpaid. There were heavy city assessments for grading and paving the streets, for gas lamps and lamp posts. The bishop gave the advice to reduce expenses and keep all real estate then owned . . . The vestry recommended that if $2,000 could not be raised, the property be abandoned to the holders of the mortgage.

A similar plight was echoed by St. Paul's Church, Flatbush, which had a hard struggle to keep the church going. St. Paul's, Woodside, a new work, "suffered in means and members from the depression of the times." Newtown was at a standstill. Riverhead sank into a deep economic depression; Christ Church, Sag Harbor was "greatly embarrassed by the distresses in the financial world." Holy Trinity, Greenport, experienced an increase in congregation and attendance at church services, "but the financial condition of the Parish was not equally encouraging."

Other parishes sustained an ability to overcome the economic distress and accomplished necessary work and helpful improvement. The Church of the Redeemer, Brooklyn, gradually extinguished mortgage debts on its property. St. Paul's, Eastern District, with a debt of $24,000, reduced its mortgage. Redeemer in Astoria built a new Sunday School building at a cost of $7,000, free of debt. St. Paul's, Patchogue, was growing both in numbers and money. Scarcely a parish failed to meet its obligations. Even poor and struggling ones made a good record in meeting their annual interest on debts contracted, in most cases, ten, fifteen or twenty years ago. An amazing record was made by St. Ann's Church, Brooklyn. St. Ann's experienced severe effects of the depression. Yet in the year of its greatest income decline, it was able to completely liquidate its indebtedness:

> During the past year the entire indebtedness of the parish has been provided for. Mr. R. Fulton Culling, on the 29th of May, 1878 subscribed $70,000 toward the payment of the debt, as a Memorial Gift, upon the conditions (1) that the whole remaining amount necessary to extinguish the debt should be at once subscribed, and (2) that St. Ann's Church should be a free church. The Vestry unanimously accepted the Memorial offering, upon these conditions. The whole amount was subscribed by members of the Congregation, and Churchmen of other parishes in Brooklyn and New York. Upon November 1, 1878, St. Ann's became a free Church. Towards liquidating the debt . . . the Senior Warden . . . and others of the Vestry and Congregation gave largely. The whole of the debt was $138,000. . . .

In the depression years the Diocese, reacting moderately to the strickening conditions, had been able to hold its own by the end of the long period. The upkeep of the episcopate fluctuated with the times. The balance on hand for the Bishop's salary in 1875 was barely sufficient to meet claims upon that fund. Larger assessments on parishes became necessary but did not meet the needed requirements. The Salary Committee in 1878, with depressed financial affairs, attempted economic cutbacks by limiting the assessment to the "actual necessities" by the treasurer. "But owing to a reduction in the interest of some of the investments of the fund, and the positive inability on the part of some of the parishes to respond" they were faced by a deficit. The only answer that seemed reasonable was an additional assessment, or a tax upon a tax. By 1880, the Episcopal Fund was in a reasonably sound condition with only a little owed on former assessment, and most parishes were up to date.

Harder hit was the missionary program of the Diocese and the charitable institutions. The adverse influence of financial conditions was felt in a decrease of needed funds and setbacks to progress. An immediate effect of the depression was the hindrance of the work at Riverhead. The Associate Mission suffered "by the financial distress of the country." The closing of a large factory, many of whose workers were parishioners of the mission, seriously interfered with any real advance. Other diocesan missions sustained their services but were unable to do any more than hold their ground. Limits had to be placed on diocesan work because of less means placed at the disposal of the Missionary Committee. The stress became more urgent in the following years. Stipends would have been unpaid and work stopped if it had not been for a "Treasurer, both able and willing to assist your (Missionary) Committee in the hours of its financial embarrassment . . . " The depth of the depression made the Committee circumscribe its operations. "For the first time in the history of the Diocese, the Committee had closed the previous year with a depleted treasury and an indebtedness to the Treasurer of over three hundred dollars." The prospect of a gloomier period ahead caused the Committee to "only partly meet applications which they felt were worthy and full of promise." The situation progressed from bad to worse. At the beginning of 1879,

> it was hoped that the depression which had hung so heavily upon the affairs of our people, would be lifted somewhat, and that with a return of our people, there would be a return of greater courage and energy in this (Missionary) Department . . . .

But the hope did not materialize. No new pecuniary responsibility was assumed; the previous rate of stipends to missionaries had to be reduced; and the treasury neared depletion. Missionary work struggled on with no recovery until 1882. In 1882, the picture for expansion seemed brighter. Besides holding the ground already sustained, some few advances were made. By 1883, the Diocese had the means at hand to begin new mission stations and to adequately sustain already existent work.

The drive for a new hospital suffered reverses equally as bad as that of the missionary outreach. With an increase in hospital need for the city, the Church Charity Foundation had begun a campaign to raise the money necessary to build a new and larger hospital. The Board of Managers on the twenty-fifth anniversary of the Church Charity Foundation felt the necessity of providing larger hospital accommodations. These were to include one hundred beds, thirty for a children's ward and a half dozen for private patients. The foundation of the new hospital was built during the summer of 1877 and was entirely paid for. The cornerstone was ceremoniously laid on June 24, 1877. Due to the financial conditions of the times, the completion of the building was postponed. The Board of Managers had committed the new building campaign to a "pay-as-you-go principle." Enough money had been raised to erect the skeletal structure but not to finish it. Nothing was done on the building in 1878 and 1879 due to "no alleviation of the depressed conditions of business affairs." In 1880, three years after the cornerstone had been laid, a renewed campaign was undertaken. The revived, and almost unprecedented, prosperity made the resumption of work on the unfinished hospital propitious. A committee of two laymen, appointed by the Bishop, solicited 100 subscriptions of $100 each; while a committee of two clergymen canvassed parishes for subscriptions for a sum equal to the number of communicants reported in the parish, over and above regular charity support. The Committees on the "Finishing Fund" and "Communicants Completing Fund" netted $8,000 and $5,000, respectively. The additional sum of $10,000 needed for completion was oversubscribed in 1882, making the completion of the hospital a foregone conclusion. On June 24, 1882, the Bishop consecrated the new building and formally opened it for public use. Five years of persistent effort with many discouragements had brought the project to a satisfactory and happy conclusion.

DEEPER CONCERNS

Living from hand to mouth had caused the Diocese and the churches to speculate about the effectiveness of the existing system of church support. The pew-rent system still retained a large following of churches. But more and more, churches were turning from this traditional means to a Sunday by Sunday free will offering. Pledged or unpledged, the offering presented a better opportunity for adding to church income. Still the new system was not the full answer. Certainly it had not worked too well for diocesan ventures. Despite scoldings and pleas, sermons and pamphlets, revenue did not increase noticeably. Wealth was present; it needed only to be tapped in the right way.

The problem of the disparity between needed church programs and the insufficient funds issued out of a deeper concern for a right attitude towards stewardship and the use of this world's goods. Millions were spent on armies, navies, on literature, science and education, in gigantic projects, on parks and roadways, on social luxury and individual extravagance, but little money was forthcoming to be spent on "the guardian of the best and noblest gifts of life, the Church." The solution rested in "God's plan", an old concept newly discovered by the churchmen of the times. The tithe principle, a definite plan for the returning to God what he had given, gained advocates none more prominent than the Bishop himself. It had been brought into the public knowledge by a minister in the Midwest. The tithe, making ten percent of one's goods the legal commitment of the individual for the work of the Church, was the answer to the disparity. Local systems of pew rent had not produced the necessary funds. It was thought that free will offerings of a ten percent pledge would alleviate diocesan and parish financial problems.

When the depression hit hard in 1876, the Diocese, in order to fully sustain the episcopate, resorted to the extraordinary means of adding a tax on tax. The extra assessment forced the question of using direct tax or free-will offering upon the local parish. The increase was very unpopular; many of the churches remonstrated against it and some positively declined because of inability to pay the increase. Other parishes, like Christ Church, Manhasset, point-blank refused on principle to pay. They had gladly and willingly given to the Bishop's support, but when a definite amount was specified, the Vestry became so incensed that they stopped the annual payment of $600 and cut back their giving to one and one-half percent of the Rector's salary, which amounted to less than $100. On a voluntary offering, the parish gladly complied. It rebelled at being told what it should pay.

Reaction to diocesan oversight or control sprang from a deepseated distrust of a greater power. Parishes lived as if they were the only and all-important community, recognizing a larger entity only when it proved convenient. It was the lot of the Diocese "to be confronted from the start with mistakes and burdens handed over from the days when dioceses were a thin varnish of Episcopacy over the most pronounced and wayward type of congregational self-will."

The diocese-parish tension exhibited its effect constantly and in every possible way. The clergy and laity showed little desire to accept episcopal direction. Bishops proposed, but clergy and laity disposed. Practically seen, each parish acted as a diocese, and each rector and vestry as the bishop. The parish was treated as the ecclesiastical unit in the diocese, taking precedence over the larger body and accepting outside dictates only by moral or personal persuasion. The assumption that the diocese was the chief homogenous factor had not been accepted. Diocesan appeals for a Theological Education Fund in 1878, resolved by the convention and verbalized in a Pastoral Letter, brought a response from about one parish in five. Attention to the unfinished condition of St. John's Hospital and to an appeal for funds had a similar fate—only thirteen parishes even bothered to respond.

Complete by-pass of the Diocese occurred regularly in the selection of a rector. When a parish became vacant, little thought was given to consulting the Bishop about a suitable candidate. Months after a rector had been chosen, the vestry notified the Bishop of its action. At no stage was the Bishop consulted. The first he heard of it was through "outside rumor," and the next by a letter informing him. The situation was acute; hence the Bishop, in a statement, attempted to make the relationship of the two units clear:

> Now a parish is an integral part of the Diocese, and what it does or leaves undone, its growth or decline, its peace or its disorder, its alienation from its sympathy with the larger life of the church, profoundly affects the Diocese. One parish badly administered, or led on by unwise counsels, or tempted into factious courses, can mar the peace and disturb the unity of the whole body to which it belongs. Its conflicts, its diseases, and distempers, intrude themselves into Diocesan Conferences, Convocations and Conventions.

But the acknowledgment of the Diocese as the total of its parishes remained unfulfilled.

THE CATHEDRAL

Amid the gloom of shortened salaries and lengthened breadlines, a great boon to the Diocese and its total life appeared in a free-will offering made by a timid, shy and overly-protected woman as a memorial to her deceased husband. Mrs. Alexander T. Stewart, late in 1876, conferred with the Rector of St. George's in his study in Hempstead. Mrs. Stewart had come to the Rev. William Moore with a plan to build an Episcopal church within his parish limits. Cognizant of diocesan policy, that no new work could be started without Episcopal approval, Dr. Moore referred Mrs. Stewart to Bishop Littlejohn. From this conference grew a long chain of conflict, tension, and confrontation. Tempers were frayed, anger was aroused, and emotions were bared; yet the first "complete and thoroughly equipped and endowed" Episcopal cathedral was erected.

Alexander Turner Stewart, an astute and shrewd merchant, had made a fortune in the department store business. Childless, he looked for a substitute on which to squander his money and to perpetuate his name. Several ill-fortuned projects, chief of which was the Stewart Women's Hotel in New York, caused him to look for a sounder investment and a more popular theme. Like the British Robert Owen, founder of ideal communities in New Lanark, Britian and New Harmony, Indiana, he conceived of erecting an ideal community in which comfortable living conditions, away from congested city areas, would surround the harassed office worker. As Lord of the Manor, Stewart planned to own all properties, build all homes, and rent out dwellings to persons whom he felt eligible and proper. His true Christian community of love and peace included schools and a church.

To implement his idea, he looked for available land which might accommodate the community he had in mind. Hempstead Plains, a barren stretch of scrub and dirt, fifteen miles from New York City had been put up for sale. Mr. Stewart made the extravagant bid of $55 an acre for 7,170 acres that extended from Floral Park to as far as the Salisbury Golf Course. Fearful of a low-rental housing area near them, the residents of Hempstead accused Stewart of wishing to devote the land to the erection of tenement houses and public charities of a like manner. Stewart in his reply briefed his case. He intended to open the plains "by constructing extensive public roads; laying out the land in parcels for sale to actual settlers; and by erecting at various points attractive buildings and residences" to attract desirable citizens. A variety of model and modest homes, moderately priced cottages for clerks, handsome villas, and country seats built on property owned by a corporation and leased to settlers composed the self-governing community with all modern conveniences, including a large hotel for visitors and friends.

By February, 1870, the land had been surveyed, streets laid out and some dwellings, adorned by white fences nicknamed Stewart's ribs, had been erected. Either ornate Victorian structures, "the Twelve Apostles," or flat-roofed small cottages, "the Disciples," appeared on the flat countryside. Non-cooperation from the Long Island Railroad forced Stewart to build his own spur railroad through the community, connecting with the Flushing line. By 1874, gas works and street lamps had been installed, Cornelia Lake dug, and the water works almost completed.

On April 10, 1876, the metropolitan area was stunned by the news of A. T. Stewart's death. The threat of abandonment made the newly organized community uneasy, but their fears were calmed when it was announced that Mrs. Stewart expected to continue the community building and to make the church in the community a memorial to her husband. Henry G. Harrison, one of her husband's architects, was commissioned to draw up the plan for the memorial church which also, was to be the tomb of her husband. Harrison's plans, an elaborate replica of a thirteenth century English Gothic church, would be supervised and overseen by Stewart's chief henchman, Judge Henry Hilton.

Lawyer Henry Hilton had made his way up the easy way by attaching himself to Stewart and by ingratiating himself into Stewart's confidence, soon becoming his chief right-hand man. An unsavory character, a confidant of crooked politicians, and completely egocentric, he surrounded himself with a bunch of strong armed, ruthless "ghouls" who lived off him. He, as Stewart before him, protected the shy good-natured widow and assumed all financial worries and mercantile pursuits. Hilton became Mrs. Stewart's agent in the department store business, and was most important in executing her forty million dollar estate, including the plans for the memorial church. Judge Hilton, in addition to his other traits, was a dabbler in religion, admiring from moment to moment the clergy whom he considered successful. In 1876, he was enamored of the Rev. George H. Hepworth, a Unitarian Mininster of New York, who was drawing large crowds and building a grand tabernacle. On July 31, 1876, Henry Harrison "went to Garden City with Judge Hilton and Rev. Mr. Hep(worth)burn by the eleven o'clock train. Judge Hilton made a speech and dug the first spadeful of sod at one o'clock. Rev. Hepburn made a prayer for Blessing to attend this memorial church to be erected at Garden City."

Work on the newly enlarged memorial church advanced rapidly; by April 20, 1877, the outer structure had appeared well above ground. In the meantime Judge Hilton's enchantment with the Unitarian minister had been jarred by rumors of financial embarrassment at the Unitarian's huge tabernacle, to the tune of a two hundred thousand dollar debt. Hilton deserted Hepworth, and being the astute manipulator that he was, he looked for a strong, permanent, authoritative body to take charge. The Stewarts were nominally Episcopalian; Mr. Stewart was even buried in an Episcopal graveyard in New York. Hilton set about accommodating his idea to the creation of a

(above) Laying the cornerstone of the Cathedral Schoo
of St. Paul, June 18, 1879.
Bishop Littlejohn makes the
formal dedication.
(left) Rare torn photograph
of Apostle House, located or
the southwest corner of
Cathedral and Fourth Street
Garden City. Photograph
taken on June 20, 1877 for
laying of Cathedral cornerstone. Note construction in
distance on right.

new Episcopal and endowed church. In working out the new church idea, Judge Hilton told Mrs. Stewart to see the Rector of Hempstead, who in turn directed them both to Bishop Littlejohn. When the Bishop heard of the magnitude of the project, he became most enthusiastic and suggested that the memorial church be made the Cathedral of the Diocese. Hilton, a man impressed by size, glamor and status, reacted favorable to the idea. Bishop Littlejohn visited Garden City and was impressed by the size and extent of the church but felt that to be a true cathedral, certain changes had to be made, especially in the chancel and the baptisery.

On June 9, 1877, Mrs. Stewart formalized her offer in a letter, which when presented to the Standing Committee, brought two searching questions: "Whether it was desirable to inaugurate the Cathedral system in the Diocese, and whether Garden City was a desirable locality for a future Cathedral centre . . . "

Previously, on May 15, 1877, at the diocesan convention Bishop Littlejohn had announced that according to the state provisions, "an act to incorporate the Cathedral of the Incarnation in the Diocese of Long Island" had been passed five days before. The Bishop had hastily explained that it was not "likely that any steps would be taken, just at this time, to carry out these provisions . . . "

Cathedrals in the Episcopal Church were a questionable novelty. The first reqularly organized cathedral in the American Episcopal Church was founded by Bishop Whipple in the Diocese of Minnesota. Previous to the Minnesota cathedral, in 1861 a pro-cathedral had been established in Chicago; the cornerstone for a cathedral in Iowa was laid in 1867; and others, were soon begun in several other dioceses. The cathedral idea had been contemplated on Long Island and a diocesan library, begun in 1875, had its name changed by 1877 to the Cathedral Library.

A reticence on the part of the Bishop and diocesan leaders to promote the Cathedral was due in part to the hostile attitude of American Episcopalians to such a foreign innovation. A cathedral was looked upon by many, if not by a majority, as fraught with great danger, being associated in their minds with European monarchial ideas and practices. By its very name, it conjured up for churchmen images of popery, corruption, useless luxury and medieval practices.

The project was also met with hostility by the clergy who questioned the unusual location. They felt the heart of the Diocese was Brooklyn, the City of Churches, and if a cathedral were to be established at all, that it should naturally be in the midst of the greatest church population and in the most active section of the whole diocese. The sandy waste plains of an unfinished village, difficult to reach except by an irregular railroad, and the proximity of the Village of Hempstead replete with its own historic colonial church, made the prospect of the center too remote and too redundant for any relevance to diocesan life.

But, in spite of dissension and disagreement, the cornerstone of the Cathedral was laid on June 28, 1877. By the time of the laying of the cornerstone, the walls were 30 feet above ground and a temporary wooden platform had been constructed for the occasion. Bishop Littlejohn, with almost 200 clergy in attendance and large crowd of interested people, struck the stone three times with the silver trowel and blessed it; the *Te Deum* was sung, prayers were offered and the congregation joined in the singing of the stirring hymn "Christ is Made the Sure Foundation."

On the persistent recommendations of the Bishop, some important changes had been reluctantly accepted. The memorial church, now a cathedral, demanded modifications, increasing the cost and changing the appearance. To accommodate a body of over one hundred clergy and choristers, the choir chancel had been extended another bay and the sanctuary enlarged from a small bay window to a large, thirteen-sided space. To effect these changes, work done had to be undone. The existing wall had to be removed as far as the transept and a new enlarged area begun. Continual conferences between the Bishop and the architect aroused the anger of Judge Hilton who accused Harrison "of fooling with the bishop." In one of his fits of rage, the irate Judge slashed across the plans of the cathedral with a large red mark cutting the size of the cathedral by one third its proposed length. A lasting tribute to his mania was the diminutive size of the cathedral with a small nave, almost squashed between a towering spire and a massive sanctuary. The cathedral was not noteworthy for its size but rather for the "completeness of its parts, its elaborate finish and its inimitable beauty."

The plans for the Cathedral and its surrounding buildings and grounds were grandiose and superlative, sufficient to enhance its centrality in diocesan life. Provisions were made for a bishop's residence nearby the cathedral, two colleges, a divinity school and a Chapter House. The last named was to serve as a mission house,

> from which a force of clergy shall go out and reach the poor and destitute in cities and every
> hamlet where parochial ministrations are not provided.

It was to be "a center of educational and charitable work with ample means for endowment and equipment. Here will be the heart of the diocese sending out the life blood to the remotest extremity."

Remotely modeled upon the Oxford plan, the system included a large Gothic structure, affording accommodations for the bishop and a large number of clergy. To the west of this building was to be the Divinity School of the Diocese, sufficiently large enough to accommodate two hundred students. A Chapter House, octagonal and sixty feet in diameter, was to be erected to stand at the end of a cloistered passage extending from the south transept porch. One half mile north a male college accommodating 500 students was to be built, and one mile south of it, a female college of the same size was to be built, with a collegiate year of forty weeks and at a cost of $300 a year. The whole cathedral foundation was to be set in the midst of a park, serviced for heat, gas and water from a separate building located a considerable distance away. The whole project was a gift from Mrs. Stewart, who promised substantial endowment for its permanent maintenance.

Church ministrations were begun amid the unfinished buildings. Sunday services, officiated over by a clergy relative of a resident, were held in a room over a store. Services were then transferred to a house (where St. Mary's School now stands) and conducted by an appointed chaplain. The two proposed colleges, changed under the influence of the Bishop to preparatory schools, began classes in the fall of 1877 in two houses loaned by Mrs. Stewart. The Bishop formally opened the schools on September 19, 1877. The entering class at St. Paul's School was 29 boarders and 17 day students; at St. Mary's, 15 boarders and 12 day pupils. This represented eight dioceses, the largest delegation coming from Long Island.

The first visible sign of the educational life of the cathedral center appeared in 1879. On June 18, 1879, the cornerstone was laid for the first of the Cathedral Schools — St. Paul's. The ceremony was attended by 3,000 spectators, as the Bishop officiated, assisted by the Secretary of the Diocese, the Rev. T. Stafford Drowne. The choirs of St. Paul's, Glen Cove, and St. Mary's Church, Brooklyn, furnished the vocal music and a military band provided the background melodies. The chimes in the tower of the Cathedral, the same ones exhibited at the Great Centennial Exposition at Philadelphia in 1876—thirteen bells for the thirteen original states, rang out the good news.

EDUCATION

Until 1877 diocesan involvement in education had a long and almost hopeless development. Pleadings and prompting on the part of the Bishop and the diocesan committee on education availed no materialization of diocesan schools. The existing apathy was due,

> to the generally acknowledged excellence of our public schools, to the many successful private schools and incorporated academies [and] to the proximity of an older city [New York] containing church schools of approved character . . . and to church schools away from home.

An apparent danger in the public schools was the attempt to gloss over with veneer the secularity of the schools by reading a few verses of the Bible without comment. This was a mechanical act not sufficient to instill religious values. Local vehicles of some education, the Sunday schools, had proven inadequate in assisting deeper understanding since very little could be done in one hour a week.

With no diocesan-sponsored school in the immediate offing, encouragement was given to already existent church schools in Islip, Jamaica, Glen Cove and Brooklyn. Most of these schools possessed the characteristic of being church-related, some having more of an interest than others. Emmanuel School at Glen Cove, a boarding school, drew pupils from eight other dioceses. Brooklyn Junvenile High School had a church character by virture of its principal's interest. A growing sentiment among diocesan leaders was that if a diocesan educational institution was founded at all, it must be centered in some of the more eligible provincial towns in Queens or Suffolk Counties.

Within one year, not one but three new schools appeared. On September 21, 1877, St. Catherine's School in Brooklyn opened under the principalship of a deaconess and a faculty of ten instructors. The school included a preparatory department for the youngest pupils, a regular six-year course of three sections—Junior, Middle and Senior, together with a special studies section and a post-graduate division. Pupils were advanced according to merit, not according to age or time spent in class. The curriculum included not only the accepted subjects but also formation of exact habits and daily religious instructions. Startlingly new, were courses in botany, fine arts and entomology; physiology and English literature were also offered. The girls attended church regularly at the nearby parish of St. Luke's Church. Beginning with forty pupils, three of whom were boarders, the popularity of St. Catherine's increased and so did the enrollment. Its central location, with commodious buildings and grounds, attracted eighty-five students by 1879, and in 1883 it had a full complement of one hundred and forty-five girls. The financial support of the schools came directly from tuition and gifts. No large endowment seemed likely, and scholarships for worthy impecunious students were badly needed.

St. Paul's School for boys in Garden City showed great progress from the opening day of classes in September 1877. The school, beginning in one house with 29 boarding students and 17 day students, took the traditional form of an English boys' school with an upper and lower school, ranging in age from 9½ to 17. Both schools studied English grammar and mathematics, with the upper school including subjects to prepare its students for entrance into college or West Point. Military drill was instituted in 1880 and became so popular that in 1883, the President of the United States detailed an officer of the army to act as instructor in military science and tactics. The boys had daily drill and exercises, encouraging a greater "esprit de corps." The new school building opened in September 1883, increasing the dormitory accommodations, assisting in better discipline and adding "facilities for illustration by apparatus and experiments." The curriculum had developed into a six-year study plan with more careful and systematic grading and with added requirements made by leading colleges. The school had ninety-one boys in 1883, of which twelve were day students.

St. Mary's School for girls did not increase as rapidly as the boys' school. Starting with twenty-seven girls, it had only added fourteen new students over the four-year period. Overseen by a deaconess, the school had three

Cathedral under construction — Note dirt roads, workmen's and supply tents, and long railroad train in distance.

sections—primary, preparatory and a four-year advanced course. The ordinary English subjects were augmented by the teaching of Latin, French and music. It was necessary in its early stages to put some girls back since they could not measure up to the accepted high standard. New buildings did not appear as quickly for the girls as they had for the boys, so activities were confined to local houses loaned by Mrs. Stewart for the purpose.

Other schools, not strictly diocesan but attempting to serve as church schools, were the Lafayette Academy in Brooklyn—a thorough preparatory school for entrance into college, a scientific school and a business school; St. Alban's, a co-ed institution where one half the students were from local churches, afforded two courses of study—academic and collegiate; the Brooklyn Junvenile High School; and the rural Young Ladies Seminary in Flushing. All church schools exhibited a common need: better financial support. They recognized an added problem of sufficient scholarship aid to educate in the correct way the best and most promising students.

The Sunday School —
A church prep school education, by reason of its very nature and scope, influenced the lives of only a few young people. Only a little over 200 students out of a potential 15,000 Sunday school children had the opportunity of a real Christian education. The overpowering influence of the state-supported public schools, in which the assertion of a secular viewpoint colored its intentions and made the educational picture more dismal. The Diocese, in desperation, looked to its Sunday schools to halt the progress of secularism.

The Sunday school had become a fixed fact and heavily relied upon for the religious teaching and training of the young. Yet the Sunday school, needed many improvements and adjustments if it was to do its job effectively. A special committee on Sunday schools was appointed to better implement the training of the young. Recommendations made by the committee changed the tenor and purpose of the Sunday activity.

The Sunday School Committee first attacked the curriculum, the course of study. There were no agreements among the various Sunday schools as to material or purpose. Many of the schools used the Protestant produced *International Series*, which although systematic, was entirely irrelevant to Episcopal education. Some parishes did not take seriously the importance of the educational opportunity. The love of popularity, the fear of not getting large and overflowing schools and the desire to hold them by appeal to the senses, rather than doctrine and conscience made the schools flippant and frivolous. The larger part of the instruction of children in the elements of Christian morality and Christian doctrine was given "in the form of stories, eagerly devoured for the plots but with scarcely a thought to either morality or doctrine they were avowedly written to inculcate." Unchecked story telling and story mongering had become an intellectual and moral nuisance which the religious press had converted into a vice. The Committee recommended,

> that a uniform system of instruction be adopted in the Diocese, having unity of teaching and
> graduation work, and of such a character as would make the Sunday School of the present
> answer the same intention of the catechist of the past.

The members of the Committee consulted other dioceses about curriculum and with their help began to produce an adequate Sunday School course of study. By 1877, Long Island, together with New York and Pennsylvania, agreed upon a graded system of teaching with leaflets and lessons. The leaflets contained, in addition to lessons from scriptures selected according to the church year, the Collect for each Sunday and some portions of the church catechism. The popularity of the new course showed in an increase from 20,000 copies in 1878, to over 250,000 copies used by every diocese save one in 1884. Over two-thirds of the diocesan schools made the leaflets their course of study.

Superintendents and teachers were also helped by the Diocese. Laymen were given the opportunity of joining in the annual series of convocations at which subjects appropriate to the needs of better instruction and better physical plants were presented by leaders.

Two very important concerns prompted the Diocese to take constructive action. They were the Sunday school library and the parents' responsibility in education. Noting a growing tendency to separate the Sunday school from home influence, the Diocese reiterated the parents' share of responsibility in the process. The family had its duties in that "parents must be brought up and told plainly that there is no possible vision of labor or responsibility which can lawfully excuse them ... " Parents were asked to direct their attention to the needs of discipline, rather than simply heeding the querulous complaints of their children. There was a need for parents' supervision of Sunday school lessons, as well as day lessons, and cooperation to insure prompt and regular attendance.

Sunday school libraries, the sources of knowledge, had degenerated into storeholds of fictitious, irrelevant fairy stories. The benefaction of books no one else wanted or cared to have prompted the Diocese to call for a rigid censorship of school libraries. The proportion of books ostensibly published for the Sunday School consisted of the "occasional insertion of some pious phrase," while for teaching doctrine they were "either so lax in their position or treacherous to the church" that they did not warrant shelf space.

The Bishop summed it up in his own words:

> More attention should be given to the material of which our libraries for children are made
> up. Some of it is worthless both in substance and form, some of it is unchurchly ... Story
> telling and story mongering have gone unchecked ... By far the larger part of the instruction
> of our children in the elements of Christian Morality and Christian doctrine, reaches them in

one way and another, in the form of stories, eagerly devoured for the plots, but scarcely a thought, either of the morality or the doctrine they were avowedly written to inculcate.

WORKS OF CHARITY

The church's ministry to the sick, the helpless and the criminal persisted in its twofold course: diocesan effort centered on the missionary work of public institutions, while parochial work sought to alleviate the plight of less fortunates in their immediate neighborhoods. Charity and concern unfolded a concentrated effort to save man's soul. Guided by the principle that evils of society can be destroyed only by changing men's hearts, church ministrations attempted to surmount personal weakness by lessening individual poverty and misfortune.

Benevolent parishes expanded their industrial schools, employment societies, and increased their charitable donations. All forms and means used before continued, confirming their belief in individualism. The Episcopal churches reflected the current conservative attitude of the well-to-do in maintaining and protecting the economic status quo. Even the outbreak of strikes and the long railroad strike of 1877 did nothing to change their attitude. They reflected the conservative viewpoint of Henry Ward Beecher in sanctifying the cult of business success and condemning the working man's effort, even going so far as to advocate force in putting down the strikers who were considered not only sinners but symbols of poverty.

A device used by some to reclaim the "unchurched masses" was the revival meeting presided over by itinerant preachers who ignored the economic and political issues and preached the "old time" religion. The City of Brooklyn was overcome with enthusiasm in 1875, swaying with fervor to the full-throated shouting of Dwight L. Moody and melting into sweetened grace by the singing of Ira D. Sankey. The mighty campaign for saving souls reached thousands with its simple message to be brave, cheerful and to accept one's lot. A reflection of the revivalist spirit permeated the Bishop's appointment of the Rev. B. S. Huntington as diocesan evangelist. His chief purpose was "to preach the word as to quicken the spiritual life of believers, to arouse the thoughtless to a sense of eternal realities, to lead sinners of every name to repentance and amendment of life . . . " The Evangelist was an itinerant, moving from place to place, adjusting his work to the local community, and delivering in quick succession twenty blows more telling on the resisting object than a thousand at considerable intervals apart. Since his commission by the Bishop in 1873, the Evangelist officiated about 259 times, conducting "evangelist missions," "the general result of which had been an increase of spiritual life and activity in parishes and a religious awakening in the church and in the community." Finding his time not completely occupied in the Diocese, he availed himself to work in neighboring dioceses. The office of Evangelist, like the revival meeting, soon passed out of popular favor. By 1878, the Evangelist had left and the diocese turned to other means.

Diocesan charitable work took on an added dimension after 1875. Two new centers of mercy were added to its three major works. In 1870, the ladies of St. Peter's Church had organized a home for little children, the Sheltering Arms Nursery. The charity afforded help to 40 or 50 children under seven years of age. In the same year the "Bethseda Band," a group of young women organized to assist the House of Rest for Consumptives in New York City, opened a similar house in Brooklyn. The home accommodated 50 sick persons and included a convalescent home in South Carolina for patients who needed the change. Financial problems, brought about by the death of their chief benefactors, caused the two institutions to look to the Diocese for help. The Sheltering Arms Nursery struggled on, cutting back its workload and limiting the number of children it could assist. The House for Consumptives fared worse. By 1876, it had become "another fair page in the history of the Diocese." The Diocese continued its responsibility in caring for young children by adopting the Nursery as a charity in 1878.

Under its protection, the Nursery enlarged and improved its administration. It added several needed improvements to its small facilities. A move to separate day care and permanent resident children and to lessen the danger of contagious diseases was hastened by a fire in the Nursery. The completion of a new infirmary in 1883 corrected the problems and increased the number of children from forty to eighty. The Nursery had the distinction of being the only institution in the city that cared for children under three years of age and that admitted children whose parents were living but were unable to pay because of incompetency or misfortune. Poor mothers, widows or wives deserted by drunken husbands were also admitted and helped as fostering mothers. The Nursery was housed in a four-story building with offices, serving and sitting rooms, four cheerful wards and the best in bathrooms, heating and ventilation.

The Orphanage and Home for the Aged expanded their work. A printing press annex to house the vocational efforts of the children was added in 1879. The educational program was enlarged and a new wing added to the existing facilities. The new wing increased dormitory accommodations and was equipped with an elevator and "all the modern conveniences, such as lavatories with marble basins, hot and cold water, linen closets, and two bedrooms—one in each dormitory for the accommodation of those persons who had nightly charge of the children." The Home of the Aged pursued "the noiseless tenor of its way" taking care of forty-two persons in the quiet atmosphere of Christian care.

The major accomplishment of the Church Charity Foundation was the expansion of its ministration to the sick. The Atlantic Avenue Dispensary took care of almost 7,000 patients in a year and gave out 10,000 prescriptions. The hospital, built at a cost of $100,000, had been the result of a long and drawnout affair.

Conceived not simply as additional accommodations for the physically ill, the hospital was meant to be a decisive church tool for the healing of both the body and the soul. A spiritual physician, the chaplain, stood ready at hand to minister to the patient's "distempered mind." To save the soul was an important part of the work of the true hospital.

That Old Demon Rum and Other Ills —

Concerned primarily with private morality and personal sin, the Episcopal church agreed that group action against sin was occasionally desirable. Temperance occupied many churchmen who fretted over America's changing mores. Sentiment for temperance was old, but vigor and the extent of organized action was new. The National Temperance Society and Publishing House was founded in 1865; the Prohibition Party in 1869; and the Women's Christian Temperance Union (WCTU) in 1874. Some worked for moderation, others for abstinence; some attacked the saloon, others aided the victim; some thought political action desirable, others placed emphasis on personal morality.

The Diocese confronted the issue in 1877. The Bishop, in his convention address, presented the problem with all its aspects for the purpose of information only, not for advocating a plan of action. He felt the problem was "drunkedness" which converted its victims into brutes, destroyed the peace of households, squandered wages, demoralized labor, engendered pauperism, fired the passions to violence in a thousand forms, swelled the police force, filled the prisons and gave the hangmen two thirds of their horrible tasks. The answer was not abstinence but temperance in all things. Each individual case demanded a different approach—"the pledge" for some, wholesome literature for others.

Nothing was done on a diocesan level until 1881. The organization of the National Church Temperance Society brought the question of diocesan action to the fore. A meeting in November, 1881, to greet the organizing secretary of the Society occasioned the start of a movement in the Diocese. An executive committee for Long Island was formed and a tentative program undertaken. Mr. Robert Graham, the National Society Secretary, visited fifteen parishes in an attempt to arouse interest. A temperance mission in Brooklyn was held in December, 1882. Three churches were used for the five-day mission. Graham spoke every evening to about 2,000 people, receiving a cordial reception and arousing some interest. Temperance guilds were formed in only five parishes. Graham also spoke in some local factories and public halls. In 1883, he addressed the diocesan convention which pledged itself "to cooperate with him in the execution of his work." Also in 1883, Graham branched out from the city, visiting Oyster Bay for two days; holding four meetings, and speaking in Jamaica where he was well received. The subject of another Temperance Mission during the Lenten Season was considered. However, practical considerations overrode altruistic aims: " . . . on consultation with the clergy, it was deemed impracticable because it could interfere with the arrangements made for Lenten Services."

Although diocesan ardor for battling the demon rum dimmed, local interest continued. Local chapters, Knights of Temperance, were formed in many parishes. A more sustained program was carried on in Oyster Bay. Graham's visit to Oyster Bay grew out of a deep concern of the parish for a rising alcoholic rate. The Brotherhood of Christ Church, Oyster Bay, had opened a "Reading and Amusement Room" where young men and boys "who otherwise spent their leisure or a portion of it, in liquor saloons and pool rooms" could find wholesome entertainment. A novel group, the Law and Order Committee, also had been formed. The village had suffered severely and long from an excessive and unlawful liquor traffic, the dealers having sold on Sundays to minors and habitual drunkards in open violation of their respective licenses. To meet this evil, the Committee, with the Rector as chairman, collected funds to retain counsel,

> and to instruct him to exhaust every legal device to bring to strict observance of the Excise Law. The plan resulted in the conviction and fining of four dealers, the closing of two saloons, and the creation of an atmosphere where young people could grow up and protest against the liquor traffic instead of the old demoralizing atmosphere of acquiescence.

No greater social service was done than by the diocesan visitor to the public institutions, Sister Eliza Coakley. Her work involving,

> speaking a word of monition here and of comfort there, praying over the sinful and encouraging the depressed, adjusting bandages, giving medicine and nourishment, supporting the fainting head and composing the features of the dead, and along the streets where poverty and wretchedness herd, and in the humble homes into which sickness and misfortune carry anguish and want, always uttering or looking for appropriate sentiments of hope illustrating them with appropriate ministries of help,

had taken on a new dimension. The deaconess realized that distributing prayer books and literature, praying and visiting were not sufficient. An important aspect of her work which consumed time and effort was that of follow-up. A concern for the institutional inmates when they left for home and the period of adjustment they had to experience, attempting to avoid the commission of the same mistakes again, pointed to the immediate need for more assistance and better implementation.

Social work in the Diocese was considered a part of the missionary program. Like new mission stations, statistics had to be given to prove the effectiveness of its work. Yet there was a deep realization that what was important was not how many had become churchmen or how many had been saved but that the church was ministering to the crying needs of human beings. Human computation could not document the effectiveness of such work. It was only when the assisted person became an accepted self-sufficient member of society that the full fruit of the work could be shown.

For better implementation of her work, Sister Eliza sought a place of operation. It would be a house where a corps of workers could live and go out to do their work of mercy. The Diocesan Women's Auxiliary, fired in imagination by the magnitude of the Sister's work, assumed the responsibility of furnishing a suitable location for the missionary center. After finding sufficient funds, they provided a house on Lafayette Street, Brooklyn. On February 8, 1882, the Bishop formally opened St. Phebe's Mission House—a home of social workers and a center of operations for all connected with it. Sister Eliza, exhausted from her work, was forced to retire and was replaced by two women associates. An increasing emphasis on follow-up of the inmates' discharge included finding homes, meals and lodgings at the mission house and finding clothing and money for their incidental expenses. The Mission House became increasingly used with applicants doubling in number—increasing meals served from 129 to 14,000 and lodgings from 45 to 490.

In addition to those works of visitation and assistance, the formation of a school for trained nurses who were to work exclusively among the poor was projected. The school was formed and a visiting nurse service began "to send the trained nurse to the bedside of the sick and dying poor." They were assisted by the faithful women associated with the agency in distributing "medicines and delicacies of the needed kind." One outstanding need to make the working force complete was a clergyman to cooperate with the nurses. Physicians' free services already had been arranged to cooperate with the nurses in the care of the poor.

MISSIONARY WORK

The missionary program of the Diocese, hampered by financial and other difficulties in the late seventies, improved after 1880 to the satisfaction of all concerned. Work continued in two areas: the distant eastern end of the Island and the teeming city population of Brooklyn and its outskirts. Queens County took care of its own needs for outreach through the local parishes. Great hope was placed on the work in Suffolk, which had been the main point of emphasis from the beginning of the Diocese.

Suffolk County had twenty-one churches and mission stations in 1875. By 1884, the number had increased to twenty-six. Some of the churches were partly parochial; that is, organized with rector and vestry but dependent upon the Diocese for support. One church, St. Mark's, Islip, which had a new church built for it solely by Mr. William K. Vanderbilt, had three mission stations—Messiah at Central Islip, Christ Church, Brentwood, and St. Mark's Chapel at Bayshore. One church, St. John's, Islip, had ceased to exist, except for its building. Other churches were largely summer chapels.

At various points along the coastline of the Diocese, population was increasing and the summer exodus from the cities turned in that direction. The advance of the Long Island Railroad into the sparsely settled areas had provided a way of reaching isolated areas. In 1870, a direct route from New York to Port Jefferson was constructed, and in 1881, a line from Patchogue to Eastport made a through line from New York to Sag Harbor via Patchogue. Spurs from the main lines had connected Far Rockaway, Valley Stream, Long Beach, College Point and Whitestone. Roads, although still far from desirable, had improved somewhat to make travelling, if not pleasureable, at least bearable. Many wealthy New York and Brooklyn families bought summer places on the Island. The Roosevelts and the Fosters discovered Oyster Bay. The Islip township had a large summer population with beautiful country homes and spacious grounds interspersed with boarding houses filled with paying guests. The North Shore became equally attractive with summer residents as far out as Greenport and Fisher's Island. As a consequence, in several places churches were built or were in the process of being built. Built as summer chapels were St. John's on Fisher Island, St. Luke's at Easthampton and St. Andrew's-by-the-Sea at Southampton. Existing churches reaped the benefit of the summer arrivals. St. Mary's on Shelter Island, few in number in the winter, had a considerable number of summer attendants. St. Paul's, Patchogue, rebuilt and underwritten by one city visitor, felt the effects of the summer population. The coastline churches were the chief benefactors of the incoming wealth; the inland parishes continued to struggle on.

Diocesan interest still surrounded the Associate Mission located at Riverhead. Under the able leadership of the Rev. Thomas Cook, a group ministry cared for the outstations where services were held and churches built. The good intentions of the Diocese were to assign six deacons to work with Cook and visit or permanently locate in some of the mission stations of the neighboring towns. The shortage of manpower and money compelled Cook to use what available resources he could so that in place of six or more helpers, he had at most, three deacons or priests and several layreaders. Because of this, he was forced to leave the parish at Riverhead; travel many miles visiting as many localities as he could as far apart as Farmingdale and Mattituck; administer the sacraments and do pastoral counseling. In the eleven years he served as the head of the Associate Mission, Cook kept up an incessant, pressured, active life covering thousands of miles, working for community improvement and "entering communities which were intensely devoted to all the prejudices and preferences of their traditional (Puritan) training." Cook spent himself in advancing the Episcopal work by personal door-to-door solicitation and by making the church respected and accepted. By his indefatigable efforts, he had established seven churches, baptized 400 and presented 1,200 for confirmation. The pressure of his work became so great that when he was taken ill in the winter of 1883, he no longer had the stamina to rally. He died on May 1, 1884.

The Associate Mission began with seven mission stations. With the fluctuation of time and interest, the number decreased and increased so that by 1884 there were ten under its care. A few showed no real progress—Port Jefferson trundled along with little life; Yaphank and Brookhaven were much the same; Sag Harbor had some renewed interest; and Patchogue took on new life with its benefactor's gift and support. But it was in two churches—one on the south shore, a recent manifestation, and one on the north shore, an old colonial church—that bright prospects were seen. St. Ann's in Sayville, formerly St. Barnabas' Chapel, in the late seventies, began to attract local residents. The work was encouraging and full of promise. A steady influx of city people seeking permanent homes resulted in increased attendance, more frequent services, and more devout public interest in church activities.

Old Caroline Church exhibited an equal spurt of active life. Dormant for many years, it had gradually come to life. Assisted by diocesan funds, the Rector, who also had the responsibility for Port Jefferson, reported that the properties had been improved and that the parish was "in good heart and growing steadily."

Queens County, the poor cousin of the Diocese, was left to its own inventions. Parishes such as Hempstead, Jamaica and Flushing had parochial missions. Other parishes conducted services in outlying towns. One parochial mission, turned parish, had to resort to the Diocese for help. St. Paul's Church in Woodside, an aided parish, experienced grave difficulties. Loss of parishioners to New York and Brooklyn had an adverse effect upon the parish, draining its resources and vitality. On the south shore a new church, St. John's, in Far Rockaway was organized by Trinity, Hewlett, which had been implemented by the railroad extension. In the Village of Merrick, an eligible piece of property was purchased for church purposes. One purely diocesan work was at the far eastern end of the county. In 1875 St. Thomas, Farmingdale, had been started with very little progress and very dim hope in its initial years.

Much more dramatic and pressing in increasing population and dynamic life was the teeming City of Brooklyn, which was spreading out to encroach more and more the suburban and country towns and villages. The pressure of city growth dispersed many Brooklynites to the Hill Section, to Clinton Avenue, to Bedford, Park Slope, as far as East New York and as widespread as Flatbush and New Utrecht, which had lost much of its rural complexion by the 1880's. Ridgewood expanded, Fort Hamilton prospered and Parkville increased.

The population movement was made possible by the improvement of transportation. There were a complexity of 42 transit lines operated by steam, horse power or cable or a combination of these. Each had its own rules, regulations, tickets and modus operandi. Before 1877 horse cars plodded along slowly transporting people from one locality to another. But in 1875 the Brooklyn Elevated Railroad was begun so that its line would extend as far out as Woodhaven (1889). Ocean Parkway was completed in 1876. It was a great residential thoroughfare which afforded bicycle paths and gave better access to Coney Island and the communities of Parkville, Windsor Terrace and Kensington along its way.

Life in the City of Brooklyn was vital, busy and, in some respects, shocking. After the great revival meetings of Moodey and Sankey, Brooklyn was rocked by the celebrated Beecher trial in which Henry Ward was accused of adultery. Many of the leading citizens came to his rescue, none more prominent than Bishop Littlejohn who was accused of "whitewashing" the facts. The city became increasingly aware of its proximate playgrounds. The "isle of rabbits" had grown into a huge seaside park, Coney Island. Four transit lines brought crowds of people, and excursion trips added to the number. Hotels and restaurants multiplied as did race tracks, bare knuckle fights and prostitutes. Rockaway, more sedate but as attractive, began to accumulate summer homes and pleasure hotels. Brooklynites wept when the Brooklyn Theatre burned to the ground and immediately took action to assist the poor victims of the fire. The Hon. Seth Low, communicant of St. Ann's Church and superintendent of the Sunday School, began his two terms as Mayor of the city and brought new and reformed principles of municipal government to the urban metropolis. Banks, always a sign of prosperity, increased and expanded by building their great "Cathedral of finance," fashioned like St. Peter's and St. Paul's Cathedrals in Europe. An awesome event which foretold "things to come," was the lighting by electric power on December 14, 1878 of Loeser's store in the downtown shopping center.

Religious progress in Brooklyn could not keep pace with the increase in numbers and property. "In the cities the building of church edifices lagged behind the advance of population while the shifting of residential districts left once prosperous houses of worship stranded and abandoned on the bleak shores of factory and slum neighborhoods." In 1878, Brooklyn had 247 churches of which one fourth were Episcopal; the others represented all kinds of religious persuasions. Even with so many churches, only a little more than one third of the population could be ministered to by them. The "City of Churches" had its concentration of churches in the most affluent sections. Some of the most populous sections were left untended and "relegated to the cruel mercies of their foolish superstitions or their heathenist indifference."

Episcopal churches in the more affluent areas prospered and grew. Holy Trinity had 750 communicants and a budget of $87,000; St. Ann's 756 and $27,000; Messiah, 881 and $31,000; Redeemer, 688 and $14,000; Grace Church, 521 and $32,000; Christ, 550 and $19,000. Outside the city limits there was only one parish that could match the numbers of the larger city establishments—St. Mark's Church, Eastern District with 456 communicants.

Its budget was only one third that of the most prosperous church.

Many Brooklyn parishes still had to contend with heavy parochial debts. Huge unfilled tabernacles had cost more than projected growth or income. In 1884, the highlight of the year was the liquidation of debts by three parishes—St. Paul's, St. James' and Ascension. The freedom from debt was attributed to honest industry and "not to money gained by the crooked arts of the typical financier, whose reputed wealth represented violated trusts, speculative snares and strong boxes with other people's property in them for safekeeping." When the Diocese began, there was considerably more than half a million dollars of debt to shoulder. Miraculously in 1884, the total debt amounted to only $125,000.

Changing neighborhoods did not present as great a threat as changing constituencies. Communities changed in character; decay crept in with fitful pace. The most evident threat was the sapping of strong support by the death or removal of persons in leading men and families.

Diocesan missions in Kings County were diverse and widespread. Churches in the city had their own parochial missions for which they were fully responsible. The Diocese underwrote and supervised work outside the immediate area. Two missions in the township of New Utrecht experienced hard times. St. John's, Fort Hamilton, an organized parish, was under the direction of a diocesan missionary who shared his time with St. John's, Parkville. They were difficult fields and awaited new life. By 1880, Fort Hamilton advanced in material prosperity and in an increased congregation. Parkville did not show a similar growth. An afternoon service held in a rented building did not enhance its effectiveness. A chapel erected in 1882 helped, but it did not cause any great expansion of membership or interest. St. Stephen's, Jefferson Avenue, did not grow materially. Sparsely settled, the little church struggled to meet the existing needs of gasline installment, paving and grading of streets and reducing its debts. The neighborhood held promise, however, for the new elevated railroad was to come through the community. St. Thomas on Cooper Avenue, planted when hopes were high for development, had very little encouragement in ten years. Scattered homes with few people did not appreciably effect an increase, but like others, it looked hopefully to the future. Trinity, East New York, had a large area of homes of lesser means; the people did not adequately contribute for its support. With an active program among the unaffiliated religious, it had about 275 communicants and a Sunday School of 486, but it could not meet all its expenses. St. Barnabas Church, with a list of communicants far above average and one of the largest Sunday Schools, had to seek diocesan aid because of its great debt. The assistance was temporary to "tide the parish over" until it could stand on its own two feet.

As the size and strength of the city grew, some of the established churches became aware of their potential and of their inadequacy in ministry. No one was more aware than the Diocese. The Diocese had made its largest missionary investment in Suffolk, but it began to realize that its point of concentration was not the wilds of Suffolk but the jungle of Brooklyn. The Missionary Committee openly attested to the need of a changing viewpoint.

> We have heard much of the ignorance and irreligion of the rural portions of the diocese, and there is too much truth in it; but for downright ignorance and unbelief, and godlessness, and vice, and crime, commend us to this city and its environs. Within the sound of these church-going bells, there are localities of squalor, degradation, and sin . . . Once it was the proud boast that this was the City of Churches . . . but the daily records of physical wretchedness, of domestic infelicity, of besotted vice, and bloody crime, have befouled the fair boast and repute of the past.

A special committee was appointed by the Diocese to investigate "the actual needs and condition of the entire City of Brooklyn in reference to the ministrations of the Church." A disheartening report was made in 1878. In six sections of the city, with a population of 116,325, there was no church work either of a parochial or diocesan nature. Several reasons were given: churches were not near enough to minister to them, the population was largely Roman Catholic or German, and other Protestant churches did have some work there. The reasons did not stand up to the outspoken need for church involvement. Further study was recommended.

The pressures of city growth drew the attention of the Diocese to the rapidly changing ethnic complexity of its urban people. The tenements of New York City were spewing their "foreign element" into Brooklyn. Irish and Germans were quickly joined by a new European group. A great migration of Italians to Brooklyn began in the late seventies and continued at flood tide until World War I. First settling in New York, the Italian laborers sought escape from the intense overcrowding in the East Side. Those who came first chose the vicinity of Hamilton Ferry along Union and President Streets. There in Red Hook grew Brooklyn's "Little Italy."

In the midst of the Italian ghetto, the Diocese licensed on December 1, 1882, the Mission of the Holy Cross. Under the guidance of Alberto Paco, lay reader and later an ordained clergyman, a room was rented from the local Episcopal church, St. Margaret's Mission, and fitted out for the Italian services. The mission ministered to a growing number of families who came to the New World and found the Roman Catholic Church largely in the hands of foreigners. Their failure to affiliate with Irish Romanists made them susceptible to a Catholic church which carefully instructed them in the Anglican system. The mission also held a night school for the Italians who wished to learn the English language. A translation of the Prayer Book into Italian was also begun.

A more established and growing group of "different" people was the Black people. Successful work among

St. Phebe's Mission House.

*Old St. Augustine's Church,
St. Edward's Street, Brooklyn.*

the Blacks had been largely delegated to the more fundamental sects, such as the Baptists. Several attempts on the part of Episcopal parishes to work with the Blacks had proven unfeasible. As early as the 1840's, a separate church, St. Peter's, had been instituted in Brooklyn, but it had to be suspended for lack of adequate support. The Rev. Samuel Haskins, "Catholic" Rector of St. Mark's Church, held services for the Blacks and helped obtain a building for services. The work continued until 1859, when the resignation of its Black rector stopped it. Grace Church, Jamaica, conducted a Sunday School for Black children. In 1879, the Convocation of Kings County, formerly the Trustee of a fund known as "the St. James Fund to be used for the benefit of colored people in communion with the Episcopal Church in the County of Kings", transferred and paid to the Diocese $1,017.78, to be kept in trust for a possible Black Church.

The Diocese in January, 1878, commenced a ministry to Black people. It was "a humble venture of the church in behalf of the black population of the city." Enthusiasm on the part of the congregation was great, but diocesan interest was small. The congregation gave as much as they could and supported contingent expenses and the minister's salary. "Working at every disadvantage, as far as location and accommodation were concerned, and compelled to meet at a most inconvenient hour of the Lord's Day," the church struggled along needing a place of worship most of all.

The Church of the Redeemer allowed the Blacks to meet in their chapel on Sunday afternoons, an exceedingly inconvenient hour. The Blacks had raised enough money to purchase a lot, yet no benefactor was forthcoming to erect a church. The paradox of the situation was that parishes of the diocese contributed thousands of dollars to support the work of Missions among the Black people of the South, yet St. Augustine's Church was allowed "at our own hours, and under our very eyes, to struggle along under disabilities which would have crushed the life out of any other mission parish in the Diocese." It seemed that the Southern Black were too far away to threaten, but the Black person in their midst was not worth any help or encouragement.

A wider and far more diversified missionary field was incorporated into the life of the Diocese with the appointment of Bishop Littlejohn as Bishop-in-charge-of-Foreign-Churches in 1874. The Diocese took on an extra dimension extending its field to include the Episcopal churches on the European Continent. Bishop Littlejohn was a greatly respected leader in the National Church. His activity in the General Convention as a deputy and as a member of the House of Bishops increased his stature and broadened his influence. Men had come to understand his eminent abilities, but none so much as his knowledge of inter-church relations in the foreign field. The Bishop had served on the Joint Commission of Ecclesiastical Reform, being the chief guide on the sub-committee regarding the Old Catholic Church. Recognizing his influence and understanding of ecumenical relations and of European affairs, the Presiding Bishop asked him to serve as chief pastor of the European Churches, an honor which Bishop Littlejohn accepted. From 1874 until he resigned the position in 1886, the diocesan lists included the names of foreign clergy, covering more remote places as Italy and Germany and more proximate places such as Cuba.

Interest in European fields had grown increasingly important. More and more Americans were traveling in Europe. Some lived there permanently; others stayed only for a few months. Young American men and women had enrolled at the universities and were looking for the ministrations of the church. On October 16, 1875, the Bishop sailed for Europe to make an official visit to the American churches. After finishing his tour, the Bishop was delayed in returning home by a death in his family. Prevented from presiding at the Diocesan Convention in May, 1876, his place was taken by the Presiding Bishop. Bishop Smith addressed the Convention and stated the reasons which led to the appointment of the Diocese to the oversight of the foreign churches, and the wisdom and efficiency with which the difficult duties of the office had been discharged. He specially called attention to the significance of the great historical event of the time, the consecreation of St. Paul's Episcopal Church in Rome.

During Bishop Littlejohn's tenure in this office, he made five visitations to the continent. In the summer of 1878, he combined his visit with attendance at the Lambeth Conference. He was well-known and in constant demand for preaching and lecturing. In 1880, he fulfilled an engagement as lecturer at the University of Cambridge while in Europe. During the entire visit, he was constantly employed in public ministrations, and regularly officiated at Sunday services. He confirmed over two hundred persons, built four churches and commenced a fifth. The Bishop nurtured the growth of churches in France, Italy, Germany and Switzerland. He consecrated Emmanuel Church in Geneva and laid the cornerstone of Holy Trinity in Paris and of St. John's Church in Dresden. He worked closely with the Rector and Vestry of the church in Paris on the erection of the church in France's capital, a church whose "dimensions and architecture" were "a credit to the American name and a magnificent exhibition of the liberality and enterprise of not a few of our leading churchmen on both sides of the sea." A church at Nice, in the south of France, occupied his attention. Services had been held there for ten years. On March 29, 1883 he attended the enthronement of the Archbishop of Canterbury.

But more important than his direction of churches was his work with the Catholic Movement in Switzerland. He conferred with the Old Catholic Bishop Herzog while he was in the United States, and he had frequent conferences with him on the continent.

> While here (United States) he confirmed several times in German congregations, and it was thought wise that the inter-communion consummated here with so much good feeling should be repeated in an as impressive and public a manner as possible in Europe, where the people are familiar at once with the methods and the consequences of Papal excommunications and anathemas.

Bishop Littlejohn's familiarity with the Old Catholic Church gave him an insight into other inter-church work. He concentrated on the Catholic Reform Movement in Italy, and he served as a member of the Lambeth Conference Committee for this area of ecumenical relations. A broadened perspective fitted him for a deep understanding of the Episcopal church's basic essence, which he put to good use.

ACT I OVER, ACT II READY TO BEGIN

The greatest engineering feat in the world, the Brooklyn Bridge, was completed in 1883. Its final erection held a threat and a promise. The bridge had made access easier to New York but also had created a gangplank over which would come new and disturbing forces that would change and develop the island. The bridge began the change of complexion that was to turn Long Island into its own small replica of "the melting pot of the world."

The opening of the Brooklyn Bridge heralded the accomplishment not of just a local work but one that belonged to the whole state and nation. The two cities of Brooklyn and New York joined together and celebrated the great opening day with revelry and festivity. The President of the United States and the Governor, attended by the two city mayors, and a large delegation of Brooklyn citizenry took part in the opening ceremony in the depot at the Brooklyn terminus. The Bishop of Long Island appeared first, "who read specially prepared sections from the Scriptures, and a prayer also composed for the occasion." Long speeches and appropriate tributes made up the rest of the program, and they were accompanied by a booming cannonade from a fleet anchored in the East River as well by bands blaring forth. A banquet in New York and a reception at the Brooklyn Academy of Music rounded out the day's proceedings. The bridge formally opened to the public, and in September 1883, a cable railway afforded a more useful crossing and a more crowded means of transit.

Bishop Littlejohn did not realize in opening the ceremony that he had closed an era. In a few short months he moved to Garden City from crowded Brooklyn. His prayer for the bridge had been in a real sense a eulogy as well as a prophecy. The bridge would complicate the life of the Diocese by injecting diffuse and ambivalent forces and ideas into his diocese, and his move would create a tension that would drastically affect all areas of diocesan life.

Yet the years 1874 to 1884 had brought a semblance of order out of confusing sidetracks and disuniting factors. The communicant strength had reached 16,670; Sunday Schools attendance numbered 16,000; clergy had increased to 107 and missionary giving had increased to $496,906.69. Amid all its organized confusion, the Diocese moved quietly on with an absence of "noise and friction." Not without its weak points, the Diocese still gave satisfaction to the Bishop, the clergy and the laymen responsible for its development. Local self-interest still presented an obstacle which at first was insurmountable, but was slowly being diminished. Overcoming this one factor, the Diocese would make even more of a real and appreciable step forward.

Chapter Six

A Tale of Two Cities

It was not until the last fifteen years of the nineteenth century, after many years of hard struggle that the Diocese of Long Island emerged, a full-strength, well-developed, firmly-rooted ecclesiastical unit. The Diocese stretched in every direction, enlarging already existing work, and initiating new-found tasks. No more significant interest held the Church than its ministry to the city. The Diocese kept pace in its charitable institutions; it completed its cathedral; it fostered its educational institutions; but it was in its urban work that the Diocese began to expand and affect. The institutional church with its parish houses and neighborhood programs was the center and strength of its ministry to the city folk. Temperance, a major issue in the former period, was joined by a concern for a growing disregard of Sunday.

The completion and consecration of its cathedral appeared as a wonderful accomplished fact, a milestone in the progress of the Island diocese. Yet, as Mrs. Stewart placed in the offering plate the implements of donation, a new task emerged which was to harass the Diocese and the Bishop, having no solution until five years of lawsuit and trial brought the matter to a conclusion. Although unsatisfactory in the long run, it was heralded as an immense step forward at the time.

THE HEART OF THE DIOCESE

On Tuesday, June 2, 1885, the Cathedral of the Incarnation was consecrated by Bishop Littlejohn in a most imposing ceremony. The day was beautiful. A large gathering of representatives from all over the Diocese, and from other dioceses, together with eight bishops, witnessed the historic occurrence. At 11:00 A.M. the procession entered the Cathedral, about two hundred in number. The clergy vested, mostly in cassock, surplice, and white stoles, all with birettas or Oxford caps, and many with academic hoods, led the other representatives of diocesan institutions, and finally the Bishop.

The procession ended; the Bishop took his seat within the altar rail. Mrs. Stewart accompanied by Judge Henry Hilton, advanced to the chancel rail where Mrs. Stewart presented to the Bishop the deeds of conveyance of the property, comprising the Cathedral, the See House, St. Paul's School and thirty-seven acres of land, together with a bond of $300,000 as an endowment fund; the total value being two and one-half million dollars. Judge Hilton read a brief statement setting forth the terms of the gift. When the Bishop had placed the instruments of donation on the altar, the doxology burst forth: the cathedral chimes joining the organ and choir; and the cadets of St. Paul's School giving an artillery accompaniment outside. At the communion service, the Queen Anne silver of St. George's Church, Hempstead, was used.

The thousands that attended the official consecration of the Cathedral admired the beautifully finished Gothic structure, invoking to some the name "candy box church". They noted the richness of the building, the variety of carved stone and precious marble, the superb organ built by Hilborn Roosevelt, and the exquisite imported English stained glass windows. The miniature cathedral made a fitting monument to the rich merchant who had found final rest beneath the altar in the crypt below. But more it had become the symbol of the untiring efforts of the men who struggled to bring it to final completion. Eight years of conflict, tension, and pain had left its visible mark on the open plains of Hempstead in the Cathedral structure. But deeper, and unseen was the mark it left upon the men involved in its construction. Stone marked the visible structure; invisible but just as lasting was the imprint of hardships and labors on men intimately involved.

The construction of the Cathedral had been a long and slow process. From the time of the laying of the cornerstone in 1877, the work was consumed with delays, conflicts, threats, and unkept promises. Henry G. Harrison, the supervisory architect, who gained a limited fame from its design, kept a strict watch over every detail, large or small, designing and redesigning as the Cathedral progressed, rejecting and approving all of its aspects. His painstaking care was enhanced by the procedure of work. Harrison created the designs which he presented for approval to Judge Hilton. Hilton, a man of "good taste but bad moods" did not give speedy approval. He would put off approval sometimes for weeks; his disapproval of many parts drew the construction out unto a long and tedious process. The detail of the Cathedral was beautiful and accurate and exhibited the talent of the architect. The price he had to pay was not commensurate with the veracity of detail. Judge Hilton in the process became the great manipulator and monarch, ordering and countermanding, pontificating and upbraiding. Harrison true to his trade, aroused the antagonism and disfavor of Hilton. Requested to draw plans for

(left) The Cathedral at Garden City
as it appears today.

(below) Sketch of consecration of Cathedral
on June 2, 1885; Mrs. Stewart presenting
deed of the property to Bishop Littlejohn.

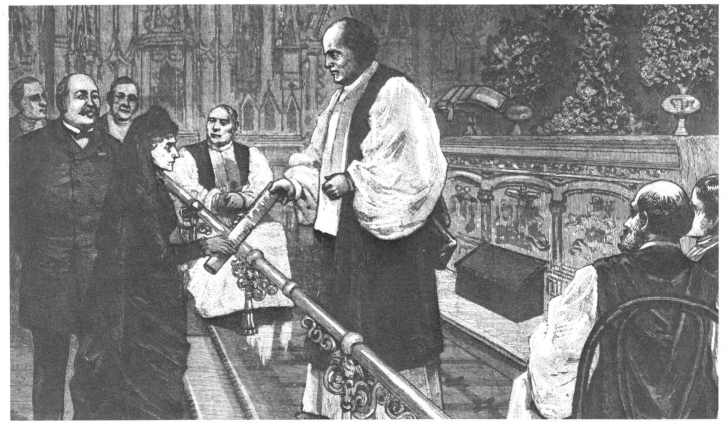

the Bishop's house, he was berated for the size of the building and for the expensive detail. Hilton wanted a plain house "of Tudor or Elizabethan style with a mansard roof," built of "brick and stone after the manner of English designs." Angered by Harrison, since he spent so many days in its design, Hilton gave the job to another architect, Edward D. Harris, who in a previous altercation between Hilton and Harrison, had won the designing of St. Paul's School. The See House and St. Paul's School, Victorian, massive and unimpressive, were the lasting monuments to Hilton's psychotic state. Not humiliated enough by the loss of the two designs, Harrison experienced the interferring hand of Hilton's agents in the construction of the Cathedral itself. Harris and the Garden City real estate agent, Cunliffe injected themselves into the cathedral building. Orders were changed, work done that shouldn't have been done, and attempts were made at change in design. The two became Hilton's watchdogs and made life miserable for the dedicated architect. The final blow came at the consecration when Hilton did not have the decency to allow Harrison to share in the final triumph. Harrison's own words engraved the anguish:

> 1885 June 2. Cathedral of the Incarnation consecrated today. A very great ceremony. Bp.
> [sic] Porter preached the sermon. Myself, wife and _____ present. My name as the Architect
> had been left out of the order of exercises purposely. The Bishop asked me as a favor to him
> that I take my place in the procession which I did. The Architect's name had been put in but
> crossed out by Judge Hilton so I was told, at his instigation.

The same difficulties and the same humiliations were experienced by the Bishop. Since the memorial church had been accepted as a cathedral, the Bishop became vitally interested in its construction. Many visits and conferences with the Judge and the Architect changed little the detail and content of the building. The Bishop was allowed little to say in the matter. He did manage to have the chancel and sanctuary made larger for cathedral purposes. His one real lasting contribution was the baptisery. Hilton wanted it as a Vestry room but the Bishop won his point. The lovely baptisery stood as the Bishop's major contribution to the Bishop's seat, the Cathedral. Two such strong personalities as the Bishop and the Judge were bound to conflict. In all, the secular prince held the trump card over the sacred prelate. Hilton had Mrs. Stewart in his hand and the money in his pocket. The Bishop fiercely stated:

> Mrs. Stewart is simple putty in the hands of Judge Hilton . . . Hilton was the worst man I ever
> met; always ready to insult me. Watched Mrs. Stewart like a cat a mouse; drew her will
> contrary to her wishes; allowed no one to see her alone, always someone in his interest.

And in final despair, the Bishop confided:

> Oh, what I have suffered from that man; what provocations, what humiliation! He has no
> regard for a clergyman's feelings. He has damned the whole thing many a time in my presence.
> He confessed to me that during two years he acted so as to offend and insult and enrage me
> and so have an excuse for breaking this whole slate. No man could be coarser, more vulgar,
> more abusive, when angry.

The most pervading threat that chilled the aggressiveness of the Bishop was not abandonment of the project but the transfer to another church, specifically the Roman Catholic. Hilton up to the time of the property conveyance stopped the Bishop with the vague assertion of giving the cathedral to another group. The possibility was reasonable and taken seriously by the Bishop.

No one person suffered more than the pawn in the game, the Rev. T. Stafford Drowne. Dr. Drowne was one of the ablest men in the Diocese. The Rector of St. Paul's Church, Clinton Street, Drowne held many diocesan offices, among which he was Secretary of the Convention and delegate to the General Convention. A close friend and confidant to the Bishop, he was appointed in 1878, minister-in-charge of the Cathedral Chapel and Acting Warden of the Cathedral Schools. Drowne soon became involved in the planning and designing of the Cathedral, being a close friend of Harrison, the architect. Arousing the antagonism of the Judge, he soon became "persona non grata" in the eyes of the chief moneyman. When the time came for the appointment of a dean for the Cathedral, Drowne was the natural choice. However, the Judge had to be reckoned with. Prejudiced already against Drowne he adamantly opposed even the suggestion of Drowne and abetted by a misrepresentation by Cunliffe, the agent and a teacher at St. Paul's, made financial difficulties the crux of his denial. The Bishop was appalled by his attitude and by the implication that Hilton have a veto on clerical appointment. He confided to Drowne that "you are secretary, standing committee, deputy, registrar and I will run this Cathedral by you and no one else." He nevertheless backed down and finally appointed another man, Samuel Cox, as the first dean. Dr. Drowne never fully recovered from the adverse and unkind treatment. He remained secretary of the Diocese and held his other offices, but did not have any permanent parochial responsibility.

OUT AND AWAY

A firm stipulation that Mrs. Stewart made, from the very first letter of offering in 1877 and verified in 1885, was that the Bishop make his home in Garden City. To accommodate the Bishop in flourishing style, a four-story, thirty-two room palace was completed in 1884. Bishop Littlejohn anxious to be near his official seat, moved out of his home at 170 Remsen Street, a few months earlier and lived at 95 Ninth Street in a house formerly occupied by St. Paul's School. On June 24, 1884, he moved into his new home.

The palace was a fitting residence for a prelate. It was "a spacious mansion, containing some thirty or more rooms, finished in ash containing all appliances of comfort, ordinarily found in city mansions." It differed in no wise "from many elegant country houses — to be ranked among the most elegant." Yet it caused many problems. The house as the Bishop saw it and as it finally came to be were two different things. The Bishop envisaged the house as a clergy center for both bishop and clergy, the clergy to pursue missionary work in the Diocese. With the dissipation and disappearances of sufficient funds, the house came to have no tenants save one — the Bishop and his family. Forced to live there alone, the Bishop soon experienced great difficulty in upkeep. He bemoaned,

> the See House was built for the finest house on Long Island. Really I can't afford to run it; it takes all my salary and all my private income, and then if we hadn't a good daughter and son-in-law in the Wessons, we could not stand it. This house should have at least an annual payment of $3,000 from the estate.

To alleviate the Bishop's financial difficulties, the Diocese did attempt some solution. The question of how to dispose of the former episcopal residence threw light on the Bishop's plight. The Diocese discussed the possible sale of the Remsen Street house and the cash from the sale put into the Bishop's salary fund. However, the diocesan leaders did not agree to the idea, and finally compromised by renting out the former house, and putting any accrued income into the Bishop's salary fund. Ironically enough, some members of the Diocese questioned the Bishop's salary. They were under the assumption that the $3,000 allotment was part of his salary and wondered why he needed any additional help from the Diocese. However, the Bishop informed them of his unmet bills for upkeep which made the situation more reasonable to all concerned.

More crucial than upkeep or housing problems was the effect of the move on the Bishop and his relation to the Diocese. In a real sense he withdrew from the center of diocesan life which was bound to have its effect upon his active participation in the diocesan dynamic. Clergy and laity missed his presence at Brooklyn and he himself lost something of that stimulus that came from city life. Garden City was still a highly underdeveloped village with under 500 residents. It was in the midst of "brown dunes and level moorlands alternate with scrubby stunted forest, primeval indeed but primitive. Village after village, presenting pictures of New England architecture . . . occasional villas dot the landscape . . . high windmills . . . streams . . . the ocean . . . In this idyllic land it is a great surprise to see on the one side of the railroad a cathedral stately and beautiful, seemingly the growth of some old city . . . " Here the Bishop was forced to live, separated not only by physical space, but also by a dimension that excluded him from urban excitement.

SOMEWHERE AND SOMEHOW

In the eight years of trial and conflict of cathedral building, the original grandiose plans for a complete cathedral system did not materialize. From a multitude of buildings to surround the diocesan center, only two buildings appeared, St. Paul's School, and the Bishop's House. The promise of an educational, charitable and missionary center dissolved in the bitterness of years. Even the already functioning school for girls, St. Mary's School, did not have a building. No promise in the conveyance for a school prompted the Diocese to pursue firmly the needed structure. It was not until 1890, after a long lawsuit that the building appeared, and again was the eminent domain of the money holder, Henry G. Hilton. His architect, Harris, designed the building. Hilton donated the new three-storied edifice that contained all the needed educational plant of gymnasium, chemistry laboratory and cooking school, in addition to lovely apartments and large classrooms. The Cathedral never did gain its promised landscaped park. Thirty-five acres were donated in 1885, a small lot compared to the grand plan that was first offered.

Disappointment also colored the final conveyance of the cathedral property made by Mrs. Stewart. Drawn up by Hilton's chief legal henchman, Prescott Butler, the donation had strings, tieing up the gift with severe restrictions. Many of the regulations were incompatible with church law. Some were vague about responsibility. All made the gift totally inadequate for practical functioning and church control. And most of all, the endowment bond of Mrs. Stewart was totally inadequate to accomplish needed work in repair, upkeep and program.

The recipient of a bad bargain, the Bishop still had to contend with diocesan objections. Many of the clergy and laity still looked upon the Cathedral as a foreign and alien conception more to enhance ecclesiastical foppery than to highlight episcopal character. The objectors felt the Cathedral would turn into "a thing of sentiment, a nursery of episcopal pride and prerogative, a well furnished refuge of clerical ease, a convenient instrumentality for getting up ecclesiastical shows and parades, that would wear the glamor of practical church work without the reality, a well-concocted scheme of Diocesan centralization that would threaten the outlying liberties of individual parishes."

The emotional block was enhanced by the practical consideration. The Cathedral was too far out in the country for conveniences. The resentments were flamed by the informed opening of the Cathedral. Except for a few finishing touches, the Cathedral was ready for services by early spring. With the approval of Judge Hilton, the Cathedral opened informally on April 9, 1885. "The Cathedral was opened with but little ceremony and a great crowd there. Everything went satisfactorily." Picked up by the press, the event had widespread publicity. The poor Bishop, beset by hostilities, immediately called a Special Convention for April 15, 1885. At the Convention all the steps previous to April were laboriously outlined. After due consideration, the Diocese accepted the Stewart offer but with the stipulation that the Convention was to be the ultimate power to the Cathedral Corporation.

Inadequate funds curbed final cathedral organization and program. A Cathedral Chapter, the executive group of the corporation, did not appear until 1890. Misrepresentation and misunderstanding delayed its formation when finally in December 1889, the move was made and a chapter made up of Dean, Almoner, Precentor and Sacristan, together with six lay members took over the direction of the diocesan center.

The great plans for missionary work under the first vision, dwindled into a hit and miss, limited struggling action. The endowment which netted only $15,000 a year was totally inadequate.

> An income of $15,000 is miserable. We have only one deacon paid out of that, $1,000. We are straining every nerve over St. Paul's. A hundred boys would make it a success. We are spending this year [1885] $2,500 to advertise it. All the rest of our endowment is reserved to meet a possible school deficiency.

A limited clerical force had to accomplish almost unlimited duties. In addition to the regular three Sunday services, the clergy had to perform all needful duties in the Cathedral Schools and had the immediate care of six flourishing missions in Queens County. The Cathedral had all the aspects of "a memorial grand in outline but full of vacant spaces."

The Diocese pursued the matter of a more suitable endowment with the powers-that-be, Hilton and his protectee, Mrs. Stewart. The matter was complicated by the death of Mrs. Stewart in 1886. In the years of his legal guardianship, Hilton had gathered under his direction most of the Stewart fortune. When Mrs. Stewart died, he had no obstacle in his way, and inherited most of the millions still left in her fortune and also became the executor of the Stewart project, Garden City. The Stewart heirs, cousins and distant relations contested the will. They were joined by the Cathedral Corporation who for three years battled in the law courts for the promised and unfulfilled adequate endowment. Early in 1887, three different lawsuits against Hilton began with charges of deceit, fraud, misrepresentation and undue influence. The cathedral lawsuit had its ups-and-downs and incurred discouragement and utter frustration among some of the clergy. Dr. Moore of Hempstead, in the summer of 1887, vented his dispair:

> Yes, Hilton has been promising to give us a good deal at Garden City. Why doesn't he do it? I have no faith in him. He doesn't care a fig for Mr. Stewart's memory or Mrs. Stewart's memory. He wouldn't spend a cent at Garden City if he could help it . . . Judge Hilton is saying to Bishop Littlejohn "I will build what you want if you will relieve me of the necessity of giving an account." I see very little chance for Garden City . . . This matter won't be settled for years. It will be good pickings for the lawyers, but the church won't get much.

The Bishop, if discouraged, did not communicate this feeling. In truth, he was not discouraged. In 1887, as hopeless as the situation seemed to most people, the Bishop accepted the situation as it was. His tenacity and faith carried the Diocese. In 1890, he loudly and joyously announced to the Diocese that the whole matter had been successfully settled. The Cathedral Corporation had an additional endowment of $500,000 and the new school building, making a total endowment of $800,000 and property and buildings amounting to over one and a half million dollars in value.

THE CITY IS THE PLACE

A growing awareness of the city problems and the church's inadequate ministry to it became clarion clear in 1885. In that year Bishop Littlejohn made his compelling address to the last convention to be held in the City of Brooklyn. His address brought up short the diocesan complacent approach to the multiplex, growing and seething environs which was called the City of Brooklyn, but which included almost all of Kings County. A tension in the Diocese about where work was most needed had produced a keen interest in the far outlying country areas in Suffolk County. The two "natural divisions", the city and the country, each had its own challenge and scope. In the non-urban region, clusters of new year-round homes sprang up among the ever-growing summer amusements and resort areas. But the immediate need presented itself compellingly and forcefully in the city. "There is no Diocese upon which the problem of Church work in the City presses more strongly than upon ours. Brooklyn not only holds today, but is likely to hold in the future, its rank as the third city in the union."

The urban scene had changed drastically because of the major influences of two classes —

> the foreign born and their old world heritage of religious revolutions and anarchies and heresies

and the other class —

> our native born people, newly absorbed from the outlying country life — many of

them . . . broken loose from home ties and old customs, and have not replaced them with new ones calculated to give stability . . . .

The opening of the Brooklyn Bridge had begun to unleash a wild stream of foreign-born, matched only by the tide at floodgates from the rural undeveloped native areas.

A noticeable change had come over the quiet city of Brooklyn. Materialism, secularism, and unbelief asserted themselves with restless aggression. Christian churches were too fragmented to minister to the urban complex. Warring Protestant sects, each asserting their own brand of salvation together with "a corrupt and corrupting Romanism that has overlaid Catholic truth and order with its own inventions and arrayed itself in open hostility against every healthy progressive impulse of modern society," had proven ineffectual.

The missionary field of the city presented a variety of opportunities. It was the progenitor of opinion that:

If there by any new ideas afloat, they find their first welcome in the city . . . Here the press has its largest circulation in proportion to population. Here men take sides rapidly. Here they are most energetic and liberal in raising means to propagate their convictions and to draw in proselytes.

It was the seedbed for future church missionaries. Families with no religious attachments, coming from the country where spiritual decay, battling "isms" and erroneous teaching had left them unaffected, became staunch members of the Church. A cross-current of churchmen leaving the city for the less populated suburban areas, became carriers of the Church. The emigrating churchmen became the basis and material for new churches. Parishes in the suburbs were settled not by the local indigent folk, nor by missionaries sent by the Diocese, but by and large by the urban baptized laity.

The city was the special field for an historic church, a liturgical community such as the Episcopal Church.

It is enough that we believe ourselves commissioned to speak for a pure branch of the Holy Catholic Church, and therefore to be possessed by the same faith and order — the same sacraments and discipline — the same gifts of the Holy Ghost, that once in the persons of the Apostles and Evangelists converted the civilized world to the Cross of Christ.

The challenge of the city, so vividly portrayed by the Bishop, manifested itself dramatically in the tremendous growth of urban population, housing and industry. The population of Brooklyn stood at 750,000 in 1885. New building, increasing at a rapid rate, filled up most of the vacant land. The dormitory character matched the economic expansion. Warehouses, the largest in the world, represented a capital of two million dollars. The waterfront received more vessels than New York. Sixty nine million dollars had been invested in industrial factories; 23 million paid in salaries and 188 million accrued in the value of products.

No more apparent was the burgeoning of Brooklyn than in the decade 1884-1894. Increasing at the rate of 30,000 people a year, Brooklyn had increased in 1890 to 806,343. By 1894, when the incorporation of all Kings County into the City was accomplished the population reached almost a million people. In 1890, Brooklyn had 10,560 manufacturers, 229 different lines of industry with more than 100 thousand workers. The warehouses and markets expanded to untold proportions.

The increasing population hinged on the development of transit communications. "The year 1891 marked the beginning of an immigration movement that changed mightily the whole complexity of life, converting a homogeneous community into a melting pot seething with foreign racial groups." The Brooklyn Bridge, the construction and extension of the elevated railroads made the immediate densely settled area, and the outlying suburban regions more accessible and more desirable. As the foreign stock moved in, the native born moved out to the more rustic but increasingly near communities. A momentous occasion which drastically enhanced the area was the application of electricity to street railways. The change from horsedrawn vehicles to electrically powered cars sped up the transit and shortened the time from the city center to surrounding areas. Within two years after 1892, horsedrawn trolleys disappeared from Brooklyn.

The city began to stir and move. The Hill Zone began to fill up noticeably. Fort Greene boasted row on row of fashionable brownstone detached houses. Flatbush was transformed from a quiet colonial town to a prosperous settled suburb. Highland Park, Cyprus Hills and all along the Brooklyn-Queens boundary substantial suburbs developed.

As population increased so the churches multiplied. By 1891, there were 291 Protestant Churches in Brooklyn and thirty-one in Kings County. In Broooklyn the Episcopal Church had achieved the ascendency with forty-five churches, closely followed by the Methodist Episcopal, the Baptists and the Presbyterians. The Roman Catholic Churches were multiplying just as rapidly; and to emphasize the growing pluralistic nature of the city, there were nine fully organized synagogues. The late eighties and early nineties witnessed the mushrooming of Episcopal Churches. Christ Church, Clinton Street, was at the zenith of its career with 700 communicants. Its chapel had the banner Sunday School of the Diocese with an enrollment of 1,030. Christ Church, Bedford Avenue, had 800 communicants and experienced unprecedented growth under the leadership of its Rector, the Rev. James Darlington, later to be Bishop. Unparalleled progress for Brooklyn churches reflected in the confirmation classes of St. Peter's Church with 93; Christ Church with 94 and Christ Church, Bedford Avenue with 114. The Hill Zone was in the heyday of its prosperity. By 1894, the Church of the Messiah numbered 1,387 communicants; St. Mary's Church, 828; St. Luke's Church, 1,241. Equal to the Hill churches was the growth of other sections. By 1894, St. Ann's Church had grown to 1,272; St. Peter's Church to 841; Holy Trinity to nearly 1,000; St. Thomas, Bushwich Avenue, had 461 in a too small building.

Within the confines of the City, some Episcopal churches had experienced erratic changes. St. Martin's Church, originated in 1853, first as the Ascension, and later as the Church of the Good Angels, had come into the Diocese as a charter member under the name of Emmanuel Church. In 1893, it reverted to the name of St. Martin's. Each change of name reflected a new congregation. The Church of St. Mark on Eastern Parkway was forced to move from its prime location by the encroachment of the Williamsburg Bridge. St. Michael's, High Street, organized in 1847, experienced grave difficulties, and came under the fostering care of Grace Church in 1871 as Grace Chapel. By 1894, it had a renascence and reverted to its original parish status and title. St. Andrew's Church on Third Avenue at the then extreme end of the city was organized in 1889 and prospered. Holy Apostles was successful from its start under the auspices of St. Paul's Church in Flatbush. Meeting first in stores and borrowed quarters, it grew to large proportions and opened its own building in 1892. The Church of Reformation, one of the original parishes of the Diocese had changed its name to Church of the Incarnation.

New work, under the direction of the Diocese and then under the two archdeacons, were spotted throughout the city. In the 14th Ward, largely foreign and predominantly Irish, a mission was begun in 1884 by a generous gift of $7,000 with three lots purchased and a chapel erected. St. Michael, as it was called, held regular services both in English and in Italian. In 1887, a new enterprise began at Bath Beach, the Church of the Holy Spirit, which met first in the Odd Fellows Hall. Along the crowded river front of the 6th Ward, a new program was initiated, The Church Seaman's Mission of Brooklyn. Near the Erie and Atlantic Basins, the center of the largest wharf and warehousing system in the world, twenty five miles long, the Seaman's Mission worked with the vast population employed in shipping. In 1889, three new churches were begun, St. Clement's Church on Atlantic Avenue near Alabama; St. Chrysostom's, among people of more ample means; and St. Timothy's Church in the "Ocean Hill section", which in 1886 was vacant land but by 1889 filled with housing and population "not rich in this world goods."

Two unusual churches appeared. On Advent Sunday, 1891, the Archdeacon of Northern Brooklyn established St. David's Church at Gates and Marcy Avenues. The new mission would service the church people in that section, but most of all was to serve as a church for deaf mutes of the City. Holy Comforter Memorial Church was established, begun and erected as a living memorial to the late Rev. Noah Schenck, longtime Rector of St. Ann's Church.

The church's ministry to the two specialized groups, the Italians and the Blacks, did not prosper as well as the other churches. Difficulty in leadership for the Santa Croce Mission caused a failing of interest and absorption into already existent parishes. The Italian former Roman Catholic priest ordained by Bishop Littlejohn in Episcopal orders, the Rev. Mr. Paco, had his own ideas of work among his native men. Paco, without consulting the Missionary Committee, transferred his main interest from the Mission in Red Hook to St. Michael's in the 14th Ward, and discontinued his work in South Brooklyn. The shift of emphasis did neither the missionary nor the mission any good. Paco resigned and it was impossible to find another Italian to replace him. The work was carried on by nearby St. Paul's Church and arrangements were made with a New York priest to hold services in Brooklyn from time to time. By 1880, the Italian congregation at St. Michael's had ceased to use the building, and the High Street church became almost entirely an English-speaking congregation. In 1889, the Diocese renewed its work by holding Sunday services at St. Margaret's Mission in Red Hook. An Italian clergyman, The Rev. Mr. Loya, a medical student, fulfilled the Sunday duty. The Italian mission continued and in 1893, the Diocese extended its work among them by holding services in Italian in Ravenswood.

The work among the city's Blacks fared a little better, not so much from diocesan interest, but by the firm conviction of its congregation. On May 19, 1890, the congregation incorporated as St. Augustine's Church called as its first Rector, The Rev. William V. Tunnel, and relinquished all diocesan appropriations. The congregation had grown without a permanent location, and at the time of its incorporation still was a tenant of loaned buildings. The Church of the Holy Trinity officially granted the congregation the right to use and worship in the church building on Canton Street, which for all practical purposes became their own church. After much pleading, George Foster Peabody purchased the chapel and gave it to the Diocese for the Black parish but only after nine moves to different locations.

On Saturday, March 15, 1890, Mrs. Charles H. Hall, assisted by her daughter, Miss Bessie Hall, and a corps of ladies established an "Industrial School for Colored Girls of Brooklyn." The project met with phenomenal success. Some other churches took a paternal interest in assisting the parish; but always in terms of the white congregations' charitable assistance, rather than fraternal intermingling. By and large the Blacks struggled alone; achieving all that they had through their own inventions.

Queens County, still including both the western section and the nascent Nassau County, could not match Brooklyn's tremendous growth. In its western area, nearest to the developing city environs, the population had increased to 87,050 while in the more remote Suffolk border region, an increase to 40,999 showed its comparative slow development. Queens County had developed along its shoreline. Most communities had developed out of summer residences turned into all year round homes. The laying out of Hillside Avenue in 1891 increased the potential for middle western Queens by making that area more accessible to city traffic. While some areas blossomed; others became static. Queens Village, a bright prospect in the seventies, had failed to realize its bright hopes. It was to the new area of Hollis that population gravitated and grew. By 1890, Hempstead approached a population of over 4,000. Mineola had 1,125 residents. The annual influx of summer vacationists and a profitable fishing industry had caused Rockville Centre, Freeport and their surrounding areas to become more settled and frequented. Macadam roads, constructed for the high wheel English bike enthusiast had opened up new parts of the Island. The formation of the League of American Wheelmen in 1880 pressured the development and extension of the hard surfaced bike paths.

Few parishes in Queens could reach the numerical proportions of the more affluent Brooklyn parishes. Flushing had 490 communicants; Redeemer, Astoria 332; Grace Church, Jamaica 260; and the Cathedral in its few short years had 160 communicants. When the Cathedral had been consecrated, the six mission stations of the Diocese were put under its jurisdiction. They included Farmingdale, Merrick, Rockville Centre, Queens Village and a new mission in 1888, Church of the Epiphany in Woodhaven. Ex-Governor McCormack of Jamaica gave the land for the Woodhaven church. St. Joseph's Church in Queens Village was not very promising. But least promising of all the missions was St. Thomas', Farmingdale. Begun in 1875, it had shown little growth. Often without a resident priest, services were held by visiting clergy. In 1885 the Rev. J. O. S. Huntington "who had a barn-like building called 'St. Andrew's Cottage' on Route 110 near the Halfway House, conducted services . . . He brought boys out from the East Side to Farmingdale in a 'fresh air project'."

By 1892, the population of Queens County had increased rapidly. Constantly receiving a large overflow from Brooklyn, a continuous succession of new communities sprang up from fifteen to twenty miles out on the several lines of the railroad. The people that came were of various nationalities, classes, and religious affiliations. Many were mechanics and laborers, Irish and German, and nominally Romanists. Others were clerks and men in small businesses, usually Protestants. They were attracted by the "prospect of exchanging the crowded rooms and high rents of the city for a country home of their own, where their children [could] have purer air and greater freedom." The lines of the railroad largely determined the lines of missionary work. Work along the central and southern lines of the railroad was done by the Cathedral, and by individual parishes on the northern side of the county.

The Cathedral had its six missions, reaching nearly the whole length of the county, all except one sustained out of its own funds. The newest mission was built in 1891 at a cost of $5,000. It took the place of Redeemer, Merrick, which in 1889 had become an independent parish. On the south side, a Mission of Grace Church, Massapequa was established; St. Michael's and All Angels, Seaford had assumed an independent state with its own clergyman. North Queens communities were under the watchful eye of the colonial churches. St. George, Flushing, still maintained its mission at College Point and Bayside while St. James, Newtown, conducted services at Bowery Bay. Organized parishes, St. Paul's, Woodside; St. John's, Long Island City, and St. Thomas', Ravenswood, were really missionary stations needing outside support to sustain ministrations. St. Paul's, Glen Cove, had in 1890 established a mission at Sea Cliff which flourished and grew. A new work at Steinway, Astoria, the creation of the Archdeaconry, began in June 1892. A rented building accommodated the growing mission composed of "working people engaged in factories" who could not afford to support the work. By 1894, the Archdeaconry of Queens had twelve missions, but only one directly under the Diocese. The others were cared for by the Cathedral and the various parishes within whose parochial limits they were situated.

The church's work in Suffolk was the feeblest and most difficult. Small populations in scattered settlements gave little support to any new missionary extension. Except for a bright spot in Northport, where in the 1880's, a group of employees of Edward Thompson Publishing Co., organized Trinity Episcopal Church, the situation remained the same as before. Suffolk had seven mission stations at Setauket, Port Jefferson, Brentwood, Central Islip, Riverhead, Greenport and a revived work at Lake Ronkonkoma, for which the Associated Mission, under the leadership of the Archdeacon, was responsible. Two other churches, Bellport and Yaphank continued under the direction of a separate mission priest. St. Thomas, Farmingdale, had begun St. Mary's, Amityville. It was apparent to the Missionary Committee that Suffolk County was not "a very favorable field for the church, and will need for some time to come hard work and patient waiting" . . . combined with liberal giving. In ten years church communicant strength had grown from 903 to 1,499, only an increase of approximately 50 communicants a year. The City, although not adequately ministered to, showed a better percentage and a surer interest.

The Episcopal Church's confrontation of the growing metropolis had proven static. Two new parishes and six new missions had been started. The loss of two parishes brought the church to where it had been in 1869. In ten years, 1873 to 1883, not even a mission was started although Brooklyn had added about 200,000 people. Since 1883, six new missions had been established, one by a churchman, one an offshoot of a neighboring parish and four by the Diocese. The proportion of church communicant to the population of Brooklyn was 1.6%, not better and no worse than the Protestant churches' record. Diocesan work in the city had avoided many large areas of population, especially four regions with an aggregate population of about 100,000. In others where population reached only a little over 20,000, there were three Episcopal Churches and fifteen Protestant. The heavily populated areas were not preponderantly Roman Catholic nor all German, but had a mixture of "Anglo-Saxons" who needed the Church.

The Church in this Diocese has distinguished itself in all work save the missionary work — the church extension work at its own doors, within its own limits. It has not come short in its liberality to general missions — in foreign lands.

But it had failed in "the desert wastes of Brooklyn." The great need demanded solution, not in ignoring it by assertion that there are enough unfilled churches to be filled, but by a shift in strategy and a change in emphasis. Two aspects had to be considered, the first was the men, the second the money.

The church extension program of the Diocese had been the responsibility of the Bishop and a small Missionary Committee. With a growing diocese and more rapidly developing diocesan life, the Bishop and the Committee had become exhausted in raising and disbursing funds. A continuous contact by the Bishop could not longer be retained without help. He decreed Brooklyn to be,

> a city with great vacant spaces where work is needed, and where souls are perishing for lack of care; a city already containing a population larger than twelve states of the Union, larger, in actual truth, than that of all the missionary effort which we *ought* to be making, there is need to put arch-missionaries into the field, to create work, and systemactically extend missions.

The suggested revival of an old and revered office, the Archdeacon, had grown in popularity in many places in the National Church. Long Island was the only diocese in the state without this "Diocesan organization" and was almost alone, among the stronger diocese of the church in the United States. The Bishop's request for archdeacons was summed up in the function of the diocesan agents. The Archdeacon would use all possible money and means,

> to found missions, to sustain cottage services, to provide shelter and apparatus for Sunday Schools, to build chapels as they are required, to furnish suitable Christian literature for the people, and Bibles, and Prayer Books, and instructive Christian reading for such as may be preparing for Baptism, Confirmation or Holy Communion.

The need was not for something that would become "additional ecclesiastical lumber to be laid away to season and dry; no new wheels in our machinery to increase the clatter and friction of those already running." Rather, the age demanded an aggressive agent to devote full time to the expansion of the church on the Island. The Bishop's request for clerical assistance resulted in the approval of the plan at the 1887 Convention.

As soon as the new office of Archdeacon had been instituted, internal problems of responsibility, function, selection, and relationship appeared. The first form of procedure for securing Archdeacons rested upon the appointment by the Bishop with the approval of the clergy in the three areas. Bishop Littlejohn took immediate steps to initiate the program. At a meeting of the Brooklyn clergy on October 17, 1887 the Bishop appointed as Archdeacon the approved candidate, C. Ellis Stevens, General Secretary of the Church Society for Promoting Christianity among the Jews, and former assistant at St. Paul's Church, Clinton Street. On January 18, 1888, at a Queens Convocation, the Rev. John C. Middeton, Rector of St. Paul's Church, Glen Cove, was approved as Archdeacon for Queens. The third agent, for Suffolk County, the Rev. Robert Weeks, Rector of Greenport and Head of the Associate Mission at Riverhead, was nominated by the Bishop and approved by the clergy in a circular letter in the mail.

The sudden death of the Queens Archdeacon and the appointment of a new candidate by the Bishop by mail brought a question of legality and proper procedure. Vague definition of jurisdiction, together with a demand for more attention to burgeoning Brooklyn caused the Diocese to consider carefully the office and work of the Archdeacons. To fully explain and clearly elucidate the new agents' role and function, together with their relationship to the existent Missionary Committee and the Areas of Work, the important *Missionary Canon* was enacted by the Convention in 1891. The canon clearly stated that:

> (1) There were to be four archdeaconries, North Brooklyn and South Brooklyn, Queens and Suffolk. The county of Kings was divided into two sections by an irregular line zig-zagging from the East River to Fulton Street and Flatbush Avenue, along Atlantic Avenue to Franklin Avenue and then back to Flatbush Avenue. The two divisions would each have its own Archdeacon.
> (2) Each Archdeaconry was composed of clergy and 3 laymen from each parish and one layman from mission stations having 50 regular communicants.
> (3) At its first regular meeting and every four years after, each Archdeaconry shall nominate to the Bishop for his appointment or rejection a clergyman to fill the office of Archdeacon, and to preside at all Archdeaconry meetings.
> (4) The Missionary Committee was to be reorganized with the Archdeacons and a layman from each Archdeaconry serving on it, together with the elected members from the convention.
> (5) The Archdeaconries thus constituted "shall have the management of Missionary operations and the ultimate control of all funds raised for the support of Missionaries, or the building of Mission churches.

(6) Each Archdeaconry should have its own Treasurer who disbursed and accounted for all monies raised in the Archdeaconries and made an annual report to the Annual Convention. Each Archdeaconry had at least two meetings a year at which attendance was compulsory.

(7) It shall be the duty of the Archdeacon, conferring with the Bishop, as to plans and details, to take the oversight of the missionary work in the Archdeaconry — to survey the ground, and to propose, as occasion offers, plans of operation, and in case such plans be adopted by the Archdeaconry, to awaken, as far as opportunity can be found, an interest therein on the part of the congregations.

Following the Convention, the approved mechanics for church extension were instituted. On recommendations of the Archdeaconries, and with the approval of the Bishop, the Very Rev. Samuel Cox served as Archdeacon of Queens, the Rev. Robert Weeks for Suffolk; the Rev. Albert A. Morrison, Rector of St. Matthew's Church, for Northern Brooklyn; and the Rev. Reese F. Alsop, Rector of St. Ann's Church, for Southern Brooklyn. All three of the Archdeacons were rectors of parishes and therefore received no stipend from the Diocese. The Suffolk Archdeacon was partially supported by the Missionary Committee's appropriations.

The need for money became more and more pressing. Voluntary gifts from parishes were not sufficient to carry on already existing work, no less new work. To increase missionary giving, the Convention of 1885 decided to tap the resources of the large Sunday School enrollment. A resolution in 1885 requested each Sunday School to make an annual offering for diocesan missions. To abet this, an offering for missions was to be taken on the Bishop's day of visitation and additional parish offerings on the fifth Sunday in the Spring and Autumn. This was increased to a quarterly collection by 1890. Although much effort was made to increase the needed income, circulars, meetings, rallies and Bishop's exhortation could not quite raise the Missionary Fund to any great proportions. In 1886, missionary giving amounted to $7,116.21; in 1890 it had increased only $2,000 to amount to $9,342.25. With the increase of archdeaconries, and the self-support responsibility of each Archdeaconry, the amount had reached $10,022.98, the largest amount ever given but not sufficient to meet all missionary needs. The Diocese still had to depend upon its two chief contributors, Holy Trinity and Grace Church, for added funds.

Diocesan giving for missions was complicated by the popular and demanding calls of the National Missionary Board. Many parishes in the Diocese contributed much to work with the Indians, or work overseas, and stinted on diocesan programs. The National $5.00 Missionary Enrollment Plan promoted the gift of $5.00 by 200,000 churchmen to raise one million dollars for missions that was to be presented at the General Convention. Even with this incentive, giving to missions was poor and inadequate.

THE REDEEMING INSTITUTION

As the Diocese emphasized the City as its focus of church extension, so in its social and charitable work, the city poor and destitute became the recipients of its philanthropy. Growing awareness of city parishes was for the "stranger outside the gate," the workingman and the city tenement dweller. For the Diocese, the implication of its concentration was a multiplication of redeeming institutions; for the parish, an enhancement of its role as the redeeming institution.

The new approach reflected a deeper understanding of the church's ministry to the City. Familiar social and economic views seemed inadequate to the new conditions of life and labor in the city. The Episcopal Church, like other Christian brethren, found it increasingly difficult to attract or hold the average working man. "When better accommodations existed, the working class commonly regarded the church, — with its fine upholstery, stained glass windows, and expensive chairs — as an institution where ill-clad worshippers were unwelcome and where the Nazarene himself would have been rebuffed." The pulpit, increasingly beholden to contributions from the rich, ignored or condoned the terrible injustices to wage earners. The church had assumed the atmosphere of a club house, where only the socially accepted worshipped, and where membership was closed but to the rich or prominent.

A deep concern for the workingman grew among a small group of enlightened reformers. Henry George and Washington Gladdens became the champions of the poor. They emphasized in their writings that economic life was not beyond the range of Christian ethics. Walter Rauschenbusch, well known social gospeler, provided the rationale for the religious involvement in the social problems of the day. The social doctrine of the Kingdom of God did not expect isolated individuals to change society but rather a "community of the ethically earnest" to found the Kingdom of God on earth.

The extension of the social gospel became the institutional church. In the 1880's the "institutional church" emerged, fostered particularly by Episcopalians and Congregationalists, with the purpose of providing centers of culture, recreation and religious education for the urban poor who were now inhabiting the sections of the city in which these churches were located. The Episcopal Church, which had few poor or workers in their ranks were among the first to be troubled about the city poor and urban workers. Morally sensitive middle class people, churchmen wanted to do something for the "underprivileged". It was an obligation of Christian charity as well as the responsibility that rested upon the affluent superior class. *Noblesse Obige!*

Parish House Religion —

Religious activity supplemented by a number of social institutions probably had its origin in the work of William A. Muhlenberg. Muhlenberg, a pioneer of many ventures, had founded on Long Island the ill-fated St. Paul's College in College Point, and had in 1870 established St. Johnland at Kings Park, a charitable institution for children and old people. He also set the example for the institutional church at the Church of the Holy Communion, New York, followed shortly by Grace Church under Henry C. Potter, later assistant Bishop of New York, and St. George's Church, Styvesant Square, New York. The general interest in social work caused the institutional church to become common in the larger cities, and no place more obvious than in the City of Brooklyn.

Pioneer work in social service had already begun in the 1870's with a ministry by some churches to the indigent poor. But after 1880 the movement took on greater and multiple dimension with the initiation of parish houses and parish house functions. Up to this time, the physical plant of the average parish included a Sunday School hall, more than likely the first church converted to instruction, and a large church, built nearby, offering workshop facilities for its members who attended Sunday, weekday, or special services. With the renewal of social responsibility, parishes began to construct, adapt, and remodel parish hall buildings. Some parishes, like St. Peter's, State Street, undertook extensive alterations. The church basement was redone to include two large guild rooms, a choir rehearsal room, and kitchen for cooking class or general use, together with bathrooms and lavatories.

Other churches, as Church of the Holy Trinity, bought parish houses. Holy Trinity chiefly acquired the building at Clinton Street and Pacific Street to furnish a house for the Women's Employment Society, but most of the church's benevolent activities tended to center there. Many churches throughout the land constructed new buildings which were more suitably adapted for the new program of the parishes.

With the multiplication of buildings, came a proliferation of organizations. The already thriving social service agencies were joined by social, cultural, and educational groups. A wide variety of purposes matched the equally wide range of persons involved. Parish Guilds increased the number of woman's groups, whether they be the newly instituted Altar Guild, or the accepted fund raising associations. The Brotherhood of St. Andrew, an unofficial national organization, joined together already existent men's groups, and assisted in forming others. Knight of Temperance Societies also furnished the local parish with a continuing means of fighting the old devil rum.

More and more an attempt to reach the working class fostered a growth of working men's clubs. The working men's clubs provided libraries, instructions, entertainment, together with monetary help in sickness or to obtain staples such as coal and flour at reduced rates. The working women were not forgotten. Some parishes instituted Working Women's Vacation Society of Brooklyn which gave "daily excursions to the seaside at Rockaway Beach during the summer, and filled their cottages in the mountains with sick and indigent married women and their children."

The church's work with young people also began to be structured, well-organized groups. The Girls Friendly Society, established in 1877, starting primarily for working girls, interested all kinds of girls, and became a major youth organization. Guilds for young women, for little girls, and for little boys were popular. Co-educational, Young People's Associations provided the youth with a social outlet as well as providing the church with funds, entertainment, and interest.

A vacation from the city was offered by the Diocese for "young girls and others of Brooklyn." The Sisters of St. John had opened a "Cottage by the Sea" at Ocean Beach, New Jersey, where girls "in need of rest and recreation with but limited means to pay the charges at the usual resorts" could come. "Everything will be provided for the comfort and healthful enjoyment of visitors. The charge for board will be $4 per week in advance . . . [with] a limit of stay, two weeks."

On a wider basis, the Episcopal Church did little to ally itself with the suffering working classes. Nationally, only a few far-sighted individuals, considered by their contemporaries, as eccentric, attempted to minister to the growing lower class. No more colorful and certainly no more dedicated a person to rise above the placid stream of apathy was the Rev. J. O. S. Huntington, son of a bishop. Best known for his founding of the Order of the Holy Cross, a monastic order for men in the church, Fr. Huntington became involved in working for the laboring classes on the Lower East Side of New York. There he came in contact with the seething, teeming cauldron of racial tension, and to it he attempted to bring the church's ministrations. Out of his work there, he drew the motivation to help the working people, founding in 1887 the Church Association for the Advancement of the Interests of Labor (CAIL). Considered a radical and a revolutionary, he pleaded for an eight hour day, child labor reform and tenement improvement. His radicalism was only surpassed by that of another Episcopalian, William D. W. Bliss, who finding no tension between the radical socialism and the Christian ethos, combined the two and founded the Society of Christian Socialists.

Long Island churchmen related very little to such novel and eccentric ideas. They were too involved in the issues of temperance and keeping holy the Sabbath. Temperance campaigning after the interest aroused in the seventies had subsided from a diocesan level to a parish level. Any attempt to confront the evils of drinking was done on a parish level through local action and local organization. Yet there was a certain element of alcoholism in the problem that the Diocese faced in the 1880's and early 1890's. For in the corrosive influence of drinking, the due observance of the Lord's Day had declined and changed. The first alarm turned to stubborn and hard-headed battle, and the heart of the matter became "saloon power".

The Lord's Day —

As early as 1890 the keen eye of the Bishop detected signs of a rising secularism and sounded a warning note on the growing disregard of the Lord's Day. Sunday for the Episcopalian in the late nineteenth century was a day of strict observance and quiet inspiration. Reflecting the first Pilgrim Fathers, the Episcopal churchmen donned their best sober dress, and participated in Sunday worship with the family. Many adults attended an afternoon service while children participated in an instruction period; some even came back to church a third time at night. In between praying, the average household occupied its Sunday in singing hymns around the family piano or organ, and in quiet reading of good and wholesome literature. The bright joy of the Resurrection found no sure place in the puritan observance. The day was one for contemplating a day of doom.

With the increased influx of foreigners, and the widespread settling of different peoples, the average Brooklynite received a stunning blow, and nowhere more apparent than in the observance of Sunday. The foreigners brought with them a different and alien culture and ethos, no more apparent and no more shocking than in the way they spent Sunday. For them Sunday was a day of enjoyment, entertainment and worst of all, drinking. They brought from the "old country" their concept of the continental Sunday.

The "margin of the county" next to the cities were subject to the "invasion of the hordes of pleasure-seekers." No more directly and seriously threatened by the evils of Sunday desecration was the limits of Queens County. A trip from crowded city streets to bucolic open Queens brought large crowds of people, bent upon mischief, and intent upon worldly pleasures. The invaders of the country interfered with the Sunday worship in many Queens parishes with their shouts of pleasure and their public games. Sunday evening trains, taking the boisterous groups back to the tenements, created pandemonium.

Political power and legal protection did not affect the growing problem, for, said the Bishop:

Magistrates and police are always tempted to obey the strongest pressures brought to bear upon them; and unfortunately the strongest pressure in this case comes from the disorderly elements in the community.

The foreigners had on their side "saloon power".

The course of action advocated by the Bishop, and pursued by the Church, had of necessity, to be local. Special regional committees in the Diocese were organized "to call the attention of civil authorities to our laws of Sunday as a day of rest and worship." They worked with the established Sunday Observance Associations in Kings County which were efficient and influential, and had held large rallies. A diocesan committee, appointed by the Annual Convention, supervised the efforts of the local group. The ultimate gain in the fight against Sunday desecration was not so much a re-enforcement of puritan ideal but rather a self-satisfaction in knowing that something was being done. The matter concerned the Diocese for many years to come.

CHARITABLE WORKS

Ineffective as diocesan efforts were to confront the growing social problems, most efficient was its ministering to the poor and destitute by its charitable institutions. The Diocese continued its five major works, under the Church Charity Foundation. A maverick, that could not be catalogued was St. Phebe's Mission House. The extension of Sister Eliza's dedicated concern for the outcasts of society, the Mission House had widened its field of operations. Permanently esconced in a building, purchased and furnished as a memorial to Harriet A. Low, an active and interest supporter, St. Phebe's had become more of a city mission work than an emergency soul-saving institution. People looked to the Mission House for number of souls saved, for growing lists of baptisms and confirmations. Yet this had not proven to be the worth of the diocesan settlement house. St. Phebe's provided services for a mobile population and by its four associates who went out into the neighborhood, by its visiting nurses' service, and by its overnight accommodations and meals, had taken on the dimension of charitable work and not church extension.

Diocesan ministrations to the city had taken on new outlets. In 1891, St. Martha's Sanitarium, on the Northeast corner of Dean Street and Kingston Avenue, was admitted as a diocesan institution. St. Martha's Sanitarium had a dual purpose: "First to provide a Home for men and women, regardless of their nationality or their creed," who were "suffering with incurable ailments other than consumption and pauperism" and "excluded by reason of their chronic distempers, from Hospitals, Homes and Asylums in general. . . . Second: to provide a place in which capable physicians irrespective of any particular school of medical practices might treat their patients in private rooms." The sanitorium in eighteen short months of existence had outgrown its facilities. It had opened an annex in 1893, named Bethany House, where at moderate cost, feeble people could have nursing care, not needing trained nurses.

St. Giles Home and Hospital for destitute crippled children opened in August 1891. Begun by the dedicated Rector of Emmanuel Church, Brooklyn, in a small house on DeGraw Street, under the direction of a deaconess Sister Sarah, it accommodated three children at first. The work grew so that the Diocese had to provide two more buildings and increased its help. The home was run by volunteer help, except for domestic workers. Its ministrations were free and "open to children of either sex and any color, nationality, or creed." Twenty-seven children, some severely and hopelessly crippled and deformed, inhabited St. Giles and received care and attention which could not be obtained elsewhere.

The diocesan institutions had the guiding care and supervision of the Sisterhood of St. John the Evangelist. Begun as an order for deaconesses, the associated women soon took on all the aspects of female monastics. The order had grown in numbers and a permanent location was needed for the Sisters. In 1891, the plan finally was achieved by the gift of a building on Herkimer Street by an interested layman, George A. Jarvis. The Sisters House furnished a home for members of the order who were disabled, a place to spend their declining years. The House also provided a place for a training school for Sisters to work in the city parishes and city missions.

EDUCATION

The Diocese did not expand its educational scope in comparison to its urban thrust. After the establishment of three diocesan high schools, interest and support waned. Pride in existent institutions replaced initiative in widening school scope. In the twenty years after 1878, American secular high schools increased from eight hundred to fifty-five hundred, while an illiteracy rate fell from seventeen to eleven per cent. The need for more schools provoked response on the part of church educators so that there were one hundred academies and private schools providing opportunity for a college preparatory training in a religious environment. Long Island did not keep step with the educational expansion. In 1871, there were 250 out of a 12,000 pupil Sunday School enrollment in church schools. By 1892, the Sunday School had grown to 20,000 and still not yet 300 attended church schools.

Long Island disinterest contrasted with renewed national church interest. Education as a primary function of the church occupied the attention of several General Conventions. The General Convention of 1892 startled the Church by asserting that Christian education had a commensurate authority, coordinate importance, and equal sanction with Christian missionary work. To engender more interest, the Convention devoted a common session to the interests of education and established a formal Church University Board of Regents. The board had the responsibility to watch over and advance the interests of the various institutions of higher learning.

The three established schools in the Diocese continued to prosper and progress in the 1890's. St. Paul's School in Garden City expanded its student personnel, enlarged its faculty, and added a new dimension to its life. Illustrated lectures, concerts by the Beethoven String Quartette, with literary, musical and dramatic entertainment by the students contributed social and cultural enjoyment. The school still maintained its military pose. The "tone of the cadets" was excellent, discipline good, and the individual boy received careful attention. "The military training contributed to regular habits, good manners and personal manliness of the corps."

St. Mary's School finally achieved a needed goal — a permanent building. The new three storied structure, with steam heat, gas light, and commodious student apartments, increased the student body and enlarged the curriculum with gymnasium, chemistry laboratory, and cooking school. The St. Mary's Altar Guild Society arranged the flowers weekly on the Cathedral Altar.

St. Catherine's Hall in Brooklyn prospered best of all the three schools. Its student body had increased to 112 pupils and eighteen boarders. A new emphasis enlarged the school's influence. The school had started a tutorial camp. Located at Holderness, Maine, the camp conducted classes and offered other unequalled opportunities. In the heart of "the most healthful and picturesque of regions" the Sisters of St. John had a farm of fifty acres at which girls, especially in the years given to education, were accommodated. The Sisters conducted "a charming summer school, where young ladies have the woods for their library, and an orchard for a study, and New England roads for a riding school, and the firmament for an observatory ... " Daily religious instruction came not as an irksome obligation, but a joyous privilege. No mention was made of the elucidation of the birds

(above) St. Mary's School, Garden City.
(left) Line of cadets in front of St. Paul's School, Garden City. Circa 1885.
(below) Early sketch showing rear view of St. Paul's School. Circa 1900.

and the bees.

The program of religious education hardly kept pace with the other diocesan activities. Sunday Schools continued to increase. Exhortations for better implementation of the Sunday School resounded; but in realty little was done. Even when presented with influence of godless and irreligious secular schools, the local schools continued to exist with inadequate teaching staff, irrelevant children's services and hymns, and outdated libraries.

POLITICAL PROCESS

The Conventions of the Diocese, meeting annually in the late Spring, had not changed radically in complexion or function from the days of its early incipiency. There were still the numerous committees and commissions, the officers, the leaders, and the same problems and needs. The paid personnel of the Diocese was still only one person, the Bishop. The three and four archdeacons, although given diocesan responsibility were still primarily parish priests with their own local interests and attachments.

The move of the Bishop to Garden City and the consecration of the Cathedral affected the general tenor of conventions' proceedings. The convention, always held in the Church of the Holy Trinity, Brooklyn since 1868, met for the first time in the Garden City locale in 1886. The shift from convenient Brooklyn to inconvenient and isolated Garden City had its effect upon the development of diocesan life. A recurrent occurrence was the mass exodus of delegates from the convention in the late afternoon to catch their trains home.

> The delegates tried the bishop's patience at a little after 4 o'clock by unceremoniously rushing
> out of the hall to catch trains bound east, and it took hard hammering with the gavel to
> restore order.

The convention did transact its business with decorum and orderliness. Always a "profitable and pleasant" affair; the smooth flow of business was attributable to Bishop Littlejohn, "a master parliamentarian." He made business glide along without any friction. Conventions characters, always plentiful, encompassed many and spotlighted the convention leaders, Rev. Dr. Charles H. Hall and the Rev. Dr. Bacchus, who were the witty members and "many a hearty laugh they gave their brethren."

The process of diocesan life was portrayed in the words of a contemporary churchman, Bloodgood H. Cutter, the "Long Island Farmer Poet" who attended the convention as delegate from Little Neck. His impressions simply summed up the deliberations and accomplishments of the convention.

> Here the Convention yearly meet.
> Here they each other kindly greet.
> Here they propose and plans suggest,
> Then they adopt what they think best.

The Convention recessed for lunch held at the Garden City Hotel where delegates let off steam from the arduous proceedings. A typical picture portrayed the scene,

> But the waiters did not us heed,
> To bring us food in time of need.
> The clergy rapped and made much noise
> As if they were yet College boys.

and no convention was complete without the annual photograph. Cutter rhymed:

> With pleasant cheer with pleasing smile,
> Front of the Cathedral stood awhile.
> The photographer in front was seen
> A getting ready his machine.

A serious consideration of the Diocese centered on the years-old issue of a federate council. Discussed and disclaimed as early as the beginning of the Diocese, the federate council, or provincial synod as it was called, lacked interest since no real purpose for its being could be found. In 1888, a renewed interest in the provincial synod came into focus. On February 8, 1888, five dioceses in New York met for a practical purpose. Antiquated ecclesiastical laws of New York State had come under scrutiny and the state proposed to update the laws with the current practices. The proposed amendment to the state law concerned the incorporation of parishes, the mode of electing vestries, and the time of the annual parish meeting. Since the General Convention had authorized joint action on the part of contiguous dioceses "in matters of common moment to dioceses" the five dioceses met and discussed the practical issues. No decisions were reached but the intent of the provincial synod showed in a willingness to pursue a "further enlargement of duties."

A current issue that aroused diocesan interest was proportional representation. Fostered by General Convention, the plan for a more proportionate representation in national and diocesan conventions, aroused briefly the interest and enthusiasm of the Diocese. For a few years, leaders discussed a plan to equalize representation according to size.

A diocesan committee, appointed by the 1888 Convention made a full report, and resolved,
> that the principle of proportionate representation of Clergy and Laity in the House of
> Deputies, in the General Convention is just and right, and should in some wise and proper way
> be put into effect.

No wise and proper way appeared, for by 1890 the subject had been forgotten without achieving any lasting currency.

CHANGING LEADERSHIP

Domain of a small elite power group, the Diocese changed little its accepted patterns of leadership. The names changed, but the same churches exerted the same influence in fashioning and channelling diocesan policy. Holy Trinity on Brooklyn Heights remained the key parish; it was surrounded by twelve satellite churches who wielded power and welded the chain links of authority. Eight-two of the 175 diocesan appointed or elective positions were gathered into the sphere of influence of these parishes. The balance of diocesan positions were evenly sprinkled throughout the rest of the island, merely tokens of patronage, not positions of influence. Out of 130 clergy, nine held the forty-four key posts; of the 117 parishes, only nine laymen had thirty-one out of a possible ninety-one coveted posts. The Diocese was still in a very real sense the extension of the affluent parishes on Brooklyn Heights.

It is true that many of the diocesan leaders, instrumental in its inception, and active from its beginning, had since become ill, feeble, or had died. Death had taken two outstanding men from the top ranks, The Rev. Drs. Jacob W. Diller and Noah Schenck. Their places were quickly filled, either by episcopal appointment or by diocesan vote, with recruits from the same parishes. The names of Reese F. Alsop of St. Ann's Church; Chauncey R. Brewster, Grace Church; James H. Darlington of Christ Church, Bedford Avenue; Charles R. Baker, Church of the Messiah; and Samuel Cox, Dean of the Cathedral, appeared as the replacements for the deceased or deficient leaders.

Some of the "old-timers" still retained their positions of prominence. Charles H. Hall, acknowledged leader of the Heights' churches, yearly retained the Presidency of the Standing Committee, along with all his other offices. T. Stafford Drowne, the Bishop's rejected choice for cathedral dean, continued as Secretary of the Diocese, as well as in his other public capacities. The two colonial churches, St. George's of Flushing and St. George's of Hempstead, continued to contribute leadership in the persons of Dr. William Moore and Dr. J. Carpenter Smith; however, Hempstead was fast being eclipsed by its favored neighbor, the Cathedral.

The layman's power-ranks had changed far more drastically in the ensuing years. Many of the diocesan pioneers had become ill or died. James Maurice, outstanding layman and legislator, Alexander V. Blake, a great donor to the Diocese, together with Seymour L. Husted, Charles R. Marvin, and Henry E. Pierrepont were just a few of the power group lost to the Diocese. But their places were filled from the same churches, and in many cases from the same families. The influence of the Lows and the Pierreponts, the Floyd-Jones and the Nicolls, was continued in the person of a younger brother or a close cousin. Names of new men, in themselves power blocs, did appear; they were Alexander V. Orr, William H. Male, and Jaspar W. Gilbert, all from the Heights' churches. The women of the Diocese had also seen some of their most dedicated workers die. Notable among them were the indefatigable Harriet A. Low; the dedicated Sister Joanna; and the munificient benefactor, Cornelia M. Stewart.

The Loyal Laity —

Better use of laymen's talents in the diocesan program received continued emphasis by the Bishop. Aware of the great reservoir of lay-power, untapped and waiting, the Bishop attempted to instill in the Diocese an acute sense of the priesthood of the laity. He formalized his ideas by admitting, on Quinquegesima Sunday, twenty-three young men into a Lay Helpers Association of the Diocese. The Lay Helpers Association gave episcopal recognition to lay participation in the church; it underscored the power of union; and it offered practical aid in the pursuit of tasks. The Association recruited new workers; in 1886 forty-three laymen from twelve parishes retained membership; by 1889 twenty-two parishes had a score of workers including parish visitors, Sunday School laborers, lay readers, Temperance Society and Parish Guild Leaders. The Association advanced the missionary program of the Diocese by supplying lay helpers in the mission stations in Brooklyn and Queens.

Women's church work prospered on the parish and on the diocesan level. Ladies continued to do the innumerable tasks they had always done. A new branch of women's work issued in the formation of altar guilds, who assisted the clergy in the work of the sanctuary. The diocesan Women's Missionary Society had been strengthened from its early years. An accepted part of most parish life, on June 11, 1885, it changed its name to conform to National Church policy by taking the title The Long Island Branch of the Woman's Auxiliary to the Board of Missions. Having met in St. Peter's Church from its inception, in 1885 it outgrew the facilities and looked for a more adequate place to meet. Finally in 1888, St. Ann's Church offered its quarters as a permanent location for the active, expansive group. The Auxiliary, at first formed to help the church's mission among the American Indians, had enlarged its scope to include foreign missions, diocesan missions, and Negro work. Auxiliary interest centered on support of St. Phebe's Mission Work from 1881 until 1887, when the Diocese retained St.

Phebe's as a diocesan charitable institution.

Women entered new fields of endeavor. Miss Jennie Moore, setting the pace for other women, became involved in the missionary extension of the church. Under diocesan direction, she made house-to-house visitations in an unchurched, neglected area of Brooklyn. She uncovered in her search eighty to one hundred church families. Her labors resulted in a church building and a thriving congregation.

The special order for women, begun first as an order for deaconesses, underwent a subtle change. From its small beginning in February 1872, the order had grown to the Sisterhood of St. John the Evangelist. There were suspicions of a possible "unwelcome phase of abnormal piety" which could possibly promote "other ills" not in conformity with the Episcopal ethos. The contingency was averted by the wise counsels which framed the Rule of the Order, and misgiving were obviated or overcome by the character of the work which was assigned. The Order's painstaking work became familiar to all the churches. Long Island churchmen took pride in their direction of St. John's Hospital, the Orphanage, the Home for the Aged, and in St. Catherine's Hall. A boon was the acquisition of a permanent house for the Sisters; this brought immeasurable stability and necessary roots.

THE EPISCOPATE

A perceptible change in diocesan leadership could be ascertained in the Bishop himself. The arduous tasks involved in establishing a diocese had left their mark upon him. Elected to the new episcopate in the full bloom of his vigor, he had, in the course of the years, lost much of his zest and fervor. Too much of his energy had been sapped in the long and tedious hours of travel to cover all the parishes for visitations from isolated Garden City. The Bishop himself was the first to acknowledge his growing incapacity. Although, in 1899, on the thirtieth anniversary of his consecration, the laudatory address, given by the President of the Standing Committee, asserted:

> Happily the time has not arrived to write our Bishop's biography or to pronounce his panegyric.

The Bishop himself, as early as 1893 had confided to the Diocese that:

> It can hardly be expected for obvious reasons, that I shall do any longer what I have done for twenty-five years past, viz: visit annually nearly every church or chapel in the Diocese.

A necessary result of his growing concern for himself was the necessity of reducing the number of visitations, "by requiring Rectors and Incumbents of neighboring churches and chapels to bring their candidates for Confirmation to the most convenient place among them for the administration of the office." Perhaps his impaired health made him more cognizant of the shortening of time. In 1894, on his silver jubilee, the Bishop prophesied:

> My labors among you are drawing to a close. The mantle of leadership and authority which has been worn for a quarter of a century, must soon pass to another. During the few years that I may hope to be with you, I crave, next to my peace with God, your sympathy, your forbearance, and your love. With them I shall be strong even in my weakness, and without them I shall be weak even in the strength that may remain to me.

Yet during his active years as Bishop of the Diocese, the Rt. Rev. Abram N. Littlejohn had been a shining luminary in the church, prominent in the councils of the wise and the influential, holding many commanding positions in the nation and in the world. The many contributions to church periodicals and the lectures and sermons delivered at home and abroad brought him recognition as the possessor of high scholarship and forethought. Trained as a lawyer before becoming an ecclesiastic, he brought to his writings and utterances a logical clarity and a concise intellectuality. He lectured at home and abroad on many controversial subjects. His great missionary address at the 1868 General Convention was only matched by his forthright thoughts on the Christian ministry. Delivered as the Paddock Lectures, entitled *The Christian Ministry in the Nineteenth Century*, the Bishop's ideas were not popular, more from method than content. He possessed the many gifts of the orator: a strong voice, an impressive style and a dignified manner. However, he could not overcome in his written works the lack of "the lighter touch and the cordial sympathy with the opponent which might have made him a popular author."

He had a high view of the episcopacy and used his untiring energy and determination to further the work of his office. By his adherence to the exalted views of the episcopate, he became an influential force in the House of Bishops. He was extremely sensitive to praise or blame; and had something of the politician's skills and methods in accomplishing his aims. He was a great believer in the power of money to do great things for the church. He was not only a great prelate but a statesman of far-seeing vision, deriving not a little of his power from his legal education.

He made mistakes, some that were highly magnified by the press and the public. His words were often misconstrued by the press and used against him. He stood ready to defend those whom he loved at all costs.

> But he never deserved the anonymous criticism which stung and hurt him, which coming none other than up to the very last years of his life, had all the more effect because it hurt his pride.

He possessed deep-seated and unswerving convictions. He had a noble view of the ministry and had no sympathy for those who had fallen from the ideal, nor empathy for those of different ideals. He was completely orthodox in his doctrine and discipline. He tried to do justice to the great theological manifestations of his time. To Evangelism, he paid homage "for the very truth for which it stood." He discerned the worth of the Oxford Movement that had "championed causes apostolic and catholic . . . [and] . . . upheld the Book of Common Prayer as squaring most accurately with the Christian spirit and usages of the earliest centuries of our care."

His unswerving allegiance to the Catholic faith brought adverse comment. In his *Personal Reminiscences*, Daniel M. Tredwell noted the conservative characteristic of his theology. At Garden City, Tredwell met the Bishop:

> with the extremely illiberal views of Bishop Littlejohn in theology. We had always supposed him an up-to-date man, but if his conversation was an expression of his views, it would be safe to say that the great bulk of his intelligent parishioners are far in advance of him in modern thought. His theology was that of half a century ago, and Doctor West himself professing orthodoxy expressed to me the same surprise that the Bishop adhered so tenaciously to a theology now nearly obsolete. 'The world', said the Doctor, 'will never go back to him or to me. However, I am not a professor of theology. Were I, I would in justice to my clientage feel it my duty to give them the best and latest in the market, and not the stale products of past ages.'

Although conservatively oriented, Bishop Littlejohn was aware of the current ideas of his times and made acute observations in regard to their contributions to the accumulated knowledge of the time. He credited the "two turning points of modern thought respecting the physical world," the theories of Newton and Darwin, with profoundly changing men's notions of the relations of God and themselves to the universe, and so setting in motion a certain modifying force throughout the domain of religion.

No such praise was in store for "Higher Criticism" in the church. Grave doubts about the "scientific" results and its "unscientific" methods made the Bishop wary of its acceptance. A similar fate awaited the Revised Version of the Bible acclaimed as a masterpiece by the secular press. The Bishop was gratified by the rejection of the Revised Version by the 1892 General Convention, claiming it could never surplant the reverence felt for the three-hundred-year-old King James Version. Yet if for nothing else, his interest in ecumenical movements and Christian unity afford him an honored place in the Church.

CHRISTIAN UNITY

Hope of church unity had interested the Episcopal Church for many years. Beginning in 1853 with a memorial to confer with other Christian bodies on possible unity, the General Convention had been besieged by many ideas and many attempts to formalize the aspirations of the church. In 1856, conversations were begun with the Swedish Church, but they bogged down in trivial detail. Abortive attempts to consider the validity of the Moravian episcopate, futile negotiations with the Presbyterians and exchange of official documents with the Russian Church manifested an interest and intent to initiate some kind of movement towards an organic unity.

After the Papal Declaration of Infallibility in 1870, no more significant event occurred than the formation of the Old Catholic Church. Largely from Germany, Austria and Switzerland, the movement of the Savarese and Campellos had aroused the sympathy and interest of the American Episcopal Church. The Joint Commission on Ecclesiastical Relations and Religious Reform had a sub-committee specifically entrusted with the relationship to the Alt-Catholic Movement in Europe. Some of the Long Island delegates served on this Committee, and Bishop Littlejohn became an influential member. His charge as Bishop of Foreign Churches had increased his knowledge and enhanced his reputation as a world church leader. His interest in the Old Catholic Churches continued throughout his episcopate. Even after giving up his overseas responsibility in 1887, he still maintained a close contact with the Old Catholics, acting as the Archbishop of Canterbury's representataive. While on vacation for rest in 1887, he pursued his interest. His vacation was abbreviated and he took time to speak in Algiers and in Seville to congregations of Spanish Old Catholics to extend to them "the sympathy of our American Church."

To Bishop Littlejohn has been ascribed the monumental landmark of the Chicago Quadrilateral. In all conversations and attempts at church unity, there was a confusion and uncertainty as to the essentials of the church and to the means of measurement. About 1870, William Reed Huntington had sketched in his published work, *The Church Idea, as Essay Towards Unity*, the suggestion of four basic principles as being the best single hope for union among the churches in America. The Bishop's Committee on Church Unity, under the direction of Bishop Littlejohn grappled with the consuming question and made a firm commitment "to enter into brotherly conference with all or any Christian Bodies seeking the restoration of the organic unity of the church." Stating that the Episcopal Church did not seek to abort other Communions, rather to cooperate with them on the basis of a common order, the Bishop declared the following to be essential to the restoration of unity:

1. The Holy Scriptures . . . as the revealed word of God.
2. The Nicene Creed as the sufficient statement of the Christian Faith.
3. The two Sacraments — Baptism and the Supper of the Lord . . .
4. The Historic Episcopate . . .

The Diocese observed the 25th anniversary of Bishop Littlejohn's episcopate with a commemorative service in the Cathedral on May 15, 1894. Five bishops participated. The diocesan clergy took the opportunity to present to the Bishop a new pastoral staff. The presentation was made by the Rev. Charles R. Baker, of Church of the Messiah, Brooklyn, in a graceful speech. He pointed out how the bishops of the church were forced to assume civil control in the troubled days when barbarous hordes were ravaging the Roman Empire. Although they adopted the purple of the prefect, they chose not the sceptre but the shepherd's crook as a symbol of their function.

New York was represented by the Rev. Morgan Dix, Rector of Trinity Church, New York, and President of the Standing Committee, who brought greetings from the mother diocese. A felicitation from the Standing Committee of Long Island was presented by the Rev. Chauncey R. Brewster, Rector of Grace Church, Brooklyn. In words of eulogy and ornamentation, he dwelt upon the happy relations between the Standing Committee and the Diocese, concluding with an apt application of the poet's lines to the island diocese.

> Sail forth into the sea, O Ship
> Our hearts, our hopes, our prayers
> Are all with thee.

The Church University Regents spoke through the President of Hobart College; the schools of the Diocese were represented by the Rev. Spencer S. Roche. The Bishop had been a staunch and unswerving advocate of Christian education. Three diocesan schools had been founded at his behest — St. Catherine's School in Brooklyn and St. Paul's and St. Mary's in Garden City. They were abiding signs of the leadership of the Bishop in this vital field.

The missionary work of the Diocese was represented by the Rev. Reese F. Alsop, Rector of St. Ann's, Brooklyn. In 1869, there were only five mission churches, four of which were in Suffolk. After twenty-five years there were twenty-nine missions and the Rector of St. Ann's predicted that by the rate of growth seen, there would be at least 170 by 1920.

Greetings from the Charitable Institutions were presented by the Rev. J. G. Bacchus. He showed the steady growth of the Church Charity Foundation with its new hospital, chapel and endowment of $200,000. Diocesan philanthropy was ramified through lines as diverse as human needs; St. Phebe's Mission; House of St. Giles; St. Christopher's Nursery; the Atlantic Avenue Dispensary; the Orphan's Press; and St. Martha's Sanitarium. The Diocese had an "honorable record" in the field of organized works of mercy.

The Sisters of St. John the Evangelist were represented by their Chaplain, the Rev. Henry C. Swentzel. In 1872, Bishop Littlejohn had set aside six godly women as deaconesses. Two of these had already come under the training of the Rev. Dr. William Muhlenberg whose tradtions lingered at College Point. Bishop Littlejohn served as their first Chaplain, and bore eloquent testimony to the patience, devotion, and self-denial of these quiet, self-effacing, hard-working women.

The Honorable John A. King, active layman from Great Neck, and Jamaica, spoke on behalf of the Cathedral Corporation. The Brotherhood of St. Andrew added its greeting through Alexander E. Orr, the spokesman for the laymen. A tri-part statement, signed by Mary Rhinlander King, Mrs. William Nicoll and Mary D. Dixon lauded the Bishop for his interest and support of the Women's Auxiliary.

The commemoration was continued in Brooklyn where special services took place at the Church of the Messiah and at St. Luke's Church. On Thursday, May 17, 1894, the commemoration events ended with a reception tendered to the Bishop and his family at the Brooklyn Club. Over 3,000 invited guests extended congratulations to the honored guests.

The anniversary program afforded an ideal opportunity to present a concise picture of the progress of the Diocese which at its beginning was simply described as "an aggregate of hopeful possibilities." A long way from the 65 churches, 85 clergy and 9,837 communicants were the 131 clergy, 130 churches and 26,923 communicants recorded at the anniversary. In twenty-five years, 97 deacons and 112 priests had been ordained; 37 churches and chapels had been consecrated. A bright note was drawn from the financial status of the Diocese of Long Island. In spite of two depressions, in 1873 and 1893, the Diocese had prospered. Endowments for the Episcopal Fund had reached $111,000; the Church Charity Foundation, $200,000; the Aged and Infirm Clergy Fund, $86,000; and the Sheltering Arms Nursery, $25,000. But most of all, the contributions for parochial objects had amounted to almost $11,000,000 with an added $1,000,000 for diocesan work; and over a million for work outside the Diocese. The value of church property aggregated $4,750,000. The history of the Diocese in the twenty-five years of diocesan life, the results of "the labors of our spiritual guide and overseer," were matters "for hearty congratulations and profound gratitude."

Chapter Seven

Ending is Beginning

The "Gay Nineties", the closing years of the nineteenth century, held more promise of prosperity, expansion and human enjoyment. While America wiled away its time in gay and gaudy pleasure, the nation experienced its first step onto the world scene as a great imperial power. Long Island shared in the jubilee. Many new elements were developing that changed even more the complexion of the island community. It boasted a growing population of over one and a half million, the benefactor of the outpouring of New York and Brooklyn's crowded tenements. Its commerce and industry was booming in spite of the recent depression of 1893. Pleasure and enjoyment were offered all around, but no more important signpost of the great pleasuredome was the opening of Steeplechase at Coney Island, complete with ferris wheel and roller coaster.

The City of Brooklyn reached out and took into its sphere more and more of Long Island, as the City began to encompass all of Kings County.

> For many years Brooklyn had grown and expanded, gradually encompassing one after another the independent towns and villages throughout the length and breadth of Kings County, until by 1896, Flatlands, the last of these, had succumbed to the onward thrust of this rapidly extending municipality. Beginning with the annexation of Williamsburgh in 1835; and followed by New Lots in 1886; Flatbush, Gravesend; and New Utrecht in 1894; and finally that "terra incognita" Flatlands.

The increasing encroachment of the city upon the suburban and rural areas had been accelerated by the construction of the Brooklyn Bridge. There was the immediate prospect of new bridges and tunnels connecting Manhattan with Brooklyn. In a few years, forecasted the prophets, Brooklyn "will have added to it some hundreds of thousands of people," and Queens "will take an upward stride in population," in the years after the construction of the Blackwell's Island Bridge, to reach a half a million population.

The decade following 1894 brought a complete change in Queens. What formerly was a farming section made up of towns and villages, and almost isolated from the mainland, lost its rural atmosphere; farms disappeared to be replaced by homes.

The City of Greater New York became a reality at midnight, December 31, 1897. After a difficult and close plebiscite the counties of Kings and Queens voted to become part of the Greater City. The County of Queens separated itself into two parts — the Borough of Queens in the west and the County of Nassau in the east. The split on Long Island had far-reaching consequences. It brought to mind the great contrast between city and country, between the cosmopolitan and the rustic. And it served as a forewarning. For as the city reached out to engulf and control more of the island, more of the island in the future would experience the same influence. Long Island was well on the way to becoming an integral part of the megapolis.

MISSIONARY FERVOR

As Long Island experienced such far-reaching changes, the Diocese of Long Island reached its most brilliant peak. The Diocese had taken deep and firm roots in the sandy soil and paved streets of the varying island community. The ecclesiastical body had achieved both the status of an accepted and influential section of the Christian Church and had received the accolade as a successful and powerful force for moral and spiritual good of the secular.

It did exhibit all the aspects of a successful, full-grown, and pervasive force on Long Island. In the thirty-second year of its history, the number of communicants had quadrupled; the number of clergy had increased two-fold; and the number of parishes had been doubled. The contributions from all sources had by 1901 amounted to about eight hundred thousand dollars. In all outward appearances, the tone of the Diocese had been conservative and moderate. Widely differing schools of thought had not hardened into parties or factions. The Diocese had not been free from "irregularities" in teaching and in ritual, but these had been corrected by the "conservative and restraining sentiment of the great body of the church." The fact that the Ecclesiastical Court had never been convened "for the trial of any clergyman for error in religion, or viciousness of life," commended this aspect.

Brooklyn Bridge. Circa 1890.

Local parishes reflected the increasing optimism of the Diocese. Churches had never been stronger nor more active. Church membership had grown rapidly. The Church of the Messiah had 1,539 communicants in 1896; in two years, attendance had increased to 1,545 so that chairs had to be put in the aisle on Sundays. Holy Trinity achieved a membership of 1,000; St. Ann's, 1,361; and St. Thomas, Bushwick, 461.

The missionary work of the Diocese had a healthy and a progressive spirit. The four archdeaconries reported good missionary activity. In the two Archdeaconries of Brooklyn, there were twelve organized missions, each with its own chapel and grounds sufficient for future use. In the Northern Archdeaconry, well-to-do neighborhoods were supplied with parish churches, most of which were in a flourishing condition. Less attractive neighborhoods contained an over-whelming majority of the population who spoke a foreign tongue. Church of the Messiah had offered its parish building "to a steadily increasing congregation of Armenians" led by an Armenian lay reader. A St. Luke's cleric ministered occasionally to a small congregation of Hebrews. Work among the Blacks increased. St. Augustine's Church had been joined by another ghetto church, St. Philip's Chapel which had been started in 1899. St. Michael's had been put at the disposal of the Italian mission. In the Southern Archdeaconry, new work started at Vanderveer Park and prospered; at Sheepshead Bay, largely a summer resort with shifting population, it did not go so well. Coney Island received the church's ministrations; services were held in the Cycle Path Club. The work of the Northern Archdeaconry was under the watchful eye of the Rev. Henry C. Swentzel; in the Southern Archdeaconry, the Rev. Reese F. Alsop, who was succeeded by the Rev. Arthur B. Kinsolving.

In Queens and Nassau, churches multiplied rapidly under different titles, signifying different jurisdictions. Seventeen mission stations, with the varied nomenclatures of Cathedral Missions, Parochial Missions, Aided Parishes and Archdeaconry Missions, varied as much as the communities to which they ministered. The Rector of Merrick initiated a needed work among Blacks in the nearby neighborhood of Smithville South. No program of parochial missions afforded such a bright note as the three belonging to St. George's, Flushing, "rightly called the maker of churches." Its mission work was a noble illustration of the principle that missions are a necessary condition of healthy parochial growth, leading to the formation of other parishes. Limited new work was started at Mineola. In 1900, Grace Church, Jamaica, established a chapel at Springfield. Suggested by the Missionary Committee in 1899, three new missions were established at Hicksville, Morris Park, and Brooklyn Manor in 1900-1901.

Oversight of the Archdeaconry of Queens and Nassau passed on the death of the over-worked incumbent The Rev. Edmund D. Cooper, to The Rev. Henry B. Bryan, Canon Missioner of the Cathedral. The work in Queens far outshadowed the Suffolk program where two aided parishes and seven mission stations struggled to keep their places in the still wild and unsettled eastern region. Experiments in services at Holbrook, Lakeland and Deer Park produced unfavorable results.

Obvious difficulties in pursuing an advancing mission program made the work tenuous and faltering. In the long years of missionary venture only a small increase in support evidenced itself. The amount from all sources for the support of missions accrued $13,969.33. The facts showed that the Diocese had not fulfilled "the full measure of its duty toward the rapidly growing population on Long Island." Yet the diocesan effort appeared excellent in contrast to "our record as helpers of the General Missions of the Church at home and in distant parts of the world." Contributions to general missionary work, especially to foreign work, fell far short of previous years giving, a situation shared by the church at large. A warning was sounded that unless conditions improved the fiscal year would close with a disastrous and alarming deficit.

Two reasons accounted for the sharp decrease in national missionary funds. The first was the current disaster in China, "the violent agitation and murderous persecution of native Christians in the East." The Boxer Rebellion had festered crimes "surpassing in indiscriminate and atrocious cruelty the persecutions in the Roman Empire of the Second and Third Centuries." The second reason resulted from the changing concept of missionary work, from "the rescue of the Heathen from the pains and penalties of sin in the future life" to a "higher missionary motive" to make all men, here and now, recipients of redemption, "so that they may partake in this present life, as well as in the future life, of the gifts, blessings and joys of that redemption."

Missionary progress in the Diocese had been hampered by insufficient personnel. Of the four archdeacons, three were parish priests. Dual responsibility meant divided energy; with either the parish or the missions suffering. The immediate prospect of new bridges and tunnels, connecting the Borough of Manhattan with the Boroughs of Brooklyn and Queens, meant a tremendous increase of population, which for Queens meant an increase to half a million. The solution rested in obtaining a man of value and power, assured of a substantial living and travel allotment, to serve as General Missionary of the Diocese under the name of Archdeacon. Many other diocese had adopted the plan of committing the missionary work to one General Missionary or Archdeacon. Proposed by the Rector of Elmhurst, the plan received considerate attention, but no immediate action.

CORPORAL WORKS OF MERCY

A unique and unusual social service institution appeared in the diocesan charitable work. A house on High Street near St. Savior's Church, Maspeth, had been donated by the Maurice family as the Font Maur Home for the Blind. No other venture like it could be found on all Long Island, even though the Island population had grown to one and a half million people, and since one person out of every 1,200 was blind, there were 1,200 possible blind candidates for such a home. The home could accommodate only a small percentage of the blind and so began by sheltering a few unusually worthy and intelligent women. The gift of land in 1896 had been added to by a similar conveyance of five acres given to the Diocese in 1897 by the same family.

St. Phebe's Mission Settlement House continued to exert a widening influence in the public institutions and in the tenement house sections of the city. Five associates, of whom one was a trained nurse, made visits to the inmates of the institutions and to the sick poor of the crowded tenements. The settlement house afforded a myriad of different aids, "bewildering in its variety and extent." It provided among its services a trained nurse and free medicine for the sick; reading matter for distribution for the poor; temporary lodging for the homeless; food for the hungry; fresh air excursions in the country "during the torrid heat of the summer for those who could not otherwise afford to go;" procurement of work and positions for the jobless, in addition to the administration of the sacraments to the sick, the poor and the neglected. Nevertheless, St. Phebe's faced the prospect of difficult times ahead. A notice was received that in 1900 no money would be paid to them by the city. A similar withdrawal of city funds affected the Atlantic Avenue Dispensary. A public service project of the Church Charity Foundation, the dispensary had treated in one year, free of charge, as many as 13,181 patients, supplying physicians and medicine for the needy poor. In 1899, the building housing the dispensary had to be closed for lack of funds. Appropriations from the city had been terminated, so that the Board of Managers had been compelled to cut off this department from its work.

On the other hand two bright new additions to St. John's Hospital, a training school for nurses and an ambulance system, added to the effectiveness of its care. In May 1896, All Angels' Cottage, east of the hospital, had been purchased and equipped by an anonymous donor. The cottage afforded living quarters and lecture room for the first class of fifteen nursing candidates. The following year, another house had to be bought to afford added accommodations for an increased registration in the three year course of study. Only five of the original class graduated in 1899. By 1901, twenty-four nursing students had registered for training; and in the same year, nine girls graduated. The Training School for Nurses had been precipitated by the initiation in 1892 of a system of "employed nurses", hired to relieve the faithful Sisters of St. John of the hard task of nursing, leaving them free to exercise the distinctive spiritual functions of their order. The ambulance service, begun in 1892, enlarged the scope of the hospital's work to a wider constituency by conveying to its wards such sufferers as needed immediate hospital care. The added services made the usefulness of the hospital greater than in any period of its existence servicing 1,115 patients, an increase of almost 50%. Ambulance calls reached a peak of 950 calls a year, and a newly renovated and updated operating room rounded out the hospital's effective ministrations.

All charitable works experienced the increasing difficulties of lack of financial support. With the withdrawal of city aid, the Church Charity Foundation had to assess its situation and find ways to underwrite its operation. A deficit had plagued the Board of Managers until in 1900, it finally amounted to $15,000. It cost about $65,000 a year to pay running expenses. The income from the endowment fund was about $12,000. Income from city appropriations, in the amount of $10,000, had been cut off. The income from paying patients and from the City Board of Education amounted to $15,000. A deficit had to be obliterated in only one way, by better support of the churches. The gloom of 1900 was changed to jubilant thankfulness in 1901. Efforts, on the part of the Jubilee Committee for the Extinguishing of the Mortgage Debt, on the part of churches, and by living within its income had cut back expenses and needed work. Curtailment had overcome bankruptcy.

The financial stricture of the times was reflected in structural laxity of the Foundation. The work of the Church Charity Foundation had functioned under a separate segmented form of policy-making and program development. Before 1900, each institution had its own standing committee which managed its affairs quite independently of the other institutions. The Board of Managers, in order to manage more economically and to better preserve unity, joined all the various services under one group which was divided into six committees, "each committee to serve for two non-consecutive months in the year, and during its term of service to have full charge and control of all the institutions of the Foundation." The new method of efficient operation went into effect on January 1, 1900.

THE GATHERING STORM

As the century came to its close, some deepseated problems became numerous and worrisome. No small matter was the increase in local church debts. Whether or not it was symptomatic of the inability of parishes to minister to changing neighborhoods, the churches in the city were forced into debt. Some parishes mortgaged property to take care of new buildings or additions to the old building; some parishes, unable to maintain the building fabric, used loans to take care of needed repairs. By the last five years of the nineteenth century, All Saint's Church and St. George's Church had debts of $47,500 and $30,500 respectively; St. James Church, set in the midst of a fluctuating population, had to increase its indebtedness from $30,000 to $45,000; St. Paul's, Flatbush, had petitioned for a $35,000 mortgage on its property and St. Mark's, Bedford, for a $40,000 mortgage. A drive for more parish endowments, in many cases, did not alleviate the financial pressures.

All churches, Episcopal or not, experienced the disheartening influence of decreasing church attendance. Golf, a new sport, drew away many enthusiastic players, willing to devote their Sunday mornings to sport on the links rather than prayer in the pews. More of a threat was the increasing bicycle craze then at its height. Men, women and children, individually or in cycle clubs rode wheels, tandems or imported tricycles. Saturday and Sunday saw Long Island invaded by hundreds of bicycle enthusiasts from the city. Clutching "Cyclist Paradise" maps, they

Members of the Kings County Wheelmen in front of their clubhouse at 1255 Bedford Avenue in Brooklyn. (1889)

arrived from New York and Brooklyn in cars especially designed for carrying the bicycle safely, provided by the Long Island Railroad. The general exodus on Sundays caused the Church Club of Brooklyn and the Brooklyn Clerical League to become concerned about the effect of the bicycle on church attendance. The Church Club considered the advantage of a portable "bicycle church, which was to be used solely as a worshipping place for wheelmen." Since the true cyclist always sought new fields and did not like to ride over the same road every Sunday, it was to be a light frame structure easily transported during the summer from place to place at convenient distances from Brooklyn. No effort was to be spared to make the church accessible by means of good roads and paved bicycle paths. The clergy believed that "the Garden City Cathedral would have many cyclists within its doors on Sunday were it not for the wretched roads from Brooklyn." As the clergy so wisely summed it up: "If the church wants the bicycle riders, it must meet them halfway."

Depressing too was the noticeable decline in the parish Sunday Schools. No numerical advancement had been made. In fact, in the years 1890-1898, the number of communicants had increased 35%, but Sunday School enrollment had increased only 9% in Brooklyn; 20% in Queens; and 1-1/2% in Suffolk. For every three communicants gained, only one pupil was added to the Sunday Schools. The number of pupils had decreased about five hundred, lagging behind not only the communicant ratio, but also the growing Island population.

The Sunday Schools of the Diocese had little if any supervision. Supervision was largely the task of the local rector, and a certain disinterestedness had fallen over the whole program. The Diocese of New York had in 1898 appointed a Sunday School Commission to increase its efficiency. A resolution in 1899 created for Long Island a similar commission of three clergymen and two laymen whose responsibility it was to supervise the instruction of young people, to better train teachers, and to improve methods and materials of instruction. Two Sunday School convocations in Brooklyn and Suffolk, and a Pastoral Letter of the Bishop brought some renewed interest. In 1901, a step forward was shown in the amended parochial reports which included vital statistics and information about the local schools.

Unrest showed itself in the clergy of the Diocese. Subtle changes in attitude and work created tensions that showed in parish programs. The Standing Committee was kept busy with contests between clergy and vestries. Zion Chuch, Little Neck, had a complaint about its Rector; Church of the Holy Apostles, Windsor Terrace, had requested advice from the Committee in regards to its clergyman. Even the Bishop's own son-in-law, the Rev. William A. Wasson, had his difficulties at St. George's Church, Brooklyn.

The number of clergy had increased so much that in addition to the regular Clerical League, a Curates Club (The K K) had formed on October 28, 1895, for the express purpose of "fellowship and discussion most interesting to the junior clerics." Both associations were concerned with the financial support of the clergy which had grown highly inadequate. The matter had become so serious that a Committee on Clerical Support had been appointed to survey the situation and to bring some recommendations before the annual convention. The average salary for a rector was $1,500; for curates, $1,085. The highest salary of a rector was $6,000 and living quarters; the lowest, $600 and no house. The average stipend of missionary clergy came to $685 and the lowest, $260. A suggestion that received attention originated in the Dioceses of Wisconsin and Ohio, called for the establishment of a sustenance fund for the poorer paid clergy.

The power of preaching, so prominent among the better clergy, had suffered greatly from new emphasis, new trends and new distractions. Preaching had been relegated to a secondary rank among the forces that shaped opinion, character and conduct. Men no longer listened or cared; they were persuaded by other forces, especially "the ever-widening area of the influence of the press, which in its Sunday issues, especially, captivates the multitude quite as much as the novel of society or a sensational drama on the stage." Other devices took the place of preaching, converting "the Church of Christ into a vast soup kitchen, or club house, or lectureship platform, or amusement hall with a 'Gospel attachment'... reaping the disastrous effects of a foolish as well as profane compromise with the world."

Apart from its local difficulties, Long Island churches became involved in the Spanish American War. America's first step on the world stage as an imperial power affected the Island and called to service the Diocese and the local churches. During the brief encounter with Spain, Teddy Roosevelt's "spendid little war", the Island served both as a training center for recruits and a receiving center for returning veterans. Camp Black on the Hempstead Plains served the same billet function it did in the War of 1812 and the Civil War. Camp Wyckoff became the receiving depot "for the sick and wounded brought back from the West India islands (Cuba) and malarial districts of the South." At times there were ten to twenty thousand soldiers in each camp.

Church efforts centered on the Montauk encampment. Transports landed directly at Montauk Point to discharge their loads, among which were many sick or wounded. Among the 22,000 inhabitants of the temporary barracks, almost 2,000 were sick and 300 about to die.

> The camp [was] astir at 7:30 with arrangements for breakfast, rushing of cavalry horses and movement of ambulances, and a sad feature of every morning was the work of the gravediggers and the carrying out of the emaciated bodies of the dead to be trundled into the government boxes provided for the purpose.

The Church responded to its call. At the request of a Mr. Woods, Canon Henry B. Bryan of Garden City visited the camp in September 1898. Stimulated by the requests for help and the need of the sick, he ministered to the troops, regularly and systematically visiting the sick and taking care of the dying. He also held regular

(above) Rare photograph of wounded soldiers being transported by rail from Montauk encampment to Brooklyn.

(below) Chapel at St. John's Hospital utilized to care for soldiers wounded in the Spanish American War.

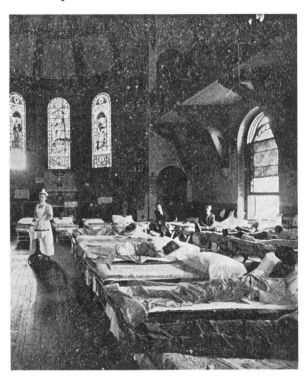

services in a tent erected by the Y.M.C.A. for the able-bodied men. The large tent afforded ample opportunity for other activities, such as concerts and programs. Bryan did a great deal of bedside ministration, distributing Bibles and Prayer Books to the soldiers. He also had a special early service for the nurses.

The diocesan hospital became involved with the war's victims. The military hospitals at Montauk became so overcrowded with the returning veterans that a call for help was issued to all Long Island hospitals. St. John's Hospital quickly seized the opportunity to help by making an offer to the government. The hospital would open its doors if railroad cars, specially prepared for the transport of sick soldiers, could bring the sick to Brooklyn by the shortest and easiest route. President McKinley accepted the offer and for three months the hospital became one large military ward. So many afflicted soldiers came that the chapel facilities had to be turned into a receiving ward. The hospital proudly publicized the fact that no soldiers died in the military venture.

The short lived war only briefly distracted the Diocese and did not help to lift it out of its doldrums.

THE DECLINING YEARS

More pathetic and more pronounced was the reduced efficiency of the Bishop himself. In the robust years of his manhood, he had thrown himself energetically into the task of firmly founding the new born diocese. He did so without any care or concern for his own health. The years of hard work had wrought their toll upon the vital episcopal authority. In his old age, he lost not only the vigor of pursuit but the stimulus of interest. More and more he seemed to withdraw within himself and his own thoughts, ignoring or evading the on-going dynamic of diocesan Island life. Living in Garden City, he had to rely mostly on the Long Island Railroad for transport. Late trains, tediously long night journeys, inconveniences and fatigue had taken their effect upon the Bishop. Over 70 years of age, he just did not possess the stamina or energy necessary to pursue the growing complexity of diocesan life. He did not keep his appointments, and the churches suffered for it. Even with centralized confirmation places, the situation did not improve. The accusation "that classes for confirmation had been presented three times in the same place without being able to secure the ministrations of the Bishop" brought forth a forthright vindication. The Bishop retorted:

> So far from having been able to keep a small percentage of my customary appointments, I
> have, in fact, made at least two-thirds of the visitations during the past year . . . and in only
> two cases failed to meet my appointments and that was caused by violent storms.

Solicitations for the Bishop by the Diocese received a flat rebuke. Suggestions of a co-adjutor to relieve the Bishop of some of his pressing problems brought a pronounced, "I want no co-adjutor."

Much of the Bishop's incapacity resulted from increasing poor health. Beginning in 1894, he suffered recurrent illness which sometimes meant he had to remain home in bed for months at a time. The Standing Committee secured the services of outside help, as far from Long Island as Los Angeles and as near as Eastern Pennsylvania. The Bishop travelled abroad more and more, being away from the Diocese for many months. While away, he did preach in foreign churches; but the time away became more frequent and more pronounced.

The most severe blow to the Bishop's well-being, from which he never fully recovered was the death of his loved wife on March 9, 1896. A devoted wife and mother, a person of keen wit and humor, always an asset to the episcopal office, she died of a heart attack, complicated by pneumonia. She was buried in All Saints' graveyard, Great Neck, after funeral services at the Cathedral on March 12. The Bishop mourned his wife deeply and was unable to be comforted by his friends or by his two daughters. To help him in his hour of grief, the Standing Committee gave him freedom of action and a relief from episcopal duties. Grief, aggravated by illness, necessitated the Bishop's leaving the Diocese. Travelling in Europe, he missed the annual diocesan convention in 1898. Only once before in 1875 had he been absent from diocesan deliberations, then to officially perform his duties as Bishop-in-charge of the foreign churches. The decisive presence of the Bishop was sadly missed at the convention so that "it required a certain effort to imagine things as going right without him." The convention was far from memorable; no resolution or discussion made it such. It was just "business as usual."

Loneliness surrounded him more and more. Dear friends and close workers died or moved away. One of his stalwart supporters, the Rev. Charles H. Hall, Rector of Holy Trinity since 1869, died. He was followed by other of the clergy, the Rev. Charles R. Baker of Brooklyn, the Rev. J. Carpenter Smith of Flushing, and the Rev. Edmund Cooper of Astoria. Certainly the death of Jasper W. Gilbert, a diocesan founding father and Vice-Chancellor of the Cathedral, caused him to feel even more deserted. Most of all, the death of two of his closest associates made him most aware of his forsaken and lonely life. The Honorable John A. King, 84 years of age, grandson of Rufus King, son of a former New York Governor, and himself a former Senator, died in 1900. John King had been a loyal supporter of the Bishop and the Diocese. One of the founding fathers, he served on the Missionary Committee, as an original incorporator of the Cathedral, as a perennial delegate to General Convention, and as an active participant in the Church Charity Foundation. King's influence was not confined entirely to the Diocese; it was evident in the founding and endowing of King's Hall in Washington, D.C., an institution of higher learning for Negroes. John King's death had been preceded by the death of the Bishop's closest associate, the Rev. T. Stafford Drowne. Long an influential man in diocesan circles, and acclaimed in the intellectual world, Drowne served for almost thirty years as Secretary of the Diocese. Active and powerful in spite of his disappointment and chagrin over the first deanship, Drowne resigned the secretaryship in 1897 because of poor health. A little more than seven months later he died. His epitaph was graven large in the Diocese:

> Staunch and stable and conservative, he closed his career as he began it, unchanged by the
> changes introduced by new schools of thought in matters of doctrine and ritual. Faithful in
> every relation and true to every duty, he has left behind him a record of priestly work which
> the Diocese will gratefully cherish in all its coming history.

> For the Bishop, the death of his wife became a greater and greater obsession.
> When he drove his horses' heads turned almost of their own accord toward the road to Great
> Neck, where in the quiet, lovely churchyard of All Saints, his wife was buried.

The Standing Committee made constant arrangements. On March 15, 1898, the President was directed "to assure the Bishop of our sympathy and sorrow in the affliction which he has sustained in the death of his wife, and if he desired to be relieved from service for a while we tender our service in securing someone to take his duties in the Diocese." The offer made no time commitment; it was at "the Bishop's pleasure."

A severe accident confined the Bishop to his home for three months and made necessary constant medical attention. His health continued to deteriorate in spite of his valiant efforts to sustain himself in his work. Frequent vacations from his home and work did not increase his success. During the summer of 1901, he went to New England for needed rest. On August 3, 1901, without any warning, he fell in the streets of Williamstown, Massachusetts, and died. Sudden but not unexpected, the cause of his death was listed as apoplexy. He died in the seventy-seventh year of his life.

Funeral services for the deceased Bishop were held on August 7, 1901 in the Garden City Cathedral. Holy Communion was celebrated at 8:30 a.m. by the Dean. At 10:30 a.m. the solemn rites, attended by nine bishops and one hundred and fifty clergy, were held. Interment followed in All Saints' graveyard, next to his beloved wife, for whom he had so long grieved. *Requiescit in Pace.*

Bishop Frederick Burgess. Second Bishop, Diocese of Long Island

Section Three
Alabaster Cities
and Fruited Plains
(1901-1925)

Chapter Eight

The Second Bishop

The first Bishop of Long Island had not grown cold in his grave before speculations about his successor became rife. Neither the death of Queen Victoria nor the fatal shooting of President McKinley quelled the discussions, opinions, rumors, and pronouncements about the second Bishop. An immediate consideration that beset the Diocese was the question of whether to choose a candidate from outside the Diocese or pick a "hometown boy". In October sentiments for a local man as Bishop gained so much momentum that the *Brooklyn Daily Eagle* said: "No outsider need apply." Disagreement over local candidates caused several new names to be discussed by local Episcopal clergy and laymen. No work on the part of the Rev. James Darlington, himself an avowed candidate, and the Rev. Henry Swentzel, the President of the Standing Committee, could stop talk about the alternative of a possible outside man. A natural candidate, the Rev. W. Huntington of New York appeared to gain some support; but by the middle of November, there was "too much talk," and sentiment again grew for a Long Island man.

The leading contender for the honor was the Rector of Holy Trinity Parish. On the death of the Rev. Dr. Charles Hall, the parish had elected the Rev. Dr. Samuel McConnell, prolific writer and the well-known author of *History of the American Episcopal Church* first published in 1890. Dr. McConnell, essentially a preacher, had the job of adjusting the Heights parish to rapidly changing socio-economic conditions in its neighborhood. His pastorate at Holy Trinity, his eloquent preaching, and his stature as a nationally known figure influenced a large part of the clergy and laity to support him for the office. After all, he was from the same parish from which the first Bishop of Long Island came.

Several of the local Brooklyn clergy names became prominent as the informal discussions continued. The Rev. Reese F. Alsop, Rector of St. Ann's on the Heights; The Rev. Canon Henry B. Bryan, Archdeacon of Queens and Nassau; and the Rev. Arthur B. Kinsolving, Rector of Christ Church, Clinton Street, and Archdeacon of Southern Brooklyn, each had his small group of supporters. A newcomer, the Rev. Frederick Burgess, Rector of Grace Church on the Heights was mentioned, but he received little support.

The Convention, called by the Standing Committee to elect a successor to the late Right Reverend Abram Newkirk Littlejohn, met in the Cathedral of the Incarnation in Garden City, on Wednesday, November 20, 1901. After settling procedures for balloting, which took all morning, the Convention re-assembled at 2:45 in the afternoon. The validity of convention delegates occupied their attention, and finally nominations were made for the privileged office. Among the hopefuls were Dr. Kinsolving, Canon Bryan, Dr. McConnell, Dr. Burgess and the Rev. James Darlington, later to become the Bishop of Harrisburg. On the first few ballots the election appeared to be a contest between three favorites, McConnell, Darlington and Swentzel. After the second ballot, a dark horse, Dr. Huntington was nominated, but received little support. The battle settled back to the three leaders. After six ballots there was still no unanimity of opinion. By 10:00 p.m. there was still no election. A recess turned the tide. A compromise candidate appeared in Dr. Burgess. From two clerical and one lay vote on the fifth ballot, he had gained such strength that on the seventh ballot he received twenty-two clerical and twenty-two lay votes. A motion to adjourn the Convention was made but lacking sufficient votes, the Convention went on with the balloting. The Standing Committee made arrangements with the Garden City Hotel "to entertain such delegates as would not be able to reach their homes that night."

A brief moment of prayer preceded the seventh ballot. On the eighth ballot, after the withdrawal of Darlington, the vote became a battle between McConnell and Burgess. It was Swentzel who, after his withdrawal, turned the tide to Frederick Burgess. On the tenth ballot Burgess had won. He received just the required number of votes in the clerical order and seven more than necessary in the lay order. The Chair declared the Rev. Dr. Frederick Burgess duly elected Bishop of Long Island. At 2:00 a.m. on November 21, 1901, the Convention adjourned after singing the *Gloria.*

THE DARK HORSE

Perhaps no one was more surprised at the final outcome of the convention than the Bishop-elect himself. Only after a long and determined battle and several inter-session caucuses, did the Grace Church Rector gain any real strength. Nominated by the Rev. John H. Sattig of Dyker Heights, he received few votes in the many early ballots, finally receiving on the tenth ballot, in the early morning hours, just the minimum amount for election.

The Rev. Frederick Burgess had had little time to make himself known to diocesan circles. Coming to Brooklyn only three years before, his sole reputation rested on his being Rector of the second most affluent highly prized parish in the Diocese. Appointed to several minor commissions, he held only two elective offices, one of which he had only held for six months. In addition to serving on the Committee on a Minority Report, the Jubilee Committee of the Church Charity Foundation and the General Relief Fund Committee, he was elected to the Ecclesiastical Court. A short-lived six months interim membership on the Standing Committee was ended by the election of another candidate.

Born in Providence, Rhode Island, Dr. Burgess came from a family of bishops. His uncle was the first Bishop of Maine. Another uncle, the Rev. Alexander Burgess, who had served as Rector of St. John's Church in Brooklyn, and who was a leading contender in the first episcopal election, had, in 1878, been elected the first Bishop of the newly organized Diocese of Quincy. The Bishop-elect, a graduate of Brown University, studied at the General Theological Seminary in New York and afterwards abroad for a year at Oxford. Serving a number of parishes in New Jersey, Massachusetts and Connecticut, he married in 1881 the daughter of Edgar J. Bartow, the builder of Holy Trinity on the Heights. They had four children, all boys.

Two events in his life tended to deepen the natural seriousness of his character. In the summer of 1879, while on his way to Great Neck, Long Island, he was a passenger on the *Seawanhaka*, which burned off Wards Island, near Hell Gate. Twenty-four lives were lost in the terrible disaster. Another tragic event occured in 1894, when his wife died. Yet, after a very successful rectorate in Detroit where his power to draw men into the church became evident, he answered a call from the Vestry of Grace Church and assumed his duties early in 1898.

The choice of Frederick Burgess as the second Bishop of Long Island was at once regarded as favorable and as likely to promote harmony and progress in the Diocese. A man of forty-eight, he was young and energetic, intending to get to work quickly and vigorously. Of a catholic spirit, there was no real question of churchmanship in the election. It was his own personal qualities and natural dignity that had finally won him the high honor and deep responsibility.

> A man of ripe learning and simple life; clear and unshaken in his convictions; caring for truth
> rather than popularity; gentle and retiring in disposition; unfailing in loyalty to his clergy; just
> in his judgements; sincere in his friendships; untiring in his devotion.

This was an adequate description of the second Diocesan.

His dignity of appearance fittingly expressed his inherent nobility of character. He commanded the respect of all, and the warm affection of those who were privileged to know him intimately. "He was a true father in God and under his spiritual sway both rich and poor and young and old rejoice." His prudent unaggressiveness made him acceptable to the general episcopacy and endowed him with qualities of pure heart, gentle mood, pleasing manner, and sound learning, all of which he brought to bear on his work. His genius for preaching without notes added greatly to his influence over men. Clergymen of all parties joined in a commendation of his administrative ability and "felt assured of a united forward movement under his guidance in every department of diocesan life." The Bishop would need all his prowess and personal capabilities as he assumed the task of guiding the Diocese of Long Island in the turbulent years ahead.

PROVOCATIVE NEW BISHOP

Cognizant of the many rapid changes that had taken place in his appointed jurisdiction, the Rt. Rev. Frederick Burgess faced squarely and honestly the task that had been entrusted to him by election and consecration. Bishop Littlejohn may have thought that he had clearly surmised the role of the second Bishop when he forecasted in 1899:

> As the first Bishop of this Diocese it was inevitable that my work should consist very largely
> in laying foundations on which others are to build. Foundations are below ground and
> therefore usually hidden from sight.

Yet time proved well that Bishop Burgess had to assume the responsibility of securing and solidifying unseen roots. He could not build a great complex structure, replete with a tremendous growth of parishes, communicants and activities, garnished with a large group of diocesan institutions, primary among which stood the Cathedral. The first Bishop appeared often and well as the great "architect" of the Diocese. The foundations he laid were very much in evidence. Bishop Burgess had his labor cut out for him. It was he who undergirded and encircled the expansive as well as the expensive entity known as the Diocese of Long Island.

Bishop Burgess early earned the nomenclature of "conserver". He felt it necessary to protect frontiers rather than to extend them. "Long Island had come to a point where the incisive call of the hour was to conserve what had been acquired in an era of rapid expansion." A week following his consecration, in a speech made at an Archdeaconry meeting, he explained his primary task. In 1908, he reiterated the way in which he viewed his episcopate: the cornerstone is easier to lay than the keystone. "This has been my idea all along," he seemed to say. "Strengthen the things that remain. Foster, not force the work. Building on what we have, do so much as the gifts of the Diocese warrant. God will give the increase." That was his faith. For him, growth had to be natural, steady and strong. Pruning accomplished a subsequent stronger growth of the "church's vines".

Bishop Burgess assumed a much larger share in deciding policy and assuming authority. A chronic weakness of the Diocese since its inception plagued the life of the Diocesan. The Diocese had been established, yet a secure relationship between parish and diocese had never fully appeared. Bishop Littlejohn, throughout his thirty-three year episcopate, had to contend constantly with blatant parochialism and self-centered clericalism. To accomplish his programs, Bishop Littlejohn temporized and concealed the disparity by referring to the peace and harmony of his jurisdiction. Bishop Burgess understood this and early in his episcopate he faced the issue unequivocally, by asserting the Bishop's prerogative. A keen judge of men, understanding the sensibilities and qualities of others, he was able to overcome opposition and in a very few years had earned the respect and cooperation of both clergy and laity. "In this 'Dominion in the Sea' may it be mine," he said in his first address to the Diocese, "to command the ship in storm or sunshine, not with any attempted tyranny but in the Master's spirit of sincerity and truth." His forthright beguiling appeal that "whether men give their allegiance to me or not is comparatively speaking, of small consequence, but it is of supreme moment to me that I never use my authority save in the cause of justice and truth," created an atmosphere in which men accepted and helped not so much because they had to but because they wanted to.

His staunch spirit gave him the courage to speak out boldly and clearly against inequalities and dangers. An important concern was the attempt on the part of men who possessed wealth, to control or subvert policy. Against this hazardous practice, the Bishop stood firm.

> The possession of large wealth, either by parishes or individuals, make them, no doubt,
> responsible for their gifts, but it does not give either to individuals or churches the right to
> usurp the authority which has been placed in the office of the Diocese.

The possession of large wealth gave no one the right to take authority away from the Diocese. In Bishop Littlejohn's final years, authority had passed from the sick aging prelate to a small group of affluent rectors and laymen. Their direction of policy rested on their control of money. "For this reason," he said, "it is not wise for the Diocese to assume such heavy obligations as to expose itself to either the capriciousness or tyranny of wealth." Realizing the bounds imposed upon his position, he nevertheless refused to concede when the best interests of the Church were at stake. Even at critical periods, not having as strong an initiative influence as he could wish, he felt no qualms in using his veto which "must be final in the action of a parish or the Diocese." He refused to accept any gifts that had strings attached no matter how badly needed. Far better it was to do no greater work than income legitimately warranted, than to have restrictive clauses placed upon it. He held to "the extension of that true Catholic spirit which leads one to give to the body corporate without expecting from all the members a uniform ritual."

A THOROUGHLY MODERN DIOCESE

Bishop Burgess at once justified himself as a modern business bishop. Aware of the size and structure of the Diocese, he knew that improved means of communication and stricter business practices were an absolute necessity. He set about the renovation of the fabric of the Diocese in terms of sound financial practices and better business methods.

Primary on his list of priorities was an office in Brooklyn. The day after his election he stressed the requirement of some room in Brooklyn where he could spend time in work and interviews. "I think the Bishop of Long Island should be the Bishop of Long Island and not the Rector of Garden City," he stated to the press. "Brooklyn is by far the largest and most important part of the Diocese . . . the head and vitals of the Diocese. Long Island is the tail. In this case the tail has been wagging the dog too long." His estimate matched that of many in the Diocese who felt the Bishop should spend at least a part of his time in Brooklyn. He did not want to fall in the same trap as his predecessor who "had lost his hold upon the Diocese at least ten years ago, all that he practically did was to attend confirmation services and it was left to a certain number of clergy to administer the affairs of the Diocese."

Responding to his friend and former Rector, Mr. Wilhelmus Mynderse began to pursue the eventuality of establishing such an office. On February 17, 1902, a plan was submitted to the Standing Committee to establish a Diocesan Mission House in Brooklyn. The logical place for it was the former episcopal residence, then rented, but easily adapted to the new use. Fully half of the parishes of the Diocese were located in Brooklyn, having easy access to 170 Remsen Street for interviews and conferences.

The use of the Bishop's old residence engendered a much wider scope of operation and purpose. The house would not only serve as the Bishop's city residence and office but also as a base for missionary operations in the Diocese. To this end, by a special act of the state legislature in April 1902, the corporation known as The Diocesan Missions of Long Island was formed, accepted by the Diocese in May, and duly organized in June 1902. The corporation held title to the Diocesan House, transferred from the Bishop's Fund and took care of the upkeep and maintenance of the diocesan center. The new corporation had the vital purpose of "something more than a safe deposit for title deeds or a clearing house for the Archdeaconries." Its prime objective lay in the origination and administration of all mission work, especially among the immigrants where sadly the Diocese had made "little or no effort to cope with the religious problems which the invasion of foreign labor forced upon our attention." In keeping with modern business, the Diocese had to keep abreast of the rapid change on Long Island. As business prepared for the new era of multiplying communities, so the Diocese had to be ready to minister to them. No hit-or-miss policy, no too-little-too-late solution but the carefully planned purchase of sites for future churches in the growing areas of the Island had to be accomplished. To this end the new corporation was largely directed. The Diocesan Missions had the added power of holding all property, real or personal, for the advancement of church expansion. A discretionary fund for the Bishop was also advocated. Special gifts for missionary work were a powerful lever in the hand of the Bishop. It relieved him of much harassment and also helped him have available cash when needed and not when appropriated.

On January 6, 1903, the Diocesan House was formally dedicated. The building, too large for the Bishop's needs had been renovated and fully equipped to serve as a center for diocesan meetings and as a diocesan library. The second floor contained the Bishop's apartment and office, "tastefully and richly furnished." Mr. Mynderse had spearheaded the project and many laymen had cooperated and donated funds for its use.

The Diocesan House fully realized its potential. Within a very few years the Bishop had re-established a firm control over diocesan life. But more, the building served the many-sided needs of the diocesan structure. Visitors streamed in by the thousands; committees and larger bodies met regularly. The house became a center for clergy supply work for Sundays, for funerals and weddings; an information booth for the various diocesan institutions, for local churches, and for church organizations; and a source of church literature. Summed up, the effectiveness of the new center rested in the constant use as "the Bishop's office, the office of the Archdeacons, an office for every society in the Diocese, in fact . . . an office for every member of the Church in the Diocese."

The "modern executive Bishop" made full use of all the new conveniences available. To improve the expeditious transaction of diocesan work, he depended on the telephone, both in his home in Garden City and in his office in Brooklyn. Keeping up with an increasing correspondence, created the necessity of procuring a private secretary, the annual salary for which was donated anonymously. Obvious to all was his use of an increasing popular convenience, the "motor car". Much in vogue, the Bishop was first among Bishops to adopt it for ecclesiastical use. Playfully calling it his "suffragan", he became a familiar figure, driving to every remote nook and cranny of the Island, untiring in his visitations.

Most beneficial of all was his staunch advocacy of publicity in church finances and his insistence upon using the best available business practices. Averse to heavy mortgages, a firm believer in the "pay-as-you-go" policy, he directed his attention to the state of existing diocesan institutions, and did everything in his power to encourage and start systematic, regular financial practices. Perhaps the need for stricter regulation and care resulted from the national scandal of a man in high church position embezzling church funds. The same unguarded condition of church funds at St. Paul's School heightened the need. At St. Paul's, when a new system of bookkeeping had been instituted and certified public accountants engaged, it was discovered that a considerable sum of money, almost $4,000, had been embezzled by a school trustee. The culprit had deftly, in the course of years, put money in his own pocket, and when the discovery was made, he absconded, disappearing before he could be brought to trial.

To prevent future recurrence of inadequate supervision of funds, the Bishop strongly prescribed tightening of controls and exacting scrupulous money procedures. In the past, in the interest of economy, ordinary business safeguards had been overlooked or lightly assumed. The Bishop had a few thoughts about better business practice for church affairs. He recommended the engaging of a trust company of good standing, not to usurp local control, but to insure church capital against loss by adequate counsel in supervising investments. Finances should be the information of all; and those entrusted with the administration of funds realize the asset of good management practices. Vestries had responsibility, as trustees, for church monies. They should, therefore, count the offerings; meet at least every three months to go over accounts and vouchers. Larger funds needed a yearly audit and special funds needed two officers' signatures for any transaction. New in church management, concise accounting exhibited the qualities of good stewardship.

First objective of diocesan scrutiny and episcopal supervision was the financial state of the Cathedral. The Cathedral, remote from the center city of Brooklyn, had suffered from apathy or complete indifference. Old hostilities, very much in evidence in its days of building, had remained. Whether due to diocesan antipathy or to Catheral self-sufficiency, a wide disparity existed between Cathedral and Diocese. It was almost as if they represented two different entities. Bishop Burgess, sensing this, did all he could to better integrate the Cathedral into the diocesan structure. In his primary address to the Diocese, he attempted an apologetic for the Cathedral, drafted in such terms as would not persuade but explain. Casting aside the old world idea, he attempted to show the real worth of the Garden City center. A Cathedral in practical terms was "a Bishop's Church", in full harmony with the American system, "where he can feel at home, where he can pronouce certain official decisions and judgments, and whither he can flee for spiritual refreshment when wearied by the complexity of the ritual which confronts him in some of his wanderings." The Cathedral had the unique quality, not of only being a beautiful piece of architecture, but of being fully recognized as it actually was, the Cathedral of the Diocese.

As a step in this direction and as a better business practice, the Cathedral Chapter, its governing body, decided to give to the convention each year a full statement of its finances, so that the convention should have that knowledge to which it was entitled. The picture presented was far from encouraging. Endowments for the Cathedral, including the Stewart grants and the "conscience" money of Henry Hilton, were insufficient for the total operation of the diocesan center. The Cathedral with its maintenance, missions, and charities had to use its surplus income to offset the yearly deficit of its two schools.

The growing financial precariousness between income and expense had caused not alarm but anxiety. Possessing buildings representing at least $2,000,000, and lands which as an investment were of no value since they could by Stewart stipulation only be used for purposes of church work and not revenues, the Cathedral corporation could be taxed fully for all improvements, such as schools, streets, lights and sewers that went on in Garden City, yet unlike other taxpayers, their land did not appreciate in value. Some relief seemed imminent with the freeing from taxation of the schools which had never been established to make money. The income receipts of the Cathedral showed a decided decrease which made the situation almost, but not quite, desperate.

Several catastrophes had drained a great deal of money from the Cathedral funds. In the winter of 1904, the power house plant had been found in a very bad condition. To build suitable tunnels for pipes, to erect a chimney, and to service the boiler had cost $45,000. Another blow came in the fall of 1905. It was found that the tall stately spire had been constructed on wrong principles and that the high stones were in danger of falling. The repair work was accomplished at a cost of $30,000. These costs had to be deducted from the general fund of the Cathedral. More "conscientious rebuilding" was necessary to put the Cathedral in good working condition.

Since its inception, the Cathedral Chapter, the executive governing group made up of men of means as well as clergy, had envisaged as its chief duty the guardianship of the schools. Surplus income from the Cathedral activities were carefully held for school maintenance. During the twenty years of existence, St. Paul's School had received deficit aid of $175,000 and St. Mary's $90,000. However, a serious practical problem the Cathedral Chapter had to face was connected with the land, about forty acres of which was practically unutilized. So deeded that it could not be used as revenue but only for charitable or religious purposes, it benefited little the Cathedral Corporation, being more of a liability than an asset. In light of the failing finances and of the doubts and uncertainties of the Diocese, only a general request for large personal gifts could help the ailing Cathedral condition. The Diocese was appealed to forget the past and assist the "wonderful instrument for good." A firm principle, a lesson hard-learned, lay in endowments and buildings; but no buildings "unless endowments go with gifts."

The discouraging financial status would have been far worse had it not been for an able dedicated treasurer, Alexander E. Orr of Brooklyn. Through years of careful stewardship, he had alleviated a more drastic setback. Sole executor of the Hilton Grant, he judiciously invested funds, and by discretion had saved them from material loss. Even with his wise supervision and with the watchful eye of the Chapter, the Cathedral could not recover. Economic pressures forced the Corporation to continue deficit spending. Repairs, maintenance, school deficits, building problems and program needs made more and more demands on the general fund. The small margin of surplus income year by year decreased from a deficit of $6,037.60 in 1904, to an excess of expenditures over income of $11,401.03 in 1908. The Cathedral financial picture did not brighten for many years.

The other diocesan institution that received a large share of diocesan attention was the Church Charity Foundation. It, like the Cathedral, faced hard times. Beginning in 1898, the future of the Foundation grew increasingly uncertain. Buildings sadly out of repair due to neglect over the years required extensive renovation. A debt of $40,000 was incurred to do the work; and then another mortgage of $40,000 had to be taken. With so large a debt incurred, receipts and contributions fell off due to a lack of confidence on the part of the public who felt that the Foundation was mismanaged. Offerings steadily decreased; more deficits grew; and so the Church Charity Foundation grew steadily worse. Retrenchment, abetted by a reorganized and united Board of Managers, and public interest renewed, produced a better outlook. The Board of Managers realized the fact "that it must show each year a true and encouraging financial statement, and that the most pathetic or poetic appeals will be of no avail if year after year there is a steady increase in deficit and continuous encroachment upon the endowment funds." The debt of $90,000 had by 1903 been reduced to $55,000. And in 1906, a gift of $40,000 by the Benson family inspired the Diocese to add to the balance so that the debt was wiped out entirely.

A hard lesson had been learned by the charitable agency. Careful and conservative management of funds, combined with strict economic measures for the purpose of living within the budget, carried the management of the Foundation successfully. Dependence on city aid to offset any deficiency was discontinued, not only because it was dangerous planning, but also because it was in a real sense immoral for a private agency to be dependent upon public taxation for support. The Board of Managers had resolved to keep expenses down to the lowest point consistent with efficiency of operation. They also, in 1904, on the strong recommendation of the Bishop, hired a superintendent to administer its affairs. Regulated expenditures, increased parish offerings and more individual subscriptions helped so that by 1905, they were able to close the year without a deficit. A firm commitment was made that the Managers would never again dig into a legacy to meet current expenditures. With the removal of the overburdening debt by 1907, the Church Charity Foundation stood on firm financial footing.

By constant referral, the Bishop was able to affect a recouping of losses and an acquisition of sufficient diocesan funds. Laxity of parish payments was reflected in a contribution of only two parishes to the increase of the Episcopal Fund. Even a threat of compulsory payment with a penalty for non-payment elicited little action and the idea was quickly dropped. Assessment of 2% for the Bishop's Salary Fund and 2½% for the diocesan fund were constantly avoided or ignored. Deficit spending of the diocesan fund which cared for the needs of the convention did not encourage any great response.

A boon to the Diocese came in the form of a sale of property. In 1873, a large grant of land had been donated by James Maurice with the intention of using it for the support of the Font Maur Home for the Blind.

When the Home was moved to Brooklyn from its Maspeth location, the property lost its intrinsic value and lay idle for almost thirty years. In the meantime additional land had been granted by the family so that the total property held amounted to a sizeable amount. On the principle of shortening diocesan cords, Bishop Burgess set in motion the eventual sale of the property. At the 1903 convention, Mr. Alexander E. Orr brought to the group a resolution "to sell or rent . . . the property known as Font Maur . . . due to a release of the land by the Maurice sisters freeing the land from restriction to sale." Three years later the property had been sold for $300,000, netting the Diocese, after sale expenses, $262,427.65. The principal of this fund was to be wisely invested and safeguarded; the income to be used by the Trustees for benevolent, charitable, and religious purposes in the Diocese. The fund became an emergency discretionary fund used for immediate needs not underwritten in other ways. The Diocesan House benefited from a grant of some of the investment accrued.

At the very outset of his episcopate, Bishop Burgess struggled with a prevalent problem of overburdened parishes, weighed down with large debts. Unsatisfactory laws, or no laws at all, either on the part of the church and state had caused fictitious church construction, erected on a pay-later basis. Vestries permitted debts to accumulate year after year with no serious notice given. Grandiose changes in property or extensive building and renovation, for which only part of the funds were raised, marked many parish paths to the mortgage bank. Episcopal approval had been sought as an afterthought or a necessary evil, saddling the Bishop with a debt responsibility for which he had no share in creating. The issue came to light dramatically in the much publicized scandal of St. Barnabas Church, Bushwick Avenue. A large debt hung about its neck like a millstone; its floating debt had become embarrassing. With few friends, the parish faced ultimate ruin when the bank threatened to foreclose. Fortunate for St. Barnabas, its doom was alleviated by the action of another Episcopal church. Calvary Church, unable to minister in its initial neighborhood, contemplated change to a new locality. Seizing the opportune moment, it paid off the debt and St. Barnabas went out of existence.

Solution to the immediate problem did not alter a similar condition in other parishes. Happily the Religious Corporation Law of New York State had been amended at the turn of the century to make mandatory the Bishop's guardianship of real property in the Diocese. According to its provisions, the sale or mortgaging of church property was expressly forbidden without approval of the Bishop and Standing Committee. Making his attitude clear and unquestioned, he adamantly stated that the full letter of the law would be used. Debts accumulated without his knowledge or bypass of ecclesiastical jurisdiction boded ill for the harassed parish. Plainly and in simple terms, he reiterated his policy:

> I do not like to talk about myself, nor do I wish to boast, but it is only fair to give the
> Parishes of the Diocese warning that I do not intend to be deprived of this prerogative which
> the State gives me, and that I can be absolutely firm in my refusals.

Taking their cue from the Bishop's remarks, parishes soon followed the regular channels of church financing. Requests for mortgages had first to be presented to the Diocesan authorities for approval before bank services were sought. Parishes heavily in debt made great strides in overcoming detrimental over-financing. Mortgages began to be reduced. The movement to gather parish endowments as a financial precaution, begun in the last years of the nineteenth century, started to accrue substantial sums. Small in the beginning of Bishop Burgess' episcopate, in the ensuing years endowments reached staggering heights adding to the stability of tottering churches. By careful management, budget trimming and prudent spending, parish indebtedness dwindled, obliterating sometimes amounts up to $40,000.

The same spirit of careful management pervaded missionary funds. Additional monies, always needed for the extension of the churches, came through the initiation of a Permanent Fund, suggested by James W. Eaton, the Treasurer, and supported by the Sunday School children of the Diocese. Through the children's efforts, provisions were made to insure loans to the various Archdeaconries to aid any particular chapel or mission station in financial distress. It was understood "that such a loan [was] to be repaid so the principal of the Permanent Fund not be impaired." A tax on parishes for the fund received widespread disapproval so that gifts and contributions were encouraged. From the fund the Archdeacons could make prompt payments to their missionary workers.

Contributions for missionary work in the Diocese remained on a voluntary basis; therefore, the parishes gave as much as they could, and as often as they were able. Parish offerings were augmented by special gifts of the Woman's Auxiliary, Advent Mite Boxes, "Barrels", Sunday Schools, individuals and offerings at Archdeaconry Meetings. The total amount varied for the various Archdeaconries; $2,900 for Suffolk; $5,225.24 for Queens and Nassau; $12,614.51 for general missionary work. The diocesan share in the General Missionary Work of the Church had up to 1901, rested on the same principal of voluntary giving. But in 1901, a new system went into effect. The General Convention of 1901, on motion of the Bishop of Montana, resolved to raise a million dollars for church advancement. Monies would be collected on an apportionment basis, in which the National Board of Missions assigned a definite amount to a Diocese which was then apportioned among its constituent parishes. The new method apportioned to Long Island in 1901, an amount of $30,031. Long Island only met less than one-third its quota in the first year. Increasing to $34,900, the Diocese still only raised a little over 33%. Even with episcopal prodding the diocesan share never attained the maximum amount requested. Through persistent efforts and constant vigilance,

. . . the Diocese came to the completion of its second quarter century financially sound and strong, and its progress was written clear, concrete, unshakeable in mortgages paid, endowments accumulated, churches built, rectories acquired, and its great philanthropies strengthened and expanded.

A popular topic of conversation among Episcopalians in the first decade of the new century was a proposed name-change. The discussion and debate had become so heated and so distorted that the Bishop felt the responsibility to speak out on the subject. Unbeknown to himself and the Convention, he had laid down long range guidelines and objectives that colored and tempered the course of his tenure. Aside from his opposition to changing the Church's name on the basis of "bad politics" and confession of weakness, he expressed the important concern for accommodating and answering the turbulent needs of the day. Couched in terms that "war has been declared — war with ignorance and lust, with infidelity and bigotry and sin," he presented his "platform" to the Diocese.

> Let the Church go on and fight its battles with the world;
>
> Let it stand in the family as the champion of women and defenseless children against cruelty and divorce;
>
> Let its voice sound in the secret chambers where statesmen form the policy of nations with its exhortation to peace;
>
> Let it speak in the midst of labor strifes whenever it can protect the cause of justice, impartially to the workmen or to the threatened contractors;
>
> Let it refuse the large gifts which come from men whose moral life has been notoriously corrupt, or from fortunes won by child labor, or by grinding the face of the poor in the gloom of the mines or amid the clatter of the mills;
>
> Let it speak with no uncertain voice when men of proved dishonesty are placed in positions of public trust;
>
> Let is show its power by stretching out its hand to the foreign hordes which the greed of capitalists bring every year in increasing numbers within our ports;
>
> Let it educate the negro and proclaim his equality in the sight of God and the nation;
>
> Let it do all this . . .

Together the Bishop and the Diocese worked to bring to bear the Church's ministry in the quest for social justice.

Country road in western Suffolk, 1900's.

Chapter Nine

The Quest for Social Justice

ASTOUNDING NEW CENTURY

When Bishop Burgess came to the episcopal purple, the American nation sensed it stood on the threshold of a brave, new and exciting world. Optimism pervaded all levels of society; hopes of the future sprang primarily from the great advances of the past few decades. Enumerating all the wonderful things accomplished in the later half of the nineteenth century, the *New York Times* sounded the clarion call to bigger and better things in its editorial of January 1, 1900. "The year 1899 was a year of wonders, a veritable *annus mirabilis*, in business and production. It would be easy to speak of the twelve months just passed as the banner year," said the prophetic editors, "were we not confident that the destruction of the highest records must presently pass to the year 1900. . . . The outlook on the threshold of the new year is extremely bright." Sunday orators and preachers assumed the same optimistic pose: "Laws are becoming more just, rulers humane, music is becoming sweeter and books wiser; homes are happier, and the individual heart becoming at once more just and more gentle."

It would seem as if the first decade of the new century would bear out the happy forecast. Growth and development held the promise fulfilled. The United States continued to grow even faster than before. By 1900, its population had reached 76 million; in 1915, it stood at 100,000,000. Swelling the already bulging population was the floodtide of immigration, with more than twelve million landless opportunity-seekers arriving after 1901. In 1907, no bounds could stop the immigrant influx; the greatest number arrived that year—1,285,390 people.

However, a decided change in the source of immigrants took place. Economic improvement in Ireland together with German legislative, industrial and commercial progress had considerably reduced the two main nineteenth century sources of foreign people. By 1890, the number coming from central, southern and eastern Europe surpassed those coming from northwestern Europe. During the last two decades of the nineteenth century Italian immigrants were twelve times as numerous as during the preceding one hundred years. Slavic sources increased about fourteen times. The trend became even more pronounced in the first part of the twentieth century. Remarkable also was the growth by 1910, of the nation's Black population to almost ten million and the Jewish to over two million.

The years of population explosion were characterized also by great changes in the social, economic and industrial life of the American people. Outstanding features showed in tremendous economic expansion, in formation of mammoth trusts, in mass production of manufactured goods and in growing agressiveness of American labor. Pride in an increasingly secular education matched an unnerving uneasiness in the growth of divorce and the advocacy of birth control. Most manifest was the decline in church attendance, relative to the increase of the general population. These changes deeply affected the thought, habits and lives of all Americans.

Transformations on the national scene quickly reflected within the limits of Long Island. Here probably the clearest evidence of the times showed in the great increase of population. The 40% increase in the last decade of the nineteenth century was overtaken in the twentieth century. At the beginning of the new century the counties of Nassau and Suffolk counted 133,030 persons. Queens numbered a little more than 153,000. It was the Borough of Brooklyn or Kings County that harbored most of the Island people — 1,166,582 persons. The remarkable growth accelerated in the first decade until by 1915, Nassau and Suffolk had a population of 200,000; Queens twice that number; and Kings County, with a population of 1,800,000 was nearly ready to dispute with Manhattan the title of the most populous of the greater city's five boroughs. Part of Brooklyn's growth rested in the incorporation of all of Kings County by 1896 which, together with the western section of Queens, helped form the Greater New York City. The remainder of Queens County, including the townships of North Hempstead, Hempstead and Oyster Bay became in 1899, Nassau County. Overpowering New York, American love of size, and plain old politics had wrought the change. Long Island became two distinct sections with the dividing line, the Queens and Nassau border, often opposed in the extremities of outlook, idea and life.

All the while, Long Island hamlets became villages, large villages became prosperous populated towns, and the disappearing Yankee farms passed into the hands of southern or central Europeans. In Brooklyn and Queens industry, commerce and business obliterated old landmarks, while in Brooklyn skyscrapers reared their towers, rivalling in a modest way the gargantuan monoliths that had begun to dominate lower Manhattan.

The evolution of mechanical methods of transportation accompanied and made possible the growth of population and accelerated the tempo of life. The horse-drawn vehicles and the cycling clubs of the 1890's yielded

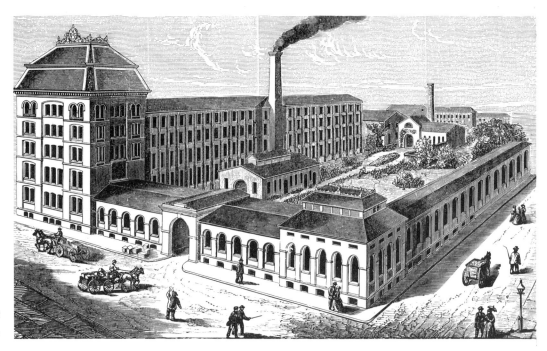

Brooklyn factory at the turn of the century.

to the automobile, which by 1910 became quite common and helped to transform street paving from cobblestone to asphalt. Rattling trolleys replaced horse cars, and the elevated trains rumbled along on steel viaducts which darkened the streets below. The Long Island Railroad had reached far into the Island with branches as far as Wading River, Riverhead, Montauk and Greenport. Service branch lines stemming from the main arteries made many small communities on the shores more easily accessible. Electric power in 1905 began to replace the time-honored steam engine. Brooklyn's solidarity with New York grew apace when the first subway opened under the East River to Borough Hall and then in 1908 to Atlantic Avenue. More arterial cords appeared to rival the world famous Brooklyn Bridge. The Williamsburgh Bridge opened in 1903, twenty years after its graceful predecessor, and was quickly followed by the Manhattan and Queensborough Bridges in 1909. As immigrant peoples flowed through these main arteries into Kings and Queens Counties, many of the residents of the older settlements were pushed out, ever eastward in concentric arcs, leaving behind them slums, shabby dwellings and vanquished brownstones of by-gone gentility. Old Brooklynites established new homes in the suburbs with glimpses of lawn and trees, thus awakening the sleepy quiet of country villages into livelier towns and small municipalities. Following new means of transportation population developed in a "series of settlements extending in an almost unbroken line from East New York through Jamaica to the pleasant little towns of Queens (Village)."

Through all the changes Brooklyn's strong local pride and pronounced individualism remained invulnerable. Social life still centered mostly in the home, although a growing diversity of amusement began to corrode its placid austere character. Brooklyn retained still its fame for rubber plants and baby bumpers. Deep-rooted proclivities simmered in the city's religious life; but Brooklyn either ignored or refused to recognize its growing secularism by affectionately recalling its foster-name, City of Churches.

MISSIONARY RETRENCHMENT

No other concern engrossed the consistent encouragement and careful supervision of the Bishop than the extension of churches in the Diocese. When Bishop Burgess took the leadership he came into a diocese that had 154 clergy in 143 chapels and churches. Communicant strength showed in 33,025 confirmed members. The total wealth was over three-quarters of a million dollars ($887,419.46). Under the policy of conservation and caution, the first seven years of his episcopate showed little advance. By the end of 1908, clergy had increased in number to 160 and churches had only multiplied by one. Communicants increase had averaged about 650 a year. After the serious panic of 1907, total wealth had dropped to $768,299.96. To all intents and interest it looked as if the Diocese had come to a standstill. Yet wisely the Bishop understood that in order to advance a time was needed for taking stock, for strengthening existing roots and for establishing sound principles. Missionary extension had to first be re-oriented before outreach could become effective.

The diocesan extension program in mission stations was near and dear to the Bishop's heart; it absorbed and held much of his time and thoughts. To effectively minister to the Island community, the Bishop comprehended the need for some central bureau of operations, and to this end the Diocesan House had been established. But even more, to adequately coordinate missionary thrust, a central agency was needed; thus came into existence the corporation known as The Diocesan Missions of Long Island. Equipped with the necessary channels of operations, the Diocese pressed for "putting greater strength into already existing missions, and to build up larger works than multiply small circles."

As in other aspects of diocesan life, the Bishop made his ideas and objectives perfectly clear. Delineating purposes and practices, he defined lines of authority and objects of final responsibility. For him,

> ...the Bishop alone has the power of initiation and location of missions and churches, although he cannot act without the advice and consent of the Standing Committee. No Missionary can be appointed except with his consent. The dismissal of the Missionary follows the same law and is left to the Bishop acting with the Archdeacon.... The Archdeaconry system is intended to be an assistance to the Bishop in his work, and rightly adjusted, it makes possible the administration of a large Diocese, but it is not intended to limit in any way the Bishop's responsibility or to take from him the privilege and duty of close personal associations with the Missionaries.

Under his approving direction, the Diocese determined general guidelines for missionary work, principal of which was the provision for future church needs. Preparation for the future rested in the purchase of sites for future churches. The same spirit had shown in the holding by individuals, "as a matter of convenience", of land or lots. In the first few years of its existence, a general transfer of properties from the Bishops and the Archdeacons, or from the Trustees poured into the new corporation, thereby centralizing under one agency the means to mission. New sites acquired were held by the Diocesan Missions. Noteworthy among the new sites was a gift of land midway between Garden City and Floral Park. The real estate firm, Garden City Estates, offered a plot of land for church purposes. The advisability of land so near the Cathedral brought forth some questions. The land was taken because it was forecasted in a very few years a large and teeming population would settle there.

> If we do not meet the religious wants of this population by the establishment of a Parish Church it will fall to others to do so by the establishment of a denominational church of some kind. The Cathedral is a Diocesan Church. It can be attended by any and all, but a Parish church with its guilds and its organizations, and the personal attention of a Priest and Pastor with the people is what this population will need and demand.

The intent of the property was to provide a future location for a parish church in Garden City, since the Cathedral was "the Diocesan Church."

Centralization of control was accomplished with the discontinuance of regional programs or parish responsibility. The first step toward accomplishing a concise command of missionary operations came with the discontinuance of the Cathedral missions. In 1902, no more Cathedral missions were to be established, but rather the money to be given to furnish missionary work for the whole Diocese.

Concern for the missionary's welfare and well-being made the Diocese aware of the inadequate salaries paid to men in the field. Good men labored for small remuneration and sometimes dimmed "the need of making adequate provision for men from whom the best must be demanded." A recommendation that "either by combination of missions, or by larger giving on the part of the people, the missionary ... be placed beyond want and disheartening care." The idea enlarged to include all clergy, encompassing the subject of "Better Salaries for the Clergy". A committee appointed in 1908 found that in several parishes as well as mission stations the priest-in-charge received below-level subsistence salaries. Since it was not possible to raise salaries without the assistance of the whole Diocese, they recommended a special annual collection for a supplementary salary fund be initiated to dispense supplementary stipend assistance, "in such proportion as the Committee ... in consultation with the Bishop, shall determine."

CITY WORK: THE ARCHDEACONRY OF BROOKLYN

And Then There Were Four —

The administration of the missionary program of the Diocese came under careful scrutiny. Since 1892, the Archdeaconry system had provided for needed episcopal assistance in the three areas of Brooklyn, Queens (and Nassau) and Suffolk. Several drawbacks became increasingly obvious, especially since Archdeacons were elected from the ranks of successful rectors of large parishes, who had to juggle parish and diocesan responsibilities resulting in divided loyalty, inadequate time and limited resources. Work in the suburban and rural areas did not seem to present as much of a problem as urban Brooklyn. Here, even with a division of work, outreach remained stationary or stagnant, with a succession of six Archdeacons in ten years. Only one incumbent served out the full term of office. In other words, the incumbent had hardly gotten acquainted with his field, formed his plans, organized his forces, entered upon his campaign, before he was discouraged or made to feel that he wasted his time and energy, and thereupon offered his resignation, leaving everything where and as he found it. The possibility of a full-time qualified missionary for at least the Brooklyn area had been broached. Responding to diocesan pressures, Bishop Burgess re-opened the question and applied some temporary measures. He appointed for the Northern Archdeaconry the Rev. St. Clair Hester who, together with interested laymen, was able to make at least the financial picture a little brighter.

Several suggestions were made, chief among which was to consolidate the two sections of the Archdeaconry under one leadership. Afraid of tampering with the Missionary Charter, the Diocese made several amendments providing for joint meetings of the two. "The subject of a paid Archdeacon was considered (May 1905), and a committee appointed to confer with a similar committee from the Southern Archdeaconry in reference to the matter." With this object in view Holy Trinity Parish, Brooklyn, offered the sum of $3,500 in 1905, first for three, and then for five years, towards an Archdeacon's salary and expenses.

It was not thought wise to alter at that time the character of the Diocesan Missions, which necessitated the membership on its board of two Archdeacons from Brooklyn, but to make a canon which should be tentative and which could lead to a subsequent change of the charter if the new method of missionary work should become permanent.

The result of the matter was the nomination of such an officer by the Bishop. In September 1905, the Rev. J. Townsend Russell became the first Archdeacon of Brooklyn, elected by both sections. Even with such an officer, the matter was not accomplished to the satisfaction of anyone. Now Brooklyn had three Archdeacons, which meant more of a reduplication of office rather than economy of action. Since the plan did not work, further investigation resulted in the demand for another officer, a General Missionary for Brooklyn. "The matter almost became a joke; the increase of titles [became] the occasion of harmless if not very thoughtful merriment." The "in-joke" produced some serious considerations. At the annual meeting of the joint Archdeaconries in Brooklyn, held in April 1908, the assembled clergy and laity voted to discontinue the office of Archdeacon of Brooklyn and to elect a General Missionary to supervise the work in the whole borough. The Rev. George C. Groves, Jr. was elected to the new office, and set up his headquarters in the Diocesan House. The two Archdeacons, the Rev. St. Clair Hester and the Rev. Charles F. J. Wrigley remained in their posts as administrators of their assigned sections.

"Hand to the Foreign Horde" —

Little zeal for missionary work characterized the Episcopal Church's ministry to the burgeoning city borough, causing stagnation in some areas and poor results in others. The Southern Archdeaconry did not have to face continual financial crises, as did its northern counterpart, due to the comparatively large offerings of Grace Church, Brooklyn Heights. The Northern Archdeaconry in 1900 was at a very low ebb, and worst of all deeply in arrears in the payment of missionaries' salaries. With the appointment of the Rev. St. Clair Hester by Bishop Burgess, in a short time, finances improved rapidly and saved the Diocese "from what was little less than scandal." In five years only one mission had been founded, the Church of the Nativity, Vanderveer Park. Given in mistaken solicitude, questionable title to the property caused the parish to incorporate. This "vicious" method of creating missions resulted necessarily in choosing men for important posts of warden and vestrymen with little training in church ways and poorly equipped for their new and untried responsibilities. A fully substantiated parish, St. Philips, Dyker Heights, did come into being, but never received help from the Archdeaconry.

In the first few years of a full-time officer, several new missions were started: St. Lydia's, East New York, holding services in an old storeroom; Holy Innocents, Kings Highway, begun in "parlor services" and transferring to a real estate office; Redemption Mission, Flatlands, meeting in the old Vanderveer Mansion; and St. Gabriel's, Nostrand and Hawthorne, stirring the most local support. Three organized parishes still received grants-in-aid of $895; St. John's, Fort Hamilton; St. Mathias, Sheepshead Bay; and St. Alban's, Canarsie. Of the three the last named was at a standstill, "owing, the Rector thinks, to the economic conditions brought about by the anti-race track legislations." As encouraging as the increase of churches may have been, it did not even scratch the surface of the swollen, teeming urban community.

Brooklyn had experienced in a very few short years one of the greatest population explosions of any city in the nation. Partly resulting from the constant flow of immigrants from the Mediterranean, partly from the emigration of Manhattan dwellers forced to leave by the raising of rents by tenement owners on the East Side, the new neighbors gravitated to the bridge areas, tightly compacting themselves in the run-down tenement areas. Over a million and a half persons lived in Brooklyn, of which six hundred thousand lived in the northern section. The northern section's problem became "the problem of the city." Among the elements that were part of it stood out "congested population, sanitation, nutrition, mixture of nationalities and races and languages, thousands who [were] not only unchurched but out of touch with any religious influence, many of whom [had] practically reverted to heathenism." Thousands of Jews, Italians and Germans had crossed the new Williamsburgh Bridge to settle in the Eastern District, Brownsville and East New York upsetting the balance of foreign born to native stock, the foreigners far exceeding the natives.

Emphasis on the Church's responsibility in foreign missions abroad dimmed in proportion "to the work in the city tenements among the cosmopolitan masses." Foreign work may have been more inviting and picturesque, but city work, more practical, promised quicker, larger and more lasting returns. Contributions to foreign missions inversely hindered the work the church should do among the urban peoples, for "every good motive and sound reason that influences a Christian to go far away to heathen lands to work for the Master or moves another to contribute funds towards this object, acts, operates and pleads for the ghettos, the dens and dives, the hotels and hives of the mission field at our very doors."

No greater motive for work among the foreign born impelled the church to Christianize and convert than fear — fear of being overpowered by the new neighbors. The growing colonies of aliens, not reached by any religious agency, would only result in "a lowering of moral tone and respect for law and order." One fact heightened the imperative, pronounced the Missionary Committee, that was already apparent:

Something must be done for the moral and spiritual uplifting and amelioration of our major population of the tenement house and of our foreign extraction, else it will drag down the educated and well-to-do minority to its lower level.

No more practical course presented itself than to assimilate and make them good citizens, to make them "one of us in sentiments, feelings, and ideas." The quickest and surest way to accomplish this was to enchurch them. To the Episcopal Church the mandate became clear since it was "our Church, which historically considered, has always been a power in the city, of commanding influence and prestige among urban peoples."

Responding to the Bishop's exhortation, realizing the need that did exist, the Diocese sought ways to work among the Jews, Italians and "Oriental Christians". The attempt to minister to the foreign-born was a novel and new step. Although the foreigners were so predominant a part of Brooklyn, no other church body cared to work with them. So far as city mission activity was concerned almost nothing was done. "There was not one single organization, or mission, or minister in all Brooklyn working with the foreigners." The Diocese realizing the great need did begin to work among the new people, following the firm course of using their native language, since little response was made to English services.

Exploratory work began among the Jews, the Germans and the Armenians. At Church of the Nativity services were held in Yiddish; and since a large Jewish population surrounded Church of the Holy Comforter, similar services were started there. For the Germans, services were conducted at Holy Cross, Ridgewood; and in Astoria, known as the "branch", Redeemer ministered to its large German settlement. A start with "Oriental Christians"

The Italian Chapel of the Annunciation founded 1906.

was made by a Mr. Hovaghim S. Hagopian, who conducted Sunday afternoon services in the Chapel of the Messiah. A graduate of a Constantinople college and General Seminary, he preached to Syrians, Persians, Turks, Greeks and Armenians; and conducted services in Armenian, Turkish and English.

But most successful was the work among the Italians. The Diocese had from time to time ministered to the Italians. Promising, yet discouraging in itself, the Italians who came to the church as children, as they grew older declined to attend Italian services, perferring to be part of a church that had no ethnic overtones.

Work at St. Margaret's, Van Buren Street, had ceased and St. Michael's Church, focus of early diocesan efforts, had in the intervening years reverted back to a "native stock" parish. Each experienced difficulties in neighborhood changes so that each faced the same crisis — possible extinction. The property of St. Margaret's was sold; and St. Michael's faced a three-fold choice: abandon its site; do settlement work; or become an Italian center. To alleviate its situation, a suggestion had been made to put an assistant at St. Michael's who could minister to the Italians. Since this did not materialize, the Diocese shifted its attention to other areas. A large settlement at Fourth Avenue and Pacific Street used Church of the Redeemer for afternoon services. St. Clement's and St. Jude's also offered their facilities for similar services. But it was at Lefferts Park that the Church's work with the Italians made the most gratifying progress. On Sunday afternoon, August 5, 1906, a new mission called "The Italian Chapel of the Annunciation" was formally opened in Brooklyn at the corner of 65th Street and 14th Avenue. Under the leadership of the Rev. Domenico A. Rocca, the small work outgrew its facilities of a storeroom, "overflowing at almost every meeting." The Sunday School grew to fifty children. Such enthusiastic response made the opening of another mission in the area highly desirable. Two new features were to be added: settlement work and classes in English requested by a petition signed "by a large number of young men recently come from Italy." By 1908, one hundred and twenty families, with two hundred baptized persons, formed the new parish. Discouraged by the lack of diocesan support the former missionary left, his work being taken by the Rev. Hubert Filosa.

Regularly established parishes in Brooklyn, in spite of the changing complexity of neighborhoods, seemed to thrive. St. Mary's had increased its membership to 1,200; St. Ann's to 1,485; St. Peter's to over a thousand and Holy Trinity to 1,200. In the outer areas, St. Thomas', Bushwick, led the churches with 1,400 members and a Sunday School of 1,000. Isolated in their white Anglo-Saxon neighborhoods, they tended to ignore or brush off the rapidly changing population. Yet they could not resist the changing tide of foreign-born. St. Ann's Church first sensed the impending crisis. Although situated in the protected area of the Heights, it still felt the threat. As early as 1886 a change became noticeable, but not great.

> The new problem . . . was the adjustment of the parish to new neighborhood conditions. Many of the old families had died out or moved away. The floating population that took their places had not the same loyalty.

As distant a parish as Redeemer, Fourth Avenue, felt the same pressures.

> The construction of the subway not only entailed damage to the property which involved the parish in heavy debt, but it completely altered the personnel of the neighborhood. Business began to encroach and old residences gave way to boarding and rooming houses. Generous supporters moved away and their places were not filled.

The church could not be kept open safely so that a small chapel, accommodating five to ten people was built to be used by the passerby.

A pervading uneasiness manifested in the shifting of locations and jockeying for better locations. Churches seized upon possible better sites, sometimes too close to other established churches, sometimes hoping to draw upon the better neighborhoods. Some churches closed, forced out by their inability to minister to the foreign-born: St. Margaret's Mission in Red Hook; Church of Our Savior in South Brooklyn, almost forty years old; Church of the Advent, Bath Beach, property sold and held in trust; St. Jude's Mission and Calvary Church, located in the heart of a populous area. Calvary sold its property to a Y.M.C.A. which certainly commented on its defeat. It bought St. Barnabas' in a less crowded section. Church of the Nativity moved to a new site as did St. John's, Parkville, which finally located at Ocean Avenue. Christ Church, Bay Ridge, sold some of its property to the Brooklyn Rapid Transit Company. St. Matthew's, an established parish since 1859, experienced grave difficulty surrounded by Roman Catholics and Jews. Its isolation rested in an amalgamation with Church of the Epiphany. Many parishes like St. Mark's, Brooklyn, had to draw upon their reserves by selling property and real estate holdings as far away as Minnesota. Even in the Queens-Brooklyn area some parishes had to re-locate. The pressure of changing clientele made city parishes move out and thereby pressure already small established parishes. Annunication, Glendale was forced to sell and the money was used for new mission work in Metropolitan District, Queens.

The rest of the borough contrasted sharply to the patchwork of peoples enmeshed in the highly concentrated urban area. Flatlands, Gravesend and Lower New Utrecht seemed almost bucolic and rural. Communities nearest the outer edge of the concentrated area did develop as an extension of the city, but less populated and more desirable. Bay Ridge and Flatbush developed into thriving suburban communities near enough to the dynamic borough center, but far enough away to offer the commuter a place of rest and refreshment. At the extreme eastern section, in East New York, life became so expansive that one of the Episcopal missions did develop to build and work. An especial significance attached to the mission, for it came about at the instigation of, and as a result of, the interest of the first Bishop. The Church of Transfiguration became a memorial to his episcopate.

Remembrance of Things Past —

The memory of Bishop Littlejohn did not die easily in the Diocese. Thirty-three years of devoted service, even in the midst of pain and illness, could not be easily forgotten, nor did the second Bishop or the people wish to forget. Reflections upon his lingering image filled the Diocese and received constant reiteration. To erect a suitable memorial to Bishop Littlejohn, a memorial fund was begun. Among his many interests the first Bishop had concentrated upon mission-building, and more especially upon the Church of the Transfiguration in Brooklyn. The small mission had its start in September 1894, meeting first in the Norwood Laundry, and then in a rented home. For nearly three years the services were continued there, until in 1897, the Archdeacon authorized the purchase of the Fulton Street Baptist Chapel for full use. The church showed little progress, even with the Bishop's interest and support by "a considerable sum of his money to its advancement." A generous gift by an anonymous donor gave the congregation sufficient funds to buy property and erect a church at Ridgewood and Railroad (Autumn) Avenues. At the groundbreaking ceremony, the Archdeacon made known that "when the proposed new church was completed it would be called the Littlejohn Memorial Church, to commemorate the great interest taken in the congregation by the late Bishop of the Long Island Diocese, by whom it was started." On September 29, 1906, after able leadership and prosperous conditions, Bishop Burgess consecrated the new structure. All-day ceremonies included a eulogy by the second Bishop that clearly showed the tremendous impact made by his predecessor on the life of the whole church. The new church was in line with "advanced" ideas and would have "a club house attachment."

In a very real sense, the lasting memorial to Bishop Littlejohn was the Cathedral in Garden City. To its erection he gave many years of tireless energy, experiencing no little share of frustration, alarm and abuse. The Diocese, in 1908, formalized this sentiment in a resolution that pledged itself "to erect at no distant day in this Cathedral, over which his (the first Bishop) soul agonized for years, a fitting Pulpit as a worthy monument to his learning, devotion, courage and genius." The idea of a pulpit did not materialize. In its place the next year, as a tribute to Bishop Littlejohn, a memorial bust, gift of one of his daughters and encased in an appropriate setting, was affixed to the wall near the baptistery. The wisdom of the final remembrance could not be doubted, for most of all, the bapistery was the work of Bishop Littlejohn.

CITY EXTENSION — QUEENS AND NASSAU.

The City extended itself outward in a thrust eastward. What was once large farms with infrequent homes and houses had given place to villages and towns, extending from Jamaica to Garden City as almost one continuous urban region. Many city dwellers, forced out by the tumerous growth of people, sought more healthful surroundings, escaping the press of the city for better light and cleaner air. Abetted by new and more rapid transit facilities in his search, the home seeker settled more and more along the path of the many Long Island Railroad branches. Very much a single-dwelling area, Queens County and Western Nassau, presented a different picture than had been the case even ten years previously. The city concentration in Queens was in the extreme western section, just across the East River from Manhattan.

The many changes about Steinway (Astoria) and Long Island City, the coming of a large foreign element, the new terminal and railroad yards and bridges,

stated the Missionary Committee,

have made many changes among the residents and attendance in the parish of Ravenswood, the mission of Dutch Kills, and Steinway, but it is a temporary and necessary condition, and the completion of the bridge will bring it, it is hoped, a new congregation and many families for these missions, and a better permanence to those already there.

Marked contrasts could be seen within the confines of the two counties. Highly concentrated areas seemed incongruous to open towns and small villages that dotted wooded shore or marked the open plain. No community reached the density of population of western Queens; most of the Island communities numbered from 150 to 2,000 people.

Nassau and Suffolk, the land of the clam-digger, enjoyed a large but transient summer population. Oyster Bay, attractive to the Roosevelts and Beekmans, had only a little over 2,000 people; Glen Cove, a city in its own right, had its well-known personalities such as Charles A. Dana of *The New York Sun*, J. P. Morgan and the Pratt family, but only a small percentage of the population consisted of permanent residents. As one progressed deeper into Suffolk, the temporal character became even more evident. Extensive uninhabited areas were relieved by a few communities, but more by the summer homes, substantial in size, although transient in character. As far out as Mattituck and Greenport, summer hotels thrived during the busy, hot summer months. The Hamptons had come alive due to the discovery by the rich of an exclusive recreation haven. Although many came to enjoy the summer breezes, the refreshing surf and the adventurous fishing, few remained to take up a permanent residence.

The playground atmosphere of the Island was enhanced by new and exciting additions. Near the city line a vast new playground had opened to attract up to 40,000 spectators. On May 4, 1905, Belmont Race Track opened its gates. The "marvel of bigness" attracted even at its early stage, a variety of people. "At such an early date 235 foreign and 314 American cars arrived for the gala occasion. Alongside the Mercedes, Packards and Fiats were the Pope-Toledos, Locomobiles, Cadillacs and even eight Fords."

A competitor to the new racetrack was the Vanderbilt Cup Race. The auto, still a toy for the more affluent, surprisingly had changed Long Island very little. Roads were still carriage trails, sometimes macadam, sometimes just ordinary dirt highways with oil to keep the dust down. Williams K. Vanderbilt, Jr. conceived the idea of using the Long Island roads for his road races. A course 250 to 300 miles long was laid out. Beginning at Jericho Turnpike in Westbury, the course went east to Jericho, south to Plainedge and then through Hempstead to Queens, then back east on Jericho through Floral Park to Westbury. Contestants "slowed down, through the large towns; three minutes through Hicksville and six minutes through Hempstead." The races, beginning in 1904, drew large crowds of spectators coming on foot, bicycle, horseback, buggies or even an occasional car. Hazardous to drivers and pedestrians, the Vanderbilt Cup Race was one of the original influences toward the building of paved roads for the use of automobiles. Because of a resulting protest, Vanderbilt conceived the idea of a motor parkway to afford a better and safer course. A corporation was formed in 1906, and a course laid out beginning in Queens County, going through Nassau into Suffolk, passing through Islip and going as far out as Ronkonkoma. Not completed until 1914, parts of the course were used as early as 1908.

In Queens and Nassau a strong missionary spirit pervaded Diocesan work. The Cathedral had eleven well-organized missions, one of which, Epiphany in Ozone Park, became a parish; the remainder were under the Archdeacon. The Archdeacon, the Rev. Canon Henry B. Bryan gave the large field full supervision, with earnestness, faithfulness and ability. The Church had met the rapidly increasing population by occupying many commanding places. Some mistakes had been made in premature building and in overloading missions with heavy financial obligations, resulting from eager persons desiring to acquire handsome property and to pledge steady support. On the resignation of Canon Bryan to take charge of work in the Panama Canal Zone, the Rev. Henry Mesier, Rector of St. John's Church, Far Rockaway, was elected with the Bishop's approval.

Much of the Archdeacon's time was taken up in preaching at the larger churches on Sundays to solicit funds. Gradually the Archdeacon was relieved from fund raising, thereby leaving him more time to concentrate his efforts on his own parish and to give real and careful oversight to all the missionary stations. Parishes guaranteed a definite amount for church extension, augmented by a special offering at the time of the Missionary Rallies. One such rally was held in Grace Church, Jamaica, on January 27, 1904. Continuing all day, the assembled group heard addresses by Bishop Burgess, the Bishop of Spokane, the Bishop of Georgia and the Archdeacon.

In the seven years from 1901-1908, under the two Archdeacons, new work had been started at nine different places. Among the more promising locations were Lynbrook, where in a few years the rented chapel was filled and a priest-in-charge assigned; Roosevelt where the congregation worshipped in a small house with low ceilings; Arverne where the local Congregational Church was purchased; and at North Corona. Three of the new works were devoted to work among the Blacks.

Parishes in the Archdeaconry had been active and ready to meet the new people who arrived in increasing numbers. Manhasset's mission, St. Stephen's, Port Washington, had grown so that it became independent in 1906. The parishes of Far Rockaway and Hewlett established a mission at Cedarhurst in 1907. The older more established parishes sought additional funds to enhance their work. Grace Church, Jamaica, sold their city holdings at 68 Trinity Place, harking back to the post-revolutionary period, to start an endowment fund. St. George's, Flushing, mortgaged its Trinity Church grant of 1790 to erect additional parish buildings. Perhaps no Nassau church received more public attention than Christ Church, Oyster Bay, which had as its most prominent worshipper, the President of the United States. Theodore Roosevelt, a member of the Dutch Reformed Church and never an Episcopal communicant, attended services there with his family. A familiar figure, "Sunday mornings he often drove to Christ Church to sit in the fourth pew," and at the bicentennial of the parish in 1906, "the main address was delivered by President Theodore Roosevelt, who spoke from the chancel aisle on the text 'What Doth the Lord Thy God Require of Thee'."

COUNTRY COUSIN: THE ARCHDEACONRY OF SUFFOLK

A busy Rector, The Rev. William Holden of St. James Church, St. James, administered the affairs of the church with sound judgment and faithfulness. In all the substantial communities the Episcopal Church had been hard at work: at Bellport, Port Jefferson and in the center of the Island at Central Islip, Ronkonkoma and Brentwood. The parish at Shelter Island, conducted as a mission, had revived its old charter and took its place as an incorporated parish. The most remarkable piece of work begun in this period was St. Luke's in East Hampton. A few weeks after Frederick Burgess became Bishop attention was focused on East Hampton as a place "where a far more aggressive work could be undertaken," and with this in mind the Bishop took the services there for a season. The hope of having more than a summer chapel found realization in the work that interested church people. Regular services throughout the year were instituted, "a resident clergyman was appointed as Priest-in-Charge, more land was purchased at a high price," and by 1909 East Hampton had become an incorporated parish with a rector and assistant who together took care of a very great area and cared for the missions at Amagansett, Freetown and Bridgehampton. The mission at Bridgehampton was made possible in 1906 by a gift of land from a generous churchwoman whose family had long been residents in the township. Services throughout the year were established at once. The danger of "having chapels where the well-to-do families who came to enjoy the cool breezes and the happy outdoor life in these attractive old villages of Long Island may go to worship after the beautiful forms of the Prayer Book," was that they had "very little effect on the [permanent] residents of the place." Occasional visits by young people "attracted for a few weeks" did not ensure continuity on the part of the worshipper for "at the end of that time they must either go back to sectarian forms of worship or lapse into indifference." No depth on the part of the community existed since "the teaching power of the Church [was] weakened unless [it could] be carried on through the whole ritual year." Summer chapels did flourish at Quogue, Westhampton and Southampton, with a parish for Indians, Blacks and Whites, with union services at Freetown. A new work of permanence began in East Hauppauge. In 1905, the Archdeacon established St. Boniface's Mission, especially designed to meet the needs of the large German settlement there.

Outside of the nine missions and one aided parish under diocesan control, Suffolk had in its large area only eleven other parishes. Unable to overcome an aversion to Episcopalian ways, unsuited to the New England staid and austere spirit that pervaded the eastern end of the Island, the Episcopal Church was deterred in deepening church roots. In all missions and churches only a little over 2,400 communicants could be accumulated. Over a thousand children attended Sunday Schools, but no church could really boast substantial financial gains. Only St. Mark's, Islip, achieved some sound finances, but others declined to only a few hundred dollars total yearly income. Even men of substance and leadership, such as E. Clowes Chorley, Rector of Emmanuel, Great River, future well-known church historian, could not effect or arouse much enthusiasm for the Episcopal way of life.

THE QUEST FOR SOCIAL JUSTICE

For the Episcopal Church, like its other contemporary religious bodies, the years following 1900 fairly bristled with social problems. The immense tide of immigrants flooding the metropolitan area, the extraordinary mobility of population, the difficulty of financing new or existing churches, hospitals, schools and other similar projects in a period of rapid growth, created situations which taxed the enthusiasm and skill of leadership to its utmost. In meeting the new problems that emerged, the Church displayed resourcefulness and vitality. Like so many of the other churches, the Long Island Church turned its attention to the role of the church in the new society. Religious activities and energies were channelled in new and unique ways, both social and political, while the Church continued to maintain its existing charitable institutions and relief organizations so typical of the nineteenth century.

WORKS OF CHARITY.

Charitable efforts did not prosper too well in the new age. No new agency or institution appeared; rather the work required all the inventiveness and skill of the constituent parishes to maintain it as it was. The multitude of institutions included the least known of diocesan institutions, the Sheltering Arms Nursery, which took care of abandoned and destitute children, and St. Giles Home for Crippled Children.

Unfortunately St. Giles Home, located in a very congested area, was forced to abandon its building, condemned by the civil authorities. Fortunately, a summer residence for the home had been secured near Garden City, which having opened in November 1903, housed both city and country activities. The diocesan church settlement house, St. Phebe's, ably continued its ministrations to the inmates of the county institutions, city jails, homes and hospitals, "for the social uplift of all kinds and conditions of persons." Convalescent poor, discharged from public hospitals were taken in until able to return to home. Social service activities included a kindergarten, a "kitchengarten", industrial classes for boys and girls, a club for girls, meetings for mothers, a library and a branch of the Penny Provident Fund. During the summer months, St. Phebe's did "fresh-air work" operating a summer vacation house, All Souls Cottage at Massapequa, where one hundred and twenty four beneficiaries were entertained, and where whole families enjoyed the summer retreat for periods varying from one to four weeks. The various institutions of the Church Charity Foundation carried on, under increasingly difficult conditions, with an increasing number of patients and inmates each year. Sadly, a long standing service, the *Orphans' Press*, had to stop operations because of the increasing competition from commerical companies.

The church's role in the new society shifted from institutional building to active participation in the campaign for social reform. Still maintaining its numerous philanthropic agencies, first in the city and then in all types of communities, the Church interested itself in social and benevolent works, extending its activities to include the physical and intellectual, as well as the spiritual. The latter quarter of the nineteenth century had seen the establishment of the institutional church, with its numerous charities, paid welfare workers and athletic clubs. In the first ten years of the twentieth century the institutional church craze reached its height, with every church, large or small, attempting through a building to achieve some kind of community identity.

The institutional church fad had its greatest play in the Episcopal Church during the first decade, 1900-1910. Varying sizes, shapes, purposes and methods characterized the church's wedge in community relations, dependent upon the affluence of the parish. The dominant parish, Church of the Holy Trinity on the Heights, could well afford its full program of community activities. Its huge parish hall became a social center, adapting to changing neighborhood conditions by the renovation of its assembly room into a gymnasium with showers in the basement, and the transformation of the third floor into furnished club rooms. A paid director supervised its athletic program. The wealthy George Foster Peabody helped by buying two additional brownstones, one for women's work, the other for men who worked in the church's social program and for a center of men's activities. A summer adjunct, Holiday House in Brookhaven, accommodated working women and girls for short rest periods during the summer vacation.

Suburban churches got on the parish hall bandwagon and joined in the rush of building new or renovating old parish halls. St. George's Church, Hempstead, completed its parish hall in 1905, "a happy place for old and young." Plays were given, clubs formed, bowling contests organized. In order to implement better its social involvement, the church built in a few more years a new gymnasium, including a swimming pool and basketball court. "The thunder from the bowling alleys, the whirl of the Indian Clubs and the click of the pool balls were most alluring and cast their spell on the entire village." Such efforts were duplicated all over the Island, no church being too small to hope for a community center. St. Matthias' (Emmanuel) Church, Sheepshead Bay, built a parish hall that included a main auditorium, a Sunday School room and a "ladies parlor".

No more pretentious or ambitious attempt at parish social identity was found than the parish hall of Christ Church, Bedford Avenue. The church proposed a five story brownstone in pure Georgian style that included modern accommodations for the Sunday School, women's work, men's work, for a gymnasium, for a kitchen, and a fifth floor apartment.

St. Peter's club room.

The intense interest in parish houses had so engrossed church leaders that in planning a new church, the first consideration envisaged a parish community hall as the initial building to be built, the church to follow after. Concerned about the widespread mania, the Bishop felt compelled to speak out. Acknowledging the prevalent philosophy that such a hall had the advantages of housing, entertainment, money-raising functions, and of "keeping young people off the streets and young men out of saloons," the Bishop felt that sometimes the disadvantages outweighed the advantages. Setting down priorities, he made it clear that the primary function of the parish hall was not to afford recreational activities for the neighborhood but of assisting the Sunday School, charitable and missionary work and of accommodating meetings of various parish groups. The perils of entertainment and money-raising affairs had become "almost humiliating." Fairs, dances, theater shows, suppers, cake sales, all sounded incongruous amid church announcements. A moral issue was involved. Nothing to impair the morals of a minor could or should be done. Money-raising had an importance, but had to be done in an honest way. No gambling should be allowed since it was very possible that a young man's "first lesson in gambling in his boyhood might be at a church fair." The Bishop did not have to be too alarmed. The parish hall fad declined after 1915; it had failed to produce anticipated results. The fun of the gym did not encourage many to cross the threshold of the church. Churches had become disillusioned; yet the movement had produced some good results. The church had pioneered in the community-center frontier just as it had in hospitals, libraries, theaters

116

and schools. The back door to church had afforded a certain amount of fun and fellowship. However, in an age of hoped-for church enlargement, the parish hall had not materialized its effectiveness.

NEVER ON SUNDAY

A perplexing problem, growing out of the temperance issue, the "due observance of Sunday," confronted the church constantly. Changing conditions and new factors in urban life had made the subject a growing issue. Beginning with the dissipation of Sunday in the nineteenth century, the tension between the old puritanical concept and the new continental observance had grown to such a point that churchmen had become alarmed at the degenerating influence on the Lord's day of peace, quiet and prayer. The change had been accomplished partly through the increasing presence of Non-Protestant immigrants and through the swelling population of 70,000 Jews. The dominant group had attempted to protect Sunday by having legislated morality in a full complement of "blue laws". Purporting to protect the sanctity of Sunday, the laws had been effectively loaded with impunity. The issue had been heightened on Long Island which had become "the playground of the greatest city in the Union." An abundance of race tracks, the prize of which was Belmont Race Track "within the sound of the Cathedral chimes," afforded sports enthusiasts the excitement of the turf. Golf links, ball fields, shooting clubs, fishing clubs and hunting clubs, lured the eager recreants. Fast weekends and house parties in the summer homes of the affluent compounded the danger. A new and exciting threat to Sunday was the Vanderbilt Cup Race which drew Sunday crowds, especially during church hours.

The enticement of the various pleasure-domes was enhanced and abetted by two long-standing evils: the theater and the saloon. The peril became magnified as one observer noted:

> Saloons are practically open all day long; theatrical entertainments go on with the knowledge
> of the police every Sunday evening, and fifteen thousand people witness ball games on
> Sunday, where a programme is sold instead of an entrance ticket.

Increasing protests had resulted in a noticeable curtailment of Sunday theaters. Cooperative action on the parts of the Diocese of New York and Long Island, together with the Brooklyn Central Labor Union, the Actors Church Alliance and the Ministerial Committee of Greater New York, had closed eleven out of sixteen illegal Sunday performances in Brooklyn. The demand for law enforcement had enabled the police and courts to give the "will of the people" more effective service. A distinct gain had been effected by "the securing of a decision by a Supreme Court Judge that the moving-picture exhibitions which, charging but a small admission fee [had] a very widespread demoralizing and immoral influence among the young on Sundays and was contrary to law."

Recognition that the issue had two sides to it made the Bishop speak his mind. Concern for the poor laboring classes made the Diocese consider the advantages as well as disadvantages. Those who sought humbler amusements,

> confined all the week in dismal city offices or shops, bound to the bench, perhaps to stitch,
> stitch, stitch through the long hours of the day, or condemned to do the same tiresome
> brainless work from early morning to late at night,

did have a certain right to "wholesome excitement or healthful exercise." But it was not the poor workers search for pleasure, but the commercialized pleasures preying upon the poor, that outweighed the opportunity for relaxation. Such law-evasions as Sunday theaters made a mockery of Sunday. Bishop Burgess felt so strongly that he wrote a prayer "for the suppression of the Sunday theaters" which he authorized to be read in all the churches.

SOCIAL OUTREACH

Responding to the Bishop's urgent exhortation of 1903 for social justice, the Diocese initiated a movement to better relate to the growing social evils of the city and the nation. An investigating committee had been appointed in 1904. In 1905, the Social Service Committee, the first of its kind in the whole church, received canonical approval and began its work. The first decided change in the official attitude of the church towards social reform occurred in its attitude to the labor movement. Up to this time the church had aligned itself with management, maintaining an aloofness or a condescending approval to the oppressive conditions of the working class. It did not seem at all to matter that workers suffered long hours at small pay, that for working sixty or seventy hours a week, the average wage was five or six dollars. The church seemed to accept as normal child labor, accident hazards, congested living quarters and unsanitary conditions. No wonder the laboring class looked upon the church as the ally of capital, as the oppressor of the working class. In 1905, the Diocese sent a "fraternal delegate", the Rev. J. Howard Melish, to the Brooklyn Central Labor Union "for the purpose of informing ourselves concerning their work and of endeavoring to remove mutual distrust between Capital and Labor."

Another involvement in the new society provided a probation officer to work with young people convicted of their offenses and released on parole. The State Legislature had in 1904, by two acts, established children's courts in Manhattan and in Brooklyn. The Jews already had a lady to work with the youthful offenders, and so did the Roman Catholics. Since the State did not have funds for such workers, volunteer societies had to provide for probationary officers. The Diocese, through the Social Service Committee, obtained the services of a young lawyer who served two days in that capacity. He soon found enough to do and the reports of the Committee showed the decided affect he had upon the courts, the young people and the Church.

A growing concern for the social well-being of young people made the Diocese move into the sphere of delinquent girls and social purity. There was at that time only one "proper reformatory treatment for girls." No institution existed for helping delinquent and immoral girls under sixteen years of age. The Brooklyn Society for the Prevention of Cruelty to Children referred the problem to the Diocese which at once set in motion the investigation of it supplying such a home for girls.

Just as pressing and more widespread was the need for sex education:

> The overcrowding of tenements and the lack of moral or religious instruction on the duties of the sex life, together with the inability of some young women to earn an honest livelihood are producing alarmingly serious conditions of sex immorality and the social evil, with their attendant physical, mental and moral degeneration.

To combat the growing danger the Committee recommended that a frank discussion with young people, judiciously separate, be undertaken. They urged "that parents, guardians, teachers, physicians and pastors be awakened to the need of individual instruction for the young on the duties of the sex life, and that some way be devised of assisting parents that desire to be informed as to the best method of thus instructing their children."

The Diocese struck out into the areas of political power, race track gambling and Sunday observance. Most appealing was their treatment of the temperance question. Their recommendations were:

1. Something might be done to encourage various substitutes for the saloon, as low priced restaurants, lunch carts, coffee houses, temperance hotels, and working men's clubs, especially encouraging the provision of halls to be rented to labor associations which are now practically compelled to rent halls connected with liquor saloons.
2. We recommend the recent action of the Borough of Brooklyn by which public comfort stations have been established near the Borough Hall and elsewhere and recommend that the number of these stations be increased, extending them to all parts of the city . . . "

The Committee also tried to assist the laborers by securing "provision for securing twenty-four hour consecutive rest each week for employees." They also recommended that every local clergyman form a similar relationship with some local union, "and express in his public speaking an interest in labor and an intelligent sympathy with its problems and efforts — the gulf between the church and the toilers will then cease to exist." In addition, the Committee recommended "as the most helpful method of restoring political power to the people" the direct nomination of party candidates such as in Wisconsin, Massachusetts and Minnesota. Such primaries reduced the power of party managers.

BLACK EQUALITY

For many years the Diocese maintained one lonely church for the large Black population in Brooklyn. St. Augustine's Church, initiated in 1875, had struggled against great odds to firmly establish an Episcopal parish. Due to the creative energy of the Blacks themselves, the parish grew into a thriving operation, became incorporated by 1890, and accepted into union with the Diocese. Recruited at first from West Indian immigrants, who wanted the ministrations of their mother church, the church encompassed all kinds and classes within the Black community. The "separate but equal" parish reflected the current viewpoint that made such an incongruity possible.

Long Island churchmen, like so many of the nation, had accepted the prevalent theory of the superiority of the white Anglo-Saxon "race". Prominent men, both in secular and religious life, had swallowed whole the attitude of Herbert Spencer and Social Darwinism. An interesting, if not oblique, manifestation of the white race theory was the Anglo-Israel Movement which clearly understood that God's chosen people were the Anglo-Saxons, commissioned especially to redeem the world. Spawned in Great Britain, the movement spread to America after 1880, with the Missionary of the gospel of Anglo-Israelism, who made a speaking tour in the various States. On one of his conversion stops he preached at Garden City, where, as he reported in a letter to a friend:

> I have now held eight drawing-room meetings and delivered five lectures. At one I converted Bishop Littlejohn and Dr. Dro(w)ne. . . .

This complacent and assured attitude colored Protestant opposition to the Roman Catholic Church, to the immigrant peoples, and to the laboring classes. Most of all it became clear in the attitude to the Black, lacking any real perception of the Black as a human being with the same potentiality for advancement.

The Episcopal Church only followed the lead of the nation. Even though some attempts had been made to give the Blacks full rights, by 1883 the matter had been almost settled by the Supreme Court decision declaring the Civil Rights Bill of 1875 unconstitutional. In 1896, the Supreme Court in the case of Plessy v. Ferguson, approved "separate but equal" facilities: segregation had become an accepted fact of life. The conclusion for the

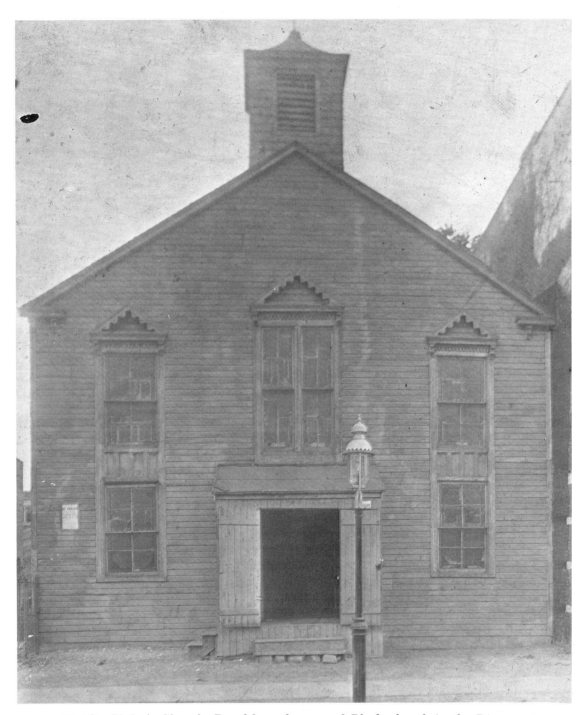

Old St. Philip's Church, Brooklyn, the second Black church in the Diocese.

superior race was that the failure of reconstruction, the low educational status of the Black, his high crime, disease and poverty rate, were simply the result of heredity. The acceptance of the Black man as inferior and incorrigeable resulted.

Pathetic was the Black's acceptance of his low estate. So beaten down and humiliated, he openly accepted his low place in society and attempted to work within this framework of reference. At a missionary meeting in the Diocese, the chief speaker of the day was "the colored missionary" who worked "so faithfully among the colored people of Long Island." Speaking to the 1903 convocation, he enumerated the scope of his work, acknowledging "improper and unsanitary conditions" which gave the impression of living "on a desert not an isle and that a soap factory one thousand miles away." Most telling was the open admission that the Blacks may have had the same appetites and desires, "although he may not have the same discretion of the white man."

Amid the claque of civilization, humanity and advancing races, a few enlightened men did try to overcome the barrier between black and white. Yet they themselves were caught in a kind of intellectual acceptance;

pragmatic President Theodore Roosevelt could graciously invite Booker T. Washington to the White House, yet in his private letters admit the inferiority of the Blacks and the grievous mistake he made in the invitation.

The same perversity and confusion clouded the mind of the President's good friend, Bishop Burgess. He could unequivocally speak out for Black rights and equality, yet he could at the same time prolong the myth by appointing a separate missionary to establish Black churches.

The whole issue presented itself dramatically to the National Church in the new century. As early as 1869, the Episcopal Church had been confronted by the burning question when the Diocese of Virginia refused a Black church full parish status in the Convention. Their avoidance of the issue, shown in the "taking under its wing" attitude also, became a part of Diocesan Convention action. A memorial by a group of interested churchworkers, in which they stated that "the present organization of our church [was] inadequate for the work of evangelizing the colored people." Dioceses throughout the nation were asked for their opinions and the issue became Long Island's dilemma.

All the current superiority complex came into full play; all the reasons for separate Black Bishops, for Black churches were vented; all the inherent prejudices made the scene. The white man's burden became clear as report after report was made.

The matter simmered well into the twentieth century. A solution offered was for a separate episcopate for the Blacks. Old fears came into play. A few Blacks in a white church were acceptable, but as their numbers increased, and too their voting power, "it was felt that such colored vote could easily hold the balance of power," and in an important matter such as the election of a Bishop, determine the results. Several voices of dissent cried out in the wilderness but were unheard. Fortunately, when the matter was discussed at the General Convention of 1907, a wise decision was made. Race was discarded and the Church provided for Suffragan Bishops without the right of succession. The issue had been resolved, but the prejudice continued on.

Disparity between black and white had heightened in regard to the first Black church. In spite of a healthy existence, the Black congregation still had no permanent church building. The appalling fact emphasized the superior attitude that it was better to live from rental pillar to donated post, than to allow the inferior to run their own affairs. They were considered incapable of owning or administering their own property. It was true that an enlightened churchman had purchased a building for their use, but the title to the property had never been turned over to them. Living off the "goodness" of the landlord, St. Augustine's plight became almost a scandal in the Diocese. Sentiment such as that expressed in the Diocesan magazine the *Helping Hand* clearly summed up the impossibility of the situation. The magazine editorialized:

> It almost seems a cause of wonder that in this great City of Brooklyn with all its wealth and
> with only two colored churches to support, that one of those congregations should be allowed
> so long a time to have no place of worship of its own. It may be we give to the colored work
> in the South, but surely that at home ought to receive our generous support.

Perhaps in answer to this plea, in 1906 the Black church received its property, but in name only. The renovated building was turned over to the Diocese "in trust for the Rector, Church Wardens and Vestrymen of said Church . . . subject to certain conditions recited in the deed."

The second Black church had begun as an answer to the expanding Black population in Brooklyn. Several Blacks had been attending regularly the white church, St. Timothy's on Howard Avenue. In a meeting of some interested churchmen and the Blacks, "the need for another Protestant Episcopal Church in uptown Brooklyn, was expressed" and services began in a vacant store on May 14, 1899. The congregation grew so large that by the end of the year a bigger building was necessary. Largely through the efforts of "one generous woman whose heart [was] deeply stirred by the pathetic appeal of the Black race," an empty Baptist Church was purchased and made suitable for services. The response was so great that a full time clergyman, the Rev. Nathaniel P. Boyd was appointed. The parochial mission became a Diocesan mission in 1904. St. Philip's Church emerged a well-grounded fully active Episcopal parish, the first in many ventures. The first charter for a Black chapter of the Brotherhood of St. Andrew was issued in 1903. The first Black branch in all the country of the Girls Friendly Society began in 1907. And when the parish hall and rectory were built, they had the distinction of being the first to be erected for Blacks on all Long Island. A third Black church joined the Church's ministry to this group. St. Barnabas' Mission, begun in 1907 in an East New York store, had "a handful of colored people" who paid regularly the "$60.00 a month toward the support of their clergyman and the services of the Church."

Not as great, but equally as compelling, was the crying need for the Church to minister to the almost 7,000 Blacks that had taken up residence in Queens and Nassau. Responding to the challenge, the Bishop appointed in 1902 the Rev. Henry S. McDuffey, a southern clergyman, to take up special work in the two counties. A house in Jamaica was purchased to serve as his base of operation and his home. In addition to the already existing Black work at North Bellmore, where a church had been erected as a memorial to a son who took a great interest in Black work, three new missions were undertaken for the Blacks. In Astoria, All Soul's Church began. In Jamaica, work was begun with the establishment of St. Stephen's Church. And in Hempstead "a mission for colored people" was first held in Liberty Hall. The mission made a great contribution to the Black population, the congregation including "the worthiest colored people of Hempstead." The Rev. Henry S. McDuffey was succeeded by a new Black missionary in 1906.

Chapter Ten

Between Two Worlds

The end of the first decade seemed a pleasant time in which to live. Many of the promises of 1900 had come to pass. War seemed far away. The Spanish American War was well over ten years in the past, and the country lived at peace. An era of gracious living pervaded the land. It was a time for social affairs, for concerts, for lectures; a time to enjoy all the modern conveniences of the day. A Long Islander by choice, President Theodore Roosevelt reigned supreme in the expanding American nation. Charles Evans Hughes made history as Governor of New York State; and George B. McClellan showed the popularity of his New York Mayoralty by being elected for a sixth year by almost five million residents of Greater New York.

It was a time for new ideas, men and organizations. The Federal Bureau of Investigation had been founded. The first commercial radio station was in operation at San Jose, California, and Arturo Toscanini had made his debut as a conductor at the Metropolitan Opera House. During the long evenings, made longer by the increasing installation of electric light, families finished their favorite newspapers, which numbered among them *The New York Times, The New York Tribune, The Evening Sun*, and of course, *The Brooklyn Daily Eagle*. After such fare, they lost themselves in the latest mystery thriller, *The Circular Staircase* by Mary Roberts Rhinehart, or in a more quaintly casual way enjoyed John Fox's *Trail of the Lonesome Pine*. The young people could be found grouped around the piano, singing the latest hit from the Ziegfeld Follies, "Shine on Harvest Moon" or "Take Me Out to the Ballgame."

On an evening, seventy-five theaters in the Times Square district enticed the average theater-goer to an offering of brilliant and distinguished actors and actresses. Crowds on Broadway, with women wearing sheath-dresses and huge hats draped in flowers or dotted veils, flocked to see the latest hit by George M. Cohan or Victor Herbert. Of an afternoon, the crowds would gather to witness the Vanderbilt Cup Race, where in spite of bad weather or muddy roads, a speed of 64.3 miles per hour broke all previous records. New vistas of leisure entertainment opened for every American. The more affluent enjoyed golf, boating and other sports, while the less fortunate were only a subway or trolley ride from Coney Island. It did seem as if good times had come to stay.

ISLAND BUT NOT INSULA

Long Island had been lulled into the same self-satisfied complacency. The good life pervaded tiny suburbs as well as staccato city life. A swelling population had compacted the urban areas and had erupted into the Island woodlands and farmlands. Long Island still presented a startling contrast between tiny town and towering city, but the gap seemed to close more and more. The long line of the city, stretching out into lush Nassau, made the scattering isolated homes become more of a solid block. Nowhere on the Island did the picture become so obvious than in Queens County.

From the time of consolidation with New York City, Queens had grown not only from the standpoint of population, but of industry. Even in 1909, the Borough of Queens, considered a city by itself, exceeded every other city except fourteen in annual value of its manufactured products. The United States census of 1909 showed that Queens County had 771 factories employing almost twenty-four thousand men and women turning out a manufactured product for that year valued at $150,000,000.

> The period from 1910 to 1924 might properly be called the "Construction Period" in the history of the development of Queens County, for during that time there have been constructed new bridges, highways, tunnels, rapid transit extensions, hundreds of industrial plants and thousands of homes of every description, the total of which exceeds half a billion dollars.

Nassau County, although experiencing a decided growth could not keep up with Queens. Suffolk still lagged far behind, and except for the sudden ripple of summer influx, retained its quiet, sleepy, bucolic atmosphere. It was, in reality, the start of the heyday of Queens, that would reach proportions threatening to the Island's Brooklyn center.

Although the Diocese of Long Island may not have kept pace with its Island constituencies, it nevertheless presented an imposing image to the rest of the National Church. By 1909, the Diocese ranked fifth among all the dioceses. Even with a strict policy of conservation and of custodial maintenance, membership and activity had expanded so much so that rumor and talk circulated to the effect that the Diocese should be sub-divided. Encouraged by a National Church law that authorized the division of larger dioceses and the formation of new Church units, Long Island Episcopalians toyed with the idea of making Long Island two dioceses. The divisive spirit did not muster too much support. The Bishop himself did not look with favor upon the projected segmentation. In 1909, speaking to the assembled Convention, he acknowledged the rank of the Diocese in the National Church, but for him this did not mean division. "Let me say quite frankly," emphasized the Bishop, "that I think Diocesan divisions have, in most cases, been carried quite far enough. Division invariably brings with it financial weakness and strain." He concluded: "The Diocese of Long Island seems to be peculiarly well built for unity." The compact Island surrounded by its natural boundary of water "has the glorious opportunity of rising to the task of spreading the influence of the Church into every borough and town and village within its borders." The Island may have been unified by its natural boundaries; the insular Church body had its own problem of unity.

THE ENIGMA OF UNITY

An unflagging search for unity dogged the uneven path of diocesan growth. In a very real sense, by the time of Bishop Burgess, the Diocese had achieved some kind of self-identity. Parochialism so rife in its early days had lessened and a spirit of cooperation among the parochial units evidenced in an acceptance of diocesan jurisdiction. Sporadic support and occasional doubt about diocesan priority still colored parish participation somewhat; but on the whole constituent parishes had accepted the fact that they were the Diocese. The most striking example of this change of attitude was in the local acceptance of diocesan judgment in parish life and in a strengthening of diocesan ties.

But as the old tension subsided, a new one took its place. In the long episcopate of Bishop Littlejohn, over and over again he reiterated the organic unity of his tenure. In the last words that he spoke to the Convention, he proudly averred:

> The Ecclesiastical tone of the Diocese from the start has been conservative and moderate. We
> have had widely differing schools of thought, but these have never hardened into parties or
> factions.

The same could not be said for Bishop Burgess' episcopate. The Anglo-Catholic movement had early in its course influenced some of the Long Island Churches, but not in the proportion that it did after the turn of the century. A growing diversity in many of the Churches became most notable. Ritualism, the aftermath of the Oxford Movement, had taken hold of many parishes.

> Colored vestments, chasubles and capes, bowings and reverences to the altar, the frequent use
> of the sign of the cross, the kissing of the stole by the priest. All such things have become
> almost common among us, and the smaller the church, sometimes, the more punctiliously are
> those ritual customs observed.

Among the more blatant practices found in some churches were the reservation of the sacrament, the illegal solitary communion service, requiem masses and obligatory confession. Most notably successful of Catholic parishes was St. Paul's, Clinton Street, Brooklyn. At first, attempts were made "to establish the parish on Catholic lines, but the effort was sporadic, without definite teaching, which aroused opposition and the Church became neither Protestant or Catholic and lost its vitality."

The population had drifted away or had become disaffected, so much so that on Easter Day 1909, the sheriff seized the Easter collection for debt. Arrangements had been made to sell the church when the parish called as Rector, Andrew Chalmers Wilson, without salary. The understanding was that he be given absolute freedom to re-establish the parish on absolute Catholic dogma. Under his leadership the large parish debt was cancelled and by 1919, the congregation had increased from 25 to 500.

A tendency to liberalize the Church took shape in many other churches. In parishes that emphasized Morning and Evening Prayer, a laxity in fulfilling the established form of services, made the services suit their own personal likes or dislikes. Clergy translated the scriptures to suit their own scholarship and compiled their own services such as on Good Friday. Other aspects were the overloading of services with music and massive choirs:

> The growth of vested choirs has not been an unalloyed blessing, and one has often to be tried
> in our Churches by the undisciplined choirs, whose behavior shocks the religious sentiments of
> the congregation.

The great stress on Morning Prayer had made it the service of the day, to the detriment of the Holy Communion service. The Bishop was distressed about the growing preponderance of Morning Prayer:

> Choral Matins does not seem to be enough for the great service of Sunday, and I could wish
> that less time were spent in getting in and out of Church, and more time in reading and
> preaching of the word.

In all the extreme emphasis, commonly called "high" and "low" Church, one standard remained supreme: "The Book of Common Prayer still remains the paramount authority in matters of doctrine and worship."

During this period the Church-at-large did suffer the indignity of several trials for heresy. Anglo-Catholics still, in some ways, opposed a conciliation between biblical criticism and the accepted theology. Some Catholics agreed that a competent, critical, but revisionist study of the Bible was essential to healthy faith of the Church. Yet the faith was under attack. Some churchmen went to the other extreme by denying the Virgin Birth. The most celebrated heresy trial to come before the Church was that of Algernon S. Cropsey, the popular Rector of St. Andrew's, Rochester. Widely known as a liberal leader, advanced in social movements, and close friend of Walter Rauschenbush, Cropsey was brought to trial for denying the Virgin Birth and asserting that in all things physical Jesus was as we are. Brought to trial before the Bishop of Western New York he resigned before sentence, and died in poverty. The trial became a sensation throughout the Church and made Long Island fearful of such influence.

Pre-occupation with inner conflicts did not deter the Church from seeking some kind of union with other Christian bodies. The Church had made overtures in the past in this area, but had stood firm on the Chicago Lambeth Quadrilateral. Movements towards unity did not have the dimension of ecumenism; it largely became a Pan-Protestant venture. At the General Convention of 1904, the Joint Commission on Christian Unity was appointed and instructed to seek cooperation of other Christian bodies in matters of common interest, such as Sabbeth observance, the sanctity of marriage, and religious education. A subsequent development in 1907 was an Inter-Church Conference on Federation. Growing out of these talks, the Federal Council of Churches was organized for closer cooperation and united action in non-controversial matters. The Episcopal Church, not a member, cooperated in matters relating to social service and religious education.

Other attempts at closer Church cooperation, such as the New and Religious Forward Movement and the Missionary Conference in 1910, brought initial enthusiasm but little lasting effect. An objection to movements and federations was that "these cooperative meetings" pushed aside "the questions of doctrine and social objects [which] have had first place." Faith did not depend on morality, morality grew out of faith.

The Commission on Faith and Order brought out some deep seated questions. The hope of bringing about greater harmony of action could not be accomplished or promoted by any premature attempts at inter-communion. This effort brought home to the minds and convictions of the Bishop and the Diocese that "any real unity must have a doctrinal and not a sentimental basis." Faith and order must be in harmony with the government established by the Apostles. The cause of Church unity did not die, it just faded away in the discussions and conferences.

THE HOPE OF MISSIONS

Rapid multiplication of churches decreased due largely to the stringent policy of caution and conservation, but in part due to the coming of war. Missionary extension did not stop; it continued on, but in a decidedly slow and watchful manner. Between 1908 and 1918 when Long Island developed so rapidly, only eight new churches were established. Most diocesan effort centered on keeping the already established churches from failing, and on bettering the conditions of mission stations, whether large or small.

The Archdeaconry of Brooklyn —

The Borough of Brooklyn had its encouraging as well as discouraging sides. In 1909, three aided parishes had achieved self-support and by 1910, two more were added to the list of fully supported churches. One of these, St. Matthias', Sheepshead Bay, after overcoming countless difficulties, encountered financial problems of such proportion that in 1914 it was sold for debt, saved only by the purchase of the Diocese which renamed it Emmanuel and continued its work. Another aided parish, St. John's, Fort Hamilton, seemed almost hopeless. Things had gone so badly that the parish was forced to seek complete assistance from the Diocese, and in 1912 reverted to mission status. Several existing mission churches grew and achieved some kind of parish identity. Holy Cross, the "working class people's" Church, St. Gabriel's and St. Lydia's all showed good signs of progress. St. Michael's, North Fifth Street, which had for many years suffered losses, became a parochial mission. After the Diocese had decided to sell the property, it was taken under the care of Church of the Ascension. Church of the Epiphany (formerly Holy Innocents) gave the greatest proof of substance, and became more established and prosperous.

But many opportunities remained untouched. Old centers of population in Flatlands and Gravesend, rapidly growing sections like Rugby and Mapleton, large population in the 17th and 18th wards confronted the Diocese. Building sites, needed for future use, had to be purchased for much less than they would cost later. A smattering of church extension attempted to meet the expressed need. In Flatlands and Gravesend a new mission, Church of Our Savior (renamed St. Agnes) started along the Sea Beach Rapid Transit Line and, as a result of an intensive house to house canvass in December 1911, St. Simon's Church became a reality. The difficulty of land and church made the Archdeaconry adopt a new and dramatic system.

A portable church, capable of seating 150 people, and withal a neat, attractive and substantial building was purchased by the Archdeaconry, erected on leased land, and rented to St. Simon's congregation for a small annual charge.

Parochial missions such as Christ Church, Red Hook "the only organized English Protestant parish in a community of about 25,000 people who are nearly all employed in the large shipyards and machine shops"; St. Margaret's and the Littlejohn Memorial Church answered a small part of the great demand.

Work among the foreign-born had only one product, the Italian church. In 1910, through the kind generosity of St. Paul's, Flatbush, the mission moved from its cramped quarters to "larger, cleaner, and lighter rooms." Named Chiesa dell'Annuzione, a Church was built and occupied in 1913 on a land site bought "partly with a fund raised in the Archdeaconry and partly with the proceeds of the sale of St. Margaret's, Van Brunt Street." The possession of "this admirable" building gave great impetus to work there, both in encouraging the faithful congregation and in attracting the attention of outsiders. The Church became a factor in the community in social service as well as in religious influence. The Archdeacon reported:

> The Italian Mission . . . has had an encouraging year, though the people have suffered greatly from the industrial depression. The Missionary has been at his wits end in his desire to relieve distress, notwithstanding the responses he has had to some of his appeals for help.

Criticism of church proselylizing did not depreciate the necessity of work among the Italians. Rather than in an attempt to convert already converted Christians, the answer rested in the Italians themselves.

> It is well known to all those at all familiar with the situation, that the Roman Church does not reach more than a minority of our Italian population. Thousands of Italians nominally Roman Catholic perhaps, are actually beyond the reach of any real influence from that Church. The fact that Methodists, Presbyterians, Baptists, and Congregationalists are all doing missionary work among Italians in different parts of our borough shows that the necessity for it is widely recognized.

The three Black congregations in Brooklyn ministered well to their varied communities. St. Augustine's Church, an incorporated parish, had become one of the established parishes in the Diocese. St. Philip's Church, after completing the parish house and rectory, "the first parish building to be constructed for Negroes in the Diocese of Long Island," went on in 1914 to erect a new church building, "the first church in this area planned and constructed by Negro mechanics." St. Barnabas', in spite of discouragements, began to show a growing congregation and good program, assisted by a large influx of new residents.

Even though the Diocese could be proud of its existing churches, there remained a great deal to be done. Except for the single effort of the Italian mission, nothing was done "to Christianize or to conserve the Christianity of thousands, hundreds of thousands," of foreigners already settled in Brooklyn. The Archdeaconry had become practically a Church extension organization.

> But other opportunities other than Church extension face us; opportunities such as are met elsewhere by Seaman's Missions, City Mission Societies, religious settlements.

Most pressing was the growing Jewish population of Brooklyn.

> More than three hundred thousand Jews live within the limits of Brooklyn borough, and though Christian work is done among them and in one place alone upwards of two hundred have been baptized, yet our Church apparently is indifferent, and satisfied to be doing nothing.

The most depressing event, and prophetic of the future of Brooklyn, was the change of status of St. Peter's Church, State Street. St. Peter's had been one of the outstanding churches of the Diocese, giving much in the way of leadership to the Diocese. An influential church, the scene of the Rev. John A. Paddock's consecration as a Bishop, it had fostered the Church Charity Foundation, the Woman's Auxiliary and other community and Diocesan projects. In 1915, the changing conditions of its neighborhood made some action mandatory. At that time the property was transferred to the Trustees of the Diocese to "maintain the Church and parochial organization substantially as they have been, until a period of three years had passed, after which the trustees should determine a policy for the future."

The arrangement cited that the Bishop should be Rector, with an associate priest to take care of parish work. The Archdeacon supervised the work and had the use of the Rectory. In September the system was inaugurated. "In this way St. Peter's came to be the Bishop's Brooklyn Church, and the headquarters of the Archdeaconry of Brooklyn."

The Church, in addition to servicing the 300 families, would be a place for "inter-parochial assemblies." A suggestion for the consolidation of St. Peter's with the Church of the Redeemer did not receive a warm welcome. The situation was allowed to continue until a crisis was reached in 1918. The fuel shortage, which found St. Peter's without coal, and the resignation of the associate priest, brought the situation to a climax. The Church was closed, the remaining congregation transferred to St. Ann's, and the property put up for sale. In December 1919, the Standing Committee authorized the sale for $50,000.

Target Center: Queens and Nassau —

A new Archdeacon, the Rev. Canon Roy F. Duffield, was appointed to supervise the mushrooming work in Queens and Nassau. Up to 1910, no new work had been started even though there was abundant opportunity for aggressive work. Seven thousand eight hundred new homes had been built on Long Island outside of Brooklyn and Long Island City in 1909, and eight thousand more in 1910.

At a conservative estimate it means an increase of about 100,000 in the population, most of it being in these two counties, because of their accessibility to the business centers.

A growing population did not necessarily mean an addition of churches. One new mission, St. Paul's Church at Richmond Hill Circle was started "near the headwaters of Jamaica Bay." At Franklin Square services were maintained in private homes for over two years, although there was no mission. A new mission was contemplated for the Metropolitan District while the new one at Corona did well. Of the nine cathedral missions, St. Thomas', Farmingdale, showed the most remarkable progress. A short time before it had been thought best to discontinue this one, but an increase in the community and material prosperity had given it new life.

The three missions for Black people gave good evidence of greater strength and growing influence. In addition to the diocesan missions, several of the parishes had their own missionary ventures. Under parish control was All Saints Mission at Cedarhurst; Grace Chapel, North Massapequa, an Italian Mission in Oyster Bay, a Sunday School at the Merrick Camp Grounds, a Black mission in Bayside, St. Andrew's, Astoria and St. Mary's, Laurel Hill. Unorganized work where services were just started included the undenominational Sunday School in the Garden City Estates, later merged with the Cathedral, and services for the white population of North Bellmore, held in the Athletic Club and in South Ozone Park.

The most successful church ventures were in Nassau County. On November 6, 1910, a Church was started in Floral Park. By Palm Sunday, 1918, the Church had a flourishing congregation and a new Church building. Far surpassing all in success were the two parishes established on the North Shore. Never experiencing a day of small things, Church of the Advent began among the wealthy, and in a few short months a parish church was erected and the congregation incorporated. Similarly, St. John's in Locust Valley began with authority from the Standing Committee to "establish a Protestant Episcopal Church in Lattingtown."

A small beginning with large expectation took place in Forest Hills "model community for lower income families, based on the English Garden City Plan." The philanthropic venture that was to turn into an exclusive residential community saw the first Episcopal services held "under very trying circumstances in a store, in private homes, and in a vacant store without heat." Begun in 1913, the work was so promising that a portable chapel was obtained, and on May 21, 1916, the first service in this chapel was held. The *Forest Hills Bulletin*, the local newspaper, wrote:

The great interest taken in the new chapel gives good promise for the success of the Episcopal Church in the community and it is hoped that now a beginning has been made all Episcopalians in Forest Hills will lend their hearty support and encouragement to the founders by their attendance at the services.

The infant mission, St. Luke's, soon turned into a healthy baby, growing rapidly as Forest Hills developed into a wealthy, thriving community.

Years of the Hamptons —

When the Bishop undertook the work in Easthampton in 1905, the only parish east of Patchogue on the south side was Christ Church, Sag Harbor. In cooperation with the Archdeacon, the Bishop appointed a Rector for St. Luke's in Easthampton. From that time on the development of the Hamptons was nothing less than spectacular. The first expansion, towards the west, started St. Ann's Mission at Bridgehampton, St. John's at Southampton and a mission at Good Ground (Hampton Bays), all the result of the former associate of St. Luke's, the Rev. Samuel C. Fish. The second wave of expansion developed eastward. A mission was begun at Freetown, St. Matthew's, and then three miles east another, St. Thomas', Amagansett, where services were held during the summer. Four miles farther east a "free chapel" in the Eastside community of fishermen and farmers, long unused "because of that freedom" was purchased and deeded to St. Luke's in 1907. In 1912, on the advice and consent of the Bishop, services of the church were brought to the easternmost part of the Diocese — to Montauk, "the point at which Long Island's day begins." At Montauk services were held in a schoolhouse, once a month "with a congregation consisting of fishermen and their families, men in the United States Life Saving Service, and summer residents."

The inaccessibility of Montauk was overcome not so much by the railroad with poor service, but by a state legislative bill which provided for a highway to that section. This made accessible such points as Promised Land and Hicks Island, where hundreds of men were employed in the fish oil refining factories during the fishing season. All Saints Memorial Mission was established with weekly services in 1914, and in 1916 the Silver Dolphin "a social center where services were held on alternate Sundays" was given to the Diocese as a gift by two

*(right) St. Luke's Church,
Easthampton
(below) St. John's Church,
Southampton*

communicants. In the Hamptons, the threat of the summer chapel, St. Andrew's at Southampton, deterred the church's work. The serious hindrance of the "chapel of ease" was that most wealthy Episcopalians attended the dunes church, thereby cutting off a good supply of money to St. John's.

Other missionary activities in Suffolk did not reach the proportions of the Hamptons. The Middle Island missions, Brentwood, Central Islip and Ronkonkoma, were notable for the installation of electric lights. The missions at Brookhaven and Yaphank were known not so much for their growth, but for the distance between them. "This field represents a drive of 20 miles every Sunday for reaching the stations, and means a like trip for visits. A motor cycle at present helps." In the case of the Hamptons and the Middle Island missions, an automobile became a necessity. Poor Mattituck had seen better days. The Church there only ministered to a small group of loyal churchmen. In a church-ridden community the possibility of closing the church became more obvious.

An important event for Suffolk County took place in 1913. After a long court battle over the right to the property of St. John's, Oakdale, Admiral Nicoll Ludlow, the sole surviving member of the family that first started the church, transferred the colonial church to the Diocese. "This Church which was originally called the Charlotte Church, after Queen Charlotte, ranks oldest of the church buildings on the Island after the Caroline Church, Setauket." The conveyance of property entailed a Supreme Court act to legalize the transfer.

The total missionary program, whether in Brooklyn or Suffolk, presented a quiet uneventful and gratifying manner. The war had its effect on church extension. "Our missions have set aside plans for development and larger work as a patriotic duty as well as the part of wisdom." The financial status of all work was good in spite of relief and war work and investment in war loans.

THE FAILURE OF EDUCATION

After a tremendously encouraging growth of the whole field of education in the 1880's, the church's involvement in this area of work showed a depressing note of stagnation, even retrogression. No more obvious effort than the Sunday School movement high-lighted the alarming tendency. Especially since 1901, the decline in Sunday School membership showed the ineffectiveness of the church to reach its children. While the number of communicants had been constantly increasing, the number of children and teachers had been correspondingly decreasing. The trend was made even more evident by the statistics of churches. Most provocative was the evidence in King's County, where in 1901, fifty-six reported 15,200 pupils and almost 1,600 teachers; by 1912, fifty-eight churches only accounted for 12,300 pupils and less than 1,300 teachers. In the outlying areas of Queens, Nassau and Suffolk it was slightly better, but not that much more encouraging. Queens and Nassau had 6,158 pupils and 624 teachers. Suffolk only 1,810 pupils and 200 teachers. The churches of the Diocese had experienced their greatest growth between 1869 and 1881, and since then the steady trickle of loss had become a rushing stream of declining numbers.

The Diocese tried to find reasons for the disconcerting picture. Allusions to the indifference of parents, lack of clergy attention, failure to interest children, incompetent teachers, antiquated methods and vestry disinterest only made the picture blacker. The appointment of a Sunday School Commission seemed at first a wise idea. A frantic scramble to devise a new curriculum, new offerings, teacher training and statistics only resulted in frustration. The Commission finally retreated from the situation by holding teachers' conferences which sounded fine but accomplished very little.

Efforts in secondary school education had been equally as frustrating. The growth of public education with its superb conditions had deterred any further advance of the Diocese. Apart from the two Cathedral Schools and St. Catherine's School in Brooklyn, no private preparatory school appeared. And the three schools themselves had been undergoing a drastic reduction and change. The number of pupils had shown a decided decrease. Efforts on the part of the Headmaster of St. Paul's School, Walter R. Marsh, had brought some good results, but not of any dramatic proportions. "The Cathedral School of St. Paul is raising again with dignity to new life and usefulness. . . . "

An athletic program had developed to its fullest with a new gymnasium and athletic field in good use. St. Mary's School, with a new additional building, had a registration of about 85 girls that increased to 104. St. Paul's rapidly advanced to a position and prestige formerly held, and had an attendance gain of 112 pupils. St. Catherine's Hall came under close scrutiny by the Diocese. Registration had fallen off and the Diocese questioned its relationship to the Brooklyn school.

> Upon inquiry it was found that though the school has always had the warm endorsement of the late Bishop Littlejohn and others in the Diocese, as the Convention has no control over it by any representative in its governing board or by any of the trustees, nor does the school report to Convention. . . . "

In 1912 the semi-official connection with the Diocese stopped, based on the idea that when officially connected to the Diocese, it would be considered once more part of the diocesan program. In actuality, the Diocese had no secondary schools since St. Mary's and St. Paul's were Cathedral Schools, having no primary link to the Diocese.

With an increased emphasis on public education, the Diocese turned its attention to implementing this means. Several problems had arisen in regard to secular schools, The growing non-church population had brought to question religious observances in the schools. A Jewish association had requested in 1907 "that every Christian song, picture or illusion to the birth, life and teachings of Christ be taken from the public schools." Little came of it since education was still within the clasp of the Christian community. The Diocese replied to the searching request by asserting that although there was no established church per se, the state did recognize "Christianity to be the established religion." Ethical and moral instruction in the school also appeared to lack any relevancy. A committee on moral and religious instruction in the public schools had been appointed to investigate the instruction in ethics from textbooks in the schools. The subject grew to such proportions that an International Commission on Moral Training had been formed in Great Britain, France, Germany, the United States of America and other countries. At the Convention of the National Education Association in Los Angeles, a special committee was appointed, backed up by a generous appropriation to investigate moral training in the public schools.

The subject of textbooks in the schools, and their content, also attracted the attention of the Diocese. A committee "to make such friendly representation to authors, publishers, Board of Education and teachers of history in public schools as will secure our youth the enjoyment of religious freedom in respect to the standards of their church." Misrepresentation in public school textbooks, whether intentional or through ignorance, had spread "false statements as to the origin of the Church of England." The crux of the matter rested on "the slander which Roman Catholic controversialists [were] constantly making that Henry VIII founded the church." Anglicans believed that Henry reformed the church and never claimed to have founded one. The responsibility of the diocesan committee was relieved by the formation of a national committee in 1913 to rectify the situation.

The many scattered efforts of the Diocese to be more relevant in education had resulted in a confusion of interest groups and a diffusion of effect. In 1910, the General Convention set up a General Board of Education to alleviate the tangental works. Following the example, the Diocese set out to coordinate its own efforts. In 1912, the Diocese had any number of disconnected educational groups. They were the Standing Sunday School Committee, the Standing Committee on Christian Education, the Standing Committee on General Theological Seminary, the Special Committee on Boys' Work and the Committee on Textbooks. At the Diocesan Convention in 1913 all of the committees were abolished and a Board of Education, duly and canonically instituted, was established. The duty of the Board, with representation of clergy and laity, was "to promote religious and moral education in the Diocese." The scope of the work was "of course, inclusive of religious education in all schools, colleges and theological seminaries, but its most important endeavor . . . directed at the parochial Sunday Schools."

The Board's responsibility had nine areas with a special committee for each: "on finance, on organization and equipment, on curriculum, on teacher training, on missions, on worship, music and art, on schools and colleges, on publicity, on parents and home." Cooperation with the National Board resulted in disillusionment. The assessment to support the national program seemed exorbitant and unnecessary.

Hopefully, the Board of Education began to work. But its efforts proved almost fruitless. The Board members found themselves "personae non gratae" in attempts to investigate "existing conditions in the Sunday Schools of the very parishes which had bidden us grapple with the problems." Requests for information had been overlooked and attempts to investigate personally had met with little encouragement. Diocesan training for Sunday School Teachers met with some success. In order to stimulate Lenten missionary offerings the Board arranged in 1916 "to present banners to the schools giving the largest total offering and the highest per capita offering." The problem of standard curriculum had been partly solved by the publication of the national "Christian Nurture

Series." The hope of ascertaining a true picture of education in the Diocese through survey statistics had not materialized, although a questionnaire had been sent out. Education was just as frustrating a problem as financing programs.

THE POWER OF PRACTICALITY

The Bishop's insistence upon sound business practices in church affairs had brought good results. Parishes, following many of his suggestions, had adopted the strict accounting of Sunday collections with the preservation of special gifts and endowments. An added precaution, firmly advocated by the Bishop, was the bonding of local treasurers. The insurance against absconding with funds, or fraud, had proven helpful on a diocesan level and so was encouraged on a local level. There was nothing derogatory in it, "but honor on the officers in such an arrangement which [was] made in most business houses and in all City governments," and alleviated the "temptation in the way of our young treasurers by our lax system and careless auditing." An added suggestion for "higher idea of business responsibility" rested on "the absolute publicity in the financial records of the Parish." Hidden accounts and secretive methods injured the people concerned, abetted by rumors and sometimes open scandal. All could be dismissed by "a full and clear statement being made to the church public."

While parishes adopted better business methods in church finances, the Diocese concerned itself with the problem of financing programs. Since 1901, the general missionary program of the church had been underwritten by the system of apportionment, a "dividing the total sum needed for foreign and domestic missions among the several parishes, basing the amount asked from each Diocese on its average annual revenue." Simply an apportionment, not an assessment, it was not compulsory but had "certain moral obligations which cannot be evaded." Year after year the Diocese had failed to meet its share, never even approaching one half the anticipated amount. A high point had been reached in 1912-1913 when $28,444 of the $63,597 apportionment was raised, but it was still only 47.4% achievement.

To provide an impetus in Diocesan participation in general program support, the Bishop appointed a small committee to pursue the matter. As a help to more parish support, the Diocese, in 1912, approved a set of suggestions that an "Every Member Canvass" to solicit funds be instituted and that a weekly offering for missions be made, adopting the duplex envelope system. A notable recommendation was "that the Diocesan Missionary Committee be directed to combine with this plan an effort towards systematic giving to Diocesan as well as General Mission work." The suggestion was badly needed. More often than not collections were sporadic, sometimes not taken, and always too little to afford adequate program support. The situation was complicated by the profusion of offerings. By Canon Law eight different annual contributions were to be made for a confusing array of beneficiaries. There were annual collections for the general missionary work of the church, for Diocesan missions, for the Episcopal Fund, for the Bishop's Salary Fund (a sum equal to 1.1/2% of stipends paid to Rectors), a Diocesan Fund (set in 1909 at 2.1/2%), for the Relief of the Aged and Infirm Clergy, for the General Clergy and Pension Fund, and lastly, for the Church Charity Foundation. A Canon on the assessment was made, but postponed for two years when it was decided that a change was "inexpedient." The idea of a unified appeal was kept alive by a resolution of the 1915 Convention which embodied the idea of a Diocesan Board of Finance, "to unify and coordinate the various assessments, apportionments, and contributions asked or exacted of the Diocese or of the parishes in the Diocese for Diocesan or extra Diocesan purposes. . . . "

Fortunately, the General Convention enacted legislature that advanced a concerted financial effort. At the 1916 Convention held in St. Louis, Missouri, several resolutions and a new Canon were adopted. The National Canon 50 "of Business Methods in the Church" specifically required all Diocesan accounts audited by a Certified Public Accountant, that all Dioceses adopt a fiscal year of January 1 through December 31, and that each Diocese have a Financial Committee,

> to maintain general supervision of the financial affairs of the Diocese or Missionary District; to secure simplicity and accuracy in collection and disbursements of funds, and cooperation between the various officers, trusts, and board of the Convention or District . . . to act as advisor of the Bishop in Financial matters and upon request, as advisors to individual parishes within the Diocese or district.

The Diocese responded by adopting the proposed fiscal year in place of the long standing May to May year between Conventions. The Bishop also appointed a Committee on Finance and Budget to pursue united action.

Besides upgrading its financial practices, the Diocese sought other ways to make the work of the Diocese more efficient and less cumbersome. Among its considerations it examined the possibility of a one day Convention, a change in the makeup of the Convention and a united action with other Dioceses.

In 1914, sentiment had been voiced for the possibility of a one day Convention. Beginning in 1868, the Convention had lasted three days, and then at Garden City had been shortened to two days. Contending that the work of the Convention was done "in the time equivalent of a working day or less"; a committee and report urged the adoption of a one day Convention. Some of the reasons were obvious. Much of the time was taken up with written reports.

On the first day the organization of the Convention was closely followed by a recess of at least an hour and a half for a pretentious luncheon. By three o'clock the last man has strolled back to his place in the meeting. An hour later, however, begins the exodus; then come adjournment to the next day.

The second day followed the same general procedure. To facilitate the Convention proceedings a number of recommendations were made: a shorter service at the beginning and an earlier session start; a simplified luncheon, possibly a buffet luncheon; an evening session; all reports printed and distributed before the Convention; all nominations made by mail in advance. It was felt that a one day Convention was not feasible and the resolution was lost to a resounding "no." Some streamlining did come about with a printed timetable of trains; and Order of Business sent a week before.

The Diocesan Convention considered the possibility of proportional representation. Of the clergy in 1914, 173 were entitled to vote. Of the parishes, there were 93 entitled to send delegates. The clergy had seats in the Convention as individuals, and each one acted for himself. It was only in the lay delegation that there was "representation as such." These delegates, it was held, and not the clergy, represented the lay constituencies. All delegations were of equal size. Each parish, regardless of size, had the right to send three lay delegates, who were entitled to one vote and no more. It was proposed to allow the several parishes to be represented by such number of the laity as was in proportion to the number of communicants in the parish, and as many votes on every question as to the number of delegates present. The system meant that each parish have one delegate and add one for every full hundred communicants until the maximum number of seven delegates. The matter was warmly debated by the Convention, but came to no decision on the matter. A motion that it be "laid on the table" was made and carried.

A pressing issue, growing out of the national agitation for woman suffrage, was the right of women to vote at church meetings. A committee of five appointed by the Bishop in 1915 had the responsibility of asking "in cooperation, if possible, with the other Diocese of the State of New York," from the state legislature such an amendment of the Religious Corporation Law, "as will make it possible for women to vote in parish meetings upon the same terms as men." The State Law was amended with the proviso that women could only vote with canonical provision by a Diocese. A memorial from Holy Trinity Parish on women voting brought the matter to a head. The special committee reported that they had discussed the matter and had asked the opinion of other dioceses. The Diocese of New York and Central New York had already authorized woman's vote, while Albany had voted it down. After referral to the Committee on Canons, the proposal "permitting women to vote at Parish Meetings" was presented to the Convention and was lost. The subject was brought up again in 1917, and again lost. Finally at the Convention of 1918, a new Canon was passed admitting women to vote at parish elections, but not eligible to serve as churchwardens, vestrymen or delegates to Diocesan Convention.

About the year 1900, the Episcopal Church began to take serious thought concerning its national organization. Suspicion of a strong central government was for over a century one of the notable characteristics of American life. The Episcopal Church reflected this fear by being a loose federation of autonomous dioceses, with central government reduced to the minimum of a General Convention that met once every three years.

Attempts from time to time to augment some kind of intermediary government between diocese and General Convention had been tried, but failed. At its primary Convention, the Diocese of Long Island looked forward to some form of cooperation between it and the mother diocese. In the last half of the nineteenth century, some joint action on the part of the diocese of New York State had been taken, but only when some crisis or pressing matter needed cooperative action. By canonical action in 1907, some semblance of needed governmental machinery was accomplished by the initiation of "Missionary Departments." The plan included that the departments of the Church be represented on the Board of Missions, thereby enlarging and expanding the national scope of action. Long Island became part of the Second Missionary Department that included New York, New Jersey and Puerto Rico. Regular meetings of the "department" were held: the 1913 meeting being scheduled to be held in Brooklyn. Before the 1913 meeting could be held, the General Convention of that year had passed a Canon authorizing provincial synods, "the most revolutionary action." There was no fear or "even the possibility of the title of Archbishop creeping into the nomenclature of the church." The old Missionary Department was abolished and the first synod meeting of the Second Province was scheduled for October 27, 1914. The work of the synod was to be simply the coordination and cooperation of the dioceses in the work of missions, in social service and in religious education. The Synod also set up a Court of Review. The Diocese of Long Island immediately took steps to unite with the Province. At the May Convention, 1914, it passed a resolution to unite with the Second Province.

THE ASSURANCE OF SOCIAL JUSTICE

As the "muckrakers" revealed more and more the social and political evils of the day, the Social Service Committee worked inside the Diocese and in its community to alleviate and reform as much as possible the depressing and corrupt consequences of those evils. First to form such a committee, the Diocese had been followed by almost sixty other dioceses instituting such a group. Work on Long Island had grown so much that a full-time field secretary was needed. The Committee went to work to raise a salary for such a worker. They succeeded by getting one-half the necessary stipend; the Diocese responded by raising the other half.

The Field Secretary turned out to be a "jack-of-all-trades". He had the responsibility of molding public opinion, building up a public conscience and of cooperating with other bodies, civic, social and philanthropic. His tasks included the most important area of assisting the local parish and of working closely with the heads of various social agencies in Brooklyn and other Dioceses. A pressing need for him to meet was the orientation of all parishes, city or country, to the fact that social service was both an urban and a rural problem. Social service could sometimes be done best in the "small community" where justice could be achieved more than in a large area. The Field Secretary addressed any number of parish groups on the needs and weaknesses of the communities to which they ministered. He represented the Diocese in civic concerns, serving on the Mayor's Committee on Unemployment, Food Supply and Bundle Day. He cooperated with the Sunday Observance Association of King's County. Much to the satisfaction of the Committee, he prevented the removal of necessary women probation officers in the local courts.

The role of the Social Service Committee had devolved into a pressure group in the Diocese and in the community. Bent on reform, they used every possible means to accomplish better conditions or sufficient premises for the good life. No area was inviolable, running the gamut from housing and unemployment to censorship of motion pictures. They campaigned against the atrocities of the unorganized labor market forming a "clergyman's Committee on Unemployment." They made arrangements with the United States Department of Labor to furnish all the parishes and missions in the Diocese with their weekly bulletin "Opportunities for Employment" to be hung in the vestibules of churches and other parish buildings so that those looking for employment might have an opportunity to know what positions were open. They worked for the relief of the problem found in the "dark rooms in the tenements." They campaigned for a federal law on marriage and divorce.

Fearful of the corrupting influence of motion pictures, especially on the young, they used every means to achieve some kind of civic censorship. Their premises succinctly expressed the belief that motion pictures caused crime.

> One third of the felonies committed in King's County are by persons under 21 and three-fourths of the felonies by persons not over 30 years of age. We believe that the teaching of the streets and of vicious motion pictures is so powerful as to counteract much of the moral training in the home and church, and that [the Diocese] ought to cooperate with other Christians in a renewed request for a city or state law requiring an effective supervision of the morality of motion pictures shown to children.

Frustrated by a mayoral veto of city censorship, they went on to advocate a State Board of Motion Picture Commission, or more adequate, a Federal Board of Censorship. Even at these two levels, they accomplished little. Going so far as to appear before the governor of the State in 1917, they were rewarded by a governor's veto of the bill establishing state censorship. The United States Congress was so absorbed in matters connected with the "great war" that the advocates of the Smith-Hughes Bill to "establish a Federal Motion Picture Commission" to prevent the showing of films "immoral or injurious to public health" did not find it possible to bring the matter to a vote.

Swept along by the rising tide of prohibition sentiment, the Diocese became involved in the temperance movement. Never in favor of complete abstinence, the Diocese hoped to instill a spirit of moderation that would alleviate the distressing problem. Closer cooperation with the National organization, the Church Temperance Society, resulted in the formation of a Long Island Branch. The three arms of the Society, promotion of temperance, reformation of the intemperate, and the removal of causes of intemperance, moved the Diocese to attempt some beneficial action. Always a favorite target, the Sunday saloon brought more invective and attempted correction. The campaign against the Sunday saloon continued unabated. It became the cause of all that was bad in the nation.

> If the Church condemns the saloon, it is not because the Church hates the workingman or his wife or family, but because the saloon is the greatest enemy of the home, because it, more than anything else, accounts for the fearful congestion of our cities where human beings have to herd at night like beasts; because it sends the man home at night with no money in his pocket and with no sense of shame, with curses in his mouth and murder in his heart.

While acknowledging the changing character of Sunday, the Church, nevertheless, made an effort to diminish the evil influence of the Sunday institution. A petition was made to the State Senate and Assembly to amend the liquor law so to prevent the opening of new saloons until the number of saloons had been reduced to one to every 1,000 of the population, and giving licenses to only first class hotels having at least 25 rooms. Year after year resolutions were passed to remove screens from parlor windows to reveal the interior.

Failing to accomplish anything by concentrating on state control of a limited trade in liquor, the Diocese organized to fight the problem in a different way. The Auxiliary Committee of the National Church Temperance Society visited parishes to arouse local support for curtailing liquor sales and for a full program of temperance propaganda. The Diocese depended on its women to carry on its temperance campaign. They, like Carrie Nation, warred against the evil, but in a less violent way. Their attack consisted in purchasing a lunch wagon and installing drinking fountains or "bubblers" on the Brooklyn city streets. The drinking fountains had been found of great service in Manhattan, "and the constant use made of them by teamsters, passerby, etc., who might otherwise be tempted to go into a saloon" proved their effectiveness. Cooperation of the Brooklyn Commissioner for the Water Supply made a widespread installation of bubblers a reality. They were scattered throughout the City and were supplied with a spigot "so a cart driver, on a hot day, can draw water for his horse also." The campaign for lunch wagons, weapons to combat the free lunch of the saloons, finally culminated in the purchase of one costing $1,500 which was put into working operation. In 1916 this first lunch wagon was opened on the plaza of the Williamsburgh Bridge. The location not being desirable, the wagon was moved to Plymouth and Adams Street, Brooklyn.

The grip of prohibition on the nation finally invaded the Diocese and it began to support the movement. Since all other measures had not produced any adequate results, they were forced into some formal action. The spread of prohibition sentiment evidenced in 1905 in the Russian government preventing the use of vodka, and the French government preventing the sale of absinthe. In Congress the House of Representatives voted 197 to 189 against National prohibition and the bill was defeated, but the margin had grown slimmer. State after state had adopted prohibition legislation, so that by 1918 the dry States outnumbered the "wets." The Diocese, confronted by the growing sentiment for legal prohibition, debated the issue. Heeding the Bishop's true estimate that "it aimed at an asceticism which the public conscience cannot support," a resolution endorsing prohibition by Federal amendment, presented by the Social Service Committee, was finally laid on the table. Sharp differences of opinion developed "not as to the desirability of temperance, but as to the wisdom of any pronouncement by an ecclesiastical body on particular political methods of furthering the temperance cause."

THE DREAM OF BUILDING

Ten years of a cautious and conservative policy had brought a certain amount of security and contentment to the Diocese. The financial prospects of the Diocese had improved greatly. Missions, long neglected, had assumed stable proportions. Parishes had grown both financially and numerically. Diocesan ventures of charity and social reform seemed to have produced marked results. Conditions had reached a point where the Bishop felt secure enough to strike out in the direction of erecting a needed diocesan building. The Bishop felt it time to develop more fully the diocesan center at Garden City.

Bishop Burgess had an abiding concern for the relationship of the Diocese to the Cathedral. Sensing a lingering tension and hostility between Garden City and the Diocese, he took every opportunity to make the Cathedral an integral part of the Diocese. In a real sense, the Diocese had never accepted the Cathedral center; regarding it as the pet project of only a chosen few, in some ways forced upon the Diocese, and so far isolated from the full stream of diocesan life as to make it inaccessible and almost useless. It did not matter that other Dioceses had to spend millions of dollars to erect a Cathedral, nor that the Cathedral, although never a parish church, had grown in influence in the Nassau community. The feeling, never openly expressed, but covertly held, persisted and had not only made the Diocese aloof, but caused an attitude of reticent separateness on the part of the Cathedral community. The Bishop tried his best by persuasion and practice to rectify the relations between the two factors.

As a step in that direction, he had instituted a full annual report to the Convention on the financial life of the Cathedral. During the early years of his episcopate money difficulties had been alleviated, and during the summer of 1910 the Cathedral Chapter completed a transaction by which it sold to the Garden City Company a tract of land, about thirty acres (now the Cherry Valley Club and Golf Course) west of the Cathedral for about $50,000. The lands had been of no use to the Cathedral except to accrue taxes and incur much caretaking expense. A firm commitment that no more land would be sold accompanied the deposit of the sale money into the Cathedral funds. The original idea for building and endowing the Cathedral had envisaged a far greater plan and a more replete endowment fund than materialized. The Stewart plan had, in addition to the three existing buildings, a chapter house, a home for deaconesses, a theological school and a seminary for women. The untimely death of Mrs. Stewart and the resultant lawsuits had cut short the magnificent plan. Monies that were reserved had to be used for building St. Mary's School, for paying deficits and for needed improvements and repairs. No further drain on the Cathedral funds could be allowed, for it would be left crippled.

When the plan for an additional building was discussed the Bishop made it expressly clear that any proposed improvement had to be a diocesan project:

> Very fairly and consistently has the Cathedral fulfilled its side of the contract, and now that a generation has passed away since this church (Cathedral) was consecrated, it is but right that it should press on to greater things. . . . The opportunity this placed before the churchmen of the Diocese is a large one. It is to make this Cathedral their own by adding to its buildings and enriching its associations and increasing its endowments.

Appealing to the conscience of the whole Diocese he sought their encouragement:

> But I am unwilling to believe that the Diocese of Long Island, as a Diocese, is ready to abandon its Cathedral as the center of its administrative, missionary, and educational work, or

that it will not, through its devoted members, provide the means, not merely to support, but to extend its Cathedral foundations . . . with a far reaching effect upon the Diocese . . . and upon the nation.

The urgent need of another building at Garden City was heightened by the tremendous growth of the Diocese. The Diocesan Convention had since 1886 met at the Cathedral, holding its deliberations in the Cathedral crypt. Beginning in 1901, the enlarged Convention was forced to meet in the nave of the Cathedral. The nave in no way was feasible or equipped for the use of a deliberative body.

> The acoustics are such that no one can be heard unless he faces his audience and speaks with deliberateness and careful enunciation and emphasis. The quick short reply oftentimes so effective in debate would be lost by most of the members, unless the one who made it occupied far more time in coming forward to claim a hearing.

Preliminary plans for the expansion of the Garden City center had been formulated by the Cathedral Corporation headed by the Bishop, and assisted by William M. Baldwin and George L. Hubbell. By a resolution of the Diocese in convention on May 21, 1912, a committee was appointed to cooperate with the Cathedral Chapter in promoting plans for erection of a Chapter House and Diocesan Hall. The final prospectus of the joint committees incorporated much more than the one building originally planned. In addition to the original idea the committee had,

> also, in view of the prospective growth of this community, felt compelled to include in our planning features, some of which may not take visible form for many years, but which an intelligent forethought should regard in the development of the area on the South side of the Cathedral.

The final plan, as accepted, included a Diocesan Hall "a large dignified chamber for deliberations of the annual Convention, with seating accommodations for four hundred clerical and lay delegates . . . The benches would be so adjustable as to permit the use of the Hall for large gatherings of the societies of the Diocese, and also for local assemblies." It also had a proper Chapter House located near the south transept door and a sacristy close to the baptisery, since "the room at present occupied is in a deep and dark crypt form which access to chancel [was] only by a narrow spiral steps or a winding stair and long walk . . . both ways being dangerous for aged and nearsighted clergy." Other buildings included choristers' quarters, rehearsal room, musical library, a Sunday School building or parish house, a library, an office building for the Bishop and Cathedral clergy for the preservation of records and for the satisfactory transaction of the business of the Diocese. All the buildings were to be connected by a long open portico.

Financing this fine plan was envisioned to be the sole responsibility of the Diocese. The Cathedral Chapter paid for the printing of publicity, the architect's fee and the outlay of the grounds. Every dollar collected was to go into the buildings and their endowment. Such a large undertaking as this could only be carried on by the Diocese, and only as the result "of hearty and cordial enthusiasm on the part of the entire constituencies." The idea, originating with the Chapter, had only the promotion of diocesan prosperity as its aim, and the sure hope that because of it the Diocese would gain immeasurably, both materially and spiritually. Underguiding this philosophic outlook the Bishop reassured the Diocese:

> I know the need for money in our mission field, in our parishes to clear off debts, or to build better churches. I sympathize heartily with any of these efforts, but I believe that not less money, but rather more, will be given to these undertakings if the Diocese as a whole unites in one true, earnest endeavor to make its Cathedral property complete and to house its Convention in a suitable and dignified home.

The joint committee at once went to work to raise the necessary funds. Reporting to the 1914 Convention, it felt the best start to be "not to endeavor to raise a large sum of money, but rather to spread information as to the possibilities for usefulness of such a structure." Some progress was made in the sum of $19,000 pledged and several promises of gifts for a choir house and a memorial library. However, troubles nagged the work. Going on the assumption that no building could be erected without all the money for building and endowment being raised, the committee experienced another setback. Other causes had influenced support.

> During the past year (1914-1915) general conditions of industry, trade and finance, taken together with the extraordinary call of our churches to bring up gifts to missions to the sums apportioned, have rendered unadvisable any urgent presentation of this great enterprise.

The campaign slowed to a standstill in the next two years, and then came the blow that was to arrest the development of the Cathedral center. It was not so much the World War but the crisis in the charitable institutions of the Diocese that cancelled any further realization. The Bishop, faced with an impeding emergency, had to admit in 1918 that,

> not too strongly can I advocate the development of the Cathedral system . . . but this

undertaking cannot claim precedent at this time . . . for the (Church Charity) Foundation puts a claim upon our generosity at this time.

THE CALAMITY OF CHARITY

Trouble seemed far away for the Church Charity Foundation in 1910. A beautiful new nurses' home, well built and fireproof, had been completed at a cost of $45,000. The year closed without debt. Under the able guidance of its superintendent, the Rev. Canon Paul F. Swett, Foundation funds were carefully administered and guarded. A firm policy of investing legacies received in the endowment fund had accumulated to nearly half a million dollars. The various institutions carried on their ministry of care and healing, with an increased number of inmates and patients. All seemed to be well. The crisis of 1901 had been carefully overcome and the Foundation stood on good solid ground.

But beginning in 1914, the Foundation experienced a wave of crises that almost spelled its doom. It became imperative that the top floor of the hospital be reconstructed and made fireproof. A new and approved operating room, and the fireproofing of all stairs, added to the desperate character. The worst aspect of all was that although all buildings needed repairs there were no funds for enlarging or improving, which was to cost about $80,000. To add to the chaos the children's home and hospitals came under close scrutiny. The three agencies, St. Giles' Hospital for Crippled Children, the Sheltering Arms Nursery and the Orphanage received children referred by the city, and underwritten by a small and insufficient allowance. Regularly visited by the State Board of Charities, the homes subsisted until caught between the State and the New York City Department of Charities. The cry that some child care centers were unfit caused the Governor of the State to appoint a special commission to investigate the charges. The diocesan institutions came in for their full share of criticism.

At these hearings all sorts of evidence seemed to be admitted, and the public, reading the public press, received an utterly false impression of two of our charities.

Headlines in the local newspapers screamed "Babies in Squalor," "Bishop Burgess, President of Nursery, Criticized by Charities' Deputies," "Whipping Children in Home." These sensational headlines made the public picture the Church's treatment as "our babies brought up in filth, our children fed as pigs, beaten and marks on body." The Diocese, in a way, resented the intrusion of such ill-tempered treatment. The Bishop insisted that "our Homes stand open to all, our books can be examined, and our children seen." But the assurance of the Diocese was shaken by the horrible death of a child at the Sheltering Arms. The Bishop informed everyone:

But in the summer of 1917, a very sad death took place . . . and the circumstances were such as threatened to bring the Board of Trustees into the Court of Justice. In company with the counsel, I (the Bishop) visited the President of the Society for the Prevention of Cruelty to Children, who told us that his Society had on file most damaging facts but that, out of deference to the Diocese, he would delay action.

Meeting the immediate situation with some temporary measures, the Bishop at the meeting of the Board of Trustees, recommended that the institution be closed and merged with the Church Charity Foundation. The policy and procedures outlined by the Bishop were completely rejected by the Board. Accordingly, the Bishop resigned as President of the Sheltering Arms, and the nursery passed out of official status in the Diocese.

The Diocese had to face another equally depressing crisis that needed immediate action. The Church Charity Foundation stood at another crisis in its history, but one so utterly different than that which confronted it fourteen years before. There the Foundation was faced with the alarming fact that it might have to close its doors and relinquish its charter because of alarming debts and disunity of management. The impending doom pivoted not on funds but on buildings.

Our buildings were built at a time when people took chances about fire which they are not willing to take now. Again and again the city has recorded awful disasters, cruel burnings of women and children, theatres and hotels destroyed.

The City Fire Department had revised its laws and ordered the Foundation to make extensive and expensive changes in its structures. On March 29, 1916, the pressing need was dramatically revealed — a fire occurred in the Orphans' House, which did serious damage to the two upper floors and the roof of the building. The fire brought home to the Board of Managers the fact that none of the buildings were fireproof. The Home for the Aged, the Home for the Blind and St. John's Hospital all needed to be considerably enlarged. To spend large sums of money on old and insecure buildings seemed a great waste, and the Board, therefore, considered plans for new fireproof buildings of greater capacity. It was thought that the present hospital could be reconstructed to serve as the Orphans' Home. The total cost of improvements amounted to $500,000.

The Foundation began its reconstruction and renewal with two new buildings — the Home for the Aged and the Home for the Blind. Occupied in the summer of 1917, they accommodated 100 inmates and cost $240,000. The work on the Orphans' Home, destroyed by the fire, was suspended and the children entrusted to the Foundation placed in other institutions. A bright note amid the pervading discouragement was kindled by the opening in November 1916, of the new St. Gile's Hospital on President Street, "an attractive, well-equipped, and home-like institution," with accommodations for forty-five patients. The Garden City house was still maintained. For the care of convalescent and chronic cases, in which surgical care was not needed, it accommodated about thirty patients. But the large amount necessary for the construction of the new building had not been completely raised, so that the new hospital and children's home had to wait until the debt could be cancelled. Of the expected $500,000 only one-third of the amount had been raised, and that only due to the unstinting efforts of a finance committee and the Rev. George C. Groves, "who obtained release from his parish, St. Stephen's, Port Washington, to raise the needed funds."

Responding to the eloquent pleading of the Bishop who, putting first things first, had clearly made the prime object of diocesan concern the Foundation, the Diocese made plans for its own total involvement. A committee to prepare plans for the 50th Anniversary of the Diocese in May 1919, "reported in favor of celebrating the occasion by securing a great offering from the people of the Diocese for the Church Charity Foundation . . . " and resolved "that this Convention approve this plan and sanction a campaign for one million dollars for the Church Charity Foundation, to commemorate this important date in the history of the Diocese . . . " The Diocese wholeheartedly gave its approval to the plan.

THE TEST OF WAR

Most Americans were astounded at the Bolshevik overthrow of the Czarist monarchy in Russia. Nostalgic thoughts of their own American Revolution colored their enthusiasm for the revolting group as the country became more and more involved in the throes of drastic change and tottering government. Sentiment that "Russia . . . is a vast country; and its people have little preparation for free institutions" gave hope to "the proclamation of a Republic." Sympathy was openly expressed, acknowledging that "Russia [had] fallen because its faith rested only on despotism and a Czar-ruled church, whose beautiful ritual and music had not taken hold of the people's heart and mind."

Americans, too, delighted in the establishment of Christian rule in Jerusalem after eight centuries of Turkish dominion. A minor operation of the war had accomplished it, giving hope for the Zionist movement and the beginning of a Jewish republic. Sorrow that in the disorder the Patriarch of the Assyrian Church had been martyred, took formal action in an expression of grief by the Convention to the brethren of the Assyrian Church, and asked "a generous and continuous help for the brave and suffering Assyrian and Armenian Christians."

But the event that shook the nation was the Good Friday declaration of war in 1917. No one event in the history of the nation had caused such a total commitment to the church's support and implementation. Involvement in the brief Spanish American War meant for the Diocese care of the wounded and ministering to the two major soldier encampments in Garden City and at Montauk. In the "Great War" the Diocese became totally mobilized, working for the eventual peace and victory "to save the world for democracy."

The Episcopal Church had given strenuous advocacy of the peace movement. The Bishop and Convention had gone on record as giving full support to "the action of the President of the United States, who has made overtures to England looking to the establishment of a permanent court of arbitration", as "a most powerful curb on war and on example to the world."

"The ideal of universal peace is so truly a Christian ideal," said the Bishop in 1911, "that we need not hesitate to put ourselves on record as in entire sympathy with the chief executive of our nation in his truly Christian efforts." Just as strongly, when the United States finally became actively engaged in the European conflict, did churchmen work for the war effort. Total commitment of all church resources signalized the manner in which the church helped. Whether it was manpower, supplies, money or services, the parishes and the Diocese did all they could to help win the "just and lasting" peace.

Parish resources included women's work in the Red Cross, by fostering membership and providing hospital and soldier supplies. Many parishes gave civilian relief to families whose men were in service; others participated in relief drives for destitute people abroad. Most parishes situated near the many military encampments provided amusement, recreation and social rooms for the men in the army, the navy and the aerial service. The Woman's Auxiliary attempted to reach all church women in a day of prayer "for victory . . . and in behalf of a new and better work which is to come after victory." Most of all, local parishes participated, with diocesan approval and mandate, in the three Liberty Loan drives. War saving societies were formed, by which war saving stamps of $5.00, or thrift stamps of 25¢, put "the patriotic service of financing the war within the reach of the slenderest incomes." Parishes like Trinity Church, East New York, bought Liberty Bonds for church mortgage reduction. A result of the financial support of Liberty Bonds, Red Cross and Y.M.C.A. had churches giving less to the general and diocesan business of the church. The shortage of fuel hit churches hard. Midweek Lenten services had to be cancelled in many churches; and some, like St. Peter's Church, had to close their doors.

The Episcopal Church cared for its servicemen. The Diocesan Brotherhood of St. Andrew formed correspondence clubs in which people were asked to write to men overseas. Books, periodicals, Prayer Books and any other literature was sent to chaplains for the men. Parishes adopted the Honor Roll system to commemorate the part their men played in the war. Blue stars on a flag were changed to gold when a serviceman was killed; lists of servicemen, plaques and bronze tablets, all gave witness to the parish's patriotic participation. St. John's nurses did their part too, serving in military hospitals in Italy and France.

Most dramatic of the churches war effort was the work of its chaplains. The great need for a large corps of

134

chaplains (700 to minister to the two million men) caused the Diocese to take a positive step in assisting men to volunteer. The "hearty approval of the volunteering of clergy to serve as chaplains," was accompanied by the stipulation that wherever possible their posts be kept for them until they returned. Parish Rectors volunteered for military service. The Rev. D. H. O'Dowd of Church of the Ascension in Rockville Centre, the Rev. Herbert E. Covell, and the Rev. John H. Sattig of St. Philips, Dyker Heights all volunteered for service. The Diocese suffered a temporary loss by the volunteering of the Rev. Charles H. Webb, Archdeacon of Brooklyn and Editor of the Department of Diocesan News. He accepted a commission that began in September 1918. The Bishop, exemplifying his own policy, assumed "some of the duties of the Archdeacon during his temporary absence as Chaplain in the United States Army."

Clergy, both at home and in service, were deeply concerned about the spiritual and moral welfare of the enlisted men. The Rev. John H. Sattig writing from Spartansburg, South Carolina, sympathized with the anguish of servicemen who "struggled between love and duty." The Diocese again and again berated the existence of corrupting influences near army encampments on the Island. The Brooklyn Navy Yard caused some concrete action.

> The Police Department was notified by us (the Diocese) of the fact that the saloons surrounding the Navy Yard in Brooklyn were selling intoxicants to sailors in uniform. A telegram was sent to Secretary Daniels of the Navy asking for a definition of the laws relating to the sale of liquor to men in uniform, as to whether it applied to sailors as well as soldiers. He replied it did. Shortly afterwards placards were posted in all saloons in the neighborhood of the Navy Yard calling attention to the law prohibiting the practice and the police promptly enforced the law.

Camp Upton at Yaphank, the primary encampment on Long Island, received the church's ministrations. The Rev. Rowland S. Nichols was appointed by the Bishop, after a visit to the camp, to carry on the church's work. He, as priest-in-charge of the missions at Yaphank and Center Moriches, took care of the families of the officers living in those villages since there was no place for them on the camp grounds. Camp Upton presented a picture of haste and confusion.

> The roads of the vicinity were not built for heavy traffic they now have to bear, and approach to the camp is difficult. Horseback or aeroplane, is at present, the best method of approach.

> In this wilderness streets, watermains and a sewer system have been planned and are in construction. Barracks are built, and electricity has been introduced. The present population is about 40,000 including soldiers and civilians.

> Making roads and erecting buildings, drilling mostly on roads or between barracks, change and confusion, in dirt and mud, is the much present routine.

Three organizations were permitted on the camp grounds, a Protestant, Catholic and Jewish service organization. Six army chaplains, five Roman Catholic and one Baptist ministered to the men. A distinct house of worship had been given official permission, but services were held in the service buildings. In October 1918, the appointed chaplain celebrated in the Y.M.C.A. building the first Holy Communion which was attended by a good size congregation. The same concern was shown in the Church's ministry to the soldiers at Camp Mills in Garden City. On Easter Day, 1918, a service of Holy Communion was attended by about 400 soldiers in the Y.M.C.A. building. To add to the service a number of the Cathedral congregation sent their automobiles to take the choir and clergy to and from the camp field.

The Bishop, even as the war ground on to more and more waste of lives and destruction and devastation, voiced a deep concern for the church's work after the war.

> The world is going to demand honesty and justice after the war as never before, because it has now had object lessons which it cannot forget.

> The men who survive this war are going to insist that greed and bribery shall no longer be rewarded, and that governments should be run on a high plane, where men give their service for their country with no hope of anything but legitimate reward.

> And now that this overwhelming crisis has come to the world, the Church will not fail her children . . . The Church after the war will not only comfort those who mourn, but will give to those who must lead a broken life the vision splendid which will light the darkness and weariness of the road.

> And when the war is over, the Church must be ready to put into practice the law of forgiveness as never before. After the war the world will look, as perhaps it does now, far more than you think, for the message of love, and forgiveness, of pardon and mercy.

Chapter Eleven

Booze, Boom, and Blasphemy

On May 21, 1919, the Diocese of Long Island celebrated its semi-centennial with appropriate ceremonies. "High dignitaries participated in a procession which formed at the See House and were led by the rousing music of the Twenty-third Regiment Band." They marched to and around the Cathedral in Garden City stopping at the front steps where the throng was met by the Bishop of the Diocese. He was wreathed in the luster of the Gothic doors and was surrounded by servicemen who had recently returned from overseas as well as clergy, choir boys and acolytes. He addressed a word of welcome to all who shared in the celebration. The long procession then reformed and walked to the long cathedral aisle to take part in the festival service of thanksgiving, the Eucharist. Following the impressive commemoration at Garden City, a solemn *Te Deum* was sung at St. Luke's Church, Brooklyn, as part of the festival musical service held on May 22, 1919.

In the Bishop's address commemorating the fiftieth anniversary of the Diocese, he looked to the future:

> The time is fast approaching when the Church is to be weighed in the balance by the new age. Stop thinking about fifty years ago and bemoaning the changed condition. . . . We must go forward and meet the era, the new aeon in the history of the world.

> The Church must accept the challenge. . . . The Church must show that it has a part to play in the National development. Mighty changes have come in men's estimate of religion through the exigencies of a war which, with its lurid light, brought out in bold relief the stern realities of life. . . . The world wants to hear . . . the Gospel.

Things had changed. It was not the same world that Long Islanders knew only a few years ago.

> During the three or four years that followed the Armistice of 1918 there came a subtle change in the emotional weather. The torch of idealism that had kindled the revolt of the American conscience seemed to have pretty well burned itself out. People were bored. In particular their public spirit, their consciences, and their hopes were tired.

Returning soldiers brought with them a deep sense of disillusionment with "the Great Crusade." Enthusiasm for the League of Nations, the President's hope for peace, petered out, and America "played in its own backyard." Trying to strive onward and upward, the electorate chose handsome but ineffectual Warren G. Harding, who talked about "normalcy" but socialized with some of the biggest grafters in the country. "Tea Pot Dome" Harding was followed by "Honest," but negative, "Cal" Coolidge. He exhibited his great genius for inactivity, but the majority of the people accepted him.

Enjoyment of trivia was accompanied by a general desire to shake off the restraints of old-fashioned puritanism and upset the revered conventions of decorum. By 1920, the rebellion against stiffness, spearheaded by the emancipated woman, became full blown. In the mid-twenties women, formerly engulfed in ankle-length voluminous dresses and topped by long hair, emerged in short pencil thin dresses with bobbed, marcelled hair. They were ready to do the latest dance craze to the accompaniment of the popular jazzband. Mary Pickford, the embodiment of sweet girlish innocence, had been pushed aside by Clara Bow, the "IT" girl.

Flappers, lighted cigarette in hand, discussed the latest book or the newest religious fad. H. L. Mencken, Sinclair Lewis, and Ernest Hemingway wooed the flaming set with their favorite dart-targets, Victorian propriety, reformers, small towns, religion and the "lost generation." The disillusionment was matched by fanatic attraction of all kinds of religious variations. Aimee Semple McPherson brought them in by the thousands with her "four-square" gospel. New cults enticed the dilettante intellectual in the city. A far cry from the delightfully sensuous fads and ideas of the urban centers was the last ditch stand of the fundamentalists in the South. The Klu Klux Klan reigned supreme and anti-intellectuals fought with anti-evolution laws and a new series of blue laws. The orgy came to its fitting climax in 1925, when the Scopes Monkey trial began to act out its facetious drama.

Many Americans still clung to their "old time religion" and their new found prejudices. Religious house parties became the rage with everyone talking about Buchmanism. The hate for Germans switched to the Bolsheviks with the red panic of 1919. Intolerance for Jews, immigrants and foreigners made the Sacco-Vanzetti case and the Black race riots famous with the crowning achievement being the Chicago Race Riot. With the reaction against Non-Americans came stricter enforcement of immigration. Contracted during World War I, immigration rose to 805,228 in 1921. Afraid of conquest by foreigners, America's government complied with quota restrictions which fixed the total number admitted to the United States to less than two hundred thousand.

Semi-centennial celebration in front of Cathedral in Garden City.

In spite of it all, Americans were buoyed up by the optimistic outlook that things were getting better and better. After a brief recession intertwined with strikes, the country settled down to a post-war business boom. The Stock Market became the local playground where stocks could be bought easily upon margin. Everyone could readily join the chorus of "How the Money Rolls In."

NEXT WEEK WE'VE GOT TO GET ORGANIZED

While Americans dabbled in Fords, flappers and fanatics, the Diocese floated along by absorbing itself in the purely mundane but absolutely necessary task of updating its structure and reorganizing its finances. Spurred by the revolutionary step of the 1919 General Convention — at which the new body, the Presiding Bishop and Council, later known as the National Council, was born — the Diocese of Long Island attempted to imitate the same spirit by concentrating on the formation of a Diocesan Council.

Fear of a centralized body, an ingrained characteristic of the Episcopal Church, had deterred any kind of national organization. As early as 1900, the need for a unified administrative group to coordinate the separate activities of missions, education, and social service had been voiced but not realized. Finally in 1919, the dream was fulfilled and the Episcopal Church had its own "curia." The Council, in addition to unifying the general church program, prepared and submitted to the General Convention a budget for the following triennium. A body which made the budget was a body with power. Finally the Council had the right to employ full-time personnel.

For the Diocese, it took a few years longer for achievement of united action, although it was badly needed. The Diocese had struggled for many years to accomplish its mission through a widely segmented division of committees, standing committees, special committees, interested individuals, and small groups of individuals. Each group with special interests had its own imperatives and its own inimitable task of sponsoring its programs. The results were confusion, conflict, and most of all, countless appeals that had no appeal. A step in the right direction had been achieved by the Diocese in its participation in the nationwide campaign. The National Church by 1919 was feeling overwhelming financial pressures caused in part by the inability or unwillingness of dioceses to support the general church program. To find a solution, a gigantic survey of the missionary, educational and social service needs, was made by the general Church. It became a huge plan for social and missionary uplift with propaganda, "some of it valuable, but most of it decidedly ephemeral and worthless . . . sent far and wide." Enthusiasm for the new movement swelled to flood-tide. "In the joint meeting of the two houses at Detroit and during the eloquent appeals, it almost seemed as if no sum up to one hundred million dollars could be too large." The bubble of bloated hope broke at the meeting of the newly organized council when only eight million dollars had been realized.

Yet in the Diocese of Long Island, the nationwide campaign had produced effects far beyond the realization of many. Responding to the "nationwide campaign of education and inspiration to be conducted during the last part of the year (1919), culminating in a nationwide every-member canvass of every parish," the Diocese set up a small committee to follow through. The outcome was exhilarating. Giving had increased 117 percent. In 1920, Long Island stood tenth in size of gifts, and although only paying 20 percent of its quota, it had increased by 71 percent over the past. Parochial support had increased 63 percent.

> The support of our Archdeaconries has been far more dependable than before. The money given to religious education and to the cause of Christian Social Service has been more than doubled. Salaries of several of the poorly paid Clergy have been supplemented by gifts from our Diocesan Fund. The Church Mission of Help has been greatly assisted in the sad yet hopeful work which it is doing to restore the fallen, and to save the children. The support of the Diocesan House . . . has been assumed and met by this Committee.

The Diocese postponed the formation of its own council. Instead it continued a small campaign committee to which was entrusted the task of supervision and distribution of funds. Its wise action and judgment were instrumental "in bringing about the very considerable success which this movement has had on Long Island." At its 55th convention in May 1921, the Diocese finally formed its central body with the adoption of Canon 6. The Diocesan Council, composed of the Bishop, eight laymen and four clergymen (appointed by the Bishop and subject to the approval of the convention) had the responsibility of "coordinating and supervising the Financial, Missionary, Educational and Social Work of the Church in this Diocese."

The Council met six times a year and gave its attention to seven areas: service and stewardship; missions and church extension; religious education; Christian social services; diocesan institutions and organizations; budget and finance; and publicity. The Council had the power of control by compiling a budget that included a diocesan united program and "such quotas as the Presiding Bishop and Council may allot to this Diocese to be raised for the work of the National Church." The adoption of the new structure had certain definite aspects. The canon gave the Council the right to demand that the principles of the nationwide campaign be lived up to in each parish. One principle was that "the large bulk of contributions shall be placed in the hands of the central board of the Diocese, for the Bishop and Council to distribute according to their discretion." This insured "better service than having many separate appeals and a struggle or rivalry on the part of various societies and undertakings for support." The tendency in the Diocese was to avoid "machinery . . . too elaborate and expensive in proportion to the product" and "to extensively employ clergymen in the position of field secretaries." The Bishop felt this was a mistake: "The multiplying of secretarial or travelling agencies for the Clergy seems a dangerous experiment, and, so far as I have been able to judge, the results have hardly warranted its continuance."

SHIFTING SANDS

The duality of Long Island became even more pronounced after the war. What had once been a small movement eastward of population turned into a turbulent torrent, as the City merged more of the Island into its diversified complex. By 1925, Long Island stood squarely divided between the congested areas of urban Brooklyn and Queens and the rural areas of Nassau and Suffolk. So pronounced was the division that the less dense eastern counties became known as "Long Island." Brooklyn and Queens, were simply "the City." In crowded Brooklyn and Queens, population stood at its highest index. Unlike its neighbor Manhattan, which had lost some people, Brooklyn had gained, registering a tremendous apex of 2,203,235; its eastern counterpart, Queens, had 714,647 people. The two combined eastern counties of Nassau and Suffolk could account for only 350 thousand, a mere drop in the bucket compared to the total Island population of 3,268,730.

Together with an increasing concentration of peoples on its western end went Long Island's pre-eminence in industry and commerce. Exceeding twenty-four states in number of people, Brooklyn ranked fourth in the nation and sixth in the world in its industrial life. Manufactured goods, valued at more than 1.6 billion dollars were produced annually in Brooklyn; 4,293 manufacturers employed almost 150 thousand workers. In commerce, Brooklyn led the world in importation and distribution of both coffee and sugar. One-fourth of the foreign commerce passed through Brooklyn's two hundred miles of waterfront. It had 187 piers for ocean freighters, five of them being the largest in the world. As a financial center and shopping mecca, Brooklyn had few rivals.

The city's industrial and commercial life spilled over into Queens but on a smaller scale. Ninety thousand men were employed at 2,200 established industries. Miles of industrial waterfrontage on the East River and Jamaica Bay offered ample space for both commercial and industrial expansion. In comparison, Nassau and Suffolk seemed relatively serene and untouched. Any noticeable activity focused on accommodating the incoming population who, pushed out from the City by dynamic industry and a swelling foreign population, had left the "ancestral homes" to seek out new homes in spacial and garden surroundings.

As the face of the Island changed, so too did its inner character. For many years the domain of the Protestant, Long Island and Brooklyn, in particular, assumed a religious pluralistic pose. The year 1900 seemed far away when Protestant churches held over half the population. By 1925, the balance between the three groups — Protestant, Roman Catholic and Jewish — had reached an equilibrium of one third each.

Brooklyn's growing and teeming population needed more and more housing. Areas such as Gravesend, Sheepshead Bay and Canarsie, less desirable at first, began to fill up with multitudinous and varied dwellings. It was Brooklyn's apartment house days, with tall cliff-dwellings rising in the most unusual places. Flatbush, essentially suburban, after 1920 saw large apartment complexes rise amid its small homes. Park Slope glittered with its "gold coast" apartments. Brooklyn Heights gave way to hotels and multi-family housing. Eastern Parkway was built up; Midwood and Brownsville received a large influx of Jews; Borough Park, built in the twenties, became a section of one and two family homes, intermixed with large apartments. Coney Island, benefiting from the extension of the subway, encouraged home development, and its beach became everyman's Riviera. Flatlands filled up; Sunset Park had the first cooperative apartment in Brooklyn; and Williamsburgh, one of the oldest sections of the city, by the mid-twenties had become the worst slum area in the metropolis. Queen's western section experienced urban development with more houses, larger housing units, and densely populated regions. "Long Island" remained aloof from radical change. Villages gradually became towns; hamlets grew into substantial villages; and streets were paved. Remote parts were made more accessible by the automobile, but they did not become intimately involved in the radical transformation. Some parts of Nassau remained rural. Suffolk resisted any development, content to retain its summer profile of a playground but able to retain its bucolic conservative and austere atmosphere.

The Episcopal Church's response to the growing diversity of Island life spattered in several utterly different directions, but none more noticeable or extraordinary than in its church missionary extension. Due to wartime pressures and stringent curbs, no new church came into existence between 1915 and 1920. Then in the following five short years, thirteen new missions were founded, not in the familiar ground of Brooklyn, but in the burgeoning region of Queens and Nassau. Except for one new church in Brooklyn and two summer chapels in Suffolk, the majority of new churches were established in Queens and Nassau. For already established churches, new conditions brought new challenges to which parishes had to adapt, sometimes in tenuous or devious ways.

The Waning of Brooklyn —

Churches in Brooklyn showed a decided disadvantage amid the changing constituency of the City. Older parishes, securely esconced in formerly lush sections, found their communicants and neighborhoods more radically changed. A steady decline in communicant strength made the churches cavernous hollow memorials to a by-gone day. Few, if any, attempted to change with their surroundings. They continued to ply their course as before, ministering to a smaller and smaller group of individuals. Some joined the ranks of defunct parishes. To that list was added St. David's, St. Margaret's and Holy Comforter. Large parishes, such as St. Ann's, St. Luke's and Grace Church were reduced to almost half their size. St. Ann's membership dropped to less than half its former 1,272. Church of the Messiah registered only 850 compared to 1,387 fifteen years before. St. Luke's had less than 500 communicants. Holy Trinity on the Heights tried to adapt by offering community neighborhood services, but its former glory could never be recaptured. A sure index of decline was shown in the Sunday Schools. All Saints' School found its enrollment cut from 566 to 299; by 1925, Atonement had only 142 of its previous 672 children; Christ Chapel, most drastically affected, had five times less its former 1,030 pupils; and St. James' was down to 78 pupils.

As most older parishes in Brooklyn showed sure signs of deceleration, a few took on new life. St. Paul's, Flatbush, reached the dazzling height of 1,603 communicants and 624 Sunday School pupils; St. Thomas', Bushwick, shone just as brightly with 1,505 members and 575 children. The far distant parishes in Queens and Nassau took up the Brooklyn slack. St. George's, Flushing, had 1,065 people and 425 pupils; Grace Church, Jamaica, 1,217 communicants and almost 700 pupils. Even remote Garden City, the despair of Brooklyn, surpassed the majority of city parishes, having 648 members and 306 children.

With their membership sharply decreased and their income curtailed, Brooklyn churches began to depend more and more on their endowments. The financial crutch, small at the beginning of Bishop Burgess' episcopate, had grown in a few cases to astronomical proportions. St. Ann's had almost a $200,000 dollar endowment; Grace Church almost half a million; and St. Paul's, Clinton Street, $100,000. Substantial endowments helped St. Peter's, Christ Church, Bedford Avenue, Redeemer and St. Mary's ease the pain of less money and half empty churches.

Missionary work in the City, first under The Rev. George F. Bambach and then The Rev. Charles G. Clark in 1924, found real expression in its existing mission stations. A quickly growing neighborhood had aided the incorporation of a former mission, Church of the Epiphany on January 17, 1923. The Italian mission showed steady but sure progress. St. Simon's still held services in its portable chapel. St. Lydia's, fourteen years old, had difficult times in changing conditions due to war and no resident clergyman. Holy Cross and St. Gabriel's had achieved self-support; but none of the missions could show the great progress that St. Philip's had under its priest of twenty years, The Rev. Nathaniel P. Boyd. In fact, two of the newest missions, Church of the Advent and St. Agnes' experienced,

> conditions . . . more and more difficult to meet and handle with complete satisfaction. The
> entire West End region of Brooklyn where these two churches [were] located passed through
> a change in population which had left very few church people in that section.

The real difficulty facing all missions and churches lay in Brooklyn's transient character.

> Brooklyn with its ever changing population and its steady flow of people out and in, presents perhaps a more difficult problem than does the other sections of the Diocese of Long Island. No sooner does our faithful Priest-in-charge begin to gather a fairly encouraging congregation then he suddenly awakes to the fact that they have, almost over night, folded their tents and stolen away.

So with diminished ranks, this priest would begin again only to find the same process repeated.

Two new and exciting works did grow out of the new Brooklyn. On the Eve of the Conversion of St. Paul, the Bishop dedicated the renovated Guild Hall of the extinct parish of the Holy Comforter and set it apart as a mission to the Jews. "To bring to them the call of the Christ in an effective way," Mr. Harry G. Greenberg, a converted Jew, had the task "of awakening the church to her responsibility for God's Ancient People." The work had the aspect of social service although services in Yiddish, Hebrew and English were held. The beginning of St. Cyprian's mission was quite different. A petition from a "mission of West Indian colored people" in the summer of 1921, to be taken under the care of the Archdeaconry, resulted in the beginning of the Diocese's fourth mission among Brooklyn's Black people.

Under the leadership of the Rev. Canon Roy Farrel Duffield, the Diocese founded ten new missions in Queens and Nassau. In 1923, the parochial mission of Grace Church, St. Albans, was taken over by the Diocese. The portable chapel abandoned by the Forest Hills Church was transferred to the new mission for church services. In that same year, services were held in the firehouse of Springfield Gardens, the beginning of St. John's Church; and later in the year St. Mark's Church initiated services for Jackson Heights in "a store loaned by the Queensboro Corporation." A fourth new mission in Corona began for the Blacks. St. Stephen's, South Ozone Park, also began in 1923. A parochial mission at Grace Church in Dunton was replaced by the mission St. John's Chapel. In Nassau a sprinkling of new works added to the already growing churches. On the South Shore a mission began in Valley Stream in 1920. It was followed by two Baldwin missions, initially begun by the Rector of St. John the Beloved Disciple in New York City. In 1922, St. Mary's Chapel, beginning as a diocesan mission, was turned over to the Rector of Advent, Westbury, for development. St. Paul's mission in Great Neck began its life in 1924.

The cover of The Comforter magazine published by the Holy Comforter Mission.

A few bright spots lightened the work and gave encouragement. Three churches were consecrated. Two churches in Brooklyn, Trinity Church, East New York, and St. Martin's, and one in Suffolk, St. Mary's Good Ground, Hampton Bays, joined the ranks of debt-free parishes. Pride emanated from the incorporation of four mission stations: St. Mary's, Amityville; St. Gabriel's, Hollis; Christ Church, Lynbrook; and the Memorial Church of the Transfiguration, Brooklyn. An unusual glamour surrounded the building of St. Luke's Church in Forest Hills. When the parish contemplated a church building after outgrowing its small portable chapel, Bishop Burgess suggested that the new church be made a memorial to his long-standing friend, Theodore Roosevelt. It had been at the invitation of the Bishop that he came to Forest Hills in 1917 where a large crowd heard him deliver "what was generally regarded as his finest wartime speech, a stirring patriotic plea for Preparedness which became known as his '100 per cent Americanism' speech." Newspapers and magazines picked up the story and amid great fanfare of quip, story and satire that elaborated the "Acts of Holy Theodore," St. Luke's was built and finally dedicated by Bishop Burgess on Sunday, March 25, 1924.

Under the able direction of the veteran Archdeacon, the Rev. William Holden, the churches in Suffolk did all they could to surmount latent hostility and few followers. The existing missions were joined by two newcomers. Growing out of a summer colony, St. Andrew's, Saltaire, began holding regular services for two months. In Westhampton Beach an extension of the work at Quoque was started with the actual formation of a congregation known as St. Mark's.

Eastward Ho —

Church extension either by the diocesan missionary program or by parochial leadership, resulted in an increased number of parishes and missions that numbered 158 by 1925. The number of churches paled in regard to the deeper meaning for the future. The trend and development of the Diocese lay in the distribution of the parishes. Portent and omen, Brooklyn, once the dynamic center of the Diocese had retrograded before the advance of the other Island sections. The fifty-seven churches and one institutional chapel fell short of the growing and spreading sixty-three parishes or missions in Queens and Nassau. True the Brooklyn churches far outstripped churches in Suffolk, Queens and Nassau in terms of money, influence and physical plant, but the die was cast. The prophesies and warnings of the Bishop and various diocesan officials had begun to come true. Queens and Nassau showed their place of prominence that would grow rapidly in the succeeding years. Symbolic and once remote from diocesan life, the Cathedral now felt life pulsating within it. The Cathedral did not come to the City; the City had finally come to the Cathedral.

HEAL THE SICK; RESCUE THE FALLEN

Eager and ardent involvement in the social issues of the day, so prominent a part of diocesan life in the Progressive Era, sank to a level of mere moralizing. The Social Service Committee, a dynamic force for social reform, were aware of the post-war tensions and requested diocesan pronouncements on the World Court, child labor, an eight-hour day and disarmament; but they channelled most of their energies into initiating and strengthening a new avenue of the church's ministry—that to unwed mothers.

As early as 1916, the Committee awakened the Diocese to its responsibility for fallen young women who needed rescue. An investigation of "methods employed by various hospitals in Brooklyn as to how they separated illegitate babies from their mothers" made the Committee aware of the plight. It bemoaned the fact that nothing was done to rehabilitate unwed mothers to prevent a second fall. A small beginning had been made in 1911 in Manhattan by Fr. Huntington O.H.C. He began the Church Mission of Help (later to become the Family Consultation Service), which attempted to minister to the unwed mother. The sympathetic work had in many cases touched Long Island, with an increasing number of cases being attended in Brooklyn and the City.

Case work on Long Island grew to such proportions that in December 1917, the President of the Church Mission of Help appealed to the Diocese for funds to pay an additional social worker to attend to the needs of Long Island. A meeting for interested clergy, members of the Woman's Auxiliary, and others was held at the Diocesan House in April 1918. About seventy-five women were present to hear the appeal of Mrs. L. Frederic Pease, secretary of the Church Mission of Help, and to hear her explain "the organized effort of the Church for the rescue and rehabilitation of wayward girls." Several made contributions to a $1,200 fund for the salary of a trained woman worker.

More extensive cooperation with the Manhattan agency began in August 1918, with the formation of a group of Associates. They joined together to further the work on Long Island, and procured a "very efficient salaried worker among girls," to cooperate with the Church Mission of Help in Manhattan. The worker, Miss Frank L. Clawson, had office hours in the Diocesan House, with use of a telephone and a room to interview the girls as well as a closet for clothes. A real need surfaced at the beginning of the diocesan branch. The Associates looked forward to having "a home, self-supporting and small, where a mother could live, go out to work and return to the baby at night." An encouraging report was made after the first full year of active work among the young women. The social worker reported that she had ninety-one cases during the year (forty-three unmarried mothers, twenty preventative, twenty-eight delinquent) all taken care of. Parish groups interested in the casework agency had furnished clothing for mother and baby as well as raising money for a milk fund.

In the beginning and up to 1924, the Church Mission of Help showed a commendable record of assistance to its girls. Over 700 girls and 400 babies had come under its supervision. Referrals from hospitals, social agencies, parishes and courts made the workload so heavy that the staff of caseworkers was increased to four. A request from the Bedford Reformatory in Westchester to take over the Long Island girls on parole made an additional worker an imperative. The agency had accomplished a great task in returning their charges to a happy and normal life.

> Some of these girls have left the diocese, some are in institutions, some in custodial homes, a few have disappeared, but the large majority are in positions where they are earning an honest wage and are leading a self-respecting life. Many are married and have happy homes.

Not currently appealing but equally as necessary was the work of the Church Charity Foundation. In all of its departments, small in number since the war, it ministered to the sick, the aged and the blind. Yet things did not go well. The year 1920 closed with a deficit even though over half a million dollars had been raised for the expansion of the Foundation. Moreover, a real need showed in physical plant deterioration. In 1922, the Bishop made public the projected needs of the Foundation: a new hospital was necessary and the old one should be converted for the use of convalescents. By 1924, full plans for the new St. John's Hospital had been formulated. The full scope of operations needed a new power house, a chapel and a hospital with 190 beds — one third would be free, one third private and one third semi-private. The estimated cost of the new plan was one and one-half million dollars. Although the need for hospital renovations and expansion was imperative, the cautious Bishop kept to his policy that no work could be done until all funds were in hand. Unfortunately the Foundation, in the midst of its germinating expansion, suffered the loss of its superintendent, The Rev. Canon Paul Swett. Work was immediately put under the direction of returned World War I veteran, The Rev. Charles H. Webb, who in one year "showed an efficient service to the charity."

St. Luke's, Forest Hills

(above) The home-like setting of the children's cottages in Sayville.
(below) Church Charity Foundation girls' building in Sayville.

Besides the regularly established hospital, nursing school, home for the aged and the blind, a new work began in this period. A valuable tract of land in Sayville had been given to the Foundation, which after careful consideration, the Board of Managers decided to use for the discontinued care of orphaned children. A new method of ministering to the homeless characterized the Foundation's new work. In order to overcome "the institutional child" product of large orphanages, the cottage system was used. The plan called for the erection of small homes in which a family atmosphere could be introduced. The care of children in the new method was far more expensive since true-hearted and high-minded attendants, skilled in dealing with children, and taking the place of mother and father were costly. However, the plan was put into effect with the Sisters from the Foundation put in charge. A "well equipped cottage for girls" was followed in 1925 with a building for boys. It cost $20,000 and was a memorial to the late Canon Swett. The cornerstone of the Memorial Cottage was laid by Bishop Burgess in the summer of 1925.

A long-standing, diversified work of the Diocese, sometimes charitable, sometimes social uplifting, had changed its character to the mundane task of ministering to the sick. St. Phebe's Mission had been converted into a convalescent home. Its other functions, so vital in the early years of the Diocese, had been gradually sapped by civic organizations or church charitable institutions. The settlement house on DeKalb Avenue entered a new phase of its existence. It filled the gap between hospital and home, taking care of convalescents until such time as they could return to their families and friends, healthy and ready to resume a normal existence. Long-term cases and chronic illnesses did not receive attention, only referrals that needed loving care with professional knowledge.

DIOCESAN MISCELLANEA

The Diocese followed its usual pursuits of money, program, and personnel. The Board of Religious Education, encouraged by the example of the Field Secretary for Social Service, made an ardent plea for a similar worker. Under the leadership of the Rev. G. Ashton Oldham, the future Bishop of Albany, the Board felt that the continuing loss in Sunday School enrollment necessitated a full-time worker. An Executive Secretary for Education was finally procured, a Miss Eveleen, who began an interesting program of Church Normal Schools, Training Courses, and educational centers at strategic points in the Diocese. The churches chosen to serve as such were St. Ann's, Brooklyn; Christ Church, Bay Ridge; and Grace Church, Jamaica. A church school service league was formed to work in five different fields of service.

The diocesan board initiated a new and immediately successful event, "Children's Day at the Cathedral." The first "day" held on May 26, 1923, with Bishop Burgess present, drew over three thousand delegates from eighty-six parishes. "The majority had never seen the Cathedral before and some didn't know one existed." The second of a long line of Cathedral Days was held in June of the following year. Ninety-six out of 160 schools took part. A banner contest for missionary offerings was recognized on Cathedral Day, with a large increase from $2,500 in 1917 to $14,000 in 1924.

Concern for education was matched by the prosaic but important concern for diocesan symbols, chiefly the official coat-of-arms. A committee had been appointed in 1922 "to investigate the origin, authority, significance and proper blazoning of the device known as the 'Arms of the Diocese of Long Island'." The coat-of-arms, originally designed by the Rev. Beverly Robinson Betts, Librarian of Columbia University, had been corrupted from the original design. Investigations showed that the ends of the three crosses which ended in three small crosses had not been properly carried out and that properly a diocesan coat-of-arms could have no other crest but a mitre. A recapitulation of the original arms was presented to the Diocese and approval was requested for it to be the official insignia of all diocesan work.

> From the arms of Alexander, Earl of Stirling, first Lord Proprietor of Long Island, he (the designer) chose a chevron, and from those of Macdonald, quartered in the Earl of Stirling's arms, he took gold for the shield, and a cross of red whose base was sharpened to a point and whose other three ends were made into miniature crosses. The sharpened base of this cross indicates, said the designer, the missionary task of our new diocese, to plant the cross in every part of our island. The "crosslet" arms show the propagating power of the Gospel, each cross planted multiplies crosses. From the arms of the ancient family of Stewart, in graceful recognition of the benefactors to our diocese of Alexander T. Stewart and his wife, the designer took the colors silver and blue and laid them in alternate wavy bands across the chevron, symbolizing the waters surrounding our island. For a motto he chose the appropriate words of the Psalmists, "I will set His Dominion in the sea", and for a crest he used a mitre, the familiar emblem of episcopal jurisdiction. Our arms thus have the virtue of correct heraldry, and are rich in historical significance and symbolic meaning.

No formal adoption of the device had been made in the Diocese. To that end, in 1924 the committee on the arms moved that the Diocese adopt it as the official designation and that it be entrusted to the Secretary of the Diocese who was to be "charged with the custody of the Arms of the Diocese . . . and so far as possible to prevent the use of misrepresentation."

CHANGING LEADERSHIP

In the twenty years of Bishop Burgess' episcopate, no radical change had come in the personnel of parish and diocese. Long rectorships had kept the same men at their parochial posts and in their diocesan offices. The power block still remained in Brooklyn with the majority of elective and appointed offices still being controlled by the Brooklyn clergy. A small percentage of clergy from the rest of the Island was allowed to participate in decision-making. The Rev. Chauncey B. Brewster, successor to the long-termed Rev. Charles H. Hall as President of the Standing Committee had his tenure cut short by election as the Bishop of Connecticut. He was succeeded by the Rev. Henry C. Swentzel who held the office all during Bishop Burgess' time and part of Bishop Stires' episcopate. The same condition prevailed in other offices. Coming to the Diocese in 1886, the Rev. Resse F. Alsop had filled many diocesan posts until his death in 1922. Among the diocesan leaders of long standing were such men as the Rev. Messrs. St. Clair Hester, Rector of Messiah; J. Clarence Jones, Rector of St. Mary's; Charles F. J. Wrigley, Grace Church Rector; J. Howard Melish, Holy Trinity; Robert Rogers, Good Shepherd; and G. Ashton Oldham, St. Ann's. The Brooklyn clergy had in their ranks one clergyman from Queens, the Rector of St. George's, Flushing. The Rev. Henry D. Waller, and the Dean of the Cathedral, played a prominent part in diocesan work. On the death of Dean Cox in 1903, the Very Rev. John Moses assumed the Cathedral responsibility, and next came the Very Rev. Oscar F. R. Treder.

By 1922, the ranks had thinned a little. On the twentieth anniversary of the Bishop's consecration, the change was most noticeable. Of the 116 clergymen who had elected the second Bishop in 1901, only forty were still canonically resident, and only ten were still rectors of the same parishes.

The diminished ranks were filled with new men. The number of clergy that held office remained small but became more diversified with leadership coming from outside the Brooklyn block. The city clergy leaders remained almost the same with a few new names appearing in important posts. They included the Rev. Wallace J. Gardner, St. Paul's, Flatbush; the Rev. Duncan M. Genns, St. Thomas', Bushwick; the Rev. John H. Fitzgerald, Christ Church, Bay Ridge. More leadership came from the clergy in the suburban areas. Important posts went to the Rev. Richard D. Pope, Advent, Westbury; the Rev. Arthur Cummins, Resurrection, Richmond Hill; the Rev. Rockland T. Homans, Grace Church, Jamaica; the Rev. Roy F. Duffield, Archdeacon of Queens and Nassau; the Rev. William R. Watson, St. Peter's, Bay Shore; and the Rev. Samuel C. Fish, St. Ann's, Bridgehampton. At this time a young candidate for Holy Orders had come to the attention of the Diocese. The Archdeaconry of Queens and Nassau had undertaken church school instruction at St. Giles' in Garden City by hiring one who "also conducted a summer school for the children at Jamaica Creek" where some of the children in that section were completely ignorant of the simplest religious truths. The name of the aspiring clergyman was Harry Jerome Stretch.

The laity who had been so instrumental in carrying on the diocesan program and policy showed a more striking picture. The older generation of laymen had disappeared. There were still members of the Floyd-Jones and Pierrepont families in prominent places but such familiar names as Webster, Marvin, Benson, Aldrich, and Husted were no longer seen. Men such as Alexander Orr, Mynderse, William Male and a score of others gave way to new men. In diocesan life new and outstanding civic leaders took an active part in diocesan life. Frank Gulden, William Baldwin, Walter R. Marsh, Augustus Van Wyck were given prominent places. Two men who were to give so much to the Diocese began their careers — Raymond F. Barnes of Good Shepherd, Brooklyn and Col. Jackson A. Dykman of St. Paul's, Glen Cove.

THE SAME OLD REFRAIN

Bishop Burgess in his episcopate had constantly prodded the Diocese to have a sane and sound conviction on proposed amalgamations, unity schemes and reconciliation to the denominations, and he continually appealed for diocesan acceptance and support of the Cathedral center at Garden City. The closing years of his term as Bishop were no different. He kept before the Diocese his hopes for the Cathedral and his counsel for christian unity.

Schemes for some kind of church unity had fermented for many years. The attempts in the pre-war progressive era halted for a time during the war, but immediately after cessation of combat, the Episcopal Church became embroiled again in overtures to denominations and plans for eventual reunion. Negotiations with the Congregationalists, the proposed canon on ordination, the Concordet of 1919, and the 1922 General Convention report, "Proposals for an Approach toward Unity," had agitated and confused the question of the Episcopal Church in its relationship to other churches. The matter was further enhanced by the final plans for a World Conference on Questions of Faith and Order to be held in Switzerland in 1927. In light of these developments, the Bishop felt constrained to speak out. Taking issue with two prevalent "advantages" of church union, he clearly asserted his own point of view, which was basically the same as proposed by the first Bishop. The big business idea of "efficiency" in a super-church; the hope of a united church becoming "a great civic power for good" which could also control the government for beneficient purposes; and the problem of freedom of the pulpit all came under his scrutiny. They just were not in keeping with the nature of the Church. For Bishop Burgess the ideal of unity rested neither in the economical nor political effectiveness but in its missionary influence.

> The Church must be united so that by its own glorious message it may inspire faith, faith to rise above materialism and believe the truth which no science can prove or disprove, that the Father hath sent his Son into the World. This is the kind of unity which when it is attained will redeem the world.

Approaches to any kind of unity rested upon the fulfillment of that purpose as it was ably and fully stated in the Chicago-Lambeth Quadrilateral and found in the essentials of the Catholic Faith.

The Bishop expressed in the same terms of unity, his hope for the Cathedral. The primary object of the Cathedral was not to provide a large preaching hall, or form a standard for ritual or model for services, but its first and foremost purpose was to symbolize and promote unity in the Diocese. "It is the Bishop's Church and as such it belongs to every Parish and to every parishioner throughout the Diocese." As such a symbol and center, the Cathedral needed the help and support of all the Diocese. The Cathedral, not like the large continental edifices but rather like the small English or Welsh Cathedrals, stood at the crossroads. It had a long and honorable history, and from the beginning it became the center of the Diocese not only in theory but in fact.

> This Cathedral situated as it is, very near what is coming to be the very center of the population of Long Island, can only be a help to the whole Diocesan life. It is rich in land, but the deeds of gift are so restricted that it can never share in the enormous improvement in land values. This is as it should be, for it places the whole future of the Cathedral in the hands of the members of the Diocese.

The Bishop had always concerned himself with welfare of the Cathedral. He had suggested and approved of a Vestry Committee, elected by the congregation with the Dean as Chairman, which would see to "the unification of the Cathedral parish's interest." Under the system the congregation had become "a generous contributor to Diocesan and missionary interests." His plans for a Diocesan Hall and needed parish buildings had stopped temporarily during the war, but were pursued again. The pressing problem for the Bishop and the Cathedral was acceptance by the Diocese. Even with all his encouragements and exhortations, the American prejudice against cathedrals and diocesan indifference to its own Cathedral, had created a chasm between the Diocese and the Cathedral. The situation had grown to such proportions that the Cathedral stood at that place where it needed full diocesan support to be made strong "through the increasing love of faithful communicants."

To show that the Cathedral was not rich on its own, Bishop Burgess had made it a policy that the Cathedral Chapter make annual reports to the convention. This was to keep the diocesan informed and to perhaps stimulate the "generous members of the Diocese" to give gifts, "large or small, which would increase the work and enlarge its endowments." The total aspect of the Cathedral called for drastic and immediate action. The Bishop encouraged the Diocese to form a Convention Committee to work with the Chapter to help, support and guide the future of the diocesan center. By this cooperation, the Cathedral would become that which it was: "The Bishop's Church, where the ordinations and other official services could be held and where the parishes could meet as in a common house."

DEATH OF A BISHOP

Bishop Burgess, active and dynamic in the Diocese, looked forward to the silver jubilee of his episcopate. In 1922, the Diocese recognized his twenty years of service, and although the strain of his office showed on his face, he still retained at the age of seventy-one the energy and power to fulfill his duties. For three more years he projected into the Diocese his hopes, his aims, and his policies. Then in February 1925, in the midst of regular routine — visiting Redeemer Parish, Brooklyn, and confirming a class at St. John's Church, Brooklyn — a severe and sudden heart attack stopped his visits and curtailed his functions.

> Neighboring Bishops came to his assistance. The Syrian Orthodox Archbishop Germanos filled the confirmation appointments during Holy Week — the only instance in Church History where an Eastern Orthodox Bishop administered confirmation with the Prayer Book Rites.

The twelve-week illness gave the Bishop an opportunity to think and consider his future. He remembered the bitter criticism and harsh feelings against Bishop Littlejohn during his illness and the avid hostility towards his insistence of not needing a co-adjutor. So a few days before the 1925 convention Bishop Burgess wrote a letter to the Diocesan Secretary. Dated May 13, 1925, it read:

> In view of the fact that I have undergone a serious breakdown which may be of a permanent character, I am constrained to ask the Diocesan Convention meeting . . . May 26th, to provide canonical relief for the work of the Bishop by the election of a Bishop co-adjutor.

Alerted to the proposal the convention at its afternoon session, under a resolution made by the Rev. Richard Pope, undertook the election of a Bishop coadjutor. Eighteen names were presented to the convention among which were the Rev. Robert Rogers, the Dean of the Cathedral; the Rev. J. Clarence Jones; the Rev. Henry

Swentzel; the Venerable Roy F. Duffield; and the Rev. Ernest Milmore Stires. The list was nominated by the Rev. Wallace Gardner, Rector of St. Paul's Church, Flatbush. The first ballot showed the favored hometown candidate, Canon Duffield, leading all candidates with Stires and Rogers trailing behind with less than half the number of Duffield's votes. On succeeding ballots the clergy held firmly behind Duffield, while the votes for the other candidates slowly swung to Dr. Stires. On the fifth ballot, with a majority in both lay and clerical vote, Stires was declared the winner and the next Bishop of Long Island. Bishop Burgess was notified of the election and graciously accepted the decision of the Diocese. Entirely satisfied with the choice, Bishop Burgess commented:

> The preparation which he has had while he has been serving as Rector of one of the largest of our Metropolitan Parishes and his zeal and enthusiasm which have always been foremost in his character, are themselves abundant justification of your expression and confidence.

As if a premonition of impending death had directed his decision, Bishop Burgess did not recover from his illness. His engagements in the Diocese were kept at a minimal. He did have a small confirmation in the See House where he got about in a small wheelchair. The "broken yet heroic" Bishop made his last public act by laying the cornerstone of the Swett Memorial Cottage in Sayville. His health failed beyond control and succumbing to the heart disease, he died October 15, 1925. He was buried in that which he loved, the Cathedral. After solemn and appropriate services, his remains were placed in the Crypt Chapel, not far from the Stewarts who had given so much in the Cathedral. A marble slab marked the resting place of the second Bishop of Long Island.

No long eulogies epitomized the simple but great Bishop. His life stood as his monument of devotion to the Church and the Diocese. Responding to the times and needs of the hastily erected Diocese, he had brought it from a position of weakness and indecision to a peak of assurance, well-being, and respectability in which honest, industry, and integrity were largely written. Cautious and conservative, his stringent but commendable policies proved valid in the end. He had made the Diocese of Long Island.

> The Bishop possessed unusual gifts as a preacher, which he was rather unwilling to use outside the regular course of duty in the Diocese. His ability as an administrator was marked. But his outstanding contribution to the life of the church in his time was his strong and rugged defense of the Faith as it seemed from time to time to be threatened.

Bishop Burgess had seen the realization of many high hopes, yet some of his fondest dreams never materialized. Adequate salaries for his mission priests were advocated but never achieved. As early as 1910, his hopes were voiced by the Archdeacons of Brooklyn and of Queens and Nassau. They joining with the Bishop commented on this vital area of need. "The missionaries' stipends are lamentably small," they said.

> The rise in prices, which we hear so much about and which have caused strikes after strikes, has occasioned perhaps more real suffering among the clergy then any other class of people. Required to lead the lives of gentlemen ... they cannot strike, they cannot even make their wants known.

A study committee on clergy stipends made report after report to the Diocese but achieved little gain or relief for the underpaid clergy.

The same frustration showed in his other aspirations. Sites for future buildings, aggressive works among the Italians, Armenians and Jews were measures he advocated with persistence but never saw fully realized. His greatest dream for a diocesan hall and for a new St. John's Hospital had to wait for his successor. His dreams others carried out.

As an appropriate and fitting memorial to the Rt. Rev. Frederick Burgess, the Second Bishop of Long Island, 1901-1925, the Diocese installed in the Cathedral of the Incarnation a beautiful pulpit. The carved pulpit of wood had five figures inscribed upon it; in the center, St. Paul; on his right, St. Chrysostom and John Wycliffe; on his left, Bishop Seabury and Bishop Burgess. The pulpit stood "on the very spot where from the old temporary pulpit you often heard the wise and loving counsels of your consecrated leader...." At the sixty-third diocesan convention, May 21, 1929, the "Burgess Memorial Pulpit" was dedicated. But as his successor ably stated on that occasion, his lasting memorial was the Diocese itself:

> The Convention journals have made his labors an important part of the history of the church; while all over the Diocese new missions, new parishes, new institutions fostered by him or whole institutions freed from debt and strengthened under his leading give eloquent proof of a zeal unselfish and untiring.

THE ONCE AND FUTURE BISHOP

Little did the Diocese or the Bishop co-adjutor realize that full leadership would fall upon the novice Bishop. "It was my hope to stand by his side, to prolong his days among us by sharing his burdens, and loyally to carry forward his plans for the development of this important diocese," confided the new Bishop to his diocese. But such was not the case. The newly elected third Bishop of Long Island had to go it alone. The deceased Bishop did not even have the pleasure of seeing his co-adjutor consecrated.

Bishop Ernest Milmore Stires, Third Bishop Diocese of Long Island.

Section Four
Between Two Wars
(1925-1942)

Chapter Twelve

A City Rector for a Country Constituency

The third Bishop of Long Island was consecrated in New York City rather than in Garden City on November 25, 1925. This was the desire of the twenty-five year Rector of the large New York parish. Acquiescing to his wishes, the Diocese witnessed the consecration of its Bishop amid the lush surroundings of New York wealth. The solemn but joyous occasion was marked by some peculiarities as well as novelties. The ceremony was simple, almost austere. The bishops and priests appeared "in simple canonicals, no copes and mitres . . . and the ornate ritualism of the Catholic wing of the church [was] absent." In the procession representatives of "evangelical Churches" marched, the first time in such a ceremony. The consecration was beamed to all the area by the new communication means, the radio. The Bishop himself preferred all to be in a simple vein. The press called it a "low church consecration."

The new Bishop for the Island Diocese was no stranger in the church. Born in Norfolk, Virginia, on May 20, 1866, he had graduated from the University of Virginia and Virginia Theological Seminary. A southern aristocrat, he had served in parishes in Virginia and Georgia before being called to a large city parish in Chicago. In 1901, he became Rector of St. Thomas' Church, New York where he served until elected Bishop of Long Island. He was married and had four sons. He had earned respect and recognition as an efficient administrator and director through his parish work and his post on the Board of Missions with the National Council of the General Convention. He added to these qualifications, those of teacher and pastor. Coming to the insular Diocese from the security of a safe and secure parochial birth, the new Bishop would have his ability tested and his strength pressured. A mature, middle-aged man, he faced a new and alien constituency that would make or break the kindly, staid and proper aristocrat.

The Rt. Rev. Ernest Milmore Stires, D.D., L.H.D., D.C.L., was formally instituted as the third Bishop of Long Island at the Cathedral of the Incarnation, Garden City, New York, four days after his consecration in the city church. He was totally unacquainted with his new jurisdiction, labelled by one bishop, "as a group of parishes considered as religious clubs without reference to the community of which they are a part" or "a redeemed waste cast up by the sea, made beautiful for a resting place and playground for the rich and poor." The patrician prelate decided to make Brooklyn the concentration point of his efforts. Relinquishing at first the See House, Bishop Stires wintered at the Hotel Bossert in Brooklyn and directed affairs from 170 Remsen Street. "The most successful parish priest in the United States" felt in the first few months of his episcopate, that the city and its problems had been neglected and that he would bring the full intent of his office to bear on alleviating or solving its problems.

After two and one-half years of diocesan life and after travelling 35,000 miles in his Island jurisdiction, the Bishop had become "well-informed regarding the details of all the problems, opportunities, and necessities of the Diocese" and had achieved "a correct appreciation of these in their general character." Witnessing the "incredible growth of great communities within a single year," he urged that intelligence and business be infused into "our religion" and that "a great movement to claim these strategic points for God and country" be started. His admiration and respect for the clergy and laity who labored hard for the church had increased greatly. The Bishop knew that he did not have to "unscrew cantankerous rectors from their jobs or vestrymen from their vestries" because he was fortunate in having in the Diocese "some of the ablest minds in the nation to whom he could turn for counsel and direction" to meet the unexampled challenge of a great opportunity.

The Bishop in his primary address to the Diocesan Convention bound himself to continue the same general program of his predecessors. He emphasized the vital areas of the missionary activities of the three Archdeaconries, the Church Mission of Help, the Board of Religious Education, the Commission of Christian Social Service, the Church Charity Foundation, the House of St. Giles, as well as providing for part of the expense of the Diocesan House, the Diocesan Council, and other essential parts of diocesan organization and activity. His overall aims, consistent with the past, concentrated on some of the things left undone in previous years. His hopes included an increase in the salaries of clergy, a better endowment of the Episcopal Fund for the Bishop's support, and plans "by which we shall be enabled to select a strategic site while the town is being projected and before it is built." But most of all the Bishop projected his fondest hope — the raising of sufficient funds "in order that Long Island might pay its way in the general work of the Church and meet the necessities for its own diocesan development." If the amount needed could not be raised by the parishes and missions, his contacts with the wealthy would afford opportunity to secure from individuals the additional money needed. In fact, his contact with the rich had resulted in the short time as Bishop in the boom to the general church program.

Our prestige (the Diocese) was increased during the last General Convention when an ever faithful layman of our Diocese pledged one hundred thousand dollars in our behalf toward the extinction of a deficit which threatened to destroy the enthusiasm and progress of our whole missionary enterprise.

The affluent rector, turned bishop, had made his effectiveness felt already.

THE ORGANIZATION MAN

Starting out at once to survey his jurisdiction, the Bishop held informal conferences in various localities of the Diocese with the clergy. The small groups were to give "prayerful and unselfish thought" to diocesan needs. The conferences were enlarged to include vestries and others so "that they could give the Bishop their great counsel." In the ensuing years the informal conferences grew into the group system by which parishes and missions were divided into a number of zones with meetings held under the supervision of a "group leader." Meetings under this form proved effective, "in intensification of parish spirit, of extraordinary development in worship, study and loyalty."

> The value of the Group System has been so completely demonstrated wherever it has been tried that it is surprising to find that many missions and parishes have still neglected to use this most successful method of increasing strength and development.

In spite of some parishes not cooperating, the system grew and a leader known as a "Key-Man" was secured for each group. Each Key-Man was assigned four or five parishes and missions with which he was in contact through a lay representative in each place.

> A message to these Key Men can be immediately communicated to every parish and mission within a few hours. Important information can be transmitted, emergency meetings can be quickly called, close and sympathetic contact can be constantly maintained.

TOWARD AN EPISCOPAL TRIUMVIRATE

Even with such a system, the Bishop expressed a need for a better program by additional help. Realizing the pressures of time and cognizant of the age limitation of his fifty-years, he attempted to devise a system whereby he could devote more time to diocesan development. Lack of adequate time would cause "an increasing embarrassment" and "a hindrance to the effective development of the Diocese" unless the Bishop could "make a more wise distribution and concentration of his time and resources for the largest good for the whole Diocese." A system was devised by which, with additional episcopal assistance, the Bishop could devote precious time to the most urgent diocesan problems. He visited one-half the number of churches in the Diocese during one year and the succeeding year, the other half. The system lasted two years. By 1928, the Bishop realized the need for a suffragan or a co-adjutor. For practical purposes it seemed best to elect a "bishop-suffragan." Besides sharing confirmation appointments, he was to "be chosen with special reference to the missionary problem of Brooklyn, in order to give (the Bishop) more time for devotion to the pressing necessities of Queens and Nassau as well as for more attention to the developments in Suffolk." He expressed the need for a third bishop, the second suffragan would be "elected with special reference to his ability to lead in the development of the Church in . . . rapidly growing counties of Queens and Nassau."

The Bishop did not express an immediacy about his request, but when conditions, financial and other, made action appropriate, the 1928 Convention jumped to the request and suspended the regular order of business and proceeded to the election of a suffragan bishop. A resolution,

> that the chairman be requested to reveal to the Convention his views as to his preference for the office of Suffragan Bishop in order that the Convention may proceed to the discharge of this heavy responsibility in the light of the views as to be received,

was followed by the Bishop placing in nomination, the Rev. George P. Atwater, D.D., Rector of Grace Church, Brooklyn. Nominations were quickly closed, prayers read, and the vote taken. The election was carried unanimously.

The election came as a complete surprise to Dr. Atwater. Only four men knew of the Bishop's purpose, and he was not one of them. Startled and confused, he asked the indulgence of the convention to consider his acceptance.

> One night's very serious and prayerful consideration has led me to the conclusion that I must ask for a reasonable period to consider the action of the Convention. Bewildered as I was yesterday by the suddenness of the events, I failed to realize that many others have some vital concern in my decision and that they must be consulted . . . .

The Rector of Grace Church, after due consideration, declined the election.

A call for a special convention to elect a suffragan bishop was issued for Wednesday, November 14, 1928. On that day, the Diocese assembled to elect such an officer. Averse to the Bishop making any nominations, the convention proceeded to nominate nine candidates, among whom were the Archdeacons of Queens and Nassau, the superintendent of the Church Charity Foundation, and the Field Secretary of the National Council, the Rev. John Insley Blair Larned. Two names were withdrawn, and the convention proceeded to its first ballot, and the Rev. J. I. B. Larned was elected the first Suffragan Bishop of Long Island.

The Suffragan Bishop-elect graciously accepted his election. On February 11, 1929, he was duly consecrated in the Cathedral at Garden City. The event was historically significant. All three bishops before him had received episcopal consecration in their former cures. Bishop Larned had the unique distinction of being the first episcopal product of the diocesan center.

Due to adverse economic conditions, the matter of a second suffragan bishop had to wait until 1933. The resignation of Archdeacon Roy F. Duffield on January 1, 1933, precipitated the whole matter. The Archdeacon of Queens and Nassau had served the Diocese for twenty years. Due to ill health, he felt compelled to resign his work. At a meeting of the Archdeaconry held at Grace Church, Jamaica on November 22, 1932, the assembled clergy and laity pondered the future development of the growing counties. Recommendations to meet the swelling population included the major idea of the "advisibility of an additional Suffragan Bishop who might combine with the Episcopal office, the duties of an Archdeacon." Important considerations were that an additional episcopal helper could relieve the Bishop of much of the detailed work that had increased; that larger duties could be exercised; and that the Diocesan's plea of 1928 could be effected with no greater cost than that of an archdeacon. Following the lead of the Archdeaconry, the Bishop called a special elective convention for January 24, 1933, to consider the advisability of a third bishop and to possibly elect such an officer. The convention hotly debated the whole issue. Opposition was so strong and tempers so short that at times the Bishop had to leave his chair several times "to answer points made in opposition" and once to speak in favor of a motion that a vote by orders be taken.

> Upon the Bishop's explanation of how the additional expense involved could be met without increasing the Diocesan assessments laid upon parishes and missions; and upon his demonstrations of the need for further Episcopal ministration, the main point at issue became a consideration of possible eventualities of more remote future.

Quelled by the Bishop's intervention, the convention proceeded to the election of the third member of the episcopal triumvirate. Six nominations were made including the Rector of the Atonement, Brooklyn, the Acting Archdeacon, Rockland T. Homans, the Rev. Messrs. John H. Fitzgerald, Wallace J. Gardner, and the Bishop of Mexico. The Rt. Rev. Frank W. Creighton, D.D. was elected on the second ballot. The convention made it unanimous.

The Missionary Bishop of Mexico was no stranger to Long Island. After serving several rectorships in Pennsylvania and New York, he came to Long Island in 1923 as the Rector of St. Ann's on the Heights. Here he served for only three years before he was elected by the House of Bishops to missionary jurisdiction of Mexico and consecrated Bishop on January 12, 1926.

> As Bishop of Mexico, Dr. Creighton found himself plunged into the delicate religious situation brought about in that country by the adoption of the new Mexican constitution. That he [was] a diplomat as well as a Churchman [was] evidenced by the successful manner in which he directed the affairs of the Episcopal Church in Mexico in the more than six years of his Episcopacy.

Political conditions forced his withdrawal from Mexico, and he became on January 1, 1931, the head of Division of Domestic Missions of the Department of Missions. He still retained his jurisdiction of Mexico, visiting from time to time. Feeling that the opportunity of Long Island was significant, Bishop Creighton accepted the call to Long Island and took his place on the episcopal team.

For more than fifty years the Diocese had managed to carry on its work with one bishop. Although Bishop Burgess did have a clerical assistant, he never did impose upon the Diocese his need for additional help. Even with an enlarged scope of work and innumerable activities, he managed to conduct the affairs of the Diocese satisfactorily. His episcopal office never wanted an increase in stipend. The second Bishop received the same salary as Bishop Littlejohn did in 1868 — $6,000 per year. When the third Bishop was elected, his salary was set at $15,000 which seemed astronomical compared to the former stipend. To ease financial worry, Bishop Stires took only one year's support. In the second year of his tenure, his salary was collected for him, but he turned it back to reduce the diocesan tax. For the next eight years, the Diocese never paid its Bishop a salary; it was done by one of the Bishop's wealthy friends. Again, when a second bishop was needed, his support was accrued from the Archdeaconry and the Episcopal Fund. The third bishop was supported by an Archdeaconry and the Cathedral Chapter. Long Island had a Bishop and two suffragans "without having to provide a stipend for any of them." The matter may have seemed to have a happy ending, but the effect on the Diocese was only the beginning of deeper and lasting tensions that plagued the Bishop's successor.

*(above) Modern ambulance which serviced St. John's
Hospital during the 1920's.*
(right) St. John's Hospital as it appeared in the late 1920's.

The cry of no money in the Diocese, met by the Bishop's provisions for additional help at no additional cost, contained subtle overtones that could not be easily dispelled. Dominant among them was the fear that the office of the Bishop might assume the dimensions of a foreign prelacy. During all of its years of existence, the Episcopal Church had a distinct aversion to any hint or attempt at a centralized authoritarian power group. Fear of popery, so much a factor in church development, seemed to hover over the church even in the mid-twentieth century. The enlargement of the episcopate offered a threat to the underlying protestant ethos and commitment. The complaint in the Diocese may seemed to have been financial, but the real fear was ecclesiastical.

The same enlargement of central authority showed in the drastic revision of the Diocesan Canon on the Diocesan Council. When the Diocesan Council began, it was still a compromise between the old form and the new spirit. The Council became chiefly a tax collection agency to raise funds for diocesan programs. The powerful and revered Missionary Committee, together with the Board of Religious Education and the Christian Social Service Commission, continued to be elected by the Convention, and operated as before, with the Council supervising policy and finance. The situation proved most confusing, with a duplication of efforts and energy in the same general areas. To effect a more coordinate action, the idea of uniting all the diocesan programs under the leadership of the Council was forcibly presented. The same old fear of "too much in the hands of too few"

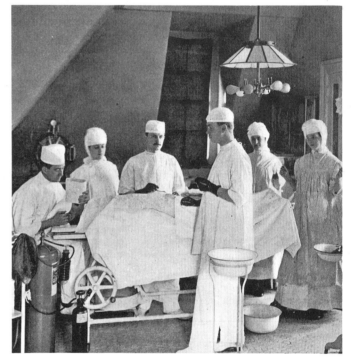

(above) Sketch of the first hospital building.
(above right) An early class of nurses posing in front of one of the two small residence cottages known as "All Angels Cottages".
(right) A view of the operating room in the 1930's.
(below) A drawing of the expanded St. John's facilities in the 1940's.

colored the acceptance of the plan. One churchman reacted to the proposal in very definite terms, to which many assented:

> This is a very radical change in our present Diocesan government. It merges the various activities and boards of the Diocese and concentrates power in eighteen men. It does away with the elective power of the Convention as to these boards.

The amalgamation of functions would mean a council consisting of the Bishop and eighteen men who would have six department functions and the power to appoint additional members on an annual basis. The plan was worth considering and in 1930 a new set of Canons created the necessary authority to unite all diocesan work under the coordinating body.

The centralization of power appeared in a combination of the various corporations and diocesan funds. In 1926, the Act of Incorporation for the Trustees of the Estate belonging to the Diocese of Long Island was again amended, as it was in 1872, to authorize and empower the corporation "to take possession of the temporalities and property belonging to such extinct church, society or congregation and hold, manage, transfer and convey the same for the use and purposes of the Protestant Episcopal Church in said Diocese." In 1927, an act was passed authorizing the merger of (1) the Trustees of the Estate, (2) Diocesan Missions of Long Island, (3) Trustees for the Management and Care of Property for the Support of the Episcopate, (4) the Aged and Infirm Clergymen's Fund Trustees, (5) the Trustees of the Clergymen's Pension and Retirement Fund, (6) Trustees of the Fund for the Families of Deceased Clergymen. By the merger, proposed and approved by the Diocesan Convention, and authorized by state law, power became concentrated in the hands of a very small group of eighteen men. The Standing Committee, which also served with the Bishop as the Trustees of the Estate, had the right "to do any act or promote any purpose or object." Procedure may have been simplified by the amendment, but power had been focused in a tight little elite group.

LET'S TALK TO EACH OTHER

An attempt to bring order through new channels of coordination created a "Council of Diocesan Organizations". The numerous and varied church organizations, both parochial and diocesan, had grown like "Topsy". To better coordinate their work and to have each group cognizant of the other's program, the Field Department undertook the council. The object was "to coordinate the work of all diocesan departments and organizations, by bringing together the working heads of all the organizations." The first meeting of the Council was held on January 6, 1932, with bi-annual meetings thereafter, at which times each organization presented its major objectives for the year. It also acted as a clearing house for all meetings to avoid a conflict of dates which "always acted as a deterrent to the object that was being promoted." The idea seemed great in the beginning, but in a few years, like so many diocesan ventures, it had passed into the file of discarded forms.

A more lasting form of communication and publicity was the beginning of the diocesan propaganda media known as the *Church Militant*. For some time the Diocese had felt the need for some means of forwarding information and describing events of diocesan import. The *Helping Hand* begun in February 1869, had in some measure included diocesan newsworthy events, but primarily, as a fund-raising venture, it concentrated on its chief objective, the Church Charity Foundation. In 1916, the appeal for some kind of diocesan newspaper was expressed by Bishop Burgess in his address to the convention when he stated: "In a large Diocese like this events of real importance and interest take place, but they seldom find even cursory mention in the Church papers, and not always accurate reports in the daily press."

The newspaper would serve as a worthy record of current history, as an organ for disseminating plans of organizations, and a place for expressive essays. A committee, appointed in 1917, reported to the next convention its proposals. "Like Gaul of Ceasar's time, the Diocese of Long Island was divided into three parts." To effect better solidarity and instill closer unity, they recommended that like sixty-one other dioceses with publicity vehicles, this diocese undertake to provide some kind of news media. As a step in that direction, they recommended the *Helping Hand* temporarily provide space for diocesan news, and allocated $500 for this purpose. The matter of a diocesan paper was not brought up again until 1920, at which time it was again deferred. A committee on publicity was appointed and a separate part of the Foundation publication was devoted to a section entitled "Department of Diocesan News". In 1925, concrete plans for a separate diocesan publication finally materialized, and the first issue of the *Church Militant* appeared in April 1926. The official publication was published monthly except for July, August and September. The object of the diocesan paper was simple:

> ...to keep every communicant in the Diocese alive to the great needs and splendid opportunities of the Diocese, to keep the parishes in touch with each other, and to receive inspirational messages from our Bishops and any clergyman who feels the urge to give to others thoughts and feelings that may mean much to the rest of us.

With the increasing influence of the diocesan vehicle of communication, the *Helping Hand* declined in circulation and subscription support. It merged with the *Church Militant*, and the diocesan newsletter became known as the *Church Militant — Helping Hand*.

Chapter Thirteen

Boom, Bust and Backtrack

BOOM: 1925—1929

For the first four years of Bishop Stires' episcopate, the Diocese rode on the overwhelming wave of prosperity that prevailed in all the nation. It seemed as if the Diocese could do no wrong. Within a few short years, all areas of diocesan life seemed to grow rapidly, whether it be the missionary program, charitable institutions, needed funds, or parish expansion. From 1925 to 1929, new missions multiplied at an astounding rate. Twelve new missions were started to meet the 4,000,000 population of the Island, with exciting prospects for many more. The Church Charity Foundation found itself with a new hospital, chapel, and enlarged nursing home. Money seemed to pour into diocesan and parish work, increasing one half million dollars. Communicant strength rose, and Sunday School enrollment increased by almost 1,000 members a year. The diocesan family, Bishop, priest and parish could join in the jubilant breathtaking ride into the clouds. Happy days had come and all seemed exhilarating on the Island front.

THE INCOMING TIDE OF POPULATION

Brooklyn sank into insignificance before the great growth of its neighbors, Queens and Nassau. The city borough had a chequered aspect in which certain sections had too many churches and others not enough. Even with the oversight of the first suffragan, the missionary extension of the Diocese could account for only one new church, Our Saviour, Gerritsen Beach — the only Protestant Church for a community of 9,000 to 15,000 people. Services were conducted by the Archdeacon and "the baby mission" seemed to have good prospects, "writing a thrilling page in the history of our diocesan work." Other churches did not fare as well. The deep concern for the foreign born, emphasized by the Synod, and reiterated by the Bishop, did not find any real materialization. The Italian mission, a diocesan work among a large colony of Italians, had grave problems. In spite of its long history, the feeling had grown that the church for which the largest appropriation was made from the Archdeaconry, had not produced the desired results. The same situation held for the Holy Comforter Mission to the Jews under the direction of the Rev. Noah Greenberg. The desired result of reaching "the people of the Hebrew Nation" and bringing to them the Gospel had fallen far short of high expectations. The Diocesan Council discontinued its missionary allotment in 1927 and the work was eventually turned over to the Christian Social Service Department. The Social Service Board raised funds for the work which they showed was a most pressing urban need:

> Holy Comforter House is located in a section of East Williamsburgh where Jews, Greeks, Lithuanians, Poles, Italians, Negroes and a few Irish are mingled. A social survey of this neighborhood would tell a story of bad housing, crowding, poverty, recently arrived and badly adjusted immigrant groups, lack of cultural and recreational facilities, cheap commercialized amusements. And that combination means warped and stunted lives, disease, crime. In this neighborhood Holy Comforter House has for years provided the one wholesome recreational outlet for the children. The little patch of ground which forms the "front yard" of the House is the neighborhood playground — the only one in the vicinity. Through the classes, clubs, and Sunday School, the workers at the mission . . . have been able to remove prejudices against Christianity . . . have given the children a taste of a more worthwhile life than the streets had to offer . . . have promoted friendship between people of various races and religions. . . .

The Diocese also recognized, through a careful and intensive study, that there were too many churches in some sections. A step in the right direction was the closing of St. Agnes' Mission which had been started in close proximity to two other churches. The Diocese disposed of its holdings and the portable chapel that had served as its church. The regret at closing a church was balanced by the admission into the diocese as incorporated parishes, two former missions, Holy Cross and St. Gabriel's.

Far more encouraging was the diocesan work among Black people. St. Philip's, the large Black church in Brooklyn attained parish status in the Diocese to the satisfaction of all concerned. St. Barnabas' and St. Cyprian's held their own with "some fair degree of success" in spite of inadequate facilities. St. Barnabas' had only a church basement "not only dark, but damp and unhealthy"; St. Cyprian's building was "no more or less than a converted barn, totally inadequate to carry on the social side of this church's work." The Diocese undertook to complete the church for St. Barnabas', which marked "the first special effort in the development of this work among our colored brethren, which [was] very much in the heart and mind of our Bishop." The four Black missions in Queens and Nassau progressed well, but Resurrection in Corona lost strength, due to a period with no priest-in-charge. This mission looked forward to the arrival of the Rev. Ebenezer H. Hamilton who, it was hoped, would make a real difference. In all this specialized work the real need was for time and money. The chief problem of work with Black congregations, "a very large group of people who are very much interested and are susceptible to the ministrations of the Episcopal Church," was the reluctance to expend large sums of money. The desire of this group of people for the ministrations of the church was not matched by a similar desire "to unfold this situation."

The Bishop appointed the Rector of St. Philip's Church, the Rev. Nathaniel P. Boyd, to assume charge of furthering the work among the Blacks on Long Island. The Diocesan Council approved Archdeacon Boyd as the first Black of diocesan stature, and he started this specialized task by augmenting rather than substituting work for the Blacks, at the same time being careful not to conflict with "the machinery operating the various missions in the different archdeaconries." Attention was given to Grace Chapel in Jamaica, and the complications involved in this mission were speedily adjusted. The people were made to feel they had a spiritual home, and it was not long before the Church School numbered 200 children. Archdeacon Boyd's work took him as far out as Suffolk to visit several "Colored Settlements", where one rector was anxious for work to start at once. But hampered by distance and funds, he concentrated the bulk of his energy in Brooklyn and Queens, and under his guidance work among the Blacks flourished with large confirmation classes, repaired buildings and a new church building for St. Barnabas'. The Bishop, on behalf of the Diocese, consented to assume partial responsibility for a new building (later known as the Long Island Building) at St. Paul's College in Lawrenceville, Virginia.

On the other end of the Island, in far Suffolk, it was not so much apathy or profusion, but under-development. Suffolk was still largely rural. The Archdeacon William Holden, described it: "Suffolk is not an industrial territory. Most of it lies outside the commuting zone of New York City. Much of it is farm land, and along the shores are fishing villages." The sparsely settled communities, sometimes redundant with churches, had a hard time supporting even the smallest work. Still used as summer havens, the Episcopal Church had its chapels-of-ease at Quogue, Saltaire, Fishers Island and Amagansett. The large field of the Hamptons continued to show "its larger sense of responsibility by having established the Parish of St. John's in Southampton, and made the other chapels their Mission field . . . ." The need here, like in Brooklyn, was for adequate support,

> To carry on these Missions as they are means varied types of money-making when the Summer comes. And the one essential for which the Church should stand — spiritual growth — and priestly contact with the people — is of necessity hampered by the existing conditions. We need men and money to support them.

A real need voiced by the Archdeacon was for a resident chaplain at St. Johnland and for the Northport Hospital for "gassed soldiers". Sunday supply by neighboring clergy did not meet the need of the men who "cry aloud for weekday services."

If the work in the two ends of the Island seemed sometimes discouraging, the multiplication of churches in Queens and Nassau enlivened and encouraged the Diocese. In the short time from 1925 to 1929, ten new churches sprang into being. The incoming tide of population had developed villages into towns, and towns into cities within a few weeks or months. Most of the new settlers, repatriated from Manhattan or Brooklyn, had mortgaged their future by purchasing homes on the installment plan, making it difficult or impossible for the new families to contribute to the building of a church or to the support of a clergyman. They could be looked to for small support only since hundreds of thousands of them were "anxious lest they may not be able to keep up the payments on their homes." The pressures of population had caused the Diocese to reassess its position, and it concentrated on developing both old and new missions, and attempting to find some makeshift means to meet the "mortgaged masses". Too often a church had to use "the upper room of a fire company building, the vacant house or empty store, a wheezy melodeon, no choir, a makeshift altar." Since the local residents could not adequately support the work, responsibility fell upon the Diocese to pursue the extension of churches in vitally growing areas. In quick succession St. Andrew's Chapel started at Oceanside, St. John's at Springfield Gardens, Christ Church at Garden City, and St. James' at Long Beach. A new work at Elmont in 1927 was matched by equally successful works in Auburndale, Bellerose and Williston Park. The youngest mission of the Archdeaconry was All Saints' Church at Sunnyside in Long Island City which started in July 1928, with the congregation meeting in the Community Room. The real difficulty was to find a place where a church could be built and services held; the high land values and building costs meant an outlay of considerable amounts of money.

MIRACLE ON HERKIMER STREET

Swelling numbers of churches were overshadowed when the superb Church Charity Foundation Center was completed. Bishop Burgess had hoped,

> for increased care of the sick poor, but he was humiliated by the antiquated, inadequate and unsuitable conditions under which a medical staff of the highest ability were forced to render

a critically important service for suffering humanity.

Even so, he was unwilling to consent to a building program that would involve the Foundation in debt or place in jeopardy its property or endowments. His successor had other ideas. The Foundation had seven hundred thousand dollars accrued from the Fiftieth Anniversary Fund and other contributions. Bishop Stires and the Board of Managers decided to use this money to proceed immediately with the erection of the Walter Gibb Memorial Chapel and the power plant, in the belief that if started, public-minded men would give to the completion of the magnificent plans.

On Ascension Day in 1926, Bishop Stires broke ground for the new buildings, starting with the Gibb Memorial Chapel, and during that summer construction proceeded on the chapel, power house, and foundation of the new hospital. On October 11, 1926, the Bishop laid the cornerstone of the chapel, assisted by the twin granddaughters of the donor, Mr. Walter Gibb. At the same time, he ceremoniously laid the cornerstone of St. John's Hospital, "though the foundation of the new hospital had been constructed only to such a point as to allow the cornerstone to be laid." Of historical importance was the trowel that Bishop Stires used, as it was the same one made in 1873 for the laying of the cornerstone of the American Episcopal Church, St. Paul's Within-the-Walls, Rome. The hammer used was the same one Bishop Littlejohn had used at the laying of the cornerstone of the Cathedral in 1877.

Several large gifts were needed to complete the hospital proper. The main building, fronting on Herkimer Street, was estimated to cost five hundred thousand dollars, and the two connecting wings, two hundred thousand dollars each. Episcopal expectation that when the building program actually began, individuals or families would welcome the opportunity to give the main building, or the wings, or some part of the necessary equipment, found swift fulfillment. In 1928, within a ten day period, 13,000 subscribers had contributed $1,170,000, about two thirds of which was given by Brooklyn.

> With generous unanimity the parishes and missions had responded to the call, and in many
> instances, the answer was thrilling and gave the diocese a new sense of its inherent power. One
> of the particularly encouraging features of the undertaking was the sympathetic cooperation of
> our brethren of the Roman Catholics, Protestants and Jews.

Equally encouraging was the statement of Brooklyn editors and businessmen: "that in their memory no other enterprise had made such an appeal with more conspicuous dignity and success." The million dollars constructed the new hospital and renovated the old one for convalescents and clinic patients. The over-subscription made possible the doubling of the size of the Nurses' Home. The affluent Bishop had "done it again."

The new hospital, as well as the other added facilities, were put to immediate good use. One hundred eighty patients were accommodated where only one hundred could be taken care of previously. The enlarged Nurses' Home, completed in 1929, had been beautifully furnished by the Woman's Board, and the attractive new quarters invited more students for the class that September, making it larger than any previous one.

The Church Charity Foundation celebrated its Diamond Jubilee in 1926, but no formal ceremonies were planned. The celebration centered "in the building operations, which signalized the expansion of the service which this noble institution has rendered through three quarters of a century." As part of the services rendered, the Canon Swett Memorial Cottage for twenty boys was formally occupied in the summer of 1926. A fitting conclusion to the outstanding charitable efforts was the dedication of the new hospital in 1929 with impressive ceremonies, presided over by the Bishop, who clearly stated that the objective was reached. The Diocese had a new and revitalized institution able to minister to its sick and dying.

BLOOMING DIOCESE

It seemed as if nothing could stop the upward spiralling of all sides of diocesan life in these few robust years. Everywhere the atmosphere seemed to be tinged with a golden glow that enlivened and enhanced the church's work. Successful parish life, whether in small country mission or large city parish, reflected the growing optimism that happy days were here and that there was a rainbow in the sky. Expansive diocesan adventures caught the infective jubilant mood, casting its nets in every direction, and catching the full draught of proud accomplishment.

Infant agency of only ten years, the Church Mission of Help, had reached quick maturity with incorporation and its own set of directors, headed by the President, The Rev. J. Clarence Jones. The object of the social work agency, as stated in its constitution was,

> this organization shall bring to young people without regard to race or creed, new hope and
> social adjustment through modern application of the ageless teachings of our Lord and Saviour
> Jesus Christ, in a combination of casework of high standards and other professional skills with
> the spiritual resources of the Church,

and this found ample expression in a growing case load of 409 girls and 190 babies. The primary purpose of assisting unwed mothers had enlarged to include vocational guidance, employment, loans, medical care and summer vacations. Mental treatment of difficult girls played more of a part, with use of the New York clinics for "mental examination and psychiatric treatment." The agency could justly say it had become a source of solace for "giving community service to all Protestant girls." The Diocese was justly proud that it had become involved in the life of the community around it.

Not as dramatic but equally as useful was the increasing role played by the laymen in the church. At a time when club and organization was the keyword, the Church had a profuse array of innumerable organizations through which each lay person, man or woman, could play his or her part in church enhancement or service. The church divided its efforts into smaller organizations which worked in their own way to make the layman an integral part of church life and to further its work in the community of which it was a part. Diversified paraphenalia of parish groups was aided and abetted by super-organizations, diocesan groups.

The Diocese had, since its inceptions, a variety of laymen's groups, pioneer and chief of which was the Woman's Auxiliary. Using woman's talents for missionary work, the Auxiliary had exerted a tremendous influence in forwarding the missionary progress of the Diocese. Under the leadership of such dedicated women as Mrs. Samuel Cox, Miss Mary Benson, and Mrs. Otto Heinigke, the Auxiliary serviced the general and diocesan missionary programs, meeting regularly first at St. Ann's Church and then in 1904, at the Diocesan House. A more specialized group, the Woman's Board of the Church Charity Foundation, organized in 1902 to replace the former "Board of Associates" and the "Co-workers", involved women "in furthering all the interests of the Foundation in the parishes throughout the diocese." Utterly different was the Daughters of the King, organized in 1895, with the specific purpose of prayer, service and loyalty to the rector.

The men of the church were not outdone by the ladies. They too, besides serving on the Vestry or as Lay Readers, had their own brand of organizational panamania. Oldest of the men's group was the national organization, the Brotherhood of St. Andrew. The Long Island Assembly followed the national guidelines of prayer and service, and an outstanding aspect of the Brotherhood's work was the annual corporate communion held on Washington's Birthday at a Brooklyn Church. The affair had, under the leadership of Mr. William F. Leggo, taken on the proportions of a mass rally at which representation of men and boys from all over the Diocese took part. The Church Club of Long Island for "any baptized layman of the Protestant Episcopal Church" had as its purpose "the welfare of the Church through study of her history, doctrines and social activities, for the maintenance of the faith, and to engage in such Diocesan work as the Bishop may advise and suggest." The chief function of the Club consisted of holding an annual dinner for fund-raising and for hearing an outstanding speaker. A short-lived experiment to coordinate all parish and diocesan men's groups was the Central Committee of Men's Parish Clubs.

There were other organizations, over and above the bewildering array of groups, clubs, societies, and guilds, that tried to meet a specific need in the Church. The Trained Christian Helpers were organized in 1897, incorporated in 1900 and recognized by the Diocese, and for some years attempted "to supply intelligent aid in the sickrooms of the poor." This Association having as many as seven sisters, four with diplomas as nurses, and with a home on Pacific Street, drew considerable attention. Like so many church groups, when its function was assumed by secular help it became just another item of diocesan history. The Little Helpers, twenty-five years old, gave an opportunity to raise money for church work. The Sisters of St. John the Evangelist, a deaconess order turned sisterhood, had its primary function usurped by the secular trained nurse corps. Still working at the Church Charity Foundation their function became spiritual assistance and guidance to the sick and needy, and they had the responsibility of caring for the girls at the Children's Cottages at Sayville. Last but not least of the layman structures was the Church Service League which was organized in 1920 and grew into an annual council, replete with diocesan units and parish groups. It, too, became superfluous with its function taken over by the Council of Diocesan Organizations.

There was no more dynamic work in the Diocese than the ministry to the youth. The Girls Friendly Society, founded in 1877, had taken deep roots in the Diocese, sometimes numbering 800 girls in its ranks and activities. A deep concern for the church to relate to boys made the Diocese appoint a Committee on Boys Work as early as 1912, "to encourage the formation of clubs in parishes and missions . . . to formulate some plan of federation of such clubs . . . in order by the concerted efforts of the boys of the diocese to increase throughout Long Island the spirit of Christian Knighthood, of true loyalty to one's better self, home, church, and country." The final outcome of diocesan interest and effort was the establishment of the Order of Sir Galahad. A semi-secret organization for boys, based on the Arthurian legends and embodying the ideals of chivalry, patriotism, and loyalty to the church, the Order quickly spread throughout the Diocese. Other organizations, such as the Boy Scouts of America and the United Boy's Brigades, although growing in many areas of the Diocese, did not receive diocesan recognition. The Order of Sir Galahad was felt to be "far superior, both as to character and to adaptability to parochial needs and conditions, to either of those organizations."

Besides the two separate organizations for boys and girls, the Diocese began its co-educational work in the establishment of the Young People's Fellowship. A council was formed in 1925 to help young people in the church who might otherwise drift away "which keeps them in touch with the church and the things the church stands for, namely: prayer, service, worship, fellowship, gifts or offerings." The program functioned under the aegus of the Board of Religious Education, becoming just one more of a multitude of activities.

On October 8, 1928, Bishop Stires laid the cornerstone of Adelphi College in Garden City. The event was significant because the Diocese had just begun to be aware of this growing area of concern. Responding to a provincial plea for work on college campuses where young people were "plunged into an atmosphere of religious carelessness, or irreligion, and of doubt" and where the church was losing "some of its finest men and women . . . the leaders of the next generation," the Diocese strongly urged support of parishes in college communities and suggested that vestries of parishes in college communities invite the cooperation of the Collegiate Division of the National Department of Religious Education in seeking to meet the collegiate need. Awareness of the problem did not mean diocesan work. Although Long Island had its growing colleges, the emphasis was on college away from home, with no work started on the local campuses.

Interest in camping as a means of Christian nurture moved the Diocese to look for ways to start a diocesan camp. Appointed in 1925, a committee on a diocesan camp reported in 1926 that some interest was expressed in a diocesan camp. A camp for boys was opened at Camp Grant of the Rotary Club of Brooklyn in the summer of 1926, where the Calverton Campsite received "our boys" and gave them "certain huts" where they were by themselves and under diocesan supervision.

SITTING ON TOP OF THE WORLD

Busy men and women eager to serve their church, and new interest in youth did not tell the whole story. The news that clergy stipends, long a matter of concern, had increased greatly in one year was exciting. The admission to seat in the Diocesan Convention all mission units was invigorating. The fulfillment of the diocesan pledge of support to the general church program was remarkable. The record of offerings and contributions, reaching an all-time high of $2,186,941.62 was truly brilliant, but most splendid of all was the diocesan state-of-affairs that added most to the mountain-top feeling. On an island that held four million people, over one-third the people of New York State, the Diocese had made an illustrious record. An unprecedented number of 183 clergy ministered in 182 churches, comprised of parishes, parochial missions, or diocesan missions. Diocesan church extension had fifty-six diocesan mission stations, not quite one-third of all Episcopal churches. There were 79,860 baptized persons; 46,663 communicants; and 23,699 in the Sunday Schools. The Diocese boasted two strong church hospitals, four homes, four social institutions, and two outstanding preparatory schools.

Every aspect enhanced the image of the Diocese as being a vital part of its Island community. The Bishop, caught in the tide of optimism, loudly proclaimed the good news of diocesan aggressiveness. In his convention address, he verbalized the feeling of all concerned. Referring to a recent church survey, he said:

> Having compiled the essential statistics of the various dioceses of the American Church, he (an eminent clergyman) rejoiced to find his diocese had a place in the first eight. I read the list with great interest, particularly because he declared that the diocese which had shown the highest percentage of substantial progress in the American Church was the Diocese of Long Island . . . . "

Then came Thursday, October 24, 1929.

BUST AND BACKTRACK, 1929—1935

On the morning of October 24, 1929, the towering structure of American prosperity cracked wide open. For many days the stock prices on the New York Exchange slid faster and faster downhill. In the course of a few brief weeks, thirty billion dollars in paper value had vanished into thin air. Although the whole credit structure of the American economy had been shaken most severely, at first business and industry did not seem to be gravely affected, and a short spurt in the spring of 1930 seemed to indicate a return to "normalcy". The short-lived hope turned to real despair in the two year decline, not only of stock prices, but worst of all, the volume of American business. A vicious cycle began. Ebbing sales, followed by declining corporate income, forced attempts to restore that income by cutting salaries and wages and laying off men. Increased unemployment, and further reduced sales lead to further wage cutting and further firing of men, and so on to complete disaster. Long breadlines and the selling of apples accentuated the plight of America. Its theme song became: "Give Us a Handout to Revive Us Again."

No single event in the history of the American nation had a more telling or more disastrous effect on the Diocese of Long Island. The Diocese had lived through similar experiences, one at the very beginning of its career in 1873, and then in 1893 and 1907, but reaction to former depressed conditions had been mild compared to the drastic effect the depression of the thirties had. Although the full effect of the economic catastrophe did not fall until 1931, the Diocese experienced a complete change of character that was to last for most of the decade, and that changed the inherent quality of the Church. The Diocese curtailed its programs and cut back its plans, but more, it realized that it was no longer the domain of the wealthy, but the home of the lower and middle classes. The Episcopal Church on Long Island emerged from its crushing blows a new kind of being.

The first to feel the effect of the 1929 crash was the National Church. A crisis in the general church brought swift action by the Bishop. Unwilling to meet the general church peril by an added tax on parishes and missions, he "undertook to make a personal appeal" to certain laymen and to friends, in order to pay the diocesan quota in full and to have a substantial sum for the establishment of new missions in the Diocese.

> They made a timely contribution to save the honor of the general church, to enhance the dignity of their Diocese, and to help forward our missionary enterprise in caring for the great incoming tide of population.

And they made possible three new mission churches: St. Thomas', Malverne; St. Andrew's, Ozone Park; and St. James', Jamaica.

Another immediate victim of the first year of the depression was the campaign for securing substantial sums to provide an adequate endowment for the episcopate, and the procuring of missionary resources for insuring salaries to new mission priests-in-charge, and for the construction of churches and parish houses in new missions. The "changed financial situation which confronted us in the late autumn" made it both "unwise and unjust" to seek large gifts from the laity. Optimistically the Bishop hoped that "in the fullness of time the larger undertaking can be brought to successful completion."

The "fullness of time" never appeared. Instead, the financial depression assuming world-wide proportions, began to affect the entire membership of the Church more and more. In the first year or two of financial anxiety, a few churches showed some bright aspects. The Church of the Good Shepherd, Brooklyn, extinguished its mortgage and was duly consecrated. Substantial material progress was apparent in some parishes paying off mortgages; in the establishment of well-equipped parish houses; in some parishes becoming self-supporting; and some missions contemplating incorporation. Diocesan life had the same surface veneer with a larger confirmation roll than ever, crowded church services, and the greatest number of people receiving Holy Communion. Moreover, the Diocese paid its national quota in full, forwarding to the central organization the full quotas of 101 parishes and missions. Twelve monthly payments, recommended by the National Council began in this period.

But these brief but bright notes did not stop the increasing gloom of hard times. By 1932, the depression was in full swing and most Americans were bewildered by economic privations and decline. As one Richmond Hill storekeeper so aptly phrased it: "Every week I think business has hit bottom, then the next week comes, and I see the bottom is deeper than I thought." All phases of diocesan and parochial life began to show drastic effects. The Diocese at first valiantly tried to keep the financial responsibilities as before, but had to admit its losses and "with regret" reduced its National Church quotas. The Bishop magnanimously offered to give 1/16th of his salary to uphold the sagging general church program, but even his efforts could not stop further drastic cuts. The diocesan budgets themselves were cut back to bare minimum, hampering and obstructing any further advance.

Naturally the first to fall under the austerity axe was the diocesan missionary program. Some churches, tottering before, were hastened to the graveyard of extinct churches. Church of the Advent and the Italian Mission succumbed by 1932, followed by the closing of St. Jude's and St. Martin's, both in Brooklyn. St. Alban's, Canarsie, suffered from the depression, and Our Saviour, Gerritsen Beach, was joined to Emmanuel, Sheepshead Bay. The valiant priest-in-charge of the joined parishes made a noble effort to save his church.

> The priest-in-charge here, realizing the worry and stress caused by the possibility of many homes being lost in that community due to lapsed payments on mortgages, talked the matter over with the local clergy of the Roman Catholic and Lutheran Churches. These three went together to the Realty Associates who had charge of this real estate development, and were able to secure for the year 1933 what practically amounts to a moratorium of this whole situation, an untold blessing to this community.

Some mission churches were transferred to parishes. St. John's Church became the work of St. George's, Hempstead; All Saints', Baldwin Harbor, the work of All Saints', Baldwin; and St. Matthias' was joined to St. Mark's, North Bellmore. Most stricken of all churches, whether parish or mission, were the Black congregations. St. Barnabas' was unable to support fully its work, even with its new church. St. Cyprian's did not produce expected results, their failure being partly accounted for by the unemployment situation. In all Black churches, diminishing income resulted from unemployment of its parishioners. The fact was "that the people who have suffered most severely in these years of stress and strain have been our colored brethren. They are usually the first to go when workers must go."

Bank holidays and government programs did not help to ease the depressed conditions. "The economic depression of the last five years," said the Bishop, "has reduced the ability of the Church properly to maintain its work, and our National Church has cut down its annual budget. . . . " The cut brought untold suffering to the missionary bishops overseas and great difficulty "in caring for 70 missions of our own in this diocese." Not only missions, but all diocesan work suffered. At the Church Charity Foundation the total payments of patients had descended drastically from its 1930 high. Church institutions fared no better. St. Phebe's Convalescent Home reduced their rates to seven from fifteen dollars a week charged to the women, girls and boys under ten housed there. And the pride of the Christian Social Service Committee, Holy Comforter House, struggled to overcome overwhelming odds. The children who came to the House, once properly dressed, began to wear "shabby things, their faces undernourished." It had to manage on a greatly reduced budget in ministering to the children who made use of its clubs, classes, library and little playground. A stop-gap measure to alleviate the plight of the Jewish community center was the naming of the House as the recipient of the Good Friday offering that usually went to the Holy Land.

Amid the crescendo of hard times, bread lines and business failures, one problem the Diocese had to face squarely was unemployment. There were in the middle of the depression years over twelve million unemployed in the nation, of which eight hundred thousand were in New York City. Some measures were taken by the Diocese to assist the hungry and destitute. St. Michael's Church, North Fifth Street, set in the middle of a polyglot parish, offered free meals to the needy discharged patients from nearby hospitals, and from the boarding houses. Street corner missions, an answer to the threat of communism, preached to the unemployed workers during the spring and summer of 1932. Meetings, held at noontime, occurred at Borough Hall, the Brooklyn Navy Yard, Northern Boulevard in Queens and in Coney Island. Old clothes to be distributed to the poor were collected by many churches. Some churches seized upon temporary help from the unemployed, and it was a boon to St. Cyprian's and Our Saviour, Gerritsen Beach, where much needed changes in the mission property were accomplished. The British Emergency Work Bureau furnished men's and women's services to churches who had work to be done, but did not have the funds to pay for it.

Emergency relief for the suffering, appeals for odd jobs, unemployment bureaus, and handouts, did not solve the underlying problem, as Bishop and Diocese soon realized.

> The problem of unemployment evoked a response from national and state legislatures, from public organizations and from private generosity . . . dealt wisely and sympathetically with the emerging problem [and] closely united all groups of people.

But the Diocese did provide a lasting protection against recurring economic problems. It soon discovered that some kind of unemployment insurance, supported by the State, was needed to help the worker. Advocating a plan in which employers contributed to a reserve fund to afford the unemployed some temporary means of livelihood, the Diocese, through its Christian Social Service Committee, pressed the issue. The Bishop himself gave assent to the plan. "When properly administered," said the Bishop, "it is as sound as any form of insurance, fire or life, based upon carefully administered actuarial experience." The problem itself had other overtones which had to be solved too. New difficulties arising out of machines replacing men, retirement annuity, and the use of increased leisure time, grew out of the turbulent times and asked for some adequate answer.

A social evil that had grown in the City, and was heightened by the depression, was the inadequate housing of the poor. Brooklyn, the one densely-populated city in the Diocese, had become a city of slums. The Diocesan Convention in 1932 went on record in favor of better housing, "the Gospel of The Tenement House Reform." The Reconstruction Finance Corporation of the national government had power to loan money to cities which requested it and to limited dividend corporations for the purpose of better housing. The recommendations of the Diocese provided for the construction of model housing at low rentals for working people. The better housing would "at once employ thousands of workers, stimulate industry and replace slum areas with decent homes."

Clergy suffered as well as laymen in the long financial crisis. The brief glimmer of hope in 1927 for better salaries and living conditions was shattered in the following years. The need for better clerical stipends was discussed by several diocesan conventions, but proved futile. The subject was brought up for widespread discussion in the Diocese. Reporting in 1935, the special committee had canvassed the clergy by mail. From the responses received, the clergy agreed in favor of a minimum wage, with subnormal salaries augmented by a fund established for that purpose. They also desired some diocesan or national agency to give information about prospective cures. Nothing, however, could be done to help the poorer clergy because of the "upset conditions of the financial world."

CAN'T GET OUT OF THIS HOLE

In 1935, Bishop Stires celebrated the tenth anniversary of his consecration as Bishop, and a series of events commemorated the occasion. On November 16, 1935, the Bishop was honored with a testimonial dinner at the Hotel Plaza in New York, hosted by his former parishioners at St. Thomas' Church in the City. The following day a window was dedicated in his honor in the church he had built. Not to be outdone, the Diocese had its own celebration. On Monday, November 25, 1935, the Church Club honored the Bishop for his ten years of service at a dinner in the Garden City Hotel. The final event in his honor was an overflowing youth rally at the Cathedral in Garden City.

The Bishop could be gratified over the "unusual vigor" of diocesan life. The Brotherhood of St. Andrew had gathered in numbers as never before, with approximately 1,500 assembled in Brooklyn for the annual Washington Birthday Corporate Communion. The House of Bishops had its "historic incident" in its first meeting on Long Island in 1932. The Annual Clergy Conference had grown in influence and in attendance. The Bishop in his travels had covered more than 150,000 miles and in the ten years of episcopal supervision had confirmed over 26,000 persons, a high figure superseded only by fourteen other dioceses. But the guarded jubilance of the Bishop reflected the sober times. The Diocese still struggled to overcome its setbacks of the past few years.

> Addressing the 1935 convention, the Bishop summed it up for his faithful followers:
> We are all conscious that, while we have the greatest desire to be increasingly helpful, the continued economic problem has increasingly limited our ability. Yet the diocese has truly regarded the condition as a challenge and has refused to be depressed by the so-called "depression". Faith and courage have been almost universal. In many instances decreased offerings have been made with increased sacrifice.

162

Chapter Fourteen

Recovery and Retirement

The depression dogged the steps of the Diocese for a few more years. Like the American nation, which, in spite of N.R.A., C.C.C. and W.P.A., and all the other governmental attempts at solution, did not reach any real level of financial stability, the Long Island unit made little heading in recouping its losses. As late as 1938, the Bishop referred to the ill-effects of the "continued economic depression." Hampered and obstructed by less funds and more stringencies, the Diocese did manage to construct new church buildings, to purchase a few sites for future development, and to renovate existing church structures; but it was not on the same scale or to the same degree as before the depression.

In the financial aftermath only two diocesan and one parochial missions began. Two new missions, one short-lived, began in Suffolk County. St. John's, Wyandanch, began in 1934 and had, by 1938, constructed a modest building. St. Andrew's, Mastic Beach, also originated in the same year to minister to a growing year-round community, from what had been only a summer colony. A third church, the parochial mission of St. Joseph's, Church of the Atonement, later called St. David's, Cambria Heights, begun in 1940, ministered to residents who found it too difficult and too far to travel to the Village Church. Encouraging, but not overpowering, were the missions that became self-supporting parishes. Among the incorporated parishes were All Saints', Richmond Hill; St. Thomas', Bellerose; and St. James', Long Beach. The Long Beach church had as its leader, a young and energetic seminarian, George W. Parsons, who when the parish incorporated, became its first rector.

The financial recession of the late thirties was aggravated by the serious threat of war. Italy and Germany, in their fanatic push for world power, threatened world peace, creating crisis after crisis in international affairs. The war spirit added new tensions to the already highly volatile battle between capital and labor. All these forces played a part as the Diocese juggled the problem of Church unity, full payment of national quota, and necessary missionary work. A severe blow to the missionary work of the church in Suffolk came with the disastrous hurricane of September 1938. Episcopal churches, especially those in coastal towns, suffered immeasurably. Throughout the Archdeaconry, church after church reported their losses, but not of the magnitude of St. Mark's, Westhampton Beach, which suffered most of all. A problem for all churches was the defective parochial organization prevalent among the majority of churches. Parish lists needed to be brought up to date. Parishes had not implemented their work by zoning and zone leaders, and developing parish visitors, and the Every Member Canvass needed serious and regular use. Sunday Schools showed an enigma. In 1926, when Bishop Stires assumed leadership, there were 20,011 teachers and pupils in 160 churches. Although the number of churches had increased to 180 by 1937, there were only 25,750 in Sunday Schools. The church education program did not keep step with other diocesan progress, aggregating only 500 in the period 1932-1938. The disparity of education was heightened by the rapid development of one congregation. The Cathedral had in 1926 only 160; in 1938 it had reached almost 1,000.

The Diocese did have its bright and encouraging aspects, none of which was more praiseworthy than the increasing role of the laymen. Lay leadership had its shining luminaries. Mr. William F. Leggo, indefatigable worker for the church, headed the dynamic Brotherhood of St. Andrew. Colonel Jackson A. Dykman, active in the Diocese since 1923, served as influential member of the Standing Committee and as Chancellor of the Diocese. Mr. Raymond F. Barnes, first Executive Secretary and then Treasurer of the Diocese, a man of "extraordinary knowledge" and "rare ability as a business man" secured great benefits to the Diocese and served to advance the cause of the Diocese in all areas. The women had Mrs. Otto Heinigke, member of the Woman's Auxiliary since its inception in 1872. She served for twelve years as its president, and received recognition for her devoted service to the Church, not only by the Diocese but also the National Church. No better witness to the strength and role of laymen's work was the annual Washington's Birthday gathering. A corporate communion and breakfast, sponsored by the Brotherhood of St. Andrew, had grown to such proportions that it took three Heights churches to accommodate the unprecedented numbers. Grace, St. Ann's and Holy Trinity Churches played host to the men and boys of the Diocese. Each year the service of witness had increased tremendously. The all-time high figure of 1938, more than 2,500 laymen had been topped by 1940, when 2,600 gathered for the annual affair. In the whole Episcopal Church there was nothing that could compare to this impressive show of lay strength.

The Diocese was also justly proud of the part played by its clergy in forwarding the mission of the Church. Two priests received episcopal recognition. The Rev. Harry J. Stretch served on the Committee on Diocesan Finance, but most of all had shown his outstanding ability as priest-in-charge of St. Albans' Church in St. Albans.

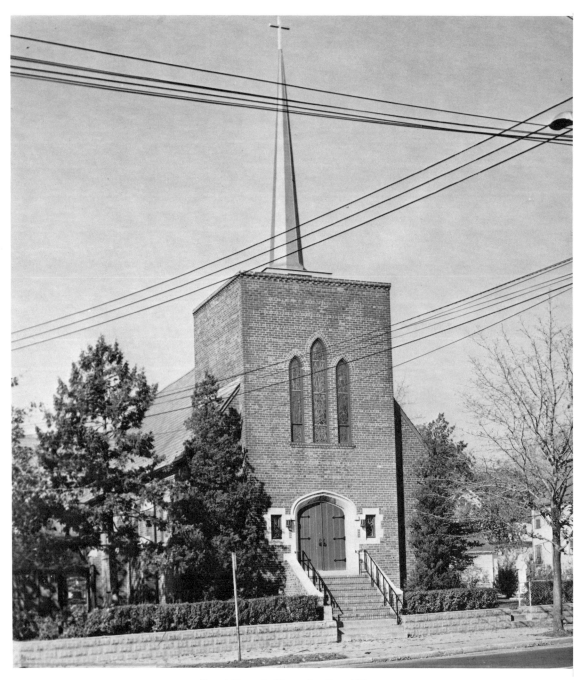

St. Albans' Church, St. Albans.

Under his inspiring leadership, the mortgage indebtedness on the church had been entirely paid off. St. Albans' had incorporated as an independent parish, and was brought into union with the Diocese in 1940. The other outstanding priest worked in Suffolk County. The Rev. Charles W. MacLean had received commendation for his outstanding work in the support of St. John's Hospital. Far removed from any use of the hospital, the Rector of Riverhead was nevertheless able to inspire and encourage county participation in the annual fund drive. The response of Suffolk under his leadership was a great example of devoted service. He had proven his effectiveness in other diocesan areas. Serving first as member and chairman of the Field Department, he became the Chairman of the newly organized Department of Promotion in 1940-1941. He originated and made the first motion picture showing diocesan life. In 1939, the film entitled "We Follow" appeared, and had such wide circulation that in the following year a second diocesan sound film was made. Containing "outstanding news events of our diocesan life," the film "Our Church at Work" again had the services of Mr. Milton W. Cross as narrator and Mr. Frederick J. Wythe as technical advisor. The films had wide circulation in the Diocese and had given the Diocese national recognition.

The encouraging notes of lay and clerical leadership was heightened by the final establishment of a long-hoped-for landmark. The Diocesan Hall, unfulfilled hope of Bishop Burgess, finally found realization in the erection of the Cathedral House. Not a diocesan sponsored project, the Cathedral House was the result of the efforts of the Garden City congregation and community. The Cathedral congregation secured funds from many sources, but most of all from its congregation and friends in the community to erect in 1938, "a Cathedral House with an auditorium seating a thousand, and many classrooms for religious instruction, and providing a suitable place for meetings of the Diocesan Convention and other important diocesan gatherings."

On Thanksgiving Day, November 24, 1938, Bishop Stires formally dedicated the new building. In the next year, the Diocese had its first Convention in the "increased facilities." Meeting first in Holy Trinity Church, then in the Cathedral Crypt, and lastly when diocesan size made that use unfeasible, in the Cathedral, the Diocesan Convention took a long step forward in having an appropriate place to meet. A propitious day was May 23, 1939, when clergy and lay delegates assembled in the auditorium for the proceedings of the 72nd Annual Convention. The Bishop in his Convention address voiced the thoughts of many and echoed the aspirations of Bishop Burgess when he said:

> We have reason to believe that our meetings will lose none of their dignity by being transferred from the Cathedral to these more commodious quarters. The Cathedral congregation and our friends in Garden City deserve our heartfelt congratulations upon this extraordinary achievement in a period of financial stringency.

A TIME TO RETIRE

Throughout his episcopate, Bishop Stires had a constant companion — the thought of adequately fulfilling the episcopal office. Coming to the Office of Diocesan at the ripe age of 59, he felt a deep concern to effectively bring his episcopal ministry to all areas of diocesan life. To this end, his request for assistance in two Suffragan Bishops had been granted, and he seemed to be content. But even with three Bishops, he had the pervading feeling of inadequacy. As early as 1934, nine years after his consecration, he had petitioned to and received approval from the General Convention for a Bishop Co-adjutor. Held in abeyance, the subject was not broached again until 1937. Then, on the resignation of Bishop Creighton, he again brought up the subject. His deep conviction was that before long a Co-adjutor Bishop should be elected. His personal reasons were enhanced by diocesan needs. The Diocese of Long Island had grown to contain one third the population of the state and 55% of the population of New York City. Growing rapidly, the Diocese had the challenge to meet the almost five million people on the Island. The Archdeaconry of Queens and Nassau alone were "equalled by only ten of the more than one hundred dioceses of our church in America." In the midst of growing community, two bishops could not do the job as adequately as three. Thoughts of an episcopal co-adjutor did not lessen the diocesan's involvement. His hopes were that for a few more years he could develop certain aspects of diocesan life that he long hoped for. They were an adequate increase of the Episcopal Fund; a fund for establishing and assisting new missions; and a revolving Building Fund.

Deep-felt appreciation of clergy and laity did not deter the Bishop's final decision. On the fifteenth anniversary of the Bishop's consecration, the clergy of the Diocese published a laudatory letter of appreciation, hoping that they might stop any rash move on the part of the Diocesan. Dated November 24, 1940, the letter extolled the accomplishments under the Bishop's inspiring leadership:

> But we desire that you shall know, we are keenly mindful of all that these fifteen years have meant to Long Island and to the whole church. But we would gratefully record a few of the highlights: a diocesan organization and a system of diocesan records that are now the envy of the church-at-large; titles to all of our church properties at last completely cleared up and catalogued; an advance in parish buildings and equipment that has averaged three hundred thousand dollars each year of your Episcopate; the wiping out of over two hundred thousand dollars in mortgage indebtedness on our mission properties; a new Saint John's Hospital, and a more recent campaign that has served greatly to widen its support; a continually developing missionary enthusiasm; a response on the part of the laity to your leadership, which has culminated annually in the largest outpouring of men at one gathering to be found anywhere in the Anglican communion; a Cathedral House at long last . . . a deepening understanding of each other. . . . For your leadership in these and countless other ways, which has served to strengthen us, and through us the whole church, we would say, Thank God.

As if cognizant of the Bishop's intentions, the clergy were not able to stop the Bishop's decision. A few months later, in a letter circulating to the clergy, dated January 13, 1941, the Bishop stated his firm decision to retire. At first hoping to retire at the May Convention of 1941, he deferred his intentions for six months, because of the crushing defeats of Denmark, Holland, Belgium and France. The Bishop gave his reasons for retirement. He was soon to be seventy-five years old and had been a priest for forty-nine years. He felt that "a younger Bishop" was needed to lead the Diocese in the "new era" that would follow the war. His decision was hastened by the General Convention ruling of 1940, making retirement of a Bishop obligatory at seventy-two years of age. Although the rule was not effective until 1943, he felt the Church had spoken: "The church is wiser than we are; the responsibility for a Bishop's retirement after seventy-two is no longer upon his conscience; he obeys the voice of the Church." The third Bishop's retirement became effective February 9, 1942.

Bishop James P. DeWolfe, Fourth Bishop Diocese of Long Island.

Section Five
The Times
They Are A'Changin
(1942-1966)

Chapter Fifteen

A Yet More Glorious Day

THE FOURTH BISHOP OF LONG ISLAND

On Tuesday, February 10, 1942, a special session of the Diocesan Convention assembled in the Cathedral in Garden City for the purpose of electing the fourth Bishop of Long Island, the successor to the retired Bishop Stires. After settling its rules of procedure and passing on the salary of $10,000 for the Bishop, the Convention proceeded to the solemn election of its Bishop. Ten names were presented for consideration, but only two were of noticeable prominence. Naturally a leading contender for the office was the then Suffragan Bishop, the Rt. Rev. J. Blair Larned. Working so long a time in the Diocese, he had achieved a good backing, especially among the laity. The other strong candidate was the recent Dean of the Cathedral of St. John the Divine, New York, the Very Rev. James P. DeWolfe.

From the beginning of the long session, the election showed a real contest between the Suffragan Bishop and the Dean. Both had their full share of ardent supporters, and both polled an impressive number of votes. Ballot after ballot showed an increasing number of clerical votes for the Dean and an equally increasing number of lay votes for the Suffragan Bishop. On the fifth ballot the Dean had the necessary number of votes for election in the clergy, and the Suffragan Bishop had the necessary lay vote. Since there had to be a concurrent vote of both groups, the Convention was in a deadlock. The usual procedure of running a "dark horse" to break the deadlock was tried. The Rev. Hubert S. Wood, Rector of St. George's Church, Flushing, was nominated as a hope of breaking the deadlock and being accepted as a "compromise" candidate. The "dark horse" ran poorly, for the two opposing forces refused to yield. Balloting continued with intermittent caucusing, recesses, prayers and "politicking". Finally, in the early hours of the next morning, February 11, 1942, on the fifteenth ballot, Dean DeWolfe had the necessary concurrent vote in both groups, and so was declared the duly elected fourth Bishop of the Diocese of Long Island. A new era in the life of the Diocese had begun.

The newly elected Bishop had enjoyed an illustrious career as a parish priest and a cathedral dean. Born in Kansas City, Kansas, in 1895, he graduated from Kenyon College and Bexley Hall Seminary, Ohio. He assumed his first cure in Pittsburg, Kansas. Three years in Kansas was followed by a twelve year rectorship at St. Andrew's Church, Kansas City, Missouri. He became so widely known that he was called to the large and prosperous Christ Church in Houston, Texas. During his parish years he filled many positions of leadership, both in the church and in the community. On February 23, 1940, he was installed as the fourth Dean of the New York Cathedral by the Rt. Rev. William Manning. His term as Dean was cut short by his election to the Long Island episcopate. He and his charming wife, together with their three children, moved into the Bishop's House in Garden City to take up duties as the overseer of one of the largest dioceses in the Church.

The Bishop-elect, after receiving the necessary canonical approvals, was consecrated the fourth Bishop of Long Island on the Feast of St. Philip and St. James, May 1, 1942. The occasion was a glorious and historic one. The Bishop was consecrated in the Cathedral in Garden City amid all the pomp and ceremony that surrounded such an occasion. He had the distinct honor, not so much of being consecrated the fourth Bishop, but of being the first Bishop of Long Island to be so ordered in the Cathedral. The Church of the Holy Trinity and Grace Church, both on the Brooklyn Heights, had been the setting for the first two Diocesan consecrations, while Bishop Stires was so ordered in St. Thomas' Church, New York. To the Rt. Rev. James P. DeWolfe went the distinct honor and privilege of being consecrated in his own church and at his own seat. The Diocese of Long Island had at last come of age.

A NEW VIEWPOINT

Even though encumbered by the drastic problems of the war years, which included returning servicemen, higher prices and greater taxation, the Diocese under its new leader turned its attention to its own specific task, the propagation of the Gospel. To this primary responsibility Bishop DeWolfe brought an entirely new and unique concept. The Bishop differed from his two immediate predecessors who undertook their duties in full knowledge of administrative and business practices. He was more akin to the founding Bishop, Abraham Newkirk Littlejohn. A theologian and pastor, he viewed all sides of life within the dimensions of the One, Holy, Catholic and Apostolic Church. An avowed Anglo-Catholic, he never quavered in his forthright statement of the Faith and never retreated from an opportunity to assert that belief. All diocesan life was the manifestation of that prime tenet of faith, the Incarnation. "The Gospel of the Incarnation," said the Bishop, "is the glorious builder of the Church's preaching and teaching." For him the constant reminder of that fact was that, as the Cathedral of the Incarnation was the center of the Diocese, so too the Incarnate Lord stood in the midst of life, and all life was His extension.

Within the ken of his Catholicity he lifted the concept of the Church to an entirely new dimension, perhaps alluded to, but not quite clearly stated by his predecessors. For the Bishops who came before him, Church extension meant the multiplication of churches in their Island communities. For him missionary work was any place, any attempt, any program where the Gospel was propagated — be it in church, on city street or among informal youth. In his first address to the Diocesan Convention in 1942 he made this clear:

> Unless the Church is able to walk among the poor and needy, the oppressed and the underprivileged of this world, as our Lord walked through the streets of Galilee, among the harlots, the Pharisees, and the poor and the working man, it will fail in its Christian mission.

For him the development and integration of personality was the great responsibility of the Church and her pastors. The parish was essentially "a cure of souls."

"No suspicion of partisan Churchmanship," said the Bishop, "attaches to the words of the Book of Common Prayer as it teaches us that Christ Himself ordained the sacraments. In her administration of the Sacraments we actually see the Church reaching into the community to affect by her own life all phases of the life about her." The mission of the Church was the extension of the Gospel of the Incarnate Lord, made evident in the sacraments and practiced in all areas of life. The mission might take different forms and make new and different paths, but it was still the same Gospel.

THE WAR YEARS

Bishop DeWolfe assumed the episcopal purple during a most trying and distressing period of American life. A little over two months before his election, the United States was plunged into World War II by the vicious bombing of Pearl Harbor on December 7, 1941. Open and complete involvement in the world conflict overshadowed all sides of life, and although the Bishop, in the primary address to the Diocese, recognized the "needs and opportunities and problems" of the Church, nevertheless the first object of diocesan outreach was the armed forces. Large issues and turbulent conditions sank in significance when compared to the role the Church played in ministering to its armed forces personnel.

Diocesan assistance to the men and women in the service was under the care and direction of the Army and Navy Commission, appointed in the fall of 1941 to answer the growing group of conscriptees. The Commission coordinated and enlarged the scope of the work of the local parishes. Prayer Books, identification cards, and war crosses, together with cigarettes and a copy of the Diocesan magazine, *Tidings*, were distributed. The Commission was not able to minister directly to the various army and navy installations and camps on the Island, so it depended on the local clergy who gladly cooperated in holding services and listening to servicemen on Long Island. The serious problem due to a lack of a resident Episcopal chaplain was overcome by the Rector of Bellport ministering to Camp Upton while the Rector of St. James, Long Beach, ministered to the U.S. Coast Guard station there. St. John's, Fort Hamilton, took advantage of the opportunity to help at the New York Port of Embarkation. Holy Trinity, Brooklyn Heights, offered its facilities for a weekend overnight servicemen's care center. The Archdeacon of Brooklyn, the Venerable A. Edward Saunders, worked closely with the chaplain of the Royal Navy, docked at Brooklyn, for which he received the commendation of the Archbishop of York. Many churches opened their buildings to men in service and men employed in the aircraft industry. Care was taken not to duplicate the work of the U.S.O., but to offer additional services. The Bishop showed his intense interest in helping the servicemen by visiting the army posts, air fields and training centers, encouraging the men and letting the men know that the Church was interested in them.

As the war dragged on to its bitter end, the Diocese became aware of the problem of the returning chaplain and servicemen. A number of clergy in the Diocese had left their parishes to serve in the armed forces. Having left the security of parish life, they would return to financial instability and no position. The Bishop suggested a fund be set up to be used "by the Bishop to assist the Chaplains, and give him a group of men that could be utilized in supply work until such time as the Chaplain should be placed in a regular cure."

The problem of the returning servicemen had no easy solution. At the suggestion of the Bishop a Committee on Returning Veterans was set up. In cooperation with the Department of Christian Social Relations this committee established Veterans' Service Centers to help and guide the returning soldier in adjusting to the problems connected with his return. Counselling service by various parish clergy was supplemented by that afforded by diocesan personnel. Most parish priests were not equipped to give adequate counselling advice to veterans with genuine, deepseated personal problems. The Returning Veterans Committee recognized this fact and so paid the expenses of the clinical training of the Rev. Arland C. Blage who became a great source of help to many veterans. The greatest lack encountered in veterans work was that of psychiatric resources. Servicemen in need were not usually ill enough to require institution care, but did require some kind of out-clinic treatment. Persuaded by the Army and Navy Commission, the Church Charity Foundation had a clinic staffed by trained personnel that helped in the veterans crisis.

The Long Island to which Bishop DeWolfe came was a far different place than his predecessor had known. The war had accelerated many of the ongoing trends that had made a small but imperceptible change. Despite the stoppage of immigration from abroad, the Diocese itself continued to grow from natural increase and by reason of the arrival of many from other areas and dioceses. Population shifts caused by overcrowding, by the encroachment of business and the spread of industrial areas, and by such civic improvements as slum clearance, housing projects, and the widening of avenues and highways, particularly in Brooklyn and Queens, had been reflected in the amalgamation of parishes, and in some instances the disappearance of others. Some of the older downtown parishes actually experienced a slight revival by reason of the erection of large hotels and apartment houses on the sites of former residences. Weekday services at noon for nearby office workers and shoppers became very popular in such localities.

As many people moved into the eastern parts of the Diocese in response to the population pressure and other changes experienced in its western end, the Church followed. The more densely populated portions of Queens County began, in turn, to resemble those of Kings County — heavy traffic, the industrialization of many old residential areas and the erection of great housing developments which, with their attendant shopping centers, seemed each a small city in itself. At the same time the suburban areas of Queens became, for the most part, built up as Kings had a score of years before, until there remained only a few open spaces in that most extensive of the five boroughs of the City of New York.

Great as the rate of population growth was in Queens County, it more than doubled in Nassau. Between 1930 and 1950, the latter county increased in population from 300,000 to 700,000, while in the same period Queens had increased its population by about 45%. The complexion of Queens may have changed, but Nassau's became radically altered. By 1953, the great estates of Nassau as well as its golf courses, woodlands and farms so characteristic of its central and northern sections, had largely disappeared. The steady stream of automobiles travelling from Elmont east towards Hicksville, and from Great Neck to Oyster Bay to the south shore of Long Island, was obliged by that time to pass almost unbroken lines of new homes and housing developments.

Part of the numerical growth of the Diocese, more particularly in the two counties of Kings and Queens that comprised the eastern section of New York City, could be attributed to the recent advent of more Blacks and Hispanics. The migration of the former from the South had been accelerated by World War II and many of these people found homes and occupations in the Diocese. The flow of Hispanics into the City and the Diocese since World War II was even more spectacular, particularly in the early 1950's. In 1953, nearly one out of every twenty New Yorkers was an Hispanic, although the proportion in Kings County was not nearly so high. In that year there were over 62,000 of these people dwelling, for the most part, in downtown Brooklyn, Greenpoint and Williamsburgh. There were 8,000 others in Queens County. The Hispanics complicated the City's social and financial problems, and yet also helped to meet the City's job needs.

Other groups of people, not already citizens as were the Blacks and Hispanics, likewise continued to come to Brooklyn. They came under the annual quota of a few thousand immigrants largely from northwestern Europe, or as displaced persons left homeless by the ravages of war. The mobile, shifting and utterly heterogenous Island community was bound to have its effect on the work of the Diocese. It colored and moulded the special emphasis for mission on Long Island.

Bishop DeWolfe makes presentation to Archdeacon Saunders on his 20th anniversary as Rector of Christ Church.

One of the first major adjustments made under the new Bishop, in the diocesan pursuit of Church extension, was the establishment of a Central Department of Missions of the Diocesan Council. Rather than having three competitive Archdeaconries vieing for money and interest, a combined Department of the Bishops, Archdeacons and lay representatives, presented to the Diocese a total unified program. One missionary budget, for local and national needs, was presented to the Diocesan Convention every year for approval. Another far-reaching change came with the appointment of three Archdeacons. In 1942, Bishop DeWolfe relieved Bishop Larned of his missionary responsibilities in Brooklyn and Suffolk so that he could "assist the Bishop in the general missionary work" of the Diocese. Each Archdeaconry was asked to nominate "parish priests to supervise local work." Before the Diocesan was elected, Bishop Larned had appointed the Rev. Charles W. MacLean as Acting Archdeacon of Suffolk, and that appointment was made permanent by Bishop DeWolfe. Since the Venerable Ernest Sinfield, Archdeacon of Queens and Nassau, had joined the Army Chaplain Corps, the Rev. Harry J. Stretch was appointed Acting Archdeacon of Queens and Nassau. His permanent appointment came in October 1944. For the Archdeaconry of Brooklyn, late in 1942, the Rev. A. Edward Saunders assumed the duties of Archdeacon. The three episcopal appointees worked directly under the Bishop and were "in constant association" with each other in the new department setup.

The Archdeaconry of Brooklyn —

Girded for mission, the Diocese faced a plethora of missionary opportunities, none more complex than Brooklyn. The "great City", or borough of Brooklyn, had undergone drastic changes. The evolution of the County had been hastened by World War II so that within a few short years Brooklyn had become the domain of the unchurched. Of the three million people who lived within its borders over 50% had no church affiliation. Few forward and constructive missionary opportunities had been seized. Some churches, facing an increasingly difficult task of ministering to new people, merged for greater strength. A consolidation of St. Matthew's and St. Luke's had substantially benefited both, and had netted the Diocese a goodly sum of money to help diocesan programs. St. Michael's, an old and revered church dating back to 1847, experienced its dying gasps. Home of A. Augustus Low, it merged with St. Mark's Church, Adelphi Street. From 1945 on, it took care of the Navy Yard district and the "good souls of low income" living in public housing projects. Parishes such as Church of the Redeemer, Fourth Avenue, found less and less worshippers in their large and commodious buildings.

In addition to the regular mission Churches, two dramatic and exciting new works began. An entire Spanish speaking congregation with its priest was received into the Episcopal Church and began parish life housed in Christ Church, Clinton Street. Another Spanish speaking congregation sprang up and used Grace Church, Conselyea Street, for its parish center. The controversial figure, the Rt. Rev. John Torok, was appointed by the Bishop as Vicar-General for Foreign Work, helping and enlarging the scope of the already dynamic congregations.

Nothing, however, could compare with the interest and support shown to the increasing Black population of Brooklyn. To the existing four Black churches two more were added. St. Philip's Church, McDonough Street, the largest Black church in all Brooklyn had outgrown its small quarters, and when the Church of the Good Shepherd found its numbers diminished and life curtailed, it agreed to sell its physical plant to the Black church. St. Philip's moved into the more commodious quarters and soon they were filled to overflowing. The old St. Philip's, whose name was changed to St. Timothy's, continued to serve the Blacks in its section who could not or did not want to move to the new church. St. Martin's Chapel, led by the Rev. Egbert A. Craig, was taken over by the Diocese in 1944, and grew so rapidly that a building campaign needed to be undertaken. No leadership in all the Diocese, black or white, could compare to that of the Rev. John M. Coleman. An outstanding leader of men, a builder, a saintly person, his talents were used to the fullest by both the Diocese and the community. A respected member of the Black community, he represented them on the Municipal Board of Education, and he recognized a real need fulfilled in the Stuyvesant Community Center.

But Brooklyn, aside from its successes, had changed. Once the dominant force in Diocesan life, once the greatest source of money and men, once the heart and mind of the Diocese, in the postwar years Brooklyn took second place to both other Archdeaconries. From being the source, it became the object of mission. The change, reluctantly accepted by the City, created a whole set of new problems that besieged both Bishop and Diocese for many years.

The Archdeaconry of Queens and Nassau —

Queens and Nassau, country and suburb before the war, had grown to be the hub of the Diocese. Under the brilliant leadership of Father Stretch, churches multiplied rapidly, and it seemed as if the missionary imperative dormant for so long would once more spring to the fore. Older communities expanded by additional housing; new areas, once open fields but now thriving communities, compelled the Diocese to plant churches in these dynamic areas. Church of the Atonement, a parochial mission of St. Joseph's, Queens Village, came under the care of the Diocese. In a few short years the church, renamed St. David's, had grown from a rented building to a new church building. Other areas such as Oceanside, Lake Success, Fresh Meadows, East Meadow and Syosset, duplicated the same spirit and the same tremendous project. But no

*(left) Vacation Bible
School at St. Michael
and All Angels,
Gorden Heights.
(below) St. Francis
Church, Levittown.*

area showed so clearly the future of the Island than the large patch of land between East Meadow and Farmingdale. Levitt Builders, after a small sortie into Carle Place, that helped St. Mary's Parochial Chapel grow to full parish status, began the huge housing development known as Levittown. In just a few short years a new community had been erected, and the Episcopal Church began work among the small Cape Cod cottages. Within nine months a mission church became self-supporting and within a few years a lovely St. Francis Church was erected. The Diocese was justly proud of its spectacular success among the newly-married, newly-housed and newly-parented people.

The Archdeaconry of Suffolk —

Suffolk's development, slower than its western neighbor, did contribute to the ongoing process of missionary expansion. St. Boniface's Church at Lindenhurst started in a rented house and soon drew many members to it. And in Gordon Heights, a small Black ghetto in Suffolk, the Diocese erected St. Michael and All Angels, an "Episcopal Church in a Rural Negro Community." Suffolk for the most part still remained rural. The ongoing tide of population did not reach as far as its inner core, and the Archdeacon himself brought this clearly to the Diocese:

This is a rural area and the work, like many other programs in rural territory, moves slowly. Our numbers of people are small, our equipment often inadequate, and the task of caring for two or three missions physically hard.... While we cannot measure our advance in annual reports or graphs, yet we know that where these Mission Clergy serve, the Kingdom of God is being firmly entrenched.

Ten years of the Bishop's episcopate had brought new life to church expansion. During these years twelve parishes had been incorporated and received into diocesan union; two parishes had been restored to union with the Diocese and nine new missions had been established. The Diocese had invested $375,000 in new mission buildings. In 1944, a budget for "assisted parishes" made its appearance and enabled at least half a dozen parishes to wrestle successfully with difficulties caused by shifting populations. The budget for the Department of Missions had increased 40% in that period despite the increased measure of self-support provided by the mission congregations themselves. Contributions by church people for all sides of diocesan life had reached the untold figure of $2,334,093.26, an achievement worthy in itself.

IMMEDIATE CONCERNS

The new Bishop inherited certain problems from the former administration. Besides making the Diocese responsible for the support of the Bishop, other financial difficulties and snags made immediate action necessary. None was more pressing than the charge of fiscal irresponsibility brought against the Diocese by the Rector of Christ Church, Lynbrook, the Rev. John V. Cooper.

At the Diocesan Convention at which Bishop Stires made public his intent to retire, the whole matter of circulatory letters containing accusations against the Trustees of the Estate belonging to the Diocese of Long Island was discussed. On May 10, 1941, the Rev. John V. Cooper issued a communication to all delegates questioning three things: "What is the present inventory value of our Trust Funds; What is the present Diocesan income and expenses, in lump sums that we can understand [and] show us an Auditor's certification of our full transactions and books." The Trustees summoned the plaintiff to appear at the Convention of May 27, and present his case — which he did. After much discussion, it was moved to appoint a committee to look into the matter. The committee was appointed in February 1942, and a deadline for a report of their findings was set for March 1943.

A lengthy and detailed report was made to the 1943 Convention, touching upon three major areas: the Cathedral, the Church Charity Foundation and the Trustees of the Diocese. The Trustees of the Estate belonging to the Diocese of Long Island was incorporated in 1871 to acquire and hold land for diocesan purposes. In 1872, the act of incorporation was amended to allow the corporation to hold parish property, real or personal, to be used for "said Church, Society or Congregation." In 1926, the Trustees incorporation was again amended to allow "possession of temporalities and property" belonging to extinct churches, societies or congregations, and to use them for "uses and purposes of the Protestant Episcopal Church in said Diocese." In 1927, the merger of six funds was authorized. The Trustees held title to and managed sixty-six individual pieces of real estate, including the Diocesan House in Brooklyn. A detailed report of assets and investments was made.

The Committee also investigated and made recommendations concerning the "Manner of Designating or Electing Trustees of the Estate." The Standing Committee, according to the incorporation act, served as the Trustees. They suggested that the work and responsibility of the Standing Committee, and that of the Trustees of the Estate were usually not, and certainly were not necessarily related to each other. They recommended that "another or different method" of selecting Trustees be provided, and that it might be better if three or four laymen were elected to that position by the Diocesan Convention. The suggestion, viable as it was, never took material form. The matter died due to a lack of interest.

Much good accrued the Diocese from the charge and the answer. The Diocese was forced to take stock, especially in regard to the Cathedral and the Church Charity Foundation. The Cathedral had a deficit in spending as well as did the two Cathedral schools of St. Paul's and St. Mary's. Of more pressing importance was the work of the Church Charity Foundation the "great achievement" of the Diocese which accomplished immeasurable works of charity, drawing the attention of the medical and surgical worlds. An outstanding house staff and a large nursing staff, assisted by the resident Chaplain, helped make St. John's Hospital and other units "an outstanding teaching hospital." The problem was overspending. Although annual reports stressed an expansive attitude, figures in the ledger did not agree. The Foundation faced a financial crisis, both in 1943 and 1944. Through stringent methods and practical outlook, a deficit of $72,000 had been reduced to $35,000. In 1944, the Foundation noted sadly that the work in the children's cottages in Sayville, maintained at a great expense to the Foundation, had to be closed. The Foundation hoped, without fulfillment, that "additional endowments or some other means of support could be found to resume work among the children." The Foundation by winnowing its expenses had achieved "a milestone", living within its means. The year 1944 looked forward to the further development of the Foundation as the Diocesan medical center and to the establishment of a "comprehensive St. John's Hospital."

The relationship of several so-called diocesan institutions was made clear. The Society of St. Johnland, founded in 1866 and located in Kings Park, had "no legal or canonical connection" with the Diocese or the

Foundation. The House of St. Giles the Cripple in Brooklyn, founded by an ardent Episcopalian, Sister Sarah, and St. Giles Home for Cripple Children in Garden City, were assumed by many to be a part of the Foundation's work. The Board of these, whose president had been the Bishop and whose membership was composed largely of Episcopalians, had no real connection with the Diocese. They raised their own funds, receiving none from the Foundation. A lay president had replaced the Bishop and the tenor of the board had changed, ending any supposed connection with diocesan charitable works. St. Phebe's Mission continued as a convalescent home for women for a while. Beset by many problems it finally closed, being sold to Brooklyn Hospital. The Board of Trustees of the institution continued to hold regular meetings after its demise. Necessary business was transacted "which included the voting of income on investments to various charitable needs." Ultimately the fund was turned over to the Church Mission of Help, which used it well.

During this period the Church Mission of Help, which eventually assumed the name of the Youth Consultation Service, prospered and enlarged its ministering. Begun as a work for girls, unmarried mothers, the Service in 1947 began to work with boys too. The agency worked with the young people whose problems were truancy, running away or unhappy home relationships. The professional staff was also enlarged to include a Black social worker. After a succession of Executive Directors, in September 1951, Mrs. Myron V. Hulse assumed the leadership in this important agency. In May 1964, the name of the agency was legally changed to Youth Consultation Service. Although faced with financial difficulties, the agency continued to expand its work and influence, meeting the ever increasing problems of teenagers and families.

EPISCOPAL ASSISTANCE

In view of the increasing scope of diocesan activities, Bishop DeWolfe felt the pressing need of regular episcopal assistance. For the first few years of his episcopate he had the help of Bishop Larned whom he inherited from the previous regime. The two Bishops, opponents in the 1942 election, never seemed to work well together. It was natural that when the opportunity of serving as Bishop-in-Charge of American Churches in Europe came to the Long Island Suffragan, he would and did accept. In 1948, the Bishop asked for the election of a Suffragan Bishop, and carefully outlined the qualities he felt necessary, among which were: a humble man; not one whom personal ambitions would cause to look for larger fields; a missionary; a man of business ability to whom the Bishop could delegate administrative details; and lastly a man of faith. The call for a special Convention for the purpose of electing a Suffragan Bishop was issued for Tuesday, October 12, 1948.

On the specified day the duly elected delegates, clergy and laity, assembled in the Garden City Cathedral for the solemn election of a Bishop. Twelve names were placed in nomination, among which were the three Archdeacons, large parish rectors and the Rector of St. Thomas' Church, Bellerose. On the first ballot the contest showed three contenders: Archdeacon Stretch, Archdeacon MacLean and the Rev. Jonathan G. Sherman of Bellerose. It took only two more ballots to determine the choice. On the third ballot the Rev. Jonathan G. Sherman received the necessary number of votes in both the clergy and lay order to make him the Suffragan Bishop of Long Island.

The swift action of the Convention in electing the Suffragan came as a surprise to many, and in some ways also surprised the Bishop. The Rector of Bellerose certainly possessed the necessary requisites, but by and large was more a scholar than an administrator. But no one was more surprised than the Bishop-elect himself, as he had no knowledge of any support or any concerted effort to elect him. Only a few days before the election, by way of another diocese, did he have any inkling that his name was even being considered. Yet on the appointed day he had proven to be the chosen candidate.

The Suffragan Bishop-elect was no newcomer to the Diocese. Born in St. Louis, Missouri, in 1907, he was educated at Kent School, Yale and the General Theological Seminary, where he served as Fellow and Tutor after graduation. In 1935, he became priest-in-charge of St. Thomas', Farmingdale. Three years later he went to St. Thomas', Bellerose, where he served as Rector until being elected Bishop. In the fourteen years of service in the Diocese, he held many leadership positions. At the time of his election he was Secretary of the Standing Committee and the Trustees, on the Board of Examining Chaplains and President of the Youth Consultation Service. He had also been in the Department of Christian Education, Editor of *Tidings*, and Provisional Deputy to General Convention. He also served for a time as Chaplain to Creedmoor State Hospital. No stranger to the ways of the Church, he himself was the son of a priest, and the son-in-law of a Bishop; his wife, Frances being the daughter of Bishop Thomas Casady of the Diocese of Oklahoma. They had three children and one on the way. After receiving due certification, the Suffragan Bishop-elect was consecrated in the Garden City Cathedral on the Feast of the Epiphany, January 6, 1949. Soon after, his fourth child Jonathan was born. The Bishop took up his duties "to share the duties and the responsibilities as well as the privileges."

ANOTHER LABORER IN THE VINEYARD

Of importance was the initiation of the office of Administrator. The Diocese had always been blessed with dedicated laymen who gave unstintingly of their time and talent. No more dedicated a layman was there than

Raymond F. Barnes, for many years the Treasurer of the Diocese. Serving in many capacities, both in the Diocese and the National Church, Barnes suffered illness in later years and on August 9, 1949, died leaving a large void in the diocesan structure. The Bishop faced with the full responsibility of "the complex administrative details" of the Diocese, in conference with the Standing Committee decided there was needed "someone to daily watch over budgets . . . to answer numerous questions by clergy and laity concerning quotas, assessments, etc. . . . and someone to represent the Bishop." To this end he appointed as Administrator the Venerable Charles W. MacLean, Archdeacon of Suffolk, to "look after the important and voluminous details that flow through the Diocesan business center." Archdeacon MacLean took up his duties in the early part of 1950, and the necessary financial arrangements were made at the May Convention. Archdeacon MacLean moved into the Diocesan House in Brooklyn to be watchdog over the Diocese and to be all things to all men. In a short time, he had "strengthened and made more efficient" the whole administrative task. At last the Bishop was content; he had his man of "definite business and executive ability."

To fill the many diocesan positions left vacant by the death of Raymond Barnes, the Bishop appointed influential laymen. As treasurer of the Diocese he named his good friend, John H. Mears, "a man of outstanding business prominence and ability, as well as a devout and active churchman." Later Mr. Mears was ordained to the perpetual deaconate and served as Volunteer Assistant at the Cathedral. He held the office of treasurer for many years. Mr. Frank Gulden, another outstanding layman, was elected by the Trustees to be treasurer of that group, also "a voluntary work without salary."

THE TRIVIAL ROUND, THE COMMON TASK

As in previous administrations, vital changes in program and policy were made to keep up with the changing times, and to make clear the mission of the Church. Re-adjustments, sometimes necessary, other times drastic, most times helpful, were made in diocesan structure, administration and leadership. New ventures were initiated and old forms enhanced, making the Diocese better able and prepared to minister to the community known as Long Island.

Girding For Mission —
In 1950, a new canon was approved updating the Diocesan Council. The canon imbued the council with "the unification, development and prosecution of the missionary, educational, youth, promotion and social work of the Church in this Diocese, of which the Bishop shall be the executive head." Membership of three years on a rotating basis was open to clergy and laymen. Women, representing the Women's Auxiliary, nominated by them, also served on the Council but only for one year. The Council had to submit to the Convention a program, supporting budget, and a plan of apportionment to support that budget.

The Department of Christian Social Relations especially became the object of scrutiny and study. In 1903, by resolution, and two years later by canon, the Diocese established a Social Service Committee, the first of its kind in the Episcopal Church and the model for the National Council. The Social Service Committee dealt with such evils as delinquency, labor problems, vice and civic corruption. During World War I, the Committee cooperated with the Red Cross, engaging in relief work and the service of voluntary chaplains. In the twenties the Committee was concerned with institutional work, and again in the thirties became the vanguard by anticipating the National Council. In 1932, it changed its name to the Department of Christian Social Relations. The forties brought the problem of war and its aftermath. In 1948, the Bishop requested the Department to initiate "an exhaustive survey and study of our Diocesan services." Ready by the end of 1949, the report was submitted to the Bishop for study in April 1950. Approved by the Diocesan Council, the Department began an expansion of its work in cooperation with other work agencies. The Department faced the problem of displaced persons, the aging, drug addiction, Chaplancies in hospitals and the growing urban tensions. On April 24, 1953, the Department celebrated its golden jubilee with a special celebration in the Cathedral House.

A United Woman's Front —
Women's work in the Diocese had many different channels, sometimes conflicting, sometimes harmonizing, but at all times vieing for the help and support of the local parishes. Nine official women's organizations included such work as the Women's Auxiliary, the Daughters of the King, the Diocesan Altar Guild and the Girls' Friendly Society. In 1950, the Bishop presented to the Diocese the hope of "a federation" which would include "the entire womanhood of the Diocese in the whole task of the Church." Each individual group would retain its individuality, the change would be "the expansion of the work of the individual units." The plan was presented at a time when the Women's Auxiliary was jointly meeting with the Convention. A joint session of both groups was held to "consider our great missionary responsibilities and opportunities." The new plan, accepted by the women, went into effect in the fall of 1950, and overlapping activities and programs were gradually eliminated. A stress on the devotional life within parish groups emphasized the fact that the "Martha" side of women's activities often overshadowed and neglected the "Mary" side.

New Thoughts of God, New Hope of Heaven —

The Diocese began to realize more fully the way of specialized vocations. Clergy ranks were augmented by the growth of religious orders. Bishop Littlejohn had, in 1872, with Mother Julia and Sister Emma, founded the Community of St. John the Evangelist. To their ranks was added in 1924, by Bishop Burgess' welcome, the Sisterhood of the Holy Nativity, which established a retreat and rest house at Bay Shore. In 1928, Bishop Stires received the Order of the Poor Brethren of St. Francis, commonly known as "the Franciscans" who settled in Mt. Sinai and named their home "Little Portion Monastery". It was Bishop Stires, too, who received the Poor Clares of Reparation and Adoration at Mt. Sinai. Bishop DeWolfe, within a week of his consecration, constituted the Brothers of St. Joseph, who eventually settled in the Children's Cottages in Sayville. In 1950, the Teachers of the Children of God, a teaching order whose curriculum was based on the "Tuller" Method set up a convent and school at Maycroft in Sag Harbor. And on November 8, 1951, the Bishop received a large group of Sisters from the Community of St. Mary. He blessed their new convent, chapel, nursery school, nurses' school and the million dollar children's hospital built in Bayside. Soon monks and nuns became a familiar sight in the Diocese and entered into all areas of diocesan life, serving in whatever way they could, but most of all as a symbol of this kind of special life.

Remarkable, too, were the annual retreats and conferences held by the Bishop for his men studying for the priesthood. Always an ardent supporter of priest and priesthood, a few months after his consecration, he held a one day conference at his home in Garden City for the then small group of seminarians and pre-theological students. The response was so great that the Bishop, when the youth center in Wading River was established, began holding three day retreats for his men. A well-known sight at the children's camp was the black cassocked men walking silently around the grounds, or the inspiring and meaningful addresses given by the Bishop, seated on his chair and talking of matters that affected most intimately the life of the Church. For both Bishop and seminarians, the three days were rich and rewarding.

The Bishop's Men —

The Bishop also wanted a more intimate relationship with the laymen of the Diocese. Laymen's work had always played a part from the time of Bishop Littlejohn. Laymen's organizations that included such groups as The Church Club of Long Island, the Central Council of Men's Clubs and the Brotherhood of St. Andrew, had given a structure within which the layman could and did serve the Church. Bishop DeWolfe had other ideas. He wanted an atmosphere within which the laymen could come to know their Bishop, both as

Franciscans at Little Portion Monastery, Mt. Sinai.

pastor and teacher. Beginning in the fall of 1945, he met four times a year with laymen at the Cathedral House in Garden City. A three-fold program of prayer, study and work included an instruction by the Bishop, and a question and answer period. Upwards of 2,500 men attended the services. Membership cards and a distinctive badge were distributed to the men who participated. A large service of witness was held each Ascension Day evening at the Cathedral.

The Hope of the World —

Nowhere did Bishop DeWolfe show his keener interest and insight than in the youth of the Diocese. In 1944, he outlined a five year plan to implement the extension of the Church among its younger members. A Diocesan Youth Roll Call showed eight youth organizations in the Diocese, among which was the Young Peoples' Fellowship, Order of Sir Galahad, Girls' Friendly Society, the Junior Auxiliary and the Junior Brotherhood of St. Andrew. An Annual Youth Convention was always an exciting and informative affair. A step forward was taken in December 1944, when the Diocesan Council voted to set up a Department of Youth, separate from the Department of Christian Education. The Department, first under the Rev. Charles T. Knapp, and then the Rev. Gordon E. Gillett, took progressive and firm action to minister to the young people of the Diocese. The Bishop plainly stated his purpose for the new missionary outreach:

> The great need among our young people is the same as that for the whole church, which is more definite instruction on the Faith and Life of the Church. . . . In the days which are to follow, it may be trite to say, but nevertheless true, that the hope of the world is with our young people. We here in Long Island must never let it be said that we begrudged any amount of time or money spent in consecrating the future hope to Christ and His Kingdom.

The Diocese did not begrudge time or money for youth work. When budgets for full time diocesan personnel were seriously cut back, the Diocese continued a Youth Director on a part time basis. On the resignation of Father Gillette, the Bishop appointed the Vicar of St. Mary's, Carle Place, the Rev. John W. Davis to act in that capacity. By 1953, the Bishop and Diocese were ready to resume once more full work among young people and Father Davis, resigning his cure, became the full-time Director of Youth Work for the Diocese.

A great stride forward for young people was the purchase of a seventy-two acre tract of land on Long Island Sound in Wading River. Youth Conferences had been a standard part of diocesan life, with a week long conference known as the Wading River Conference being held at the Boy Scout Camp in that Suffolk Village. Beginning in 1944, taking advantage of the vacated children's cottages at Sayville, the Diocese held a series of five to seven week conferences for children of all ages. In 1947, the Diocese took advantage of a legacy left by Mary E. Benson, and bought a beautiful tract of land set on the bluffs overlooking Long Island Sound. Prefabricated buildings were quickly erected and in July 1947, the Bishop blessed the youth center, named Camp DeWolfe by the young people of the Diocese in honor of the Bishop. The first season at the camp there were less than sixty campers a week, and a small staff took care of all the children's needs. As the years went on, the interest and enrollment grew and the camp began to outgrow its small facilities. Children from all over the Diocese enjoyed the fun of camp, swimming and nature, while receiving a good church education from the diocesan clergy who came week by week to camp.

Juvenile delinquency, which became a major problem to the whole nation, stirred interest and action on the part of the Diocese. The Brothers of St. Joseph, a new order, were given the responsibility of working with delinquent boys. The Brothers completely renovated one of the large buildings at the Sayville Cottages, turned over to them for their work. Never overcrowded, the Sayville work assisted boys in a difficult period of their life, in adjusting to their problems and solving them.

NEW TREASURES STILL OF COUNTLESS PRICE — EPISCOPAL CHARITIES APPEAL

Responding to the Bishop's request, the Diocese went on record in 1949 in favor of "a Diocesan Chest", a combined appeal to include the Bishop's Call, the Church Charity Foundation and the Church Mission of Help. Unable to make the combined appeal in 1950 because of an appeal for "One World in Christ" by the National Church, the first Diocesan Chest, named Episcopal Charities Appeal, began on June 10, 1951, under the leadership of the Hon. Edward A. Richards and the Hon. Charles S. Colden. The fund allotted 60% of receipts to the Church Charity Foundation, and the rest went to the Church Mission of Help and the Bishop's Call. A total of $90,192.53 was collected in 1952. The results of the first two campaigns, although not up to expectations, showed that a united appeal for charities had won the cooperation of contributors who formerly supported the participating agencies, and had secured new contributions from those who appreciated the one campaign a year rather than several appeals as before.

By 1955, the Appeal totalled $161,044, an increase of more than 161% since 1950, the last year in which the diocesan charitable institutions held separate campaigns for their support. The volunteer Executive Director, the Ven. Canon Charles W. MacLean, was justly proud of the work the Appeal had accomplished.

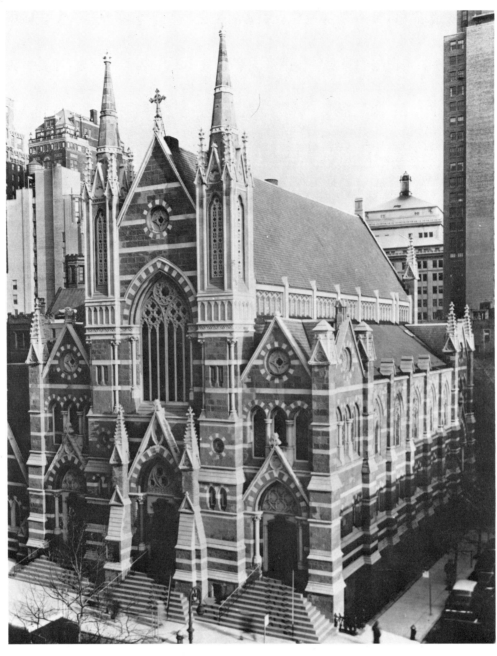

*St. Anne's Church,
Brooklyn Heights.*

A DIOCESAN CHURCH

In 1950, the Bishop received from the Vestry of St. Ann's Church, Brooklyn, a communication offering the facilities of the church, its altar and buildings for diocesan purposes. It proved a great boon for the Diocese. Known as the Mother Church of Brooklyn, for many years St. Ann's played host to innumerable diocesan functions, making it in some sense a diocesan center. Strategically located on the Heights, because all principal subways converged at nearby Borough Hall, and easily accessible to Manhattan and Brooklyn generally, it seemed a natural choice for some kind of diocesan center. St. Ann's Church had also undergone, like most churches in the surrounding area, a drastic change that made its effectiveness in the neighborhood far less real and vital than in its hey-day. The Bishop accepted the kind offer of the church and named St. Ann's as the Diocesan Church in Brooklyn. At last the hope of Bishop Burgess, in attempting the short-lived plan of making extinct St. Peter's Church a diocesan center, found fulfillment. On May 9, 1950, the Bishop celebrated in the chapel and gave meditation to the congregation of priests and laity. The life of the Diocesan Church had officially begun.

On Whitsunday evening, May 28, 1950, the Bishop conducted a service of witness at which he outlined his plans for the Diocesan Church, and for the strengthening and bettering of church life in Brooklyn. This was the beginning of what soon developed into the Bishop's Lenten Mission. Beginning in Lent 1951, the Bishop held a series of Sunday night teaching missions at the Diocesan Church. More than 1,500 people crowded in on Sunday nights to hear the Bishop's outstanding addresses and be a part of the magnificent singing of hymns. Questions and answers gave the mission an informal atmosphere within which the Bishop, as pastor, could be with his people and they with him. The Bishop possessed a fine voice and loved to sing. One of the great and pleasurable moments of these missions was to hear the Catholic Bishop sing "What a Friend We Have in Jesus".

SPEAKING OUT

The Rt. Rev. James P. DeWolfe, Fourth Bishop of Long Island, had no reticence in speaking out on issues that he felt needed his voice. Two years after his consecration he deemed it necessary to speak his mind on pacifists and isolationism. His assertion certainly left no room for doubt as to which side he was on and for what he stood. The same quality colored his criticism of John D. Rockefeller and the imminent Protestant Council of New York. Always on the side of Catholicism, he made clear his opposition to the Pan-Protestant venture and affirmed his complete reliance upon the tenets of the Chicago-Lambeth Quadrilateral. But no issue received such widespread publicity, nor caused so much friction in the Diocese and the nation, as did the prolonged incident known as the Melish Case.

The Melish Case —

It was purely a parish problem; one that had happened before and would happen again. Two parties no longer lived amicably together and so sought outside arbitration. The petition for the dissolution of pastoral relations has always been fraught with deep conflicting emotions and discordant sentiment, always ending in hard feelings. The simple case of Holy Trinity Church, however, had its complications: a long-tenured, beloved rector, a once influential parish, a profound filial attachment, a sacrificial father, a strong-willed son, and a most unusual agreement. Add to the situation the dimensions of the times, the Red Scare, the Cold War, the House Un-American Activities Committee and the intense spirit of anti-communism. The simple decision to seek outside help in the Ecclesiastical Authority, the Bishop, charged the situation more. Inflated public opinion, the shift of emphasis from rector-parish to rector-bishop, and the long legal battle between all three distorted the situation even more. Newspapers colored the scene; sides were taken for or against the Melishes. The purely parochial problem became a national problem. The widespread publicity, the interminable suits in the civil courts, all made the Melish case a household word and drastically affected Holy Trinity, the Bishop and the Melishes.

In 1904, the Rev. John Howard Melish accepted the call to Holy Trinity Church, Brooklyn Heights, with one very strong proviso. He came with the firm understanding that in all matters of parochial policy he would be the major determiner, not the Vestry. During his long ministry at Holy Trinity, he associated himself with many then liberal and radical movements, among which were the Central Labor Party of Brooklyn, the Fusion Party of New York, the case of Algernon Cropsey, and the defense of his assistant, the Rev. Bradford Young, a prominent socialist.

When in 1939, Dr. Melish's son, the Rev. William Howard Melish, became the Assistant Minister at Holy Trinity, the Rector and the Wardens and the Vestry petitioned the Rt. Rev. Ernest M. Stires, to seek his consent for the right of Dr. Melish's son to succeed his father at the time of his death or resignation as rector. In a letter dated August 11, 1939, Bishop Stires stated that, "No vestry can bind their successors, no bishop can bind his successor or even bind himself as to what action he will take when a situation arises which has not yet arisen. . . . "

In June 1946, the Assistant Minister, the Rev. William Howard Melish, was elected Chairman of the National Council of American-Soviet Friendship. From this time on, his activities outside of the parish were considered by many of the congregation to be radical and pro-communist. The whole matter created tensions in the parish, when Mr. Tom Clark, Attorney General of the United States, issued his lists of "subversive organizations" that included the Soviet-American Friendship Council.

In 1947 and 1948, the membership of the Church of the Holy Trinity had diminished to the extent that the Wardens and Vestry in May 1948, adopted a resolution requesting the son to resign as the Assistant Minister of the parish and petitioned his father to bring about such a resignation. When both refused, the Vestry referred the matter to the Bishop and the Standing Committee of the Diocese.

In December 1948, Bishop DeWolfe, accompanied by the Chancellor and able lawyer, Colonel Jackson Dykman, made a formal visitation to the parish and listened to prepared statements by both vestry and rector. No action was taken, but in January 1949, the Vestry, by a vote of nine to two, petitioned the Bishop to dissolve the pastoral relation between the parish and rector.

A "Committee to Retain the Rector" was immediately formed. The Bishop, on March 2, 1949, sent a message that, in his judgment, the pastoral relation would be dissolved as of April 4, 1949. The Bishop's letter contained a memorandum from the Standing Committee of the Diocese upholding the Bishop, referring to "dissension" in the parish and the assistant's "detrimental outside activities."

On March 7, 1949, a parish meeting was called to consider the removal of nine vestrymen who voted against the rector. Before the meeting to fill the vacancies could be held, the affected vestrymen filed in the civil court papers for a restraining order to prevent the holding of a special election and asked that they be reinstated.

A temporary injunction holding everything in status quo was issued. On April 16, 1949, Justice Meir Steinbrink of the New York Supreme Court, held a formal trial. The Vestry, through counsel, asked the court to declare the special meeting illegal, to forbid a new election, and to sustain them in the exercise of their offices, and to enforce the Bishop's judgment. The Counsel for the Bishop and the Standing Committee took a similar stand, declaring that a vestry was the corporate body in an Episcopal Church, and alone entitled to act in such matters.

Judge Steinbrink decided in favor of the Bishop and the Standing Committee of the Diocese and the legal Vestry, on the ground that under the Canons, the "Committee to Retain the Rector" had acted illegally. The decision affirmed on appeal to the Court of Appeals, was refused for review by the United States Supreme Court. The Civil Courts upheld the Bishop's actions.

Three years after the official termination of his office, Dr. Melish delivered what he called his last sermon. The sermon lauded Moses as a "revolutionary leader" and that all human progress had been the product of "the revolutionary spirit of man." In poor health, Dr. Melish spoke from a wheelchair. His son continued to fill the vacant pulpit as "Acting Rector". The matter dragged on for many more years.

The Cathedral Controversy —

Unable to restrain himself from unequivocally confronting matters, spiritual or ecclesiastical, the Bishop's conflict in his own Diocesan Church helped to threaten his reputation and his work. One of the chief points of emphasis made constantly by the Bishop was the centrality of the Eucharist. Throughout his episcopate, basing his views on the Catholic ideal, he constantly reiterated that the Eucharist be the chief service on Sunday. The paradox of the matter was that in the Cathedral of the Incarnation the chief service continued to be Morning Prayer. Prodded and urged by some of the Anglo-Catholics of the Diocese, the Bishop issued his statement in 1951. He proclaimed:

> In order that there might be a symbol of this type of worship throughout this Diocese,
> beginning this Fall (1951) the chief service of worship every Sunday at our Cathedral will be
> the Holy Communion.

The Cathedral in Garden City had been from its very first moments a community church. No other church existed in the suburban community for many years until in the first decade of the twentieth century the Roman Catholic Church began. There were five Protestant churches in the community by 1952, but Protestants still continued to consider the Cathedral the Protestant church and supported it liberally and well. The institution of the Eucharist at each service shocked and repelled many of the Cathedral attendants. Widespread publicity in the press brought open conflict and soaring tempers. The Dean himself, caught between Bishop and congregation, was thought to be working against his immediate superior. To quiet any talk the Dean, together with the Canons on the staff, issued a statement to the congregation of the Cathedral in April 1952. It was followed by the Bishop preaching in the Cathedral on Low Sunday, April 20, 1952, at which time he appealed to the Garden City congregation to be the pace-maker for the Diocese. Realizing the diverse character of the Church, the Bishop nevertheless made it plain that the Cathedral was an Episcopal Church and as such abided by the tenets and practices of the Church.

"The Cathedral is the Bishop's church," he clearly stated. "The Cathedral, just because it is the Cathedral, must set the standard for the whole Diocese in all respects. Certainly the Cathedral staff and I believe the Cathedral congregation, for the most part, understand and approve and accept that proposition." The Bishop was being a little hopeful. The faithful Episcopalians remained to make the Diocesan Church stronger and more effective. But many more left, irate and indignant against the Bishop, remembering for a long time his usurpation of "their church." Most went to the Garden City Community Church which prospered on the added numbers and income. The Bishop, surrounded by his friends, and the Cathedral sure of its identity did survive, perhaps a little worn and battered, but able to pursue its Church ministry.

The identification of authority in the Cathedral engaged the Bishop, the Cathedral Chapter, and the Vestry Committee, a local community non-decisive group, for many years. The Cathedral's life was made no easier by the death of its Dean, the Very Rev. Hubert S. Wood.

SMOOTH SAILING

The unnerving and tumultuous events of the first twelve years of the Bishop's tenure did not openly affect the advance of the Diocese. Everywhere there seemed to be expansive life and active dynamic progress. A purely mundane accomplishment, but far reaching in its scope, was the establishment of the Diocesan Investment Fund. The Fund, open to all organizations in the Diocese, non-profit making, solved the problem of investing local and diocesan endowment funds. Administered by the Trustees of the Diocese, annual reports began appearing regularly after 1954, showing a good investment for all concerned. Missionary receipts increased over 200% from giving in 1944. The Annual Campaign for Episcopal Charities Appeal prospered, increasing each year in money and influence. Extension of churches resulted in the firm establishment of St. Bede's, Syosset, adding to the growing number of active Episcopal churches in the Island communities. Renewed interest in the diocesan center was engendered by the establishment of the "Friends of the Cathedral". Statistics for the twelve years brightened the picture. Communicant strength had grown from 62,404 to 68, 025; baptized persons from 97,686 to 116,572. Most dramatic of all, offerings and contributions rose from a little over 1½ million to 3½ million in 1954. The Diocese appeared to all intents and purposes to be alive and well and living on Long Island.

Chapter Sixteen

The Golden Evening

The last twelve years of Bishop DeWolfe's administration held the dream fulfilled. At perhaps no other time in the history of the Diocese did so much happen and was so much accomplished. Charitable works, always a prime concern of the Diocese, made great strides forward. Missionary outreach, expanding in some areas, contracting in others, came to full fruition. The Cathedral, suffering little from its recent controversy, had emerged strong and sure of its identity. The work of the episcopate, enlarged and demanding, made the services of a second suffragan imperative. The centralization of the Diocese in Garden City was accomplished by the removal of the Diocesan House from Brooklyn to Garden City. Work among the laity and young people knew no bounds. But most noteworthy and more far-reaching in its permeating influence was the expansion of the diocesan educational program, with the establishment of another diocesan landmark.

ANOTHER DIOCESAN LANDMARK

In the original plans for the Cathedral complex proposed by Mrs. Stewart there was to be, among other buildings, a seminary. Death, money and unfriendly persons made the original plan an impossibility. It was left to be done, almost eighty years later, by another interested woman, Mrs. George Mercer, Jr. Her offer coincided with the purposes of the Bishop and together they made possible another diocesan landmark on the Cathedral grounds.

The Bishop, deeply interested in the education and vocation of the priesthood, nurtured an idea whereby men of late vocation could study for Holy Orders. The old method of instruction, assignment to a parish priest as private tutor, did not seem to work well. He also envisaged a center of sound church instruction for lay people of the Diocese. To this dual purpose the Bishop proposed the establishment of a school of theology "to provide systematic and adequate instruction in theological subjects for men preparing for Holy Orders, unable to attend Seminary . . . and to provide sound instruction on an adult level for interested lay people of the Diocese." The school of theology, the Bishop emphatically stated, was not to be "a short-cut to the priesthood." The school would meet regularly on weekday evenings and on Saturday mornings. This would include regular classroom instruction, student-to-student contact, regular church services and the opportunity for the Bishop to exercise his role as the leader of men who would someday be priests.

The hope became a reality. In February 1955, the school formally opened with a celebration of the Holy Eucharist at the Cathedral. Registration for classes was held three days later. From then on classes were held regularly at St. Paul's School in the evening and the Cathedral House on Saturday mornings. The faculty, composed of diocesan clergy, was headed by the Rev. Albert Greanoff who resigned as Dean in December 1956. In his place the Bishop appointed the pedantic Rev. Robert F. Capon. A library was begun as a memorial to the Rev. J. Clarence Jones, long time diocesan leader. The incoming class numbered forty-six.

The hope realized soon found a permanent home. Through the kind intervention of H. Clinton Corwin, a member of the Standing Committee and active Cathedral communicant, interest in the project was kindled in Mrs. George Mercer, Jr., a wealthy New York woman. Following a small scholarship donation, she made a large bequest to the Diocese for the specific purpose of erecting the George Mercer, Jr. Memorial School of Theology. On May 15, 1956, at the 89th Diocesan Convention, amid fanfare and pomp and circumstance, ground breaking for the new building took place on the southwest corner of the Cathedral grounds. The School of Theology building answered a specific need. As the Bishop told the assembled Convention:

> While it is not our present intention to found a Theological Seminary . . . the new Theological School building will provide centralized teaching activities . . . and at the same time bring into corporate relations and fellowship those who otherwise have pursued their studies more or less in isolation, under the personal guidance of their respective tutors.

On December 27, 1958, the Bishop formally dedicated the new building and consecrated the Chapel of the Good Shepherd in the presence of its generous donor, Mrs. Mercer. The "L" shaped building, contemporary in design, with a slight Romanesque influence, consisted of five classrooms, a cafeteria, administrative offices for the Bishop and the chapel. Classes were held immediately following in the new building. In June 1959, four "Mercerized" men graduated to take their place in diocesan life. Since that time a steady stream of graduates have flooded the Diocese and spilled over into other dioceses and missionary fields.

George Mercer, Jr. Memorial Building, Garden City.

In 1965 another windfall for the school was announced by the Bishop. Under the terms of the will of Helen B. Mercer three bequests were made to the Diocese: a trust of $800,000, the income to be used *solely* for the maintenance and repair of the George Mercer, Jr. Memorial Building; a trust in principal amount of $7,000,000, the income to be used *solely* for Theological Scholarships at the School or other accredited Episcopal seminaries in the continental United States, to be awarded by the Bishops and Trustees; and a provision in her will for air-conditioning the school building, enlargement of the parking areas and landscaping of the grounds. Certainly the Bishop and Diocese could rejoice over such a fine and worthwhile gift.

THE TRAINING OF THE YOUNG

The establishment of the School of Theology did not sum up completely the educational advance of the Diocese. Ever since its inception a constant concern was the education of its young. Many attempts were made to enlarge and deepen the educational life of its younger constituents. An attempt at expanding preparatory schools had finalized into two secondary schools, the Cathedral schools of St. Paul's and St. Mary's. Sunday schools, or church schools as they came to be called, had their ups and downs, fluctuating in numbers and influence. To enhance their effectiveness there were always well-meaning attempts to write new curricula, to add new trappings of Lenten Mite Box offerings, Birthday Thank Offerings, Cathedral Days, Daily Vacation Bible Schools, innumerable Teacher Training Courses and Institutes, and Fall Assemblies. Varying degrees of success followed each attempt challenging the Diocese to do even more.

A new and exciting approach to education made its appearance in this period. Taking a cue from the Roman Church, Episcopal churches on the Island and in the nation, began to establish parochial schools. The day school movement was aided and abetted by the tremendous expansion of church physical plants, always including an "educational building." A wide range of parochial day schools included a full spectrum from simple nursery schools to fullblown kindergarten through high schools. To guide and assist parishes in the development of day schools, the Department of Christian Education formed a Division of Boarding and Day Schools, supplemented by an Episcopal Schools Association. An appreciated assistance was the establishment of the Teachers of the Children of God on Long Island. Abbie Loveland Tuller, founder of the Order and known as Mother Abbie, brought her own inimitable educational philosophy known as the Tuller method, to help in schools started in Westbury, Freeport, Lake Success, College Point, St. Augustine's, Brooklyn and a boarding and day school at Maycroft in Sag Harbor. Other day schools such as the Webster Day School in Queens Village, Woodhull School in Hollis, Christ Church, Clinton Street, Brooklyn, St. Paul's in Patchogue and St. David's, Riverhead fared well, expanding student population faculty and physical plants.

The two Cathedral schools prospered as well. Record enrollment soared at both, as high as 320 students at St. Mary's and 250 at St. Paul's. Building programs enhanced the already existing facilities. In 1957, St. Paul's added new faculty cottages; and in 1963 a new field house, one of the largest on Long Island, was dedicated. A new library wing was to be built. St. Mary's added a new science wing on the west end of the gymnasium building, with physics and chemistry laboratories. An additional wing on the main school was in the planning state, designed to house the "Little School" a kindergarten through fourth grade coeducational program. The Rev. Nicholas Feringa, Headmaster of St. Paul's for ten years resigned on June 30, 1963. He was briefly replaced by Mr. Kenneth Dolbeare. In 1965, a new Headmaster, Dr. Claude C. Casey, was appointed and took up his duties as guide for the dynamic boys' school.

By 1965, boarding and day schools were in full bloom. At an Episcopal Schools' service in the Cathedral on October 28, 1965, over 1,000 students from schools all over the Diocese attended. The day school movement included twenty-two schools, fifteen with nursery schools, seventeen with kindergartens, sixteen with elementary grades and four with high schools. They were located all over Long Island with a concentration of schools in Nassau County.

A pressing problem presented itself. The large group of young people who finished their grade work wanted to continue their education in an Episcopal school. The already existing higher grade schools were either too expensive or too limited in facilities to accept the influx of students. Taking the problem in hand, a small group of Nassau clergy discussed together the possibility of founding a Diocesan High School. Under the leadership of the Rev. Robert H. Pierce, Rector of Transfiguration, Freeport, and the Rev. Christopher L. Webber, Rector of Christ Church, Lynbrook, an Episcopal High School Committee was formed to "explore the possibility of an Episcopal High School in Nassau County." Gaining momentum and interest, the Committee looked into possible sites for the school. Believing Nassau to be the best possible location, they pursued the quest and applied for land at the abandoned Mitchell Air Force Base, Uniondale, or at North Bellmore. Both applications were rejected. Early in 1964, government-owned land adjacent to Mitchell Field and Hofstra University, "the cultural Center of Nassau County," became available. An application for the land was made. The Federal government approved the Diocese's application, "the first milestone on the road to a new junior-senior high school."

The plans for the 8.7 acre tract elaborately detailed in the March 1966 issue of *Tidings* included an educational building with a chapel, and a multi-purpose sports field. The junior-senior high school would accommodate five hundred students. To raise the necessary funds a professional fund-raising concern was hired, which found "widespread interest and support." Arrangements were entered into, in which the land would be held in escrow and reserved for the use of the Diocese. The whole matter was presented to the Standing Committee at a special meeting held on June 25, 1964. Their response was less than encouraging. After hearing the case they concluded it was unwise to proceed with the project, mainly due to lack of money. Because of "many uncertain parts of so important an undertaking" they "reluctantly" recommended to the Bishop that "in their judgment they would not proceed any further at this time. . . . "

The recommendation of the Standing Committee on this matter did not seem to dampen the Bishop's ardor in pursuing the matter. Although acknowledging in his 1964 address to the Convention that the Diocese was "in no position to finance it at the present time," at the Convention held May 18, 1965, he announced the appointment of the Rev. E. Frederic Underwood, Rector of Church of the Advent, Westbury as the "Rector of the Diocesan Schools and Director of the Department of Christian Education." The appointment included supervision of the Cathedral Schools of St. Paul's and St. Mary's and "the new Episcopal High School to be built at Mitchell Field." To all intents and purposes the high school seemed at the point of being built.

COMFORT EVERY SUFFERER

Equally dynamic and just as exciting was the whole field of charitable works. The chief acts of diocesan mercy concentrated in two institutions, the Church Charity Foundation and the Youth Consultation Service. Although progress reports were made annually on church-related institutions such as St. Gile's Hospital and Home and the Society of St. Johnland, they quickly sank into insignificance. St. Phebe's Mission, carried on by a skeleton corporation for a few years, dissolved and its fund was transferred to the Y.C.S. with the Bishop's encouragement, both the C.C.F. and the Y.C.S. became the chief recipients of the Episcopal Charities Appeal. They prospered and grew, encouraged by E.C.A.

Episcopal Charities Appeal, under the directorship of Archdeacon MacLean, found new sources of money and new insights into raising more. Every year beginning in May, the campaign began and reaped good rewards. Mr. Joseph Patrick, one of the Drive's Chairmen, initiated an Endowment Fund with a gift of $14,000. A gift from the Wilbur Brundage Estate added $1,750,000 to the endowment fund. Under the leadership of such laymen as Robert C. Hattersly and Milton W. Hopkins, the appeal fund grew. By 1963, receipts amounted to $236,396.59, an outstanding achievement and witness. The campaign for funds tapped both churches and church people, as well as receiving support from outside persons and businesses.

The Youth Consultation Service assumed more and more the identity of a total counselling service. Its change of name showed its transition of services. At first ministering to unwed mothers, it had incorporated into its social work case study problems of juvenile delinquency and school drop-outs. In 1953, the case work agency extended its preventative care to children under twelve years of age, adding to its technique play therapy. It moved its office in 1962 to a more centrally located one on Sutphin Boulevard with a "play therapy" room part of the office layout. Various personnel changes were made and it became well known in social work circles for its highly qualified casework staff. Mrs. Hulse continued as the Executive Director.

The Church Charity Foundation concentrated its ministry on the sick and suffering in the Herkimer Street complex. The hospital patient care increased tremendously. The service of the hospital to its community showed in health services, emergency clinic and out-patient department. The hospital undertook two training programs, one for licensed practical nurses and one for hospital orderlies. The Home for the Aged and the Blind tended more and more towards infirmary care. The School of Nursing with enlarged quarters completed in 1956 also produced many graduates. Spiritual care and bedside ministrations by the Chaplain, the Rev. Charles E. Gus, complemented completely the outstanding care given by the Foundation institutions.

A milestone in the work of the Foundation and in the life of the Diocese was passed when the Foundation announced the beginning of another hospital. Ever since 1851, the Foundation had concentrated its health efforts in Brooklyn, but in 1960, the Board of Managers studied the possibility of acquiring or building a new hospital outside of Brooklyn. In January 1962, seventy-four and one half acres on Route 25A, about a mile and a half west of Smithtown, were purchased. On June 18, 1964, the Bishop and diocesan officials took part in the ground breaking ceremonies for St. John's Hospital, Smithtown. A fully air-conditioned four story structure with a capacity of 163 beds was planned. The hospital would provide all the usual services of a general hospital. A feature was the chapel for use of visitors, ambulatory patients and staff. The estimated cost of the project was over $4,500,000. Construction was to be finished in eighteen months, at which time the proper dedication ceremony would take place.

MISSIONARY PROGRAM

The advances in education and charity were matched by the development of the missionary outreach program by local churches and the Diocese. The changing complexion of Long Island caused contractions in some areas, enlargement in others, stabilization in many, but in all a valiant attempt to make the church relevant to the lives of the people in their communities.

Urban Long Island —

More and more in these years, the City reached out and absorbed into its "megalopolis" the small farmlands, little villages and open spaces. The dividing line between city and country, between New York and Long Island, once at the Queens-Nassau line, now advanced farther on the Island until mass housing and population reached on the North Shore to the Town of Huntington and on the South Shore to the Town of Babylon. The urbanization of the western section flowed into the east bringing with it crowded conditions, closer contact and city problems. The means of transportation, built for a different condition, were unable to keep up with the mushrooming population. The Long Island Railroad, line of the "dashing commuter," shuttled thousands everyday between the suburban hearth and the urban mecca. Sometimes on time, many times late, the line coped as best it could. Accelerating train fares did not help either the line or the rider. The automobile, once a luxury or recreation pastime, now became a necessity. The local general store, center of community life, gave way to large impersonal shopping plazas, huge food marts and specialized commercial areas. Community life, such as it was, became fragmented and the harried parent became a taxi service for children involved in Scouts, Little League or local school activities. Poor Island roads, never meant to bear the trememdous traffic, became choked and crowded. Local arteries at rush hours filled to overflowing. The Long Island Expressway, the "longest parking lot in the world" was jammed with bumper to bumper traffic as far out as Huntington. The Northern and Southern Parkways, once ways of scenic drive and natural pleasure, became asphalt jungles of beeping horns, overheated engines and massive traffic jams. From Brooklyn Heights to East Northport, there were wall-to-wall people.

The Archdeaconry of Brooklyn —

Rapidly changing Brooklyn of the forties had radically altered. Large housing developments mingled with older apartment houses and once grand brownstones or two story homes. Urban renewal helped much to better the decaying communities, but still had far to go. Atlantic Avenue presented not only for the occasional visitor but also, and more so, for the city dwellers, a depressing scene of infestation and decay. Urban evils, rising crime rates, drug addiction, harried firemen and police, and unsanitary living conditions became the rule instead of the exception. Perhaps most shocking Brooklyn, once the "City of Churches" had become the land of the unchurched. There were over one and a half million people and the majority of them had no religious affiliation.

The trend of rapidly changing neighborhoods, the influx of many different racial groups, and the exodus of thousands to the suburbs made the Episcopal Church's task extremely difficult in this urban center. The Archdeaconry struggled against overwhelming odds and tried many different avenues of attack. Some succeeded, others failed.

Two approaches to solve the Brooklyn enigma that succeeded were the "Aided Parishes" and the "Associated Mission." The latter began in Brooklyn with four newly ordained, newly graduated men, assigned by the Bishop to work under the direction of the Archdeacon. These four men and certain other priests composed the Associated Mission, the purpose of which was to coordinate the work of the Church in various Brooklyn parishes where neighborhood conditions had changed. Meeting regularly, the group attempted a ministry to the unchurched. United together in "prayer, study and action," the Associated Mission assisted the Archdeacon in difficult areas, hoping that the closer cooperation of work would make the Archdeaconry work more effective.

Older established parishes had fallen on hard times. Church buildings, too large and too costly to operate, began to deteriorate. Changing neighborhoods with people of lower income moving in complicated the situation. Churches expended greater effort and energy to maintain church physical plants than to minister to their communities. To alleviate these pressures a little, the Diocese initiated the program of aided parishes "to help parishes in changing situations."

Some churches, like Redeemer on Fourth Avenue, increasingly ministered to smaller and smaller numbers, keeping plant and church open only as necessary. Others began to amalgamate following the examples set by Messiah and Incarnation; St. Luke's and St. Matthew's, and St. Stephen's and St. Martin's. Our Saviour, Gerritsen Beach, closed and became part of St. Simon's. St. Timothy's, condemned by and sold to the City for a housing development site, joined St. Mark's, Brooklyn Avenue. In 1959, Calvary and St. Cyprian's joined the list of amalgamated parishes.

Death Throes of a Parish —

At the 1960 Diocesan Convention a properly signed petition came before the assembled body. The Rector, Church Wardens and Vestrymen of Holy Trinity Church, Brooklyn requested the extinction of the church. The reasons given were plainly stated: in addition to other things the parish did not have twenty-five persons of full age; had no contributors; and there seemed to be no qualified persons to serve on the Vestry. After careful examination of the petition and canon law, the Convention unanimously voted the extinction of the parish.

The story of the church's demise reached back to the time when on Dr. Melish's removal, his son William Howard Melish continued as an assistant pending the election of a new rector. Differences soon developed between William Melish and the Vestry, and at the request of the Vestry, the Bishop assigned as supply priest, the Rev. Herman S. Sidener. The Vestry later elected Dr. Sidener as Rector and was duly instituted by the Bishop on February 8, 1956. Thereafter litigation ensued to sustain the right of the new Rector and the Vestry to the custody and control of church property and funds. They were finally successful, whereupon full control of the church and property was restored to the new Rector and the Vestry.

Under the Canons of the Diocese of Long Island and the Religious Corporations Law of New York State, extinct church property was assigned to the Trustees of the Estate of the Diocese. After the action of the convention, Holy Trinity was operated by the Trustees who allowed the Church Army in the United States, the Guild of the Blind, a Spanish congregation and many other groups to use the facilities until the Trustees assigned the church and two of its residences on Pierrepont Street to St. Ann's Church, the nearby parish. Before the final court decision, Bishop DeWolfe stated that Dr. Melish could retain use of the rectory for his lifetime, and that the Trustees would underwrite the maintenance of the building. In addition they matched in like sum his annual grant from the Church Pension Fund, paying him until his death in 1969.

Gloriously Alive —

"The church in the Archdeaconry of Brooklyn is gloriously alive," said the Archdeacon in his annual report to the Diocese. "It's existance in the midst of a stark urban culture has forced it to ask basic questions. . . . It's continuance and life depend upon its ability to serve the burning needs of the people in whose midst the church is set." The truth of this statement found grounds in the real source of the Brooklyn renascence, the Black and Hispanic churches. Church vitality found its release in the Black congregations. Six parishes in the Archdeaconry had a membership of over 1,000 and of these four were Black. They were St. Augustine's, St. George's, Marcy Avenue, St. Mark's and St. Philip's, MacDonough Street, the last named numbering 2,033. St. Philip's suffered a great loss in 1961 with the death of its Rector, the Rev. John M. Coleman. To fill his place the parish called the Rev. Richard B. Martin from Virginia on June 27, 1963. As a fitting memorial to Fr. Coleman the new junior high school that opened in the Bedford Stuyvesant area was named the John M. Coleman Junior High School. It was opened in September and appropriately dedicated on November 26, 1963.

Vital and enriching, the work among Spanish-speaking peoples increased to five parishes. The Spanish congregation moved from its Grace Church, Conselyea Street location to larger quarters — Church of the Holy Family, Atlantic Avenue. The Spanish congregation at Christ Church, Clinton Street, prospered as did the Church of St. Michael and St. Mark. Two other parishes, St. Andrew's, Fourth Avenue and St. Anthony of Padua also worked among these new residents of the Brooklyn area. A great service to the Spanish community emerged in an unusual use of the radio medium. The Rev. Luis A. Quiroga of Holy Family broadcast every Sunday afternoon on Station WBNX in Spanish on a program called "Beams of Light." Unusual too, and a great credit to the Diocese, was the inauguration of work among the blind. Taking advantage of the services of the Rev. Harry J. Sutcliffe, himself blind and a priest received from the Assyrian Orthodox Church, the Diocese began an information service in 1959, organized as the Episcopal Guild for the Blind.

The Archdeaconry and Diocese suffered a great loss at the death of its Archdeacon, the Venerable A. Edward Saunders. Active in all phases of Brooklyn life, but most especially on the Brooklyn waterfront, he left a legacy of unfinished business and great contribution. The Bishop, in his place, appointed Fr. Martin, Rector of St. Philip's, MacDonough Street. Fr. Martin was highly qualified to take up his diocesan duties, having served in Virginia as an Archdeacon. He assumed the Brooklyn post on January 15, 1965.

The Archdeaconry of Queens and Nassau —
Queens County, next door neighbor to Brooklyn, presented a similar urban condition, not as startling but just as challenging. Full urban life had spilled over into Queens, making it a miniature reflection of Brooklyn. Some of the northeastern shore areas attempted to retain their picturesque scenery, but by and large huge housing developments eroded the greenlands. Populated areas such as Jamaica and Flushing dramatically demonstrated the presence of the City and more and more turned to face that direction.

But the most striking transition came in Nassau County where the Post-World War II housing boom continued into the middle sixties. More and more the land of small villages, large estates, green golf courses, and ideal suburban living succumbed to mass housing, apartment houses, gigantic shopping malls and congested traffic. Levittown, the experimental prototype, became the accepted blueprint for building speculators. By 1960, however, building came to an abrupt halt. Few farmlands remained to be developed, all available land was swallowed up. The attainment of zero population and the permanent settlement of the World War II veteran gave the county of one million inhabitants an older and more mature face, promising the emergence of the senior citizen. An important aspect was the growing religious pluralism. The influx of different ethnic groups altered the religious complexion of the county. The Roman Catholic and Jewish faiths became the dominant controlling factor; the white Anglo-Saxon Protestant rated last in population and influence. The change created more problems for the struggling settled churches, prominent among which was the Episcopal Church.

Growth and solidification of population pressured the already existing Episcopal churches and missions into positive action. Building campaigns for new or enlarged physical plants exploded all over the Archdeaconry. Established churches built new churches, parish halls, or made large additions to their small plants. St. Gabriel's, Hollis, razed its historic church to erect a new one, judged the "best church built in Queens in 1960." St. George's, Hempstead, tore down its historic Guild Hall and erected a huge "educational" building; St. John's, Lattingtown, a 1915 church, undertook a mission building campaign; St. Paul's, Glen Cove built a new rectory and planned a new parish hall. Their efforts were duplicated in varying degrees all over both counties. Diocesan missions joined their older institutuions in the building spree. St. Bede's, Syosset; St. James the Just, Franklin Square; St. James the Less, Jamaica; St. John's, Hempstead, all constructed new church buidlings. Large growth in numerical strength added new life to most churches, the Cathedral leading the way with 5,000 members and 1,300 in its Church School. No more remarkable record could be found than that of Grace Church, Massapequa. Founded in 1844, the small 125-seat church was the only church in the village until 1949. The tremendous swell of population caught up the church in its rise, and by 1964, it had a membership of over 3,000 and a church school of 950. Unable to accommodate so large a congregation in the existing building, the church began a fund resulting first in a large parish hall and finally in a huge contemporary church. The original church was kept for sentimental reasons.

Black churches in the Archdeaconry matched, if not in numerical strength, at least in vitality, its western brethren. Church of the Resurrection, East Elmhurst, under the leadership of the Rev. Harold L. Wright, later Suffragan Bishop of New York (successor of the tireless Rev. Ebenezer Hamilton) expanded its plant and enlarged its work. Churches in the Jamaica area, St. Stephen's and St. James the Less, had a total membership of over 1,200. St. John's, Hempstead, whose building burned, relocated on South Franklin Avenue in a new and enlarged modern church. Predominantly white churches all over Queens and Nassau felt the influx of Blacks. Grace Church, Jamaica; St. George's, Flushing; and St. Alban's, St. Albans, all began to change and welcomed into their congregations Black people as active members.

Two new mission churches sprang up to meet the population demand. In February 1956, a new church, St. Jude's, was begun in Wantagh. Their church buildings came ready made. Hofstra University, Hempstead, donated two completely equipped barrack-type buildings which became church, parish hall and church school. In 1963, the ten-acre tract of land in Plainview, donated by Edwin P. Shattuck, became the site of St. Margaret's Church. A church building was begun and completed by 1965.

The Archdeaconry of Suffolk —
Most spectacular was the growth of Suffolk County. By the mid-sixties its population had almost doubled. The closely developed mass housing of Nassau continued as far east as the Town of Huntington and Babylon. The congested area spattered off as far out as Wading River and Bellport. The only really rural area left on Long Island was on the North Fork. The dividing line between city and country, between New York and Long Island, had advanced far east. Long Island was rapidly becoming Metropolitan New York.

Response of the established parishes and missions seemed almost inadequate to match the great influx. Before

(above) Spanish-speaking congregation
at the Church of the Holy Family,
Brooklyn.
(right) St. John's Church, Hempstead,
under construction.

World War II Suffolk churches had a combined membership of 9,212 with a communicant strength of 5,787. By 1964, they had 27,151 members and 14,750 communicants. Church school pupils numbered 6,096 in 1940 and by 1964, there were 21,956. Churches found their physical plants totally incapable of effectively ministering to such numbers. Alterations and enlargement of educational facilities and churches became a necessity, and at times an emergency. The five largest church schools in Suffolk reflected the large growth, none more dramatically than Trinity, Northport, which in 1940 had 85 pupils; in 1965 there were 491.

As in Nassau, building campaigns became the rule rather than the exception. New parish houses, school facilities, and enlarged chuches sprang up. St. Peter's, Bay Shore, showing the greatest development with a totally new plant, a credit to the Rector, the Rev. Canon Sydney R. Peters. St. John's, Huntington, constructed a large modern school building, but perhaps most commendable was the story of St. Mary's, Lake Ronkonkoma. A small church made duplication of services unavoidable. Juggling of buildings did not effectively help, thus a campaign for larger facilities began.

Other areas where new communities sprang up or old villages received new life presented a different challenge. To effectively minister to the people, new sites and buildings had to be acquired. St. Boniface, Lindenhurst, begun in a single family house, had so outgrown its small building that a new large church was built on Sunrise Highway. In August 1958, church services in the local firehouse were held for the people of Deer Park. In the early summer of 1963, two acres and a house was purchased, and in mid-August a twelve-year-old church, purchased from the local Roman Catholic Church, became the permanent home of St. Patrick's. On June 28, 1958, the Bishop formally opened St. Thomas of Canterbury, Smithtown. Planned at first as an Associate Mission

187

where three priests would live and service the people of King's Park, Commack, and Centereach, the "Mission House" became the parish for Smithtown. It soon outgrew its united facilities and a new church was built. In 1958, plans were made by the Archdeaconry to begin work in Rocky Point. The projected work finally materialized when on December 5, 1965, the Director of nearby Camp DeWolfe conducted services and organized the parish known as St. Anselm's, Shoreham.

Missionary Postscript —

Of all three counties, Suffolk seemed the place to be. Between 1950 and 1960, its population had increased by 141.5% and it looked as though the next ten years would offer a like increase. Not matching this tremendous increase, the Archdeaconry of Suffolk in its life after World War II did increase its membership three times as much from 9,212 to 27,041. Communicant strength had increased from 5,789 to 14,867. Under the leadership of Archdeacon Harry J. Stretch, who succeeded Archdeacon MacLean in Suffolk, the Episcopal church worked to meet its challenge. The Archdeaconry of Brooklyn reflected its changing communities with membership decreasing from 31,323 to 20,889 and communicant strength down from 21,848 to 15,805. Steady and stable growth manifested in the parishes and missions of Queens and Nassau, with church membership increased from 57,943 to 68,475, as did communicant strength from 33,425 to 43,144. Total church strength numbered 116,406 and communicants 73,816.

An important missionary policy for the Diocese was adopted. The Department of Missions mandated that old parishes consistently receiving financial aid from the Diocese be dissolved and their property turned over to the Trustees. Such parishes should revert to mission status, their Vestry become the Executive Committee, and the Bishop appoint the priest-in-charge. Where possible and when feasible, such congregations should be joined to other congregations, adding strength and new life to existing ongoing parishes, and be under the direction of one priest. The effect of this "purple paper" determined the life of many parishes in the future.

(right) Bishop's Day at Camp De Wolfe, Bishop DeWolfe with Jed Davis, son of camp director, and Billy Boardman, the Bishop's grandson.
(below) Beginnings of St. Patrick's Church, Deer Park.

SOLDIERS, FAITHFUL, TRUE AND BOLD

As important as starting churches and erecting buildings was the missionary outreach program to all the people of the Diocese. The dynamic work done by the young people and the lay men and women increased in effectiveness and was a cause for pride.

Under the leadership of Bishop DeWolfe no work prospered more than the Department of Youth, College Work and Camp DeWolfe. The work among young people expanded to include Acolytes, Young Adults, Girls Friendly Society, Episcopal Athletic League and Canterbury Clubs with College Chaplaincies. By 1965, the college work program readily utilized, in cooperation with the Second Province, a college worker whose home base was Brooklyn College and whose interest became urban college work.

There was no more compelling example of the dynamic youth work than in the growth and expansion of the Diocesan Youth Center, Camp DeWolfe. From a small beginning in 1947, they had enlarged its program, multiplied its numbers and erected a million dollar plant. Set on a cliff overlooking Long Island Sound, the camp began in prefabricated buildings erected quickly to accommodate campers in its opening season. Slowly and surely over the years the temporary buildings were replaced by lovely St. Luke's Chapel, a large well-equipped dining hall and smaller buildings housing the work crew, the infirmary and the arts and crafts program. The crowning achievement, a multi-purpose recreational hall, was dedicated in 1963 to the memory of Elizabeth DeWolfe, deceased wife of the Bishop. Parish participation in the camp measured almost 80%. A high caliber church camp program served over 1,200 campers during the summer months. The Bishop took just satisfaction in the number of vocations found during these summer months.

The yearly youth program featured youth rallies at the Cathedral, sometimes with 1,000 young people in attendance, annual youth conventions, Autumn Balls in honor of the Bishop, and a four-point program of worship, study, service and fellowship. A different kind of youth activity made its appearance in 1960. Under the able direction of Mrs. Louis Ferraro, active Cathedral communicant, the Cornelia Assemblies were formed. The presentation of young women to the Bishop amid formal gala surroundings not only highlighted the service of youth, but also benefited yearly the Bishop's Call.

No less commendable, men and women achieved a prominent place in the on-going life of the Diocese. With the guidance of such presidents as Mrs. Benjamin T. Young, Mrs. Geoffrey C. Hazard, and Mrs. William Hannah, the Federated Women's Auxiliary continued its active program of meetings, service projects and support of the United Thank Offering, a national project. In accordance with a resolution passed at the National Triennial Meeting in 1958, the Auxiliary, on May 14, 1959, changed its name to the Episcopal Churchwomen of the Diocese of Long Island. The change of name did little to dampen their ardor or interfere with their program. Men too had their full share in advancing the Mission of the Church. The Brotherhood of St. Andrew, with such fine workers as Everett MacSaveny, Walter Jones, William Mason and Gilbert Lowerre, pursued their work-study-service program. Although fluctuating in numbers it still constituted the major diocesan organization for men. The annual Washington's Birthday Corporate Communion and Breakfasts, once held only in Brooklyn, spread all over the Diocese attracting as many as 3,000 men and boys. To recognize the service of its outstanding leaders, Bishop DeWolfe instituted the awarding of the Diocesan Distinguished Service Crosses. A long list of names appeared. Individuals like Col. Jackson A. Dykman, Hunter Delatour, Dermot Ives, Frederick Stokes, Rudolph Heinsohn, and Mrs. Locke Page, aided and abetted the task of the Diocese wherever and however they could.

THE CENTER OF THE DIOCESE

A perennial enigma for the Diocese was the Cathedral in Garden City. Beginning with the first Bishop, each Bishop and his administration had to deal with this baffling entity. When isolated from the rest of the Diocese it caused few problems, but as the population advance enmeshed it, and its isolation shattered, real problems became apparent. Tensions between Diocese and Cathedral grew apace. Circumstances, not people, made the puzzle pressing. Greater and greater use of the Cathedral for diocesan affairs brought an examination of the role of the Cathedral, its purpose, and its administration. Bishop DeWolfe attempted to solve the question in 1952, but still the relationship of Cathedral to Diocese needed to be explained and understood.

Ward of the Diocese —
The Cathedral in Garden City had its full share of problems. The untimely death of Dean Wood made more difficult the solution of serious situations faced by the Cathedral. The first attempt to add stability to the Cathedral came with the appointment of the Very Rev. James Green, a member of the New York Cathedral Staff, as Dean in October 1953. Unfortunately Dean Green's tenure was cut short by his death in August 1955. Over a year later, on December 19, 1956, the Bishop nominated to the Cathedral Chapter, the electoral body, in his place the Rev. Harold F. Lemoine, Rector for fourteen years of St. Joseph's, Queens Village, and very active in Diocesan affairs. He was installed as Dean on March 2, 1957. Now the Cathedral could tackle its outstanding problems.

As in the past, its problems concerned money. The Cathedral Schools had difficulty overcoming unfavorable economic conditions. In addition, school buildings required extensive repairs which increased overhead. The result was the income available to the Cathedral Chapter, its governing body, had been insufficient to finance its full liability. In order to meet operating deficits and emergency obligations, the principal of endowment funds had to be tapped. The small contribution of the Diocese towards the upkeep of the Bishop's House and grounds did not offset the recurring deficit in the Cathedral Foundation. Scanty reports to the Convention each year, and little support by the Diocese, made the situation even more urgent.

These factors were symptomatic of something deeper and more disturbing. Whether because of one or the other, the relationship between the Cathedral and the Diocese was tenuous. A part of this unusual relationship was the fact that the Cathedral was also a parish church with its own Vestry Committee, whose congregation gave generously to the support of its "parish church." The congregation as such carried on their parish life as did any other parish, and were many times in their attitudes just as congregational and parochial as other churches. The Cathedral House, built largely by contributions from local residents, often became the battleground. Use of the building was granted by the congregation for diocesan use, many times grudgingly. The relationship between Diocese and Cathedral was distant, often difficult and at time almost extinct.

To unite Cathedral and Diocese, to mend the break and give each a full understanding of its relationship, the Bishop attempted to show the true place and function of a Cathedral. "The Cathedral is the Mother-Church of the Diocese," the Bishop said over and over again. "It is the seat of the Bishop of Long Island," he also stated. Making clear who had the governing responsibility, he outlined the way in which a true Cathedral operated. The Dean was the Bishop's vicar, nominated by the Bishop to his office. The operation of the Cathedral was "the ultimate responsibility of the Cathedral Chapter" not of the local Vestry Committee. Congregationalism had no share in the management, program and policy of the diocesan seat. The Cathedral schools were in every sense "Diocesan Schools." Summing it up, he pointed out that the Cathedral, in a true sense, was the "Ward of the Diocese."

Much work had been done in the "Ward of the Diocese" largely due to the efforts of one of its communicants, David Ferguson. He brought about the grant from the Taylor Foundation used solely for the purpose of properly and suitably rebuilding and re-amplifying the Cathedral pipe organ. The Crypt Chapel, where lay the bodies of the Stewarts, was completely redone. St. Mary's School, through his efforts, erected needed science buildings. Building improvements, however, did not provide a solution to the solvency problem. The Cathedral would continue to be plagued by it even with sound management, added contributions and careful spending.

Full Circle —

The final step in the centralization of the Diocese in Garden City, begun with Bishop Littlejohn's move to the See House, occurred in the closing year of Bishop DeWolfe's episcopacy. The Diocesan House, 170 Remsen Street, the first residence of the Bishop of Long Island and used for many years as the Bishop's office in Brooklyn, and as the business center, came under close scrutiny. In 1959, the Diocese entered into negotiations with the Brooklyn Union Gas Company to exchange buildings. The Diocese would move from 170 to 180 Remsen Street and so have larger quarters for diocesan activities. Nothing came of it. Plans to move the business office to Garden City had been contemplated but never accomplished. In 1964, the Diocese received an offer of $152,500 from St. Francis College, a next door neighbor, which wished to enlarge its facilities. The offer was too good to be turned down. Propitiously, the Cathedral had been left a spacious home at 92 Second Street, Garden City. One half block from the See House it seemed an ideal location for the Bishop's home. Since the house was a gift to the Cathedral, the Diocese purchased it from that body. While the Bishop was in Florida that winter, he was moved from the old historic See House to his new residence. The Bishop's old residence was turned into the Diocesan House, a building of office desks, filing cabinets and jangling telephones. The Bishop commended the move of consolidation of diocesan offices. "This project places our Diocesan House in the center of Diocesan activities." The Diocese was now completely centralized in Garden City. The move begun in 1884 was completed in 1965. Diocesan activities in Brooklyn centered in 157 Montague Street, which housed the Archdeaconry office and other diocesan organizations.

THE WORLD PRESSES IN

The diocesan pursuit of its mission occasionally turned its eyes out into the world that surrounded it. National and international concerns made such change of vision necessary and right. Events, both of a local nature and ones of wider reach, directed the course of the diocesan imperative and made the Diocese "sit up and take notice." Controversial issues confronted the American citizens which needed solution. Nuclear weapons, disarmament, "peaceful co-existence", cold and outright war, juvenile delinquency, alcoholism, drug addiction, and the welfare of senior citizens aroused public interest and church action. No two issues were more appealing to churchmen and in greater need of concerted effort than ecumenical relations and civil rights.

Ecumenical relations from time to time engaged the attention of both Diocese and Bishop. From its beginning a deep concern for understanding and concerted action permeated its inquiries and colored its reactions. Church unity, a subject about which other bishops and other times had much to say, came under scrutiny. The formation of the National Council of Churches of Christ in America, a Pan-Protestant conglomerate received little support from most Episcopal churches on Long Island. Pressures upon the Diocese came in the proposal of amalgamation of churches into one church. The Church in South India; the "Reformed Catholic" Church of the Blake-Pike proposals; the Ceylon and Northern India schemes; and the ordination of women in the Church of Sweden, all caused discussion and heated argument. The final authority and solution to the quest was always a reiteration of the Chicago-Lambeth Quadrilateral, the work of the first Bishop of Long Island.

Church unity gave way to Church Understanding. The Episcopal Church undertook to better relate itself not only to other Christian bodies, but also to the non-Christian, specifically the Jews. In the Diocese, to cope effectively with ecumenism, several attempts were made. In 1955, to better approach the Orthodox Churches, an Orthodox-Anglican Fellowship began, reflected in the Commission on Church Unity including such in their conferences, even changing their title to the Commission on Catholic-Orthodox-Protestant Churches. Joy was expressed in 1961 when the Philippine Independent Church and the Spanish and Lusitanian Reformed Churches came into communion with the Episcopal Church. Vatican I and Vatican II helped present an atmosphere within which better understanding could be achieved. But it was the relationship between Episcopal churches and the Jewish people which showed marked development and improvement. The traditional evangelistic approach to the Jews had not produced any great results. Out and out proselytizing had provoked more bitterness than conversion. A change in approach showed in the formation of a Commission on Christian-Jewish relations. Long Island had the highest concentration of Jewish people in any comparable area in the country. The Commission conceived the missionary strategy involved in Christian-Jewish relations which was "the presentation of the Gospel to the Jews in such a way that they will be ready and able to listen to it." Seminars, occasional literature and other means of communication were used to involve all the Diocese in this primary movement.

The Civil Rights Movement began to have its effect on the Diocese. The drive for racial equality had its most noticeable beginning on February 1, 1960, when four Black students "sat in" at a Southern lunch counter. Events developed rapidly. Freedom "riders" of the Congress on Racial Equality; Governor George Wallace in 1963 "standing in the school house door"; the March on Washington for jobs and freedom; the Civil Rights Act of 1964; but most of all and most dramatic the march from Selma headed by the Rev. Martin Luther King, Jr. brought the whole subject of equality before the nation. The Diocese itself could not escape from its confrontation. Although the Diocese had a good share of Black churches, it did not escape its share of evaluation. St. John's Hospital, set in the midst of a Black ghetto, was accused of not having enough Blacks on its staff, and of offering segregated hospital rooms for patients. The Bishop himself spoke out on the subject, especially of legislating morality. In his address to the 1964 Convention he concluded that "legislation by the State" did not result "in achieving men's universal recognition of the Fatherhood of God as a reality, nor the Brotherhood of Man as the ultimate consequence of such adopted legislation." The real test of its worth came in the commitment of the individual to their responding love to our Lord Jesus Christ and then obedience to the will of God. The quest for social equality did not end but continued on. Many other factors would keep the matter pressing, chief among which was the election of John E. Hines in 1964 as Presiding Bishop of the Episcopal Church.

A CALL FOR HELP

In 1943, at the second Convention over which the Bishop presided, he vehemently affirmed to the assembled body, "I have enjoyed being your Bishop. Hard work you know, doesn't kill a person — not even a Bishop — worry does that." By 1956 he felt the full effects of fourteen long years of struggle, tension and misunderstanding. He confided, "There is a loneliness about being the Bishop of a Diocese.... There have been many headaches and heartaches ... tensions arising from every quarter." A very sensitive person, he struggled valiantly to overcome any feelings of hostility within himself, always attempting to accommodate himself to those forces and persons opposed to him. His position became more disquieting by the beginning of his illness. Several minor attacks had slowed him down; in 1961 he suffered the first of a series of major breakdowns that were to affect so much his relationship to the Diocese. Realizing full-well his increasing incapacity, he requested from the Diocese another Suffragan to assist in Episcopal labors, missionary tasks, "and the overall activities of one of the largest jurisdictions in the American Church." The Diocese responded to the Bishop's call for help and the date of November 4, 1961 was set for the election.

On Saturday, November 4, 1961, the special Convention for electing a second Suffragan Bishop of Long Island assembled in the Cathedral at Garden City. After the usual procedure of setting convention regulations, ten names were put in nomination. It became evident from the first ballot that the contest would be between two major candidates, the Rev. Albert A. Chambers, Rector of the Church of the Resurrection, New York, and the Administrator, the Ven. Canon Charles W. MacLean. Ballot after ballot showed the same tendency as in other episcopal elections: Father Chamers was elected by the clergy; Archdeacon MacLean by the laity. After the eighth ballot the Convention came to a standstill. A short but tense battle over legal procedures caused an abrupt halt to the proceedings, to be reconvened at the call of the bishops. Fourteen days later, on November 18, the second session of the Convention was held. Six names still remained on the ballots. Ballot after ballot was cast with no decision made. Finally on the fifteenth ballot, the clergy capitulated to the laity and elected as the second Suffragan, Archdeacon MacLean.

Archdeacon MacLean had labored long and well in the Diocese of Long Island. A native of New Hampshire, he graduated from St. Stephen's College and General Seminary. From 1928 to 1930 he served at the Church of the Epiphany in New York City. The three years following were spent in St. John's Church, Dunton, L.I., before becoming Rector of Grace Church, Riverhead, in 1933. In 1942, he was appointed Archdeacon of Suffolk, earning the praise of both church and community for his great share in raising funds for the Central Suffolk Hospital in Riverhead. In 1950, he took up his duties as Administrator. He served the Diocese in many ways: Trustee of the Diocese, member of the Standing Committee, Director of Promotion, Director of Episcopal Charities Appeal, Assistant Treasurer of the Diocese, Treasurer of the George Mercer Jr. School of Theology where he also taught, Vice President of the Diocesan Council, and Registrar of the Diocese. To fill his place the Bishop appointed the Rev. David J. Williams as Executive Secretary of the Diocese, taking over some, but not all, of the Administrator's duties. He began his duties as second Suffragan on March 1, 1962.

On St. Valentine's Day, February 14, 1962, the new Suffragan Bishop was duly consecrated in the Cathedral of the Incarnation. At the request of the Presiding Bishop, Bishop DeWolfe officiated, assisted by Bishop Sherman and Bishop Donegan of New York. After the colorful ceremony more than 500 persons attended a luncheon in honor of the new Bishop at the Garden City Hotel. The new Bishop immediately demonstrated his usefulness to the Diocese. The burden of diocesan oversight increased tremendously with the sudden and severe heart attack suffered by Bishop Sherman at the General Convention held in the fall of 1961 at Detroit, Michigan. Although other Bishops outside the Diocese came to help, much of the weight of responsibility fell on the new Bishop. Despite the protracted illness of the Bishop and Senior Suffragan, diocesan appointments were fulfilled. The Junior Suffragan had "lightened the burden of the heavy schedule" the Bishop's calendar had accumulated.

SOON, SOON TO FAITHFUL WARRIORS

On October 17, 1962 for the twentieth anniversary of the Bishop's consecration, the Diocese hosted a testimonial dinner at the Garden City Hotel. A tremendous turnout filled the ballroom. Mr. Clifford P. Morehouse, President of the General Convention House of Deputies, presided at the festivities. Honored guests included the Speaker of the New York State Assembly, the Mayor of New York, the Presidents of the Boroughs of Brooklyn and Queens, and the County Executives of Nassau and Suffolk. Guests speakers, the Bishop of New York and the Presiding Bishop, the Rt. Rev. Arthur C. Lichtenberger, gave laudatory addresses. At the close of the dinner, Bishop and Mrs. DeWolfe received the many guests.

An unfortunate and unforeseen blow fell upon Bishop DeWolfe with the death of his wife, Elizabeth. So much a part of his life, she died on January 5, 1963, after a prolonged illness. There was a service on January 7, 1963, at the Cathedral and she was buried in the churchyard of St. James' Church in St. James. The Bishop never fully recovered from her death. Close friends and family could not fill the gap left in his life. He tried to escape in long vacations and in delegating into the hands of a few associates the responsibility of administering the complex diocesan structure. Friends and associates pressed upon him retirement, but he adamantly refused. He made clear his views on the subject early in his episcopate. Nor was a Bishop-Coadjutor to his liking; he was not one to share authority easily. Perhaps sensing impending death, he wrote his own eulogy while at the Diocesan Convention. In his Annual Address to the Assemblage on Tuesday, May 25, 1965, he listed the achievements of his twenty-three year episcopate. The financial state of the Diocese was so sound that it was able to contribute more than pledged to the National Church program. Total financial contributions measured over five million dollars. In the years since its inception in 1951, the Episcopal Charities Appeal distributed $1,120,000 to the Church Charity Foundation, $350,000 to Youth Consultation Service and $374,000 to the Bishop's Call. During the fourteen years, the Appeal received endowment gifts with a market value of two million dollars. During his twenty-three years the missionary operations of the Diocese grew and expanded. The Department of Missions purchased thirty-five rectories and built thirteen; fifteen mission churches had been built and three purchased; seventeen parishes had been erected and two buildings purchased for parish hall purposes; thirty-one parcels of land had been acquired for mission sites. During this period repairs and improvements had been made to mission properties at a cost of $400,000. Financial records showed the purchase of new sites, buildings and new construction in this period to be in excess of $3,000,000. The Diocese also acquired the valuable site of Camp DeWolfe, on which in fifteen years many new buildings had been constructed to meet the ever-increasing numbers of children in attendance.

Expressing repeatedly his hope that while on a confined schedule he would be "restored to full and sound health" did not ease the situation. Illness made him more and more unavailable. Finally realizing this, on November 3, 1965, at a special meeting of the Standing Committee, the Bishop announced that on the advice of his physician he was going to take a leave of absence from the Diocese. During his absence he requested the Standing Committee to be the Ecclesiastical Authority. His fears became reality when late in November, on the night of the widespread electrical blackout, he suffered a severe crippling attack. Amid blinking firetrucks, police cars, ambulances, doctors and friends, in a lightless house, he almost died. On the next day accompanied by his favorite nurse, Bette Davis, he was taken to St. John's Hospital, Brooklyn, where he remained for months. He came home in January for one day and was taken back again to the Brooklyn hospital. While in the hospital his close associate and dear friend, the Venerable Harry J. Stretch, Archdeacon of Queens, Nassau and Suffolk, died on January 13, 1966. Three weeks later on Sunday, February 6, in the late afternoon, the Bishop died.

Tuesday and Wednesday, February 8 and 9, a clergy watch was kept at the Cathedral where the Bishop's body lay in state. On February 9, 1966, the Bishop was given the Church's last rites amid the pomp and ceremony he loved so well. A large outpouring of clergy and laymen filled the Cathedral to take part in the Burial Office and Requiem, and witness the two Suffragan Bishops pontificate alternately. After the service the body was placed in the receiving vault at nearby Greenfield Cemetery, Hempstead. The Bishop's body was finally interred, not in St. James where his wife was buried, but in the Crypt of the Cathedral where lay Alexander and Cornelia Stewart and the second Bishop of the Diocese, Frederick Burgess. As if to erase any lingering thoughts of the Bishop, his family auctioned off publicly all his personal possessions.

It was not until December 16, 1967, that a fitting memorial was dedicated to his memory. Just as the Baptisery was Bishop Littlejohn's memorial, and the pulpit Bishop Burgess', so too a fitting remembrance in the Cathedral was built. A large display case called a Diocesan Treasury was installed in the north wall of the Cathedral Undercroft. The glass doored repository was to house diocesan memorabilia for viewing and appreciation. The memorial address given by the Bishop's good friend, the Rev. Canon Harold S. Olafson, President of the Standing Committee and Chancellor of the Cathedral Chapter, summed up Bishop DeWolfe's contributions to the Diocese. No more poignant tribute to him was made than that of his list of daily intercessions — heading the list was the name of the former Rector of Holy Trinity Church and son, the Melishes, Senior and Junior. "That brethren," said Canon Olafson, "is a notable example of Christian love."

Annual conference for postulantes and candidates for Holy Orders, given at Camp DeWolfe.

Bishop Jonathan G. Sherman, Fifth Bishop, Diocese of Long Island.

Section Six
New World A'Comin
1966

Chapter Seventeen

A Time of Troubled Waters

On the death of Bishop DeWolfe, the ecclesiastical authority, the Standing Committee, took immediate steps to choose his successor. They issued a call for a special session of the Diocesan Convention to be held on Saturday, March 19, 1966 at the Cathedral in Garden City. The alacrity of decision and call gave the Diocese little chance for caucuses, recommendations, discussions or just plain "politicking". Little time was really needed. It was well known that the election would be a contest between the senior and junior Suffragans. A small element in the Diocese favored an "outside man", but they garnered no large support.

THE FIFTH BISHOP OF LONG ISLAND

The special Convention to elect the Diocesan, after a celebration of the Holy Eucharist in the Cathedral, was called to order by the President of the Standing Committee on the prescribed day. After fulfilling all the legal logistics of such a Convention the call for nominations was made. Eight names were offered, including the two Suffragans, a bishop from another diocese, and five local clergy. A long and close race between the two favorites seemed imminent, so the Convention settled down to wait and vote again and again. The Convention, on being reconvened to hear the results of the first ballot, was completely surprised that there was an election in both orders of clergy and laity. The Fifth Bishop of Long Island was the faithful long-standing Suffragan, the Rt. Rev. Jonathan G. Sherman. More suprising was the overwhelming number of votes cast for Bishop Sherman, and the small number of votes cast for Bishop MacLean who came in third, after the "outside" Bishop. Most surprised was the Diocesan-elect himself. A humble man, a scholar, and a man totally faithful to his office and his immediate superior, he did not contemplate so total, so swift and so convincing a victory. Rumors even had it that he would not take the option of running for the office. He did, and was given an overwhelming acclaim.

Bishop Sherman had labored industriously and conscientiously, both on Long Island and in the National Church. His diocesan work consisted of serving as the Director of Christian Education, President of the Youth Consultation Service, Vice President of the Nassau County Council of Churches, Delegate to the Anglican Congress, and first Chairman of the Diocesan Commission on Mutual Responsibility and Interdependence (M.R.I.). Outside the Diocese he had leadership positions in the Episcopal Service for Youth, serving as Vice President and President; he was a member and then Chairman of the National Joint Commission on Architecture and Applied Arts; President of the American Church Building Fund and member of the National Joint Liturgical Commission. His interests ranged from a better understanding between Christians and Jews, speaking out boldly and marching for the cause of Soviet Jewry, to a closer relationship between the Anglican and Orthodox Churches. He served as Chairman of the Commission on Relations with Orthodox Churches and on the Anglo-Orthodox Consultation. His interest was recognized by his appointment by the Archbishop of Canterbury in 1968 to the Anglican delegation for proposed discussions with the Orthodox Churches. Dear to his heart was his first love, the Holy Scriptures. His scholarly approach to diocesan life was always scriptural, and one of the happiest chores he had was teaching Old Testament, whether in the Mercer School or in the local parish.

Immediately following the election, the elated prelate gave his acceptance speech. Giving full support to the Faith of the Church as expressed in the Creeds, the Offices of Instruction and the Collects of the Book of Common Prayer, he went on to tell the assembled group that they could expect things to happen. He promised:

> I am sure that you agree with me that in the Diocese of Long Island we have a vast potential
> that lies waiting to be uncorked. I hope you share my eagerness to see those bubbles
> effervesce and to see that cork hit the ceiling in all these drives.

In reporting the election, *The New York Times*, on its front page, summed up the election as "a tribute to the 'High Church' in the Anglo-Catholic wing of the denomination." They further observed: "Like his predecessor, Bishop Sherman has been a key figure in the Anglo-Catholic movement" and that "the Bishop fits the image of a 'correct Churchman' in Episcopalianism."

Since Bishop Sherman was already episcopally consecrated it was not necessary to make him a bishop. He had to be "enthroned" in his seat at the Garden City Cathedral. After receiving the necessary approval of other dioceses, the enthronement took place in June in the Cathedral, with a multitude of dignitaries, clergy and laymen, chief among which was the Roman Catholic Bishop of Rockville Centre and the Greek Orthodox Prelate. The enthronement was accomplished in true Episcopal fashion when Dean Lemoine fulfilled the time-honored ritual and ceremoniously placed Bishop Sherman in his *cathedra*. As the words of the *Veni Creater* poured forth in solemn tones the era of a new episcopal oversight had begun.

Bishop Sherman speaks at the dedication of St. John's Hospital, Smithtown.

WELCOME ABOARD

On his accession to the Episcopal throne, Bishop Sherman enlarged the leadership staff of the Diocese. He had as his assistant, Bishop Maclean who was "constantly" at the Bishop's side with his "clear eye and steady hand." "Whenever I differ from him," the Bishop said, "I do so with fear and trembling." Decisions had to be made as to the Archdeaconries of Queens and Nassau, and of Suffolk; the Brooklyn Archdeaconry had its able leader, Archdeacon Martin. The death of Archdeacon Stretch in January 1966, had caused a vacancy in the two diocesan jobs. Temporary or Acting Archdeacons had been appointed, subject to the approval or disapproval of the elected Bishop. At the 1966 Convention Bishop Sherman thanked the two temporary officers and then appointed in their places the Rev. William G. Penny, Rector of St. Joseph's, Queens Village as Archdeacon of Queens and Nassau, and the Rev. Paul F. Wancura, Rector of the Church of the Ascension in urban Greenpoint, to be Archdeacon of Suffolk. Because of the foreseen population explosion in the Diocese, the Bishop requested an episcopal addition to give adequate direction to this expansion. The Convention approved the request and the election of another Suffragan Bishop was held.

The electing Convention was called for Saturday, October 8, 1966. On that day the assembled delegates heard nominating speeches for fourteen candidates, all local clergy except for one outside bishop. The balloting began and at first it seemed a three-way contest between Rev. Dr. Dougald L. Maclean, Rector of St. George's Church, Flushing, the Ven. Richard B. Martin, Archdeacon of Brooklyn, and the Rt. Rev. Albert E. Swift. As the balloting continued it became a contest between Dr. Maclean and Bishop Swift. On the eighth ballot the former had a necessary majority in the laity, but not the clergy, and the latter had close to a majority in the clergy. In accordance with pre-agreed arrangement, the balloting stopped at 6:00 p.m., with no election. On Saturday, October 29, 1966, the balloting continued, but with a difference. Obviously someone or some group had done some "behind-the-scenes" work, for the candidacy of Archdeacon Martin assumed new life. By the time of the sixteenth ballot the Archdeacon had the majority of votes necessary in the laity and on the seventeenth had the necessary votes in the clergy. On the concurrent majority vote in each order the Chair declared the Archdeacon elected Suffragan Bishop.

Archdeacon Martin held many Diocesan offices, chief among which was Chairman of the M.R.I. Commission and member of the Standing Committee and Trustee of the Diocese. He served in many Brooklyn community leadership posts, and also on the Board of the Protestant Council of New York and the Church Army of the United States. He had the distinction, when appointed Archdeacon, of being the first Black to achieve rank above priest in the New York area. On his election to the episcopate he became only the second Black to be elected Suffragan in the whole nation. On February 2, 1967, in the presence of clergy, friends and family, he was consecrated a bishop in the Church by the Presiding Bishop, John E. Hines; Lauriston Scaife, Bishop of New York, and the Bishop of Long Island. A reception for the new Bishop was given in the Cathedral House immediately following the service. Bishop Martin, in addition to his episcopal duties, retained his responsibility as Archdeacon of Brooklyn.

In 1966, the Bishop engaged the management consultant firm of Rothrock, Reynolds and Reynolds who recommended the abolition of the office of Executive Secretary and the appointment of a full-time professional Director of Diocesan Relations. The Bishop then appointed to serve in this capacity John J. Mead, who became the Promotion and Communications Director with duties consisting of "internal management, advisor, public relations executive, spokesman, and Editor and Business Manager of *Tidings.*" He held direct responsibility to the Bishop. His contribution to the life of the Diocese was a "management seminar" for Diocesan Council Members and the diocesan professional staff. As Chaplain or "Clerical Assistant to the Bishop", Bishop Sherman appointed the Rev. Donald Latham who took up his duties in the Bishop's office October 17, 1967.

ON THE TIDE OF OPTIMISM

In the early years of Bishop Sherman's administration the Diocese of Long Island was swept along by a wave of optimism, partly due to the years before, but more likely accountable to the favorable aspects of the future. In his 1967 address to the Convention he cheerfully asserted:

> As we look forward to the next twenty years we shall see that the whole of Long Island will become part of a great metropolitan area embracing counties in Connecticut and New Jersey as well as New York, and we are already having to think in terms of our part in the Church's mission to this expanding city. The old boundaries, political and ecclesiastical, are utterly obsolete, and unless the Church is content to become an historical curiosity, isolationism in a Diocese, as in a parish, must become a thing of the past. God is bringing in a new world.

The Centennial Celebration of the founding of the Diocese emphasized this forward look. Characterized as the celebration of the next hundred years, the Diocese undertook the necessary steps to make the Centennial Celebration a "look ahead" as well as a "glance back." In December 1966, Bishop Sherman appointed a special committee, heading by Bishop MacLean, who planned the appropriate events. The celebration got off to an auspicious start with the visitation of the Most Rev. and Rt. Hon. Frederick D. Coggan, Archbishop of York, Primate of England. In honor of his visit, the Diocesan named the newest mission in the Diocese, St. Cuthbert's Church, Selden-Centereach, "after the saint in our new calendar who was consecrated in Yorkminster by the Archbishop of Canterbury on Easter Day, A.D. 685." The Archbishop began his visit at the Annual Ingathering of the Quota Service for the Episcopal Churchwomen in the morning and afternoon of Thursday, May 25. He was whisked from there to a rally at the Brooklyn Academy of Music, where he addressed the assembled multitude. On Friday, May 26, he appeared in St. Peter's, Bay Shore, for a rally at that end of the Island. On Saturday, May 27, he conducted a Quiet Day for the clergy of the Diocese. He ended his visit by preaching in the Cathedral at the morning services on Sunday, May 28.

A series of scholarly seminars on such subjects as politics and education, planned as part of the centennial observance, found fruition in one such event. On Friday, December 1, in the Colden Center at Queens College, a panel seminar was held dealing with the subject of "Religion and Political Power." The panel consisted of Dr. William H. Booth, Chairman of the New York City Human Rights Commission; Dr. Andrew Cordier, Dean of the Graduate School of International Studies at Columbia University, and former Executive Assistant to three Secretary-Generals at the United Nations; Dr. Arthur C. MacGill, Associate Professor of Theology at Princeton University; and Dr. Daniel Callahan, well-known publicist, lecturer and author. Well-received, but not too well attended, it was thought best to forego any such events. The Centennial Celebration concluded at a Dinner Dance held at the Garden City Hotel on Wednesday, October 16, 1968. The speaker for the evening was the Rt. Rev. Reginald H. Gooden, Bishop of Panama and the Canal Zone.

"This is a great Diocese," Bishop Sherman asserted in his early Convention addresses. Facts seemed to bear out his assumption. If nothing else the financial picture proved it so. Even though the missionary objective achieved only 70% of the anticipated assigned parish giving, each year brought an increase in monies available. The rosy glow reflected in annual increases until 1968, when missionary giving stood at the all-time high of $561,254.12. The Diocesan Assessment, fund for the upkeep of the Episcopate matched its pace, increasing just as noticeably as missionary funds. The challenge of new works to be begun, new insights to be learned, and new programs to be initiated, heightened the expectancy of "bigger and better things." But the time, like the river, had reached its crest and soon would recede to reveal the imprint of unfulfilled dreams and lessened insights in the sands of Long Island.

ROUGH SEAS AHEAD

Long Islanders, like every other American, experienced a time which to some was a temporary aberration, to others a time of transition; to all it was an observable shift of emphasis in all phases of American life. They faced a series of unrelieved crises surfacing in every dimension of national life. Climactic and traumatic was the Watergate affair ending in the "White House Horrors."

The years 1966 to 1974 emerged as a time of causes, courts and confrontation. The role of the courts in this period changed from adjudication to morality. Social and economic causes became a way of life. Flambuoyant and sometimes notorious in the beginning, by the middle seventies many had been forgotten. Achievements and successes did not overcome the sense of moral failure and national bankruptcy, intensified by the most pressing issue, the Vietnam War. Escalation of the war resulted in a loss of public confidence and support dwindled into searching and unnerving questions. Americans who had weathered the "generation gap" were faced with a more overpowering stress called the "credibility gap." Even the ending of the war in 1973 did nothing to alleviate the tension as the unravelling of the Watergate web became the burning issue. The resignation of the President and his subsequent pardon only confused the nation and threw it into a deeper abyss of distrust and discouragement, and again widened the credibility gap.

What affected Long Islanders most, whether they lived in urban centers of Brooklyn and Queens, or in the suburban and rural areas of Nassau and Suffolk, was the increased economic crunch. Although spending more in leisure time activities, supporting more and more the sports market, buying more and more arts and antiques, the general American public became the victims of adverse economic conditions that hurt and limited savings. The Stock Market collapse in 1970, and the recession that followed, made matters worse. Unemployment soared, hindered by wage and price controls. The already inflation-ridden economy suffered another blow in the "energy crisis." Beginning in the spring of 1973, and culminating on the Memorial Day weekend, the problem became a crisis. By the fall of 1973, a serious shortage of natural resources affected large areas of consumer products. In 1974, the economy continued its downward trend, impeding action in many domestic problems, not the least of which was urban decay, education and scientific research. The housing boom, so essential to Long Island development, was adversely affected by the rising inflation. After 1969, the price of homes skyrocketed, and to add to the troubles, a drastic decrease in new home building occurred.

By the middle seventies American optimism became restrained as dissatisfaction grew. Lack of confidence in American standards, and most of all in the political system, added perplexity and disillusionment. Reacting to the times, American society became markedly conservative. Liberal causes persisted but had lost much of their vigor. Little radical action or innovative movement found credence. The "nostalgia craze" became the game, symptomatic of the wistful longing for better times in former days.

FALLING BAROMETER

The Episcopal Church since its inception, had always been regarded as the Church of the fashionable, the wealthy and the "comer". Claiming as nominal members many old wealthy families, it stood as the paragon of a staid, affluent, ultra-conservative prayer house, best characterized by Clarence Day in *Life with Father*. The nomenclature "God's frozen people" to many seemed aptly appropriate for a group of people who appeared cold and aloof, going through such liturgical gyrations as stand up, sit down, kneel. Sometimes apart from the world around it, it prided itself on a rich liturgy, sound faith, social prestige, and above all on possessing an historic episcopate. Many within the Church felt they had the right combination of the Protestant and the Catholic to justify it as the "bridge church". Pride in its own ethos made churchmen largely await the day when all Christian Churches would settle on it, and so it would become *the* Christian Church. A continual quality, always present in Episcopal ranks, were the extremes of churchmanship high and crazy; low and lazy; and middle and hazy. Somehow or other all stripes of churchmen were able to live under the same roof, bound together by the unfailing allegiance to the Book of Common Prayer and the office of the Bishop. Even when the wealthy patrons had left its ranks, their places taken by more and more of the middle class, the Episcopal Church still retained its stereotyped image. It was to all intents and purposes a prosperous and cold entity, peculiarly gifted.

As much as it might try, the Church could not help but be affected by the radical social change around it. An increasing demand for relevancy, aided and abetted by the "God-is-dead" movement, and the demands of the "secular gospel", made deep inroads into its stability and solidarity. Badgered by "radical chic" liberals, both inside as well as outside the Church, and fascinated by the Madison Avenue concept of "image", the Church involved itself in a self-effacing overhaul that, in the long run, sapped some of its vitality and confused many of its adherents. The election of John E. Hines as Presiding Bishop of the National Church hastened the process and pointed the direction. Formerly staid and conservative, the Church now became commonplace, down-to-earth and relevant.

In the rapid process of change, marked strains appeared in the relationship within the two large areas, personnel and structure. The Church was never without its three way stretch between bishops, clergy and laity, overlaid and complicated by the triad of National Church, diocese and parish. When tensions equalized, or a common cause united, stable relations existed and the Church was able to function well. Imbalance or polarization caused wide disparity, and the alienation of the third party always ensued. Reacting to such forces, vitality and aggressiveness changed to chaos and confusion, and the Church faltered. To complicate the balance, a major and pervasive sympton appeared. A "great gulf fixed" came between top management and the grass roots. Incredulity, disillusionment, compounded by anger and frustration, seeped into all areas of church life. The credibility gap appeared first in the relationship of the bishops to the clergy, but soon the same negative feeling permeated all personnel and structure relationships so that conflict and controversy became the chief means of communication.

The change of image, accelerated by the rapid disintegration of unifying bonds, brought also a drastic change in church policy, especially as it affected the Church's major area of concern, missionary work. The Episcopal Church had as its chief missionary thrust, either at home or abroad, the establishment of Episcopal Churches. It's foremost quality lay in the propagation of the good news of Episcopalianism, winning souls to the ways and teachings of its unique formularies. Following such a policy, the Episcopal Church flourished best in large population centers, concentrating its manpower and its finances in areas that contained a certain cosmopolitan air, or in the safe suburban atmosphere of middle class propriety. Churches grew strong in numbers and magnificent in imposing buildings and pleasant programs. Responding to the current theological philosophy, not the least of which was found in Harvey Cox's *The Secular City*, the Church revamped its missionary policy.

Paramount in the new look was the precept of sacred secularism, an anomoly in terms that stressed the urbanization of life in which common life was diversity and the disintegration of that life important. The Church had to turn its focus from "other" world to this world. An absolute necessity was to respond to social change, or face the alternative—death. The Church had to discard its past orientation with its superfluous attributes, preservation and permanence. An avant-garde corps was to assume the role of a servant who bound himself in the struggle for the secular city's wholeness and health. In all, replacing the metaphysical, the political became the best form of attack.

"A basic decision must be made by anyone who feels himself claimed by the Christian gospel," theorized Mr. Cox in *The Secular City*. "Either being a Christian is something religious and quite distinct from secular affairs, or Christian Faith is a human posture conceivable for a man who is part of his secular culture." Following his line of thought, the Church did not stand outside the process as prophet, but involved itself in it as a suffering servant. Individual pietism had to be abrogated for social activism. The religious ghetto had to break down its walls of isolation and become a part of the world around it. In this novel philosophy the Church's salvation rested not in the establishment and extension of parishes, not in any church programs, but in a complete immersion in the social problems of the times. The major expenditure of time, money and personnel needed to be invested in the definition of issues, in the confrontation, and in their ultimate solution. As the times changed, so changed the work of the Church.

So imperceptible at first, and then more and more as the National Church and the Diocese of Long Island immersed themselves deeper and deeper in its new focus, issues became all important, and confrontation the mode of solution. In the diocesan program, the novel outlook found implementation in community outreach, in finding and elaborating issues, and in protesting man's inhumanity to man. The diocesan emphasis on church extension, departmental programs and missionary enterprises lessened in intensity and soon became forgotten. Symptomatic of the new image was the diocesan public relations magazine *Tidings*. From a simplistic explanation of diocesan and parish current events, the paper took a more editorial bias. Front page picture and story offered the problem, and the Bishop's dialogue became the vehicle of expression in confronting the issues of the day.

Implicit in this change was the realignment of its constituents. High and low, evangelical and catholic, so much a part of church life, melded into a new set of standards and labels. The conversion of the ecclesiastical into the political brought forth a new set of tensions: conservative, liberal and radical. In the shift to politicization, the common bond became man's commonality, his humanity. No more was the emphasis on church-centered or even church-oriented programs. Power to control, and especially political power, became not just the means but the ends to proclaiming the good news of the secular gospel.

STORMY WEATHER

Caught up in the headlong pursuit of relevancy, the Diocese faced a full spectrum of highly volatile and controversial issues, adequately foreshadowed by social problems of the past. Since the initiation of the Social Service Committee in 1904, many problems were brought to the floor of the legislative body, the Convention. The pages of the Convention Journals are filled with a long string of "whereases and therefore be it resolveds." As a point in fact, the role of women as participants in decision making on all levels of church life had been discussed as early as 1948. But like all other social problems, this issue was secondary to the major thrust of the diocesan program-planning and Church establishment. Issues, although discussed and voted on, did not intrude into the every day diocesan mission.

The distinquishing quality of the period 1966 through 1975 was that the issues became the program. The whole force of diocesan energy went into the definition, the confrontation and the solution of the various major issues. The attack on the problems was not theological, nor moral, but basically political. Power to solve rested in power to control. Solution often rested in some form of legislation, whether canonical or civil. At first the issue-centered approach was limited to the diocese and the National Church, but as controversy became more heated, and results more publicized, all levels of church life became involved. The credibility gap and distrust of higher offices, and of each other, made the situation more tenuous. A wide gap grew between the local parish that had as its objective the expansion of membership and influence, and the bureaucracy which had as its objective church relevancy and "meaningful experience." Both wound up in the same trap and the same dilemma — fighting for survival.

Issues confronting the nation were the same as those confronting the Diocese. The Diocese spoke out on penal reform, and in May 1970, it went on record for the repeal of sex legislation. The resolution as adopted stated that "while adultery, fornication, homosexual acts, and certain deviant sexual practices among competent and consenting adults violate Judeo-Christian standards of moral conduct, we think that the penal law is not the instrument for control of such practices when privately engaged in, where only adults are involved, and where there is no coercion — we favor repeal of those statutes that made such practices among competent and consulting adults criminal acts." Following the lead of the Executive Council and the tragedy of Attica, the Convention in 1972 resolved to support all existing programs which offered viable alternatives to prison for youthful first offenders. The Bishop was encouraged to appoint a Diocesan Commission on Penal Reform to study crime and punishment.

The Diocese tackled the issue of ecology, so popular and so absorbing. The 105th Convention affirmed man's stewardship over all God's creatures and placed a "high priority" on study and learning the complexities of our world, and so "stir up the ecological consciences within the Body of Christ." The problem of child adoption was also considered. A resolution was made and passed that any child eligible for adoption, still in foster or institutional care, should have the courtesy of all religious restrictions which discriminated against parents of diverse religious backgrounds removed and that such restrictions should be dropped and adoption made irrevocable. Welfare reform also came under discussion. The Convention approved a resolution, sponsored by the Department of Christian Social Relations, advocating principles that called for national legislative action, relief of municipalities and states from welfare costs, and the establishment of a "guaranteed adequate income."

The Convention confronted and solved a long standing inequity in equal rights for young people. The youth of the Diocese had for many years been an active segment of diocesan life, contributing much to its well being. Thought of as the "future of the church" young people resented their second-class citizenship, working for full and equal rights in decision making. Young people made known their demands, and under pressure the Convention responded. In 1971, the Convention agreed to create a new Canon giving leadership privileges to those over eighteen years of age. Canon 33, as adopted, stated that "qualified young persons over eighteen years of age had the right to vote in parish elections, to serve as vestrymen and wardens, to be elected delegates to the Convention of the Diocese, and to hold elective offices of the Convention." Young people under eighteen years of age had the right when so chosen by the parish to serve as youth delegates to the Convention, with a seat and voice, but no vote. Two representatives from the youth delegations were elected to serve on the Diocesan Council, again having a voice but no vote. At the Convention of 1973, a Board of Managers consisting of elected members, as well as Archdeaconry and Trustee representatives, was created to supervise the program and policies of Camp DeWolfe. Before this the camp was under the jurisdiction of the Department of Youth.

Abortion Reform

An highly emotional issue with deep theological overtones engaged the attention of the Diocese for several years. In response to the movement for abortion law reform and the need for a clearer understanding of the complexities of abortion, the Diocese, in 1968, memorialized the General Convention, petitioning them to adopt a resolution supporting abortion law reform based upon the fundamental principle:

> Where the decision to terminate life has been arrived at by proper safeguards against abuse, and where it has been clearly established that the physical or mental health of the mother is threatened seriously, or when there is substantial reason to believe that the child would be born badly deformed in mind or body, or where the pregnancy has resulted from rape or incest.

With the enactment of abortion laws in Hawaii, Maryland and impending in New York, the issue needed further clarification. In May 1970, the Convention adopted a resolution creating a Commission to define "human life" and "human being", and to analyse the issue and clarify the role of the Church as teacher and pastor with regard to the affect of abortion on society and individuals. The Commission on Abortion Reform made their report in 1972 and affirmed a woman's freedom to exercise her conscience with the advice and counsel of her physician and priest. They clearly established the time limit of twelve weeks of gestation, during which beyond reasonable doubt, the mother's physical and mental health would be seriously disrupted over a sufficient period of years, any stage at which the life of the mother was endangered, when pregnancy resulted from rape or incest, or where the child would be deformed. Although the abortion controversy raged on, and abortion on demand became more and more an accepted practice, the Diocese turned its attention to other matters. Having solved this deep theological issue it moved on to other areas that demanded its concerted effort and attention.

Church women had always played an important role in the ongoing life of all sides of the Church. Women's organizations of the parish, diocese, and National Church, religious orders, Church Army sisterhood and religious education offered active and interested women a vast opportunity to serve their Church. By and large considered service people, fund raisers or housekeepers, women were depended upon enormously by the Church for their interest and support. In some cases, plans could not survive without their presence and effort. Still, when it came to decision-making or policy-forming, they were given second place. Formally organized under such diocesan titles as the Women's Missionary Society (1872), the Women's Auxiliary (1919) and the Episcopal Churchwomen (1958), their function remained the same. Meeting separately in the Diocese, taking part in the National Triennial Meeting, and raising millions of church dollars through the United Thank Offering, they were still not allowed any participatory role in determining policy.

The struggle for equal rights for church women, involving a part in Vestry, Convention and other elective offices, harked back as far as 1948 when the Rev. John H. Melish proposed a canonical amendment to allow them to serve in such capacities. The suggestion predated the moment for action, and women, although canonically franchised to vote in parish meetings, still did not have the right to hold office. A disparity between canon law and the New York State Religious Corporation Law did not receive attention until 1957. Proposed in 1956, and approved in 1957, the resolution read:

> That a committee be appointed for the purpose of approaching like Conventions of Dioceses located in the State of New York so that the legislature be informed of the desire of this and like Conventions, if they be so minded, to revise the Religious Corporation Laws relating to Protestant Episcopal Churches governed by such act, particularly paragraph two of Section 40, Article III, being Chapter 53 of the Laws of 1909 concerning the rights of women to vote at a meeting called for the purpose of incorporating a Protestant Episcopal Parish.

The Committee on Canons moved, and it was seconded and carried, that a special committee of this Convention study this proposition and report at the next annual Convention. The proposal upgraded an archaic law but still did nothing for the participation of women in key roles.

The movement for equal rights for women, gaining impetus from the national spotlight, proceeded slowly. The subject was discussed by the General Convention in 1964 and 1967, but was roundly defeated. The Diocese upstaged the National Church by taking a giant step forward. In 1966, the Convention amended Canon 28 which dealt with women among qualified voters, and added the section stating: "Women who have the qualifications prescribed by law shall be eligible to the office of Churchwarden or Vestryman. No person, otherwise qualified to serve as a Delegate to the Convention, shall be ineligible by reason of sex." The General Convention finally, in 1970, allowed women as delegates to that august body. It was at that same convention that the ordination of women to the diaconate was regularized. Quickly taking advantage of their new participatory role, women began to fill the ranks of vestries and Diocesan Convention delegations. By 1971, thirty-eight women served as convention delegates, and a momentous decision was made when Catherine G. Collings, communicant of St. Luke's, Sea Cliff, an active diocesan worker, was elected to the Diocesan Council. The Diocese still had to bridge the gap by electing a woman as a regular delegate to the General Convention. Although nominated, no woman achieved this distinct honor and privilege.

On May 4, 1972, the Episcopal Churchwomen celebrated its centennial at a service of thanksgiving in the Cathedral followed by a formal luncheon. Bishop Sherman commended the auspicious occasion:

> Now with women seated as regular deputies to General Convention, and as delegates to our Diocesan Conventions, and elected as Wardens and Vestrymen in a growing number of parishes, and serving as Lay Readers and Deacons, they are no longer strangers and sojourners, but fellow citizens of the household of God.

But the unsettling times did not leave the matter of equal rights for women there. As much as the Bishop rejoiced, and as much as the Church accepted, still there was another battle to be fought, one which would attract far more attention and untold publicity, both from the Church as well as the public press. The Diocese, with every other diocese, had to face squarely the issue of women priests. The opening wedge in the battle to ordain women as priests began as soon as women were made deacons. Formalizing the fomentation and facing the issue in 1972 the House of Bishops, the national executive group, prepared proposals for canonical and constitutional changes to afford full ordination to women. They presented them at the General Convention in 1973. Reaction to the move became immediate and intense. An history-shattering decision such as this was bound to have its effect on all levels of church structure, especially as it pertained to the Diocese.

The issue of ordaining women as priests did not much affect the Diocese until this time. Women had been ordained priests elsewhere, but with the formalization of the House of Bishops, the matter could not be ignored. At the regular Diocesan Convention held on May 16, 1972, a resolution was passed memorializing General Convention not to re-interpret nor proceed to alter the National Constitution and Canons to permit the ordination of women to the priesthood. A Diocesan Commission to study the question was formed and a canvass of other communions and opinions urged. The Commission under the chairmanship of the Rev. George Raymond Kemp held four study meetings. A poll of the members was made and found that:

> Opinion seemed to be fairly evenly divided between those who would approve the ordination of women to the priesthood, if this action received ecumenical consent, and those who would favor the ordination of women to the priesthood at the present time, but not at the price of schism.

The Commission presented a resolution to the 1973 Convention to memorialize General Convention that before any final action be taken "it issue a call for serious and formal ecumenical dialogue on this matter between this Church, the Roman and Orthodox Churches, and such other churches as may already have had some experience of women in the ordained ministry." They also urged a canvass of clerical and lay opinion within the Church as to "the possible effects upon this Church of such ordination of women, or of the refusal of it." A minority report was also presented. The Convention, after much discussion, accepted the majority report only.

The matter was further complicated and made a public issue by the action of a group of retired bishops. On July 29, 1974, Bishops DeWitt, Corrigan and Welles ordained, without authorization, eleven women to the priesthood in Philadelphia. The action came under immediate fire. Besides being highly publicized, the matter seemed destined to create havoc in the Church. In his address to the 1975 Convention, Bishop Sherman made clear his stand:

> I continue to deplore the actions of Bishops, seminary deans, priests, deacons, and lay persons who by threats or in other ways seek to anticipate and to force the hand of the General Convention. . . . What particularly disturbs me most is the impatience displayed by those who seek the ordination of women to the priesthood. Having been a member of the House of Bishops since 1949, I do not recall any serious discussion of this subject prior to the Lambeth Conference of 1968. . . . I pledge my loyal obedience to whatever decision the General Convention may make in this matter. I will not be a party to any schism in the Church.

To prepare properly diocesan delegates for the General Convention in Minnesota, and to arrive at a responsible consensus, a seminar was planned in which all points of view would be expressed, and the subject thoroughly discussed.

Black is Beautiful

Highly inflammatory, not only for the National Church, but for the Diocese as well, was the issue of civil rights. The achievements of the early sixties in a drive for Black equality led to a new drive with more advanced goals. Notwithstanding the advances made, new demands and new goals became paramount. In the early sixties the burning issue was whether Blacks would be allowed to ride the buses, and where they would sit. In the late sixties and early seventies emphasis shifted. It was whether Black people would be allowed to drive the bus, whether masses of Black people had the fare to ride, and whether Blacks had a rightful place as executives and directors of the bus companies and the unions with which it dealt. The standard around which the movement rallied was the quest for Black Power.

Revolted by the ineffective ministry of what was known in Black ghettoes as "plantation charity", the movement concentrated on the means of self-determination. Plantation charity, a variation of the Thanksgiving Day baskets for the poor, afforded the benevolent giver a "good" feeling in helping "inferior people" while the recipient, whose helplessness intensified, was expected to be grateful to him. Such charitable acts, abetted by the attempts of church groups who invaded the inner city and did good works among the ghetto minorities, did not really help those who were being aided. For Black leaders the only answer to true equality was the seizure of power and the development of a more positive image. Black power meant basically politics and money; Black people would attain equal status only when they developed political and economic strength, first in their own communities and then in the outside private and public sectors. For the non-Black, Black power meant Black violence, encouragement to riot, and a resurgence of rabid Black nationalism. Their fears seemed confirmed by the outbreak of riots and violence in the major cities from Los Angeles to New York City. Deep-seated anxiety welled up at the mention of "Burn, baby burn." A corallary of black power was the nurturing of pride in their cultural heritage, their "Blackness." The drive for self-realization, self-identity, and dignity through consciousness of their history led to an emphasis on Black History and the Afro-American culture. It raised the Black man to a position of dignity on a par with other men. Blacks gained some new hope in the black domination of professional sports. Idolized were O. J. Simpson and Walt Frazier. An added dimension, rejection of integration as a goal and strategy, grew out of a hard realization that the methods of the white-dominated civil rights organization did not naturally improve the conditions of their lives. The use of radical development, the emphasis on racial supremacy, the enlargement of Black Nationalism, and the use of violent insurrection were the tools to insure a black share in the American dream.

Cries of "Power to the People" and "Black is Beautiful" did not measurably affect or stir up all levels of the Church until 1967. Before that the plight of the poor Blacks in the ghettoes was purely academic and as much as the General or Diocesan Conventions would propose, local churches disposed. A certain smugness pervaded the attitude of churchmen, especially on Long Island. There were Black churches in the Diocese and they had an equal vote in Conventions, even if not in decision-making positions. The election of Bishop Martin proved to many how "enlightened" the Diocese had become.

At the General Convention held in Seattle in 1967, a bold step was taken: a program to aid the Black in his quest for power. The program supported Black power, committing without strings a substantial amount of money to Black people for developing power bases, capitalizing economic development in the ghettoes and providing persons with indigenous skills. The decisions of the Seattle Convention, known as the General Convention Special Program (G.C.S.P.) made bold steps in "the racial revolution" by appropriating $2,000,000 each year for three years to assist in urban cities, and to underwrite the poor in ghetto areas and the dispossessed and oppressed people of the country, thereby achieving the "healing of our National life." Against poverty and racism the program provided manpower and money for works set up by the poor themselves to gain political and economic power. Funds were assigned by a screening and review committee with no reference to "race, creed, or ethnic origin." It was the priority in mission.

The violent assassinations of Senator Robert Kennedy and the Rev. Martin Luther King, Jr. made the need more pressing. Commenting in May 1968, Bishop Martin made the telling statement: "Black people are beginning to wonder whether the white man can be trusted to play the game of democracy fairly." Diocesan response to the new program came in the appointment of a Commission on Urban Work, directly under the Department of Missions, whose responsibility it was to explore ways of implementing the G.C.S.P. on Long Island and to be supportive of clergy in distressed areas. A pilot project was planned for the Bedford-Stuyvesant Area. Commenting on the G.C.S.P. Bishop Martin labelled the program a top priority of time, personnel and money. "It seeks to help the poor help themselves," he affirmed. Knowing diocesan reaction, he defended the program by cautioning that any new effort needed a period of trial and error. The Diocesan Convention heartily supported the program by resolution, pledging to make a "meaningful contribution" in this most worthwhile endeavor.

Grave difficulties and serious questioning dogged the path of the program as soon as it began. Indiscriminate giving and the failure to abide by the non-violent criteria brought the program under heavy fire. A Special Convention II, meeting in South Bend, Indiana on September 3, 1969, took up the problem and attempted solution by appeasement and amendment. Affirming the general intent of the program, the Convention assigned $200,000 to the National Committee of Black Churchmen and $100,000 to the National Indian Work. The program suffered a severe blow in the appearance of James Forman and the demands of Black Manifesto. The demand for "reparations" of $5,000,000,000 from the Christian Church, and specifically $60,000,000 and 60% a year income from all assets of the Episcopal Church hit hard all churchmen, whether in the National Church or on the Parish level. The added threat of violence and terror caused untold fear and aroused heated anger. Churchmen looked more closely at the program, especially as it concerned the Diocese of Long Island. The Rev. Calvin Marshall III of the African Methodist Episcopal Zion Church, leader in the Bedford-Stuyvesant project came under heavy fire. Grants to Black militant groups such as the B.E.D.C. and the radical Allende group, coupled with the invasion of dioceses or areas without the consent of local authorities, made the issue hotter and more turbulent. In October 1969, the Bishop made clear the voluntary nature of the program, on a resolution, adopted unanimously, by the Standing Committee. The resolution read:

> Resolved that, the Bishop of Long Island . . . proclaims a Sunday within this calendar year, to call attention to these resolutions of the Special General Convention II and invite financial contributions to the special funds authorized.

At the Diocesan Convention in May 1970, the impact and procedures of the program were scrutinized. Strong feeling made the passage of a resolution swift and forceful. The resolution, as approved by the Convention, urging a specific regard for existing diocesan organizations as channels of communication and action, and an inclusion of the parish as a viable effective arm, succinctly stated that grants by the National Church be made only with diocesan approval, and that high priority be given to the utilization of existing parishes in the inner city or wherever there was a significant minority presence, to accomplish a ministry that was "more obviously and effectively taken in the name of the Church and the Lord of the Church."

Diocesan implementation of the program's intent centered in the work of the Commission on Urban Work. Begun in 1968, it had the task of "focusing attention on social, political and economic issues and conditions which abort life and community in the inner city." Their hope was to be the advocate and voice of "the powerless and voiceless people." For three years it had a paid staff that included the Rev. Louis Ferrara as Director of Social Action, while also serving as Executive Director of the Department of Christian Social Relations, and a Mr. Charles Hale who pounded the pavements of the Brownsville-East New York section of Brooklyn as a "sidewalk lay minister" of the Episcopal Church. Under the aegis of the Commission, a corporation known as the Absalom Jones Housing Corporation, so named in honor of the first American Black Episcopal priest, was formally organized and addressed itself to the housing needs in the Brownsville-East New York area. Annually in January the Commission sponsored a Martin Luther King salute. In 1974, the Commission awarded to Medgar Evers College the "Martin Luther King Scholarship Award." Also in 1974, the Commission held its first annual Achievement Awards dinner. At the dinner the Hon. Paul Gibson, Deputy Mayor of New York, was honored for his outstanding contribution to the Church and for his leadership in civil affairs in the City. It also provided consultation for rehabitation of houses, counselling for young prisoners, work in prison reform, assistance in consumer education and improved landlord tenant relations in central Brooklyn. With governmental cutbacks and Diocesan reorganization, the Commission suffered serious setbacks. Lacking funds, the Commission assumed the task of serving "as a conduit within the Diocese of the current information, contacts, resources (personal and governmental), and to move the Diocesan community closer to concerns of social justice," to evaluate current changes in social legislation, social resources, and to study changing procedures for the delivery of social services.

Diocesan assistance in the drive for Black power took various forms, mostly dealing with movements and organizations outside the diocesan structure. In November 1966, Fr. Ferrara and Mr. Leon E. Modeste, diocesan churchman, were appointed by the Mayor of New York to serve on the Council against Poverty, a group dedicated to the allocation of Federal and City anti-poverty funds. The Diocese, through the efforts of Bishop Martin, played a large part in organizing Project Equality. A nationwide program for inter-racial justice, it utilized the hiring and purchasing power of religious bodies and coordinated the efforts of religious institutions, congregations, schools, hospitals and homes. Signed pledges from businesses were required in order to promote opportunities for minority persons at all job levels. Its aim was to overcome employment discrimination by companies and unions in such general services as banking and construction. Because of his interest and leadership, Bishop Martin was elected President of its Board of Directors. He served as Coordinator to expedite the program thrust in the Diocese. The Diocesan Council assisted the program by recommending that the Diocese and local churches deal only with Equal Opportunity firms. Bishop Martin also became a member of the Advisory Committee on Equal Opportunities at the State Campus in Farmingdale. Under the guidance of the Urban Commission, the Diocese in May 1970, urged Congress to declare January 15 as the Rev. Martin Luther King, Jr. Day. Equal opportunities in employment in the Diocese did not fare as well as some other aspects. There were some white priests in integrated or predominantly white parishes, but not one Black priest in a white parish. The unfortunate death of the Rector of Christ Church, Bellport, led to the calling of the Rev. Herbert Thompson, black priest from Brooklyn, to this predominantly white parish. No other parish, white or black, was as daring.

The Black movement in the Diocese, as well as the nation, gradually melded into that most divisive issue experienced by the American nation. Black power became absorbed in the pros and cons of the issue that Americans faced; and somehow the aims and objectives of black equality and black power became a part of the demands and protestations involved in the issue of the Vietnam War.

The Vietnam War

The most divisive issue suffered by the American people could not help but become an issue for the Diocese itself. The unfulfilled promise of cessation accompanied by an escalation of battle; the huge dumping of money into the military, accompanied by the undercutting of domestic programs; the disillusion heightened by the MyLai Massacre, all created a wide gap between the doves and the hawks, with most Americans caught in the middle. In his opening address to the 1966 Convention Bishop Sherman commented on the undeclared war:

> At this point my own personal view is one of confidence in the integrity of our President as he painfully commits the military power of this nation in the cause of freedom against aggression, while exercising the utmost caution and restraint in the use of that power.

By 1971 (five years later) he, like his constituents, had had enough of the war:

> As a citizen I have come to believe, and as your spiritual leader I feel bound to state that the war in Vietnam must stop. I have come to believe this not only for the sake of the Vietnamese, but also for the sake of the survival of our own society in this country . . . our cities, our health, our education, and our civic freedom and order. I do not question the lofty motives that caused us to be involved, but I am convinced that our very ends are being frustrated by our means. This is the hard lesson that we have learned through incalculable sufferings, and cost of lives, and the destruction of God's good earth.

The Diocese, like the Bishop, was confused and frustrated by the attenuation of the war. Voices were heard on the far extremes, the doves and the hawks, but little action came from the "silent majority." Related problems of the military-industrial complex, prisoners of war, conscientious objectors, and amnesty faced the Diocese, which was hoping for some solution. A growing anxiety over steadily rising military costs brought forth a response on the part of the Bishop. In his 1969 address he lamented the "present defense budget" whose capacity was for eight times "overkill" — that is the ability to destroy the Russians eight times over. "I believe the time has come," clearly stated the Bishop, "to make a salutory venture in the direction of sanity, common sense, and the interest of the human race."

No response on the part of the Diocese was forthcoming. Related to the military was the Strategic Arms Limitation Talks (S.A.L.T.). In May 1970, the Diocesan Council was instructed to develop education and action programs to gain support for the arms limitation talks between the United States and Russia, emphasizing the reduction of military spending and the suspension of deployment of nuclear weapons system. The Convention, also in that year, confronting the problem of the Anti-Ballistic Missile System, did not make a firm resolution of the deployment of the anti-ballistic system and the national priority of the alleviation for poverty, deprivation and disadvantaged among large segments of the population. The Committee on Miscellaneous Business asked to "be discharged from further consideration" of the issue "since the material covered therein had already been acted upon by the Senate of the United States." On the treatment of prisoners of war the Convention officially demanded adherence to the Geneva Convention by the Republic of North Vietnam, demanding the cessation of inhuman treatment of helpless American prisoners of war, and meaningful negotiations to end the war.

Young men and the draft, a highly explosive issue, also came under scrutiny and recommendation. Following the lead of the General Convention in 1967, which recommended counsel and legal advice for conscientious objectors, the Convention resolved that the Diocesan Council "study ways and means to formulate and execute a plan that would offer draft counselling to young men of the Diocese of Long Island who have problems of conscience with regard to the prospect of the military draft." Recognizing that there were men in federal prisons because of dictates of conscience, the Convention urged "a ministry for young men now imprisoned." The problem of amnesty had no easy solution. A resolution on the subject was presented to the May Convention in 1972. It called for "a clearly defined policy of amnesty." After a period of debate the resolution was defeated.

At the 1971 Diocesan Convention, a most radical resolution on the war reached the floor for discussion entitled "Peace in Southeast Asia." It called for immediate and total withdrawal from Vietnam, an end to "the imposition" of Thieu, Ky and Dhiem on the people of South Vietnam, a pledge to form a "provisional coalition government to organize democratic elections" and to withdraw any and all foreign troops. The resolution was hotly debated and discussed. Amendments to the resolution were offered, but rejected. Finally the resolution was withdrawn by those who presented it. In 1973, the Bishop commenting on the end of hostilities, and the return of prisoners, summed up the effects of the unwanted war:

> On our knees we thank God for the cease-fire in Vietnam and for the return of our prisoners of war. But there is in our hearts no jubilant mood of victory. There is rather the heavy awareness of the terrible loss of life, of bodies maimed and minds warped, of our national resources wasted, and a far off land made desolate. Perhaps the greatest casualty in the war was that of our National spirit, torn and divided, confused, distracted and exhausted.

For him the nation had to recapture its lost ideals and honest image among the nations of the world.

The Issue of Liturgical Reform

No other issue had such a devastating effect on the Episcopal Church as the movement for liturgical reform. Sacred to the Episcopalian was the Book of Common Prayer. When all else failed a rallying point or a battle cry could always be found in Prayer Book allegiance. It was true that the Prayer Book had gone through a number of revisions, the last being in 1928. Even in the midst of the political upheaval of the American Revolution and the subsequent formation of the American Prayer Book, the essential form and substance of the book remained, except for a few minor changes, the same as that of 1662. Subject to differences of churchmanship, Anglo-Catholics and Romanizers added accretions to the Lord's supper to conform to the Roman rite, and Evangelicals emphasized the Protestant in Morning and Evening Prayer, but in spite of these it still remained the same Book of Common Prayer.

In the liturgical reform movement the Episcopal Church did not stand alone. Many Protestant Churches, whose worship facilities resembled large speaking auditoriums, began to alter their structures and assume proportions of sanctuary, altar and ecclesiastical accutrements. Too, the Roman Church, following Vatican II, evaluated its liturgy and made far-reaching changes, not the least of which was the translation of the Roman Mass into the vernacular.

A cry of relevance, more meaningful experience, and modernization permeated the quest of liturgical renewal. The National Standing Liturgical Commission evaluated and advised needed changes and improvements. In 1967 a draft of "The Liturgy of the Lord's Supper" was authorized and the Seattle General Convention approved its trial use.

The experiment with the "trial use" was to be an experience of the whole Church, with hoped for reactions from the "grass roots". By and large the revised service had a small and limited use. Avant-garde parishes undertook the new liturgy, but the majority of parishes kept to the traditional Prayer Book form. The 1970 General Convention continued the program of liturgical renewal. In true Anglican fashion the National Church published, in 1971, a service book entitled *Services for Trial Use, Authorized Alternatives to Prayer Book Services*. Including all services for the Church, a choice was given between two styles, an up-dated traditional style and a contemporary modern version. Encased in the "green book" one had a choice of two daily offices, and in the case of the Eucharist, three rites. The aim of the National revision was to have a trial period, with the hope that by 1976 the draft proposed book would be accepted and finally in 1979 be accepted as the Book of Common Prayer.

In preparation for the use of the trial services, the Diocesan Liturgical Commission began in 1968 a program that aimed at helping towards a better understanding of the liturgical process. Conferences and workshops for clergy and laity were held. Still there existed a wide disparity between those parishes which used the trial use and those that did not. Many congregations did not provide the opportunity to use the new rites, and where the services were used, it was sporadic and dilatory. To have a widespread use of trial services, Bishop Sherman, in February 1972, mandated the use of Rite II from the Feast of Pentecost until Advent Sunday, 1972. The reason given was that experimentation with the service would afford the opportunity to make a "fair judgment" on them. To refuse the experiment, was for the Bishop, "to act irresponsibly in relation to the Church as a whole." Upon recommendation of the Diocesan Liturgical Commission, the Bishop mandated the use of the proposed Prayer Book changes at all official diocesan services in the Cathedral and elsewhere.

Questionnaires were sent to all parishes in the Diocese soliciting their reactions to the new usage. The tabulation of the parochial responses was in the hands of the Diocesan Liturgical Commission — "on the basis of the responses as well as the consensus of the Commission." The tabulated report was submitted to the National Joint Liturgical Commission in April 1973 in time for presentation at the General Convention. The Rev. Leo Malania, a priest of the Diocese, had the immense task of coordinating all responses for the National Church. The 1973 General Convention continued the study and use of the revised rites, offering a second set of authorized services, aptly named the "zebra book". The continuance of the trial use did not much change the worship habits of the parishes in the Diocese. In response, a dissonant cry sprang up against the liturgical reform. The National Society for the Preservation of the Book of Common Prayer found many like-minded adherents in the Diocese, and began a concerted effort to gain strength and voice to oppose any Prayer Book changes.

The Hope of Ecumenism

A continual concern, not so much an issue as a hope, was the conversations, conferences and plans for some kind of organic church unity. Looking both to the Protestant Churches on the one hand and the Orthodox and Roman Catholic on the other, the Diocese, following the lead of its national counterpart, strove to advance ecumenical relations with its Christian brethren.

A change of the name indicated the direction in which the movement went. Starting as the Commission on Church Unity, its name was changed in 1967 to the Commission on Relations with Catholic, Orthodox and Protestant Churches, which in turn became the Commission on Ecumenical Relations. Two important new developments affected the cause of ecumenical dialogue. The first was the progress of the organic plan, known as the Consultation on Church Union (COCU). The other was the emergence of the Roman Catholic as an active participant signified by the mutual rescinding of excommunication by the Roman Catholic and Orthodox Church, in force since 1054, by the Second Vatican Council, and by the historic meeting of the Pope and the Archbishop of Canterbury in 1966.

The Consultation on Church Union, initiated in 1960, progressed slowly. Involved in it were the original four, the United Presbyterian Church in the United States, the United Church of Christ, the Methodist Church and the Episcopal Church, later joined by the Evangelical United Brethren, the A.M.E. Church and the Southern Baptists in the United States. As the Diocese wrestled with the proposals of COCU, it retained its insistance that in any attempt or discussion of Church union, the 1888 Chicago-Lambeth Quadrilateral be the yardstick of evaluation. In 1967, the Diocesan Commission reported its activities. The publication of COCU's *Principles of Church Union* did not hold much hope for Episcopal involvement because of the problem of the ministry, specifically as it referred to the "historic episcopate". The whole plan became almost archaic with the new and welcomed emergence of the Roman Catholic Church. With it a basic assumption changed from some structural unity to a way in which all Communions could have understanding and reciprocity, still preserving their separate traditions. The Bishop recommended the beginning of ecumenical discussion at the "grass roots", alluding to the experience of one of the local Commissions on Faith and Order, specifically that of the Nassau County Council of Churches. The Diocesan Commission felt that the "grass roots" seemed against the principles of COCU, not wishing to lose the Episcopal identity. In 1969, the Commission reported "nothing new" in ecumenical relations. The publication of the final proposals of COCU again brought the plan before the diocesan purview. Individual parochial study was encouraged, the results of which were sent to the Committee, who in turn collated and sent the results to the National Joint Committee on Ecumenical Relations. The formal plan of COCU suffered a setback with the departure of the Presbyterians. A decline of interest in the proposed large, centrally administered body showed disinterest in that particular form of administration. The General Convention in Louisville in 1973 voted to continue relationship with COCU since the organic plan of union was considered passe.

With the more active participation of the Roman Catholic Church, the Diocese looked more in that direction for some help and guidance. At first impervious to church cooperation and union, the Roman Catholic Church in general, and the local churches in particular, began to seek out other Churches following Vatican II. As an indication of this, at an Adelphi University service held in the Cathedral in Garden City, which for years was solely Episcopal, all three major faiths were represented. Besides Protestant, Jewish and Episcopal Chaplains, the Roman Church allowed a priest to take part and to preach the sermon. With the Roman Church's interest, ecumenical interchange, informal and seldom publicized, grew in most communities in the Diocese.

A permanent Anglican-Roman Catholic Commission, formed in 1970, gave the movement new direction and understanding in the two Communions, by announcing a substantial agreement on the meaning of the Eucharist.

In 1971 the International Commission unanimously agreed to a statement on the Doctrine of the Ministry. A National Workshop on Church Unity sponsored by the Roman Catholic Church became "the one annual gathering of Episcopalians concerned with ecumenism in the Church" to which the Diocese sent a representative. A cloud descended on the Anglo-Roman ecumenical dialogue with the controversial ordination of women priests. Although some liberal Roman clergy and laity looked to and supported the Church in its expansion of the priesthood, by and large, and in official circles, it threatened the cordial relations between the two. Moreover, the issue was feared as disruptive to the increasing dialogue with the Orthodox Church. Better and closer relations with the Orthodox Church had been a long standing objective in the diocesan pursuit of ecumenism. Bishop Sherman, intensely interested in this area of concern, had risen to national and international prominence in the developing relationship between the two Communions. Since its inception in 1968, he served as the American representative to the Anglican Theological Commission for Joint Doctrinal discussions with the Orthodox. He attended the Anglican-Orthodox Joint Doctrinal Commission that met at Hertford College, Oxford. He also met with Orthodox leaders in Cyprus, joining in the discussions of the promotion of inter-communion between the two Churches. Planning to attend the funeral in Turkey for the Ecumenical Patriarch Athenagoras I, he cancelled his trip as a supportive gesture to the Archbishop, Primate of the Greek Orthodox of North and South America, who was barred from attending. As a diocesan demonstration of ecumenical felicity, and to preserve the presence of all Churches engaged in official ecumenical discussions, the Bishop and the Convention passed in 1970 a resolution to all to send representatives to the Diocesan Convention. The Bishop did his part to make known his stand. As a protest in response to reputed suppression of religious teachings by Soviet authorities in Lithuania, he spoke at St. Patrick's Church, Glen Cove, at a rally and then marched with other religious leaders to the Russian Embassy in Glen Cove.

The ecumenical movement, at first an attempt at Church unity in response to a growing religious pluralism, changed its complexion and its participants with a shift to understanding and cooperation with all religious bodies. In relations with the Jews, dialogue had been hampered by the distinct attitude of Episcopalians to evangelize and convert. Such an attitude which caused aloofness and sometimes hostility to intervene between the understanding of Christians, presented even greater difficulty in the dialogue between Episcopalians and Jews. A Commission on Christian-Jewish Relations, left lapsed, was reactivated following the Diocesan Convention of 1970. The Commission adopted at its beginnings a statement of policy:

> While not denying the obligation of every Christian to bear witness to Jesus as Lord, the Commission emphasizes that its work is the promotion of mutual understanding and goodwill between Christians and Jews, and it rejects any suggestions that its work is to evangelize or convert Jews.

After identifying issues causing tensions between Christians and Jews, the Commission went on to plan seminars and conferences that would help foster a better understanding between the two. In 1971, a lecture and panel forum was held focusing on the topic "A Christian Considers Israel", a discussion of the problems concerning the state of Israel. In 1972, the issue selected for attention was anti-Semitism in the forces of Christian tradition, "Anti-Semitism in the Gospels". After 1974, the Commission restated its policy and purpose, mainly "to establish and maintain an amicable relationship between Christians and Jews on Long Island," based on "mutual understanding of the continuing validity and integrity of our respective religious-cultural traditions." The subject for the current project was an investigation of the inter-religious dimension of religious education. The Commission planned a conference for religious educators on Sunday, April 13, 1975, at which the topic was to be "Jews and Christians; What do we teach about each other? Christians and Jews; What should we teach about each other?"

The Effects of the New Emphases

The Diocese and its constituent parishes were visibly shaken and unalterably affected by the concentration on the social and political problems they attempted to solve. Some of the issues were no more than restatements of abiding theological or social truths, but others, not so easily solved, and more than just controversial, caused deep-seated anger and anguish. By 1973, many churchmen had grown weary of issues and wished to be free of political and social concerns when it came to their church life. People in suburban and rural parishes found it difficult to understand efforts to improve conditions in the Inner City. What all Long Island churchmen understood were the hot issues of women priests and Prayer Book revision. By 1973, the Diocese felt the full effects of the social and political unrest around it. The movement for Black Power began the reaction of the "grass roots" which coupled with the other burning issues of the day, had an adverse effect on diocesan and parish life, creating insurmountable tensions and resulting in two major conditions: credibility gap and a dwindling of diocesan monies.

CAUGHT ON THE REEFS

The Diocese suffered immeasurably from its shift in program emphasis and its proclamation of its new "image". Prolonged confrontation of current issues incubated more problems and fostered deeper tensions,

The group caught in the middle of the power struggle were the clergy. By and large a group of dedicated men, they struggled as best they could for survival in their parishes, trying to accommodate or soften each new issue or tension that fell in the turbulent times. Their battle for survival, sometimes fought alone, sometimes fought with the help of their brother clergy, and their reactions to each new crisis made them more intensely aware of the many inequities that existed in the clerical scale of justice. Except for the chosen few who served in the powerful positions of the Standing Committee (and in turn served as Trustees of the Estate, of Episcopal Charities Appeal, and of the School of Theology), the other elective positions opened to them offered little opportunity for effective decision-making. Their feeling of disenfranchisement was heightened by the chaotic deployment of local clergy into local vacancies. Too often when a parish became vacant few eligible clergy knew about it, and only found out when the vacancy was filled. Especially irksome was the glaring truth that many of the more substantial parish positions went to clergy outside the Diocese. Little mobility was offered the local faithful priest who might move from mission to small parish, or from curate to rector, but always in the parishes that offered less money and influence. An over-abundance of clergy, accentuated by the influx of Mercer School Clergy, who competed in the job market, made the clergy wary and unsettled. Their plight was heightened by the sharp rise of inflation without an accompanying increase in stipend. In fact, many clergy were far below subsistence level, earning as little as $3,000 a year. At the other end were the few more affluent rectors who made as much as $18,000 a year. Inequities in salaries and job opportunities, competition in a sated clergy market, and demotion to a second rate citizenry in decision-making, all widened the already growing rift between the Bishops and the clergy. Deep distrust, frustration and abject uncertainty colored the deteriorating relationship. The Diocese had its own credibility gap.

A renewed interst in some kind of clerical cooperative venture grew out of this tenuous relationship and caused the recandesence of the long standing, not too populous Long Island Clerical League. The clergy had had, since the latter part of the nineteenth century, some form of mutual society. Official and unofficial clerical groups had been formed, sometimes along churchmanship lines, sometimes for special interests. In the past thirty years associations had come and gone, among which was the Seabury Club, the Anglican Society, the American Church Union, and the still active, highly-selective Rector's Club. Each catered to its own members and were bound together by a commonality of interest or position. But there was no central powerful group to whom most of the clergy might look for supportive concern. Open to all the clergy in the Diocese was the quasi-official Long Island Clerical League, a group used mainly for discussions, speakers, and rap-sessions. No real power was inherent in its persons, its structure or its place. Clerical unrest, a national as well as a diocesan phenomena, sought some viable means of expression, and that came to be the Clerical League.

Attempts, formal and informal, on the part of the clergy to bridge the widening gap between the Bishops and the clergy, had proven unsatisfactory and at times frustrating. Special committees on pastoral relations, infiltrating the fiber and weakening the core of diocesan life. Relevancy, a word with different meaning for different groups, touched off a series of enigmas that resulted in more problems. In the diffusion and fragmentation of doubt and uncertainty, two discordant notes became prominent: the polarization of "top management" and "grass roots" and the inordinant use of the word "political". Indicative of the mood of the Diocese and representative of the thinking of many was the voice of Brooklyn. Both clergy and lay people in that Archdeaconry had serious doubts about "closed corporate structures". They asked "embarrassing and erstwhile forbidden questions about Diocesan investments, endowments, trusts and trustees." Current favorite idioms became part of diocesan dialogue, adding a new dimension to the already harassed Diocese. Such expressions as "the establishment", "loss of confidence", "credibility gap", "decision-making", "power struggle" and "distrust" were increasingly used to describe the diocesan climate of opinion. A clue to the undercurrent thought and ideas was found in the Preparatory Commission's publication for the Special Session of the Diocesan Convention to be held in February 1972. Encased in typical phrasings, it stated clearly the temper of the times using such highly colored thoughts as "the restoration of real and meaningful power", "politicized to the highest degree", "wider range of decision makers", and "properly politicized democratic system". In so many words it tackled the problem of control over positions and money. Theoretically it demanded a desirable shift of power from a small elite to a wider more representative group. The real point and "hidden agenda" in such a political ploy was the struggle for power between two bureaucracies within the same system. A power bloc in the Diocese that had gained steadily in influence, although not in numbers, was the coterie around the School of Theology. Opposite to them, and opponent of them, was the small group of chosen officials centered in the Department of Missions. The unhealthy financial situation, set in the confusing circumstances of mistrust and disillusionment, played into the hands of the one power bloc; control of finances, supposedly the province of the elected members of the Convention's executive body, the Diocesan Council, had passed into the control of the non-elected members, with the result that "crucial decisions" came under the guidance of "those few who were in sufficiently authoritative positions to resolve the conflicts as they thought best." In the power struggle, which reached its climax in the election of the Bishop Coadjutor, the "coup" backfired. However, slowly leading up to that crucial moment was a series of "tests", not the least of which was the relationship of the Bishops and the clergy.

conferences and talks with the Bishop, did little to alleviate the situation. Feeling they had no strong ground on which to stand, and looking for some means to make their voice heard, the Clerical League turned political. The results of their efforts was the enshrinement in the Diocesan Canons of their proper place in the Diocese, a specific legal entity known as Canon 24. Initiated by the Clerical League, the Convention in 1971 gave it formal recognition by voting to accept it into the Canons. Incorporating all deacons and priests canonically resident in the Diocese as members, the League had as its purpose:

(1) the furtherance of the profession of the Priesthood as an integral part of the Mission of the Church in the Diocese of Long Island

(2) the provision to the Diocese of a forum to which can be referred all matters relating to the priestly profession

(3) the deepening on the part of the whole Church, of its awareness of its role as the outward sign of the Priesthood of Our Lord Jesus Christ.

An important concern for all clergy was the matter of adequate salaries. The Clerical League originated the move to make some kind of aggressive and forward step in securing adequate compensation for the clergy. Responding to their urging, the Bishop appointed a Commission to study clergy salaries, which undertook a census and made some needed recommendations. Following their report, the 1971 Diocesan Convention adopted a resolution authorizing an increase in the minimum annual salary for the mission clergy from $7,000 to $7,500, effective in 1972. A subsequent annual cost of living increments was highly recommended. Unfortunately the resolution affected only mission clergy salaries. Encouragement of parishes to match the diocesan minimum did not cause widespread salary increases. For the mission clergy, a standing resolution for a cost of living increase assured them a stipend of $9,750. Compared to the national clergy income, the Diocese ranked forty-ninth out of ninety-two dioceses in median income when viewed against the National Bureau of Labor Statistics. In intermediate income for any family on Long Island, the clergy ranked ninetieth in regard to clergy salaries around the country. The Bishop, by exhortation and letter, attempted to encourage parishes to match the diocesan minimum and consider cost of living increases. Some did respond, but not in any overwhelming numbers.

The overplus of ordained clergy created a climate of anxiety, especially for those men between forty-five and fifty-five who found themselves locked into positions they had served for some time. Parish autonomy in selecting its rector created many problems which even the Bishops did not overcome. To standardize the calling process, besides the canonical notification of vacant parishes, a procedure was set forth that included a parish profile, an assessment of parish goals, and a personal data questionnaire for a priest interviewed. The clergy became computerized when the Presiding Bishop pushed the first button to produce a profile for the newly established National Clerical Deployment Office. A Diocesan counterpart was opened. The clergy had now become a series of numbers.

THE ROCK OF NO FUNDS

A most noticeable effect of the issue-centered program came in lessened giving and insufficient funds, a problem which had to some degree plagued the Diocese since its inception. The problem was not so evident in the area of the upkeep of the episcopate, known as the Diocesan Assessment, since it carried penalities for parish non-payment; the direct evidence was in the area of the Missionary Objective or Quota, a voluntary giving of monies to support the program of the Diocesan Council. The Missionary Committee, back in the early years of the Diocese, had struggled to raise funds for mission programs. In each succeeding decade the giving fluctuated, affording expansive work in periods of affluence and cutbacks in times of financial stricture. The devastating effect of the "Great Depression" had been finally overcome by the time of Bishop DeWolfe's episcopate. The Diocese continued on the high wave of sound financial backing, but that situation changed drastically after 1969.

The Commission on the Ingathering of the Quota had reported in 1967 on the approaching problem of insufficient funds. "Lending urgency to the efforts of the Commission was a decrease in receipts for 1966, to an amount representing only 70% of the assigned quota." The situation seemed calm compared to the following years. National crises and the Stock Market collapse of 1970, with its incumbent recession, coupled with the angry reactions to the Black demands for reparation, played havoc with parochial support of the diocesan program. By 1970, the situation before the whole Church and before the Diocese was critical. Cuts in missionary support required the National Executive Council to slash its budget by more than one million dollars. The Diocese of Long Island for two years contributed only $175,000 of the $430,000 assigned to it. The Diocese was in such bad straits that on the basis of anticipated receipts it could only pledge $50,000. As of May 1, 1970, the diocesan program had $14,000 less than the former year's receipts in the Missionary Objective. A warning by the Bishops that it might be necessary to cancel some diocesan programs and some work of the Diocesan Council Departments, added to the seriousness of the situation. The attrition of funds was accelerated by the withholding of funds from the Diocese as a reaction against the radical programs of the G.C.S.P., whose "undemocratic, uncanonical, congregational" action threatened the "episcopal ethos," and was extremely "divisive" to the Body of the Church. At its March meeting, the Diocesan Council voted to engage the Diocese in a special September campaign to make up what was lacking, in order to reach at least the $175,000 minimum. The Convention, acting upon the suggestion, did not approve. A report on the Council and Bishop's plan for raising the needed money, stated that sharing "the pain" caused by those withholding Missionary Funds because of their opposition to the Church's involvement in social activism, they though it "ill advised" to conduct a fund drive until goals and objectives were clearly defined.

Other causes also had contributed to the financial plight. The economy confronted every parochial unit with rapidly escalating costs during a period when there had been a general decline in church attendance and the number of contributions. One factor involved was that the time was one of "decentralization" when an increasing numbers of members proudly and honestly questioned not only the diocesan program, but also diocesan priorities. The Diocesan Council considered the "special campaign" prospect and made a "wise and right decision" by rejecting it. They favored raising the necessary cash through the normal channels "democratically" approved by the Diocesan Convention. By February 1972, the situation worsened. The Treasurer, Mr. Kenneth W. Miller, successor to the Rev. Mr. Mears, informed the Diocesan Council that they faced a deficit of $70,000, calling for a 12% slash in the total missionary program, including an already decreased commitment to the work of the National Church, the work of the departments, and possibly mission priests' salaries. The Bishop tried to encourage support and interest in subscribing to the deficit. In his address to the Convention he tellingly stated:

> With 70,255 Communicants and 103,562 Church members listed in our 1971 Journal, can any
> member of this Convention tell me that it is beyond our capacity to raise $70,000 for the
> Mission of Jesus Christ, starting at home, and reaching out into all the world.

The answer to this and other questions lay in the work of a special convention and its preparatory commission.

At the May 1971 Convention a suggestion from a regional meeting of clergy and laity from the Huntington-Port Jefferson area was considered. They proposed that a special diocesan convention be held in February 1972 to consider the financial crisis and the whole range of diocesan finances, with a preparatory commission to plan fully the convention. The suggestion became a reality when the 1971 Diocesan Convention approved the plan and set February 5, 1972, as the day for the special session.

The Commission, composed of five lay persons and six presbyters, began meeting on May 24, 1971, and held regular meetings up to the time of the special session. After analyzing a consolidated balance sheet to determine what assets there were, determining what was "liquid" and what was "locked up" in special funds or real estate, they explored other methods of raising funds used by other dioceses. Then, in the form of a lengthy report, they made their startling innovative suggestions. Their proposals did not touch the matter of diocesan program priorities, but a new process of budgetary action. Their recommendations simply stated were direct: a single budget for all diocesan expenses, balanced against known pledges and other income for the then current year. Up to this time the financial system was based upon a double budget, which had developed historically from two major funds, the Missionary Committee's fund and the Episcopal Fund. The two had gone through several transformations, but had come to the point where they still retained their individual identity as the Missionary (Quota) Objective and the Diocesan Assessment. The Diocesan Assessment, primarily for the upkeep of the episcopate, had enlarged to include all salaries, housing and expenses of secretarial staffs, business offices and related matters. There was a penalty if the assessment was not paid. All other Diocesan expenses came under the Missionary Objective, which included Archdeacons' and mission priests' salaries, Diocesan Council Department budgets and related matters. There was no penalty attached to non-payment of the latter, hence one was obligatory, one optional. One was a sheltered budget in which everything proposed was accomplished, and the other was exposed to the whims of payment. If endowments came to the Diocese they were poured into the asset side of the sheltered budget. To overcome this disparity, a single budget was proposed that included all items of the Diocesan Assessment, all proposed programs of the Missionary Objective, and the work of the Episcopal Charities Appeal. The single budget was to be kept in matching total expenditures against a reasonable expectation of support. The guide for parochial support was to be the current expenses rather than income. The budget was to be voted upon as near the beginning of the year prescribed as could be. Former practices meant that in the summer of 1971, for instance, the Diocesan Council would begin planning for 1973, leaving a one and a half year interval within which conditions might change to alter or correct the proposed budget. Finally, there would be no tax but a free will offering; that is there was to be a single uniform stewardship asking for all units, based upon a 25% amount of local current expense.

There was much canonical revision and amendment involved in making the plan a viable means of diocesan support. Canon 15 of the Committee of Diocesan Finance needed revision, calling for the replacement of the Committee on Diocesan Finance by an elected Committee on Program and Budget, the chief agency of the Convention whose responsibility was a balanced budget, the "last responsible agency short of the Convention itself." Also Canon 15, the former Committee on Delinquent Diocesan Units, was converted into a new and enlarged Committee on Stewardship. The Preparatory Commission also recommended a revision of Canon 13, so as to remove all staff persons except the Bishop and Treasurer from the Diocesan Council, and also make it smaller in number. The heads of the various Council Departments were to come from the Council membership. The Council also had the responsibility of initiating the budgetary process through its Finance Committee, submitting it to the Program and Budget Committee for balancing and adjustments. A clear timetable of the way in which more persons were to be involved depended on the recommendations of changing the day of the Diocesan Convention from the third Tuesday in May to the third Saturday in February.

The Special Session of the 104th Diocesan Convention was held on February 5, 1972, in Garden City according to the tight schedule of the Commission. The Convention approved basically the budgetary plan with an exception. When the Convention considered the Canon on Episcopal Charities Appeal, an amendment was made, seconded and passed, deleting that section that put E.C.A. directly under the umbrella budget. The movement to control E.C.A. had come this far but had failed. E.C.A. continued on as it did in the past, canvassing not only outside gifts, but also parishes and missions in the Diocese. The plan, as amended, was presented to the regular session of the Diocesan Convention on May 16, 1972. It passed as amended, and so became the diocesan form for raising and allocating monies.

With the new process in hand, the campaign to raise the budget began. Hearings were held in counties in October and November. A preliminary program and budget of $1,298,386 was sent to the Committee on Program and Budget, which was balanced against pledges from churches and other income. In the year 1973, only $701,610 was raised; $44,600 less than the amount pledged. In 1974, the amount raised was $697,951; $25,155 less than the amount pledged.

Because of decreased giving, stringent measures had to be taken. Paring the budget to expected income meant only one thing: the ax had to fall, with some department heads being dismissed and the departments being manned on a voluntary basis. Among the departments being cut were Educational Ministries, Communications, Stewardship, Christian Social Relations, and under the Bishop, the position of Clerical Assistant. The Department of Educational Ministries (formerly the Departments of Youth, College and Christian Education) had experienced a change of leadership before. Canon Davis, for almost twenty years Director of Youth, College and Camp DeWolfe, had resigned in September 1968, to assume the duties of Rector at Historic St. George's Church in Hempstead. The post was left vacant until 1970, when it was filled, but only for a short time. By the spring of 1973, the post was again vacated, and administration of the department was in the hands of volunteers. Mr. John Mead, Director of Diocesan Relations, found employment in the National Seabury Press. Mr. Fred Long soon left, as did the Rev. Louis Ferrara. They were joined soon by the Rev. Donald Latham, Clerical Assistant to the Bishop, who became the Rector of the Church of the Ascension, Rockville Centre. The paid staff positions of Archdeacons weathered the storm, their office being termed Program Assistant and Archdeacon. The winnowing of paid staff members found completion in the resignation of the Archdeacon of Suffolk, who became the Rector of Caroline Church, Setauket. Bishop Martin, faithful worker in the Diocese, also departed from the Diocese and assumed duties in 1974 at the National Executive Council in New York. By the middle of 1974, the Diocesan staff consisted of the Bishop, the Senior Suffragan, soon to retire in 1975, and the Program Assistant and Archdeacon of Queens and Nassau. The Diocese had radically changed. In a strict adherence to budgetary principles it had lost much of its manpower and its strength.

BEAMS FROM THE LIGHTHOUSE

No one single event had such a telling influence on the Diocese than the Anglican Congress held in 1963 in Toronto, Canada. The Congress, attended by ecclesiastical representatives from all over the world, issued a call to all churches. It formally called upon all churches and diocesans to take up the task of overhauling structure and evaluating program. The Rt. Rev. Stephen F. Bayne, Jr., executive officer for the Congress, alerted all churches via the Seabury Publication, *Mutual Responsibilities and Interdependence in the Body of Christ*, stating clearly that "the time has come when this unity and interdependence must find a completely new level of expression and corporate obedience." He reported the findings of the Congress which firmly recommended "that every Church begin at once a radical study of its own obedience to Mission. Included in this should be a study of its structure, of its theology of mission, and of its priorities in decision." The General Convention, meeting at St. Louis, Missouri, in October 1964, made a response to the report and heartily endorsed it for use in all dioceses. To implement the M.R.I. program in the Diocese of Long Island, a special Commission was appointed in January 1965, with the then Suffragan Bishop Sherman as Chairman. On his election as diocesan, the Bishop turned over the direction of the Commission to Archdeacon and then Bishop Martin.

Companion Diocese —

One of the ways in which M.R.I. was to be operable was for each diocese to have a partner diocese. The Diocese of Long Island elected to have a companion relationship with the domestic Diocese of Southern Ohio. From meetings, conferences and visits, a new viewpoint on the planning process was shared by the two. As an overseas partner the Diocese accepted responsibility for certain Projects for Partnership in the Province of Uganda, Central Africa, known as the Province of the Martyrs. With gifts from the Episcopal churchwomen, Confirmation offerings, Mite Box offerings and special parish gifts, Long Island helped Uganda in funding such projects as training of women workers, of radio and television personnel, the purchase of a jeep for the supervision of the women's work, and scholarships for theological education at Bishop Tucker College. In 1973, the companion diocese was changed. At the May 1972 meeting of the Diocesan Council, Bishop Sherman appointed a special committee "to explore and make a recommendation" of a new companion diocese. Two dioceses out of six were considered: Nassau and the Bahamas, and the Diocese of Colombia, South America. The two suggested companion dioceses were presented to the Council and Colombia was chosen. A resolution approving an M.R.I. companion relationship between Long Island and Colombia was moved, seconded and passed at the Diocesan Convention in February 1973, with the proviso that after three years a review and renewal be made by both dioceses. As a beginning to the new relationship, the Rev. Guillermo Marquez, a Colombian priest, came to work in the Diocese, and Fr. Louis Quiroga, himself a Colombian and priest in Long Island, escorted a group of Long Island Episcopalians on a tour of Colombia.

Structural Change —

The M.R.I. Commission, acting under the mandate and authority of the Anglican Congress, the General Convention, the Diocesan Convention, and the Diocesan Council, proceeded to examine the structures and forms governing the corporate life of the Diocese. The first structure scrutinized was the annual Convention. The Commission recognized the annual gathering as the legislative body, but detected that it was "also the family of God, meeting to do God's business." It, like every other diocesan structure promoted the peculiar fellowship, unity and involvement that belonged to the Body of Christ. The Commission wrote into the purpose of the Convention: fellowship, maximum participation and involvement, and frank dealing with current problems resulting in clearly defined policy. They proposed certain changes in the format of the Convention, especially the changing of the date of the Convention to the third Saturday in October. An Ad Hoc Committee on the structure and function of the Diocesan Council was also appointed. Some of the proposed changes in the Convention format were accepted. The Convention began in 1969 at the new hour suggested, had a light lunch and heard the Bishop's address and budget report before lunch. The awarding of the Distinguished Service Crosses, and other awards, was dropped from the order of business. No evening banquet, as suggested, became a reality, nor did October become the month for the annual meeting. Upstaged by the Preparatory Commission, the changed annual date was February, not October.

The Ad Hoc Committee on the Diocesan Council took three years to germinate its findings. Under the leadership of Bishop MacLean opinions were gathered, studies made, and suggestions accepted. Feeling now ran high that the Council was an entity to itself instead of performing its accepted role of interim body between Conventions, subject to Conventions. When the Council on its own merit made some radical decisions on controversial issues, many in the Diocese took offense. The membership of the Council and the dominance of non-elected members also was carefully examined. The result of the Committee's findings were presented to the 1971 Convention as an amendment to Canon 13 of the Diocesan Council. The amended canon, as adapted on May 18, 1971, clearly stated that the duty of the Council was "to carry out the program and the policies adopted by the Diocesan Convention." It had charge of the unification development and prosecution of the Church. It also served as "the program planning and policy making body" between sessions of the Convention. In no case did the Council have the power to reverse any action of the Diocesan Convention or consider any matter tabled by the Convention. The membership of the Council was shorn of its non-elected members, except for the Archdeacons. It consisted of the Bishop, Archdeacons and ten clergy and ten laity elected by Diocesan Convention, and one clergyman and one lay person elected by each Archdeaconry. The Council also had the responsibility of forming a long range planning Committee "for the ongoing review of the work of the Council, its program and its planning process," composed of four Council members and six chosen from the Diocese at large. The membership of the Diocesan Council was enlarged according to the provisions of the Canon. A highly innovative step was taken when the Department of Missions was also enlarged from its small clique to include lay and clerical representatives from each Archdeaconry.

Growing out of the M.R.I. structural change was the emergence of the Long Range Planning Committee. Under the chairmanship of the Rev. Albert H. Palmer, the Committee began an exhaustive survey of the Archdeaconry system. Understanding that there was some need for a system that afforded an exchange of ideas, guidance, physical assistance, direction, funding and flow of information, the Committee questioned the whole intent and performance of the Archdeaconry system. They felt a need for a clarification of the Archdeacon's role, the establishment of definite goals, and the inclusion of all parish units, who by self-exclusion had created a gap in performance. Two alternatives were examined by the Committee: a strengthened Archdeaconry system or a so-called regional approach. Gathering all their material together, the Planning Committee's program was delayed by the absorption of the Diocese in the Budgetary process. Ready to present their plan in 1974, it was further delayed by the executive session of the Bishop with his clergy in February 1974.

Another major structural change, not initiated by either the M.R.I. Commission or the Long Range Planning Committee, but by the General Convention, was the establishment of a Commission on Ministry. For many years, theological students studying for Holy Orders, appeared before a Board of Examining Chaplains, who examined them in specific fields of study, and if they approved, prepared and delivered to the Bishop and Standing Committee all required canonical certificates and forms. Replacing the old Canon 23 of the Board of Examining Chaplains, the Diocesan Convention in May 1971 adapted a new canon entitled, "Of the Commission on Ministry." The new Commission included not only priests, but also lay persons nominated by the Bishop, who "at the direction of the Bishop, the conduct and evaluation of the examination of persons for Holy Orders was assigned to the Commission on Ministry, the said Commission shall make all reports required by the Canons." Exclusively the domain of the clergy, postulants and candidates for Holy Orders now came before both clergy and laity, who had the task of determining both personal and theological fitness of those presented to them.

CHARTERED WATERS

In spite of discouraging financial strictures, seeming apathy and .confusing diocesan structures; the Diocese continued, as it had since 1869, its three pronged offensive in the fields of education, charitable works, and missionary extension. Each area took on a new perspective: in education, response to a new movement, and the establishment of new entity; in charitable works, the enlargement of facilities and the enhancement of services rendered; in missionary extension, the emphasis on community outreach and the accommodation to a radically changed community.

Education —

The drive for the proposed Episcopal High School continued until the fall of 1966. An elaborate system of committees was set up to undertake a diocesan-wide campaign to raise funds for the project. All seemed in readiness to proceed. But in the evaluation of the situation, it seemed wise both to the Bishop and those interested to cancel the drive and proceed in another direction. Frustration resulting from difficulties associated with the site itself caused discouragement, and so the plan was dropped.

Because of an increasing role in education, both in the Diocese and parishes, a new thrust had to be made. In his address to the 1967 Diocesan Convention, Bishop Sherman stated that the initial steps had been taken to establish an overall Episcopal Foundation for Education, the purpose of which was "the overall planning for Christian Education in Long Island as we move into our second century." On May 31, 1967, the Episcopal Foundation for Education was duly incorporated under the State Laws of New York. Its purpose was,

> to assist in developing, supervising and coordinating programs for education in the parishes and missions of the Diocese; to assist in the orderly development of Parish Day Schools and other educational facilities; to promote a program for graduate fellowships in education for clergy and laity of the Diocese of Long Island, but not necessarily limited thereto; to collect and receive funds for the educational work of the Church in the Diocese of Long Island.

The Foundation did not have the power to operate any educational institution. Headed by the Bishop, it had twelve trustees, six appointed by the Bishop and six elected by the Diocesan Convention. A new Canon 28 regularized the Foundation's place in diocesan life.

The phenomena of parochial day schools on Long Island was most noteworthy. Nationally in the years since 1963, there had been a 72% increase in pupils. Total enrollment increased yearly, with the largest increase in the nursery and day care levels. Erratic development demanded some kind of overall direction. In 1967, the Bishop issued a long list of standards for certification of Episcopal Schools in the Diocese. A Division of Boarding and Day Schools, the Department of Christian Education, and the Episcopal Schools Association, was joined in May 1970 by a Commission on Boarding and Day Schools. Established by the Diocesan Convention, it set to administer standards for certification. An Episcopal School within the Diocese was defined as "any school sponsored by a parish or Diocesan unit, offering daily curriculum of studies embodying any of the grades, kindergarten through grade twelve." They also had the responsibility of adapting a program of certification for both nursery and grade schools. They administered the Diocesan Standardized Testing Program. Ultimate control of the school, it was assumed, rested with the rector, wardens and vestry, or with the Bishop in the case of a diocesan unit.

The unfortunate death of the Rev. Dr. E. Frederic Underwood on April 24, 1969, caused adjustments to be made in the overall direction of the educational program of the Diocese. Dr. Underwood, until his death, served as the Rector of the Episcopal Schools of St. Mary's and St. Paul's, the Campaign Director for the Episcopal High School, and the Director of the Department of Christian Education. To give better direction to the overall educational program, under the aegis of the Episcopal Foundation for Education, the Office of Boarding and Day Schools was established. Created on August 1, 1969, a director was appointed a month later. Mr. Robert C. Courtemache of Massapequa took up the duties of directing the whole program of counsel and assistance to the many parish day schools. Under his leadership a research and review of current materials used by the New York State Board of Regents and State Accrediting Bodies was made. A Diocesan Cooperative Purchasing Guide was set up, affording educational units in the Diocese as much as 50% discount on materials needed. He served as liaison officer to the National Association of Episcopal Schools and coordinated activities for the Long Island Episcopal Schools Association. Outstanding were the Episcopal School Days, at which some 4,000 children attended from thirty-six and then forty schools. Helpful too were the all-day conferences and workshops for teachers and staffs of the local parish schools. Mr. Courtemanche resigned in March 1973, and was succeeded on a part-time basis by Dr. William Atkins, Associate Dean of the Hofstra School of Education.

The Cathedral Schools of St. Paul's and St. Mary's made some needed improvements and additions to their respective physical plants. In 1969 the cornerstone was laid for Ellis Hall at St. Paul's School, a wing on the main building that included a modern library, laboratories, classrooms, as well as equipment and storage space. On May 11, 1968, with Dean Emeritus Mary H. Russell present, the new wing, consisting of library, assembly hall and twenty classrooms, at St. Mary's School was dedicated. Miss Russell, Dean of St. Mary's since 1937, was followed by Miss Martha K. Robbins, who was elected Principal in 1969. Leaving in 1972, she was followed by Mr. John B. Walmsley, who took up his duties as Principal of St. Mary's School. St. Paul's School prospered under the Headmastership of Dr. Claude C. Casey. Dr. Casey was recognized as a leader of one of the top fifty boarding and day schools. St. Paul's received recognition as an outstanding prep school in *Town and Country Magazine.*

Forecasts of tremendous growth in the field of higher education, a 40,000 to 124,000 increase in college students by 1985, made the Diocese do some long range planning in this "priority" area. In the summer of 1966, the Bishop appointed a Commission on Higher Education composed of clergy, professors and college administrators. A beginning in the field was made by the appointment of a priest by Bishop DeWolfe, under an arrangement with the National Executive Council, to work with the faculty members of Brooklyn College and explore the whole concept of the Church's ministry to the campus. The Commission recommended close cooperation while maintaining respectful detachment with the New York-centered Ecumenical Foundation, a college and university oriented work. They also recommended the appointment of a canon theologian to personalize and represent diocesan concern in the academic field. Confusion of purpose and lack of sufficient funds not only negated any kind of canon theologian, but also forced the departure of the college worker in Brooklyn. In 1969, the Diocese engaged in the cooperative Stony Brook project. The mushrooming State University at Stony Brook caused local religious groups to look for some way in which to minister meaningfully to the university students. Since the Diocese owned a large piece of property near the campus, it seemed ideal that if and when a full time "Center for Religion and Society" be established with a full-time director, the property be used for that purpose. A series of meetings and discussions involving university administrators, diocesan officials, and local clergy were held, but nothing materialized.

The School of Theology continued its education of pre-theological and theological students. One of the needed requirements for accredidation by the New York State Board of Regents was an adequate library. In May 1973, construction began on an addition to and a re-arrangement of the already existing library facilities. A two-level reading room with space for 75,000 volumes, (large enough to serve as an auditorium as well), an enlarged lunch room, student lounge, new quarters for the diocesan bookstore, an adequate office for the Dean, and additional classrooms were part of the plan. The buildings were formally dedicated by the Bishop in 1975.

In April 1970, a group of Long Island churchmen became deeply concerned about increasing state aid to parochial schools and the implications of such aid for the historic and unique American concept of separation of church and state. In May of that year, by a two to one vote, the delegates at the Diocesan Convention passed a resolution to urge, for that time, the retention of Article XI, Section III of the Constitution of the State of New York. The Diocese, like most other religious groups, including the Roman Catholics, favored the retention of the article known as the Blaine amendment. The amendment forbade the use of public funds "in aid or maintenance" to any religious school or institution. It did promise, however, "for the transportation of children to and from any school or institution of learning."

A sad loss in the program of the Department of Christian Education was the discontinuance of Cathedral Day. At its October meeting in 1968 the Diocesan Council voted to stop the annual children's event. Because it had become largely a project for Brooklyn children, with other church children in the Diocese not attending, the whole purpose of the day seemed lost, and so any future Cathedral Days were cancelled.

Charitable Work —

The annual appeal for the all-encompassing fund, Episcopal Charities Appeal, prospered even in the face of adverse economic conditions. In 1968, the Appeal's endowment funds had reached $2,200,000. The annual drive for funds had grown from $309,942.47 in 1969 to $387,417.93 in 1974. Under the general chairmanship of Carl V. Brandebury and Carl Fischer, with such mottoes as "Every Cry Answered," "More in '72," or "Reach for a Star," the Appeal produced more and more support from local parishes and outside sources. The monies raised, as in the past, helped its three beneficiaries, the Bishop's Call, the Youth Consultation Service and the Church Charity Foundation.

The Church Charities Foundation improved and expanded its health care facilities. On August 20, 1966, St. John's Hospital in Smithtown was formally dedicated. By September 19, it began receiving patients, and on May 8, 1967, had full capacity. The existing facilities at St. John's Hospital in Brooklyn received needed expansion and modernization. A sixth floor was added to the building, increasing the hospital's bed capacity by sixty-two. The former School of Nursing building was renovated to house the Out-patient Department, Emergency Room and laboratories. The Foundation continued its Home for the Aged and the Blind. It added to its health services a Psychiatric Clinic, a double unit Methadone Clinic in Brooklyn, and in cooperation with the New York City Health Department, an Ambulatory Care Unit at Brooklyn's Bedford Health Center. Plans were formulated to expand the Foundation's program to include nursing homes and to establish health care facilities in Queens and Nassau. One possible location considered was the Hempstead General Hospital and Nursing Home.

The Youth Consultation Service, recognized leader in the field of social work agencies, added a broadened dimension to its ministry with the incorporation into its services of "Satellites" in the Babylon-Islip area and in

Westhampton Beach. The qualified staff concentrated its efforts in the crucial area of supportive case work with families where children were in great jeopardy because of pressures of poverty and lower income.

In Nassau County the agency sponsored a Day Activity Center at St. George's Church, Hempstead, where recovering schizophrenics between the ages of fifteen and thirty took the next step from hospitalization to continuing education and vocation. In 1968, the agency celebrated its fiftieth anniversary of service to the Diocese. A continued evaluation and reshaping of its services made the agency rethink its priorities and redirect its program. Indicative of this, the 1973 Annual Meeting of the agency voted to change its name to the Family Consultation Service.

MISSIONARY OUTREACH

Diocesan expectations for missionary expansion and church extension were high in 1966. Following the lead and forecast of Island planning groups, census takers and demographic prognosticators, the Diocese "tooled up" to meet and minister to the future population explosion. The seven and one half million people, four and one half in Brooklyn and Queens, the rest in Nassau and Suffolk Counties, was slated to double in size by 1980. Downtown Brooklyn as a center of employment; the Brooklyn Navy Yard industrially developed; an increase of 800,000 jobs on the Island; expansion of office buildings, large campuses, and large apartment houses: all were painted in glowing colors as part of the future of Long Island. The Diocese of Long Island, already ranking fifth in the National Church statistics of clergy, baptized members, communicants, and finances, had the potential of increasing and surpassing all bounds. In the face of the prospective growth, the top priority for the Church was "long range planning." The Planning Process, "the methodology," by which a Diocese sought to "define and to articulate its goals in obedience to mission and to involve maximum participation of its personal resources, clergy and laity, with a particular emphasis on lay expertise," in the implementation of those goals was to be paramount. Process demanded constant reference to what was happening in terms of social change — urbanization, cybernation, poverty, education, housing, employment, social conflict — with a constant resort to experts and decision makers in government, education, health and business and economics.

Gearing up for the tremendous task, the Department of Missions and the Diocesan Council made certain adjustments. Clarifying the role of the Archdeacon, which came under close scrutiny, and adverse criticism, the Diocese amended Canon 13 on missionary operations, updating the archaisms, and spelling out the Archdeacon's duties as "oversight of the Missionary work in his Archdeaconry" and the coordination and administration of all work of the Archdeaconry. Control by the Department of Missions over mission churches was firmly and unequivocally set. The Bishop and the Department issued a "directive" that no repairs be made to mission properties without the Bishop's approval. They, together, set a policy that required all building funds, endowment funds, and special funds in excess of $500.00 be deposited with the Department for safe keeping in a savings account. Funds were withdrawn only upon request of the Archdeacon, the priest-in-charge and the local Executive Committee. The policy practiced in regard to aided parishes became law with the approval of Canon 67 by the Diocesan Convention in 1968. Under the new canon aided parishes of three years duration lost their parochial autonomy and became, in essence, a diocesan mission. They had to transfer the title of all real estate, endowment and trust funds to the Trustees of the Estate, to be administered by them and the Bishop. All policies applicable to diocesan missions applied to them as well. If an aided parish, giving assurance of stable life and finances, applied for parish status, and once more became autonomous, all properties were to be returned to them. The canon became effective January 1, 1969. Its usefulness was fully demonstrated.

The Archdeaconry of Brooklyn: Quandary —

Because of the times Brooklyn's slated growth did not materialize. In fact, it more likely approached the forecast of the National Urban Coalition which predicted that by 1980 most cities would be "black, brown and bankrupt." The non-white population of New York State tripled, making up 10.1% of its population. Most non-whites were concentrated in the New York area and in Brooklyn, but the spread of non-whites had branched out onto Long Island, increasing no less than 47%. In face of the "flight to the suburbs," deteriorating neighborhoods, tightened federal funds, and a decreasing interest in cities and urban problems, the Archdeaconry of Brooklyn struggled valiantly to fulfill its mission. Strategy for urban mission included joint team ministries, cooperative use of buildings, cooperative community planning, and sharing human resources. Termed by the Archdeacon, Bishop Martin, as "one of the most blighted boroughs," it was not able to afford the "luxury" of parochialism and inter-parish rivalries. Indicting the Church for erecting too many buildings, he averred the only course of action made possible was closing, clustering, merging or consolidating church properties. Sale of property accrued few lasting benefits to the churches of Brooklyn. True, there were many strong and healthy churches ministering to their neighborhoods with three — St. George's, St. Mark's and St. Philip's, MacDonough Street — having well over eleven hundred communicants. Others made up in spirit what they did not have in numbers. But, on the whole, the Archdeaconry fought for its survival. Of thirty-eight congregations in Brooklyn, sixteen or 47% in varying degrees received assistance from the Department of Missions.

Such conditions found relief in the consolidation or closing of churches. In 1970, Church of the Holy Family, the Spanish speaking congregation moved from its own building to Church of the Holy Trinity. Then it

*(right) Confirmation at St. Philip's,
McDonough Street in Brooklyn.
(below) The Senior and Junior
Suffragans, The Rt. Rev. Charles
W. MacLean and The Rt. Rev.
Richard B. Martin.*

moved to Christ Church, Clinton Street. On December 6, 1970, it applied for mission status and became the mission church of Christ Church and the Holy Family, using the relinquished Christ Church plant. St. John the Baptist Church, for a while, shared its building with the Ocean Parkway Methodist Church, and shared a priest with Emmanuel Church. It soon disappeared. In the fall of 1969, the Rector of Trinity, East New York, became the Vicar of St. Lydia's. A closing of prominence was the official cessation of St. Ann's Church, the mother church of Brooklyn. Its members and activities transferred in 1969 to the Church of the Holy Trinity, which became the Diocesan Church. The Holy Trinity parish hall, "nerve center" of church life in Brooklyn housed the Suffragan Bishop's office, the Long Island Assembly of the Brotherhood of St. Andrew's, the Diocesan Department of Christian Social Relations, Episcopal Guild for the Blind, and the Guild for the Deaf. A joint ministry between St. Matthew's, Woodhaven in Queens and Transfiguration in Brooklyn afforded little hope for the Brooklyn Church. On September 12, 1971 it closed. Church of the Epiphany struggling for so many years closed on October 30, 1970, its membership transferred to St. Simon's.

A rash of fires played havoc with some Brooklyn churches. On August 22, 1966, a fire gutted St. John's, Fort Hamilton. Due to the efforts and labors of its Rector and congregation, the church was beautifully rebuilt. At the beginning of 1969, a fire totally destroyed the Church of the Messiah and Incarnation. At first the congregation worshipped in the local Roman Catholic Church, but when there seemed no hope of rebuilding the congregation joined nearby St. Mary's Church. In 1969, St. Augustine's Church was destroyed by fire. On August 30, 1970, ground was broken for a new church, but finally the congregation purchased a large abandoned Roman Catholic Church.

Community outreach was shown in the ingenious use of existing church buildings. Under Title 7 Older Americans Act, non-profit organizations had the opportunity to provide meals for Senior Citizens. Such programs were started at St. John's, Fort Hamilton, and at All Saints Church. The work included not only serving meals, but meals taken out to shut-ins, arts and crafts, social activities. St. John's served 175 and All Saints, 180. St. George's, Brooklyn, instituted a nutrition program for those over sixty years of age, including hot meals for shut-ins as well as meals served on the premises. St. Andrew's Church, Fourth Avenue, undertook a program for children, initiating a Day Care Center. St. John's Church, St. John's Place, sponsored in part the Park Slope Improvement Corporation which, in addition to its rehabilitation of brownstones and 102 low rent dwelling units, had a day care center; Bishop Martin served on its board. The Church of St. Michael and St. Mark helped its local area by offering its facilities to the Board of Education for its use. Housing for the elderly found a resource in Messiah and Incarnation. The 80-86 Greene Avenue Corporation, an ecumenical, non-profit group, had the option of using the church property as the site for multiple apartments. The Absalom Jones Corporation worked at the same purpose of M-1 site housing for the Brownsville-East New York area and the rehabilitation of residential units in Brooklyn.

The Archdeaconry of Queens and Nassau: Quiescence —

Missionary enterprise in Queens and Nassau came almost to a standstill. Saturated with buildings, both residential and commerical, with no room for expansion, the parishes and missions within its confines had to adjust to difficult situations and transient congregations. Queens County reflected more and more the urban influence, coping as best it could. The population influx to Nassau County had stabilized with almost a million and a half people living within its borders. By 1970, agriculture had all but disappeared, and the only large patches of green remained in some areas of the North Shore. Older and more settled Nassau communities such as the Village of Hempstead, experienced urban renewal with huge apartment complexes and federally funded low and middle income housing, and senior citizen apartments. All churches, whether mission or parish, suffered from less financial support and fewer parishioners. In 1965, church membership in the Queens and Nassau churches stood at 68,475; by 1974 it had reached a low of 44,047. As an indication of this trend, Grace Church in Massapequa in 1965 had 3,280 members, with 510 children in its Church School; by 1974 the number was cut in half to 1,575 members and 177 in the Church School. Zion in Douglaston had 745 members in 1965; by 1974 it had been cut to 351; St. George's, Flushing had a membership of 1,408 in 1965; by 1974 it had 1,033. St. Francis, Levittown in 1965 had 856; by 1974, there were 425 members. The Cathedral, always large, lost 1,000 members in the same period, its Church School shrinking from 800 in 1965 to 436 in 1974. With less members and financial strictures pressing upon every church, some long standing mission churches had to close. Five missions were closed; with another on the way. St. Mary's, Auburndale, closed, its members going to St. Margaret's, Fresh Meadows; Trinity, Elmont, its members joining St. James the Just, Franklin Square; St. Andrew's, Ozone Park, its membership scattered. In 1970, St. Andrew's, Belle Harbor, joined the list of closed churches. St. Stephen's, South Ozone Park, was "phased out." St. John's Church, Far Rockaway, consolidated with nearby Trinity, Hewlett.

Some unusual community outreach programs began in this period. Novel and contemporary was the Chaplaincy at the Protestant Chapel at J. F. Kennedy International Airport. In the late spring of 1966 Episcopal services were begun at 12:10 p.m. The Diocese and the New York Council of Churches provided the necessary funds to secure a chaplain, and one of the priests from the nearby parish began duties as such. Unusual too was a work begun by Church of the Annunciation in Glendale. An experimental work with a two-year senior citizen's program grew into the Glenridge Senior Citizens Center. A great blow to the Diocese came at St. James Church, Elmhurst. One of the original colonial parishes it suffered a setback when fire completely gutted its old building. Fire also played havoc with St. Clement's Church, Baldwin Harbor. It burned out in 1966 and a new structure was soon constructed. A special ministry appeared at Grace Church, Jamaica. Under the leadership of the Rev. Eugenio N. Loreto, services for a Filipino congregation were held regularly, being said in the Tagalog language, using the Misang Filipino.

In the light of such circumstances, the response of the Archdeaconry was limited and at times sparse. Theorizing, the Archdeacon gave such answers as he could:

> The need is to develop a process that will develop skills which will be helpful in generating a remedy for on-going renewal . . . There is no right set of answers . . . the Archdeaconry is the regional system for Episcopalians . . . Let us all join the decision-making process and labor together.

The Archdeaconry of Suffolk: Quintessence —

Of all four counties in Long Island, Suffolk offered the most promise. In 1960 Suffolk had fewer inhabitants than its neighbor, Nassau; by 1970 it had gained three and a half times more residents, jumping from 666,784 to 1,127,030. The concentration of population was in the five western towns accounting for 90.2% of the total county's population. Population growth slowed dramatically after 1970. Adverse economic conditions, inflation, high interest mortgages and recession caused a slump in house construction and resulted in a contraction in projected growth. By 1973, construction had come to a virtual standstill. Such conditions were bound to show in the missionary expansion of the Archdeaconry. No new diocesan missions were established after 1967. St. Anselm's, Shoreham, begun in the winter of 1965, showed the greatest growth. Holding services at first in the local Lutheran Church, it soon purchased a site for future development, and to act as an interim building purchased a telephone storage plant on Route 25A and converted it into a multi-purpose plant. The advent of Leisure Village, a senior citizens living complex, added greatly to the already growing congregation. In 1966, a parochial mission, St. Edward's, joined the Suffolk churches. The Church of the Holy Trinity, Greenport, purchased a house in Southold and began holding regular Sunday services in that community. The last Suffolk mission established in this period was St. Cuthbert's in Selden. On November 6, 1966, a group of interested churchmen held services in the V.F.W. building in Centereach. Five years later the church had a congregation of over two hundred families, its own priest-in-charge and a church and rectory outgrown by the local Roman Catholic Church. A tragedy occurred in 1969 when the Black church, St. Michael and All Angels in Gordon Heights was partially destroyed by fire. The church was officially closed on October 7, 1970. The Diocese turned the property over to the Town of Brookhaven, donating the land and the fire insurance money of $25,000 to the Town for a town community recreation center. With no new work, support and participation was given to an ecumenical project known as the Smithaven Ministries through the cooperative efforts of churches in the area. A place in the large shopping complex, Smithaven Mall, was occupied. Task forces offered information and church referrals, child care, counselling, and other helpful aids to the transient shopper. A financial crisis in 1972 endangered the work, but through the efforts of the local real estate owner, and a move to smaller quarters, the ecumenical work was assured more years of service.

Suffolk parishes and missions felt the ill-effects of the times. Decreasing membership and lessening church school rolls showed in such established parishes as Trinity, Northport; St. Ann's, Sayville; St. Mark's, Islip and Grace, Riverhead. One former diocesan mission, incorporated as a parish, erected a new church plant: St. Mary's, Lake Ronkonkoma, incorporated in 1972, razed its 104 year-old structure and erected a new Norman-Gothic structure, more able to accommodate the quadrupled congregation.

THROW OUT THE LIFE LINE

A movement that could not be ignored for long by the Diocese and its churches was the growing pre-occupation in many Christian churches with individual pietism. Manifestations of the need for some kind of spiritual direction erupted in such novel ways as "Jesus freaks," "Children of God," and the whole "Moonies" movement. In the more traditionally oriented and established churches, surfaced the Pentecostal Movement, the Charismatic Movement, Faith Alive and Youth for Christ. The "born-again" Christian appeared in many churches, not the least of which was the Episcopal. Recognizing the influence and assaying the value that these various outgrowths of the same spirit showed, in 1972 Bishop Sherman issued a "Call to Renewal." As an "attack on the spirit of war-weariness and cynicism and despair" resulting from the Vietnam War and the "prevailing secularism" of the times, the Bishop called for an intensive period of prayer, Bible study and spiritual outreach. The climax of the Call to Renewal was to be the visit of the Bishop of Coventry, the Right Rev. Cuthbert Bardsley, Chairman of Evangelism for England.

Preparation for the diocesan campaign began in March 1972, with the visit of two of his assistants who met with diocesan groups. At the Clergy Conference the shape of the Diocesan Mission was "hammered together." Again in January 1973, another aide of the Coventry Bishop was sent. A Clergy Conference in October 1972, a Pre-Lenten Retreat for Clergy in February 1973, and a series of coordinating meetings led up to the visit of the Bishop of Coventry in the fall. A special prayer for the Call to Renewal was written by Bishop Martin. Bishop Bardsley visited the Diocese from October 25 to November 2, 1973. The visit consisted of two major gatherings, "teach-ins" in the day at strategic locations in the Diocese, and services and rallies in the evenings. At the teach-ins he spoke informally to the gathering of clergy and laity, and at the rallies he preached. The response to the call was "enthusiastic." Establishment of local prayer groups and Bible Study groups was encouraged. Such spiritual opportunities were taken by some of the parishes. Bishop Sherman himself reached many parishes with his "Tour of the Scriptures" and encouraged the continuance of the interest. The diocesan prayer had been picked up and incorporated into devotional manuals in other dioceses and parts of the Anglican Communion. With the departure of Bishop Bardsley, Bishop Sherman encouraged parishes to continue the spirited movement, stating clearly that the Call to Renewal had only begun.

ON THE HORIZON

As soon as Bishop Sherman was elected and installed as the fifth Bishop of Long Island, rumors and speculations as to when he planned to retire circulated the Diocese. Feeling the need to quiet any thought of his imminent retirement, he squarely faced the issue in his Convention address of 1971. Speaking to the assembled Convention he said loudly:

> On the subject of the Episcopate I beg your indulgence for a personal word of clarification as to the future. With canonical changes affecting the retirement of Bishops, I find some of my brothers in the House retiring at the age of sixty-five. God willing I shall reach that age on June 13th, 1972. This fact has understandably given rise to some speculation as to the date of the next episcopal election in Long Island. I think it only fair that you should know my intention in this matter. While a Bishop may retire at sixty-five, he is not required to retire until seventy-two ... My doctors assure me that ... I am in reasonable health. So it is my hope that I may be able to finish this course in faith. This could mean eight more years for me in active duty.

In early February 1974, the Bishop met with his clergy in executive session. At that meeting he announced to all present that he had experienced an "energy crisis" himself and that he felt the time had come to elect a Bishop-coadjutor. Reiterating the same before the Diocesan Convention on February 16, 1974, he also elaborated on it more. For the "smooth and orderly transition of the episcopate," he asked for a special Convention to be held on November 16, 1974. Detaching himself from the process, he recommended the Standing Committee be responsible for "planning a procedure." Again he stated clearly: "Please take note of the fact that I am saying nothing at this time as to the date of my retirement."

219

The Convention responded to his request and set up the procedures for the election of a Bishop Coadjutor. They recommended that a Nominating Committee be formed, consisting of one clergyman and one layman from the Standing Committee, one clergyman and one layman from the Diocesan Council, and one layman and one clergyman from each county, elected at special county meetings of Convention delegates. The committee, utilizing the Planning Committee, had the responsibility of developing a "profile" of the needs of the Diocese, and of calling for and receiving, and itself propose names for consideration. Two pre-convention meetings in each county were planned for the purpose of "involving delegates to the Convention in developing criteria and standards for the selection of a Bishop Coadjutor." They were to select no more than five persons whom they felt were qualified to be presented to the special Convention for the ultimate selection.

The Nominating Committee set to work immediately to find the right persons as candidates for the office. By the cut-off date in August, forty-two names had been received, of whom thirty-nine had been personally interviewed. By the end of September the Committee had narrowed down the number to ten, six from outside the Diocese and four from within. Much in-fighting, pressuring, and politicking went on from the very beginning. One of the finalists had been campaigning in the Diocese for more than a year. The Rev. Robert Terwilliger was well-known in the Diocese because of his frequent speaking visits, and his leadership in Trinity Institute, New York City. The full Nominating Committee met in an October overnight conference at which all the ten candidates came before the Committee personally for the last final evaluation. Certain to be nominated was Dr. Terwilliger. One candidate at least seemed assured to the Mercer coterie who had been working hard and long on a campaign to persuade the Committee. The final five were chosen, among whom, besides Dr. Terwilliger, was a Dean from Chicago; Bishop Martin; a priest from New York; and a priest from Louisiana.

When the last ten were notified of their approval or disapproval, there began a last minute campaign on the part of a small group of dissonants. Counting on a feeling of antipathy for Dr. Terwilliger, and playing to the general sentiment that no local man had been chosen, the Mercer coterie organized a caucus. A series of phone calls and personal contacts netted a small group of clergy who met at the Deanery in Garden City, who went about a circuitous route of selecting their own candidate. The long drawn out clique-dominated meeting, adeptly maneuvered, came up finally with their own candidate, who happened to be one of the Mercer faculty. All at the meeting were firmly to support the candidate and not be swayed.

The Nominating Committee, in order to acquaint the voting delegates with the few nominated candidates, set up a series of regional meetings, at which each appeared singly and spoke. Not to be outdone, the Mercer group set up similar meetings at which their candidate spoke. A little before the date of the Convention, answers to key questions given by the five candidates, with a profile of each candidate, was sent to all the voting delegates; so too the Mercer candidate.

On November 16, 1974, the duly elected clerical and lay delegates, after a celebration of the Holy Eucharist in the Cathedral, assembled in the Cathedral House. After setting the usual procedural rules, the Bishop made a brief statement about the duties of the Coadjutor. After this the Convention went into a Committee of the whole. The Chairman of the Nominating Committee gave the report for that group and presented the names of the five candidates. Two nominations were made from the floor, both being local clergy, one of whom was the dissonant candidate. The report of the Committee on Program and Budget followed, presenting the financial arrangements for the support of the Coadjutor, including a salary of $24,000. After accepting their report the first ballot was cast. It showed an expected large vote in both clergy and laity for Dr. Terwilliger; and a surprising number of votes for the Rev. Robert C. Witcher from Louisiana. On the second ballot both candidates gained more votes. The third ballot showed Dr. Terwilliger near victory, with Fr. Witcher not too far behind. Before the casting of the fourth ballot, the Mercer candidate suddenly withdrew. Not knowing which way the voting would turn, the assembled delegates were surprised to learn that on the fourth ballot the Louisianian had been elected the sixth Bishop of the Diocese of Long Island.

The Bishop Coadjutor-elect was in many ways a stranger to the Diocese. Except for a few men in the Diocese who had been with him at seminary, or those who knew him from General Convention, he did not have a wide spread of personal friends. Born and raised in Louisiana, his whole life, except for wartime service, had been spent in that State. He attended Tulane University, Seabury Western Seminary, and Louisiana State University, where he received his M.A. and Ph.D. degrees. After his ordination in 1953, he served as priest-in-charge for mission churches, Rector of St. Augustine's, Baton Rouge, Canon Pastor of the New Orleans Cathedral, and finally as Rector of St. James Church in Baton Rouge. His Diocesan and National church positions included Youth Director, Chairman, Department of College Work, President of the Standing Committee, Examining Chaplain, and delegate to the General Convention; all in the Diocese of Louisiana. He also served as Trustee of the University of the South and of Seabury Western Theological Seminary. He was the author of a history *Founding of the Episcopal Church of Louisiana 1803-1838*. He was married and had two children, a girl and a boy.

On Monday, April 7, 1975, the Feast of Annunciation Transferred, the Bishop Coadjutor-elect was consecrated in the Cathedral of the Incarnation. In all the glory of the revised Prayer Book rite, the Presiding Bishop, John M. Allin, together with Bishop Sherman and the Rt. Rev. Iveson B. Noland, Bishop of Louisiana, and friend of the Bishop-elect, consecrated Robert Campbell Witcher a Bishop forever in the Church of God. A reception was held in the Cathedral House honoring the new Bishop and his family. Long Island had its sixth diocesan who, in not too many years, would assume full leadership in the Diocese.

Postword
by The Rt. Rev. Robert Campbell Witcher

I have always had the highest regard for the Diocese of Long Island, but must confess that I have not known and still know very little about it. But as I have been introduced to it over the past several months, it appears to me that the real greatness of the Diocese is still in a potential stage. There have been tremendous accomplishments in the past and yet I think that there are great things in store for the future as well. Not only because of its strategic location and its enormous size, there is a potential for service to this area and to the Church because of the peculiar make-up of this Diocese. There are such diverse elements in it — geographic, social, economic, ethnic — city, rural, rich, poor, black, white — that the Diocese has the potential for setting an example for the whole Church to follow. The trick is to bring all of these elements into a cohesive family unit, rather than allowing them to be devisive. This Diocese has a unique ability to use political forces and a communication system which is second to none. It is my hope that the politics will be used for carrying out the will of Our Lord and the communication system for proclamating the Gospel and Christian truth in order that we may build ourselves together into one family in Christ. From my own point of view, I would very much like to be as *available*, as *accessible*, as *open* as I possibly can. And to do this, at least for the next year, I must spend as much time out of my office as I possibly can. I would like very much to make a pastoral call on each priest and if he has one, his family, and upon the lay-leadership of the Diocese as well. This will give me the data which I will certainly use and will stop, look and listen many times along the way to begin to formulate a kind of picture which will help me become the kind of pastor and leader that I must become to do my job properly. I cannot, on my part, offer you any great miracles. I can only offer you to be myself with the few talents that I do have to offer, but to offer them fully, freely and generously, to love you and serve you, to love God and serve God.

You have in this Diocese a magnificent set of talents in terms of both clergy and laity, and I hope that God will give me full grace to help you to put it all together to become the great Diocese that God has called us to be. I believe very deeply in the Lord Jesus Christ and in His Holy Catholic Church. I am deeply committed to a sacramental type of ministry and have the highest respect for the traditions of the Church. I also believe that we have to proclaim this with an intense kind of evangelistic fervor. I think it was Billy Sunday who called the Episcopal Church a sleeping giant many years ago. Somehow, we keep slumbering on, dissipating our energies, scrapping over family affairs. I am ready to put this aside and get on with the true proclamation of the Gospel to the millions of people who are standing by waiting to hear the good news. If every person, for example, brought only one person to Baptism and/or Confirmation, how tremendous it would be for the Church.

The opportunities are very definitely here and I want to stop, look and listen to find out how best we can take advantage of these opportunities for Christ and His Church. I do not expect to spend any time at all worrying over the negativisms of our day, even those in our Church. I definitely do want to accentuate the positive. There are tremendous problems which I think that we do have, clergy deployment, missionary strategy, failure of stewardship, but I hope you will view these with me as opportunities. To the laity I would like to say that what happens will largely depend upon you. At the recent last General Convention of the Episcopal Church, people were going around with a button which said 99%. It indicated that more than 99% of the people in the Church are laity. We have some of the finest talent in this country who are members of the Episcopal Church and many of them live in Long Island. I would say that one of the things that I would definitely like to do would be to use the tremendous talents to put together a family in Christ which is exemplary in every way in this Diocese. Human beings, even Christians, being what we are, do not always have to agree. But we also don't have to lose charity. I think that the laity can probably do this if we clergy can properly motivate them and make their talents known. There are many other things which I would like to say, but only want to suggest now that as I begin a new life with you, that I am going to stop, look and listen to Almighty God, to the voice of His Son through His Church, and to the voice of the Holy Spirit through you, and I invite you to do the same.

Bibliography

PRIMARY SOURCE: *Journals of the Conventions of the Protestant Episcopal Church in the Diocese of Long Island*, 1868-1975.

OTHER DIOCESAN MATERIAL:
Journal of the Protestant Episcopal Church in the Diocese of New York, 1864-1869.

Publications: *The Helping Hand* which became the *Church Militant* which is now *Tidings*, the official diocesan news publication. *Long Island Calendar, 1902.*

Unpublished Material: MSS *Legality of the Election of Bishop Littlejohn*, Diocesan Archives; MSS *Diary of Henry G. Harrison*, Diocesan Archives.

CHURCH HISTORY: GENERAL SOURCES
Hastings, Hugh, supervisor; *Ecclesiastical Records of the State of New York*, 3 volumes, Albany, 1902.

CHURCH HISTORY: THE EPISCOPAL CHURCH
Addison, James Thayer; *The Episcopal Church in the United States*, New York, 1951.

Albright, Raymond W.; *A History of the Protestant Episcopal Church*, New York, 1964.

Bayne, Jr., Stephen F. ed.; *Mutual Responsibility and Interdependence in the Body of Christ with related background documents*, New York, undated.

Chorley, E. Clowes; *Men and Movements in the Episcopal Church*, New York, 1946.

DeMille, George E.; *The Episcopal Church Since 1900*, New York, 1955.

Executive Council, The; *Church and Society in Crisis, Social Policy of the Episcopal Church, 1964-1967*, New York, 1967.

Hodges, George; *Three Hundred Years of the Episcopal Church in America*, Philadelphia, 1906.

Manross, William; *A History of the American Episcopal Church*, 2nd edition, revised and enlarged, New York, 1950.

McConnell, Samuel D.; *History of the American Episcopal Church*, New York, 1891.

Perry, William Stevens; *The History of the Episcopal Church, 1587-1883*, 2 volumes, Boston, 1885.

St. Clair Will, Theodore; *The Episcopal Church, Heritage of American Christians*, Milwaukee, 1934.

Tiffany, Charles A.; *A History of the Protestant Episcopal Church in the United States of America*, New York, 1895.

SECULAR HISTORY: GENERAL
Allen, Frederick Lewis; *Only Yesterday*, New York, 1964; *Since Yesterday*, New York, 1961; *The Big Change*, New York, 1961.

Faulkner, Harold U.; *The Quest for Social Justice, 1898-1914*, New York, 1931.

Gossett, Thomas F.; *Race: The History of an Idea in America*, New York, 1965.

Lord, Walter; *The Good Years from the 1900s to the First World War*, New York, 1962.

Mowry, George E.; *The Era of Theodore Roosevelt and the Birth of Modern America*, New York, 1962.

Mowry, George E.; *The Twenties, Fords, Flappers, and Fanatics*, Englewood Cliffs, 1963.

Meyers, Gustavus; *History of the Great American Fortunes*, New York, 1937.

Nevins, Allan; *The Emergence of Modern America*, New York, 1935.

Schlesinger, Arthur M.; *The Rise of the City*, New York, 1933.

Slossons, Preston W.; *The Great Crusade and After, 1914-1928*, New York, 1930.

Sullivan, Mark; *Our Times: The United States 1900-25*, Vol. 5, 6, New York, 1933.

Wechter, Dickson; *The Age of the Great Depression, 1929-1941*, New York, 1948.

STATE SOURCES AND URBAN STUDIES
Ellis, David H.; Frost, James A.; and Carman, Harry J.; *A Short History of New York State*, Ithaca, 1957.

Flick, Alexander C., editor; *History of New York State*, 10 volumes, New York, 1937.

Nevins, Allan and Kraut, J. A., editors; *The Greater City, New York 1898-1948*, New York, 1948.

Van Pelt, Daniel; *Leslie's History of the Greater New York*, 2 volumes, New York, undated.

LONG ISLAND SOURCES
Bailey, Paul; *Historic Long Island in Pictures, Prose, and Poetry*, Amityville, 1956.

Bailey, Paul, editor; *Long Island, A History of Two Great Counties, Nassau and Suffolk*, 2 volumes, New York, 1949.

Gabriel, Ralph Henry; *The Evolution of Long Island*, New York, 1921.

Hazelton, Henry Isham; *The Boroughs of Brooklyn and Queens, The Counties of Nassau and Suffolk, 1609-1925*, 3 volumes, New York, 1925.

Munsel, W. W. and Co.; *History of Queens County, New York 1683-1882*, New York, 1882.

Overton, Jacqueline; *Long Island Story*, sequel, Bernice Marshall, *The Rest of the Story*, Port Washington, 1961.

Pelletreau, William S.; *A History of Long Island from Its Early Settlement to the Present Time*, New York, 1903.

Ross, Peter; *History of Long Island*, 2 volumes, New York, 1903.

Ruther, Frederick; *Long Island Today*, New York, 1909.

Smits, Edward J.; *The Creation of Nassau County*, Mineola, N.Y., 1960; *Nassau Suburbia, U.S.A.*, Garden City, N.Y., 1974.

Stiles, Henry R., editor; *The Civil, Political, Professional, and Ecclesiastical History, A Commerical and Industrial Record of the County of Queens and the City of Brooklyn from 1683-1884*, New York, 1884.

Stiles, Henry R.; *A History of the City of Brooklyn*, 3 volumes, New York, 1870.

Syrett, Harold C.; *The City of Brooklyn, a Political History of Brooklyn, 1865-1898*, New York, 1944.

Thompson, Benjamin F.; *History of Long Island*, 3rd edition, 3 volumes, New York, 1918.

Weld, Ralph Foster; *Brooklyn is America*, New York, 1950.

Wilson, Rufus Rockwell; *Historic Long Island*, New York, 1902.

LOCAL SOURCES:
Brooklyn Savings Bank, The; *Old Brooklyn Heights, 1827-1927*, New York, 1927.

Callendar, James H.; *Yesterdays in Brooklyn Heights*, New York, 1927.

Carven, Rev. Charles E.; *A History of Mattituck, Long Island, New York*, privately printed, 1906.

Discen, Vernon; *The History of Central Islip*, Brentwood, New York, 1954.

Erwin, Francis; *Oyster Bay and History, A Sketch*, privately printed.

Kent, Charles M.; *A Historical Sketch of Merrick, Long Island*, New York, 1900.

Mager, Roger W.; *Roslyn Then and Now*, Roslyn, New York, 1952.

Maudville, G. H.; *Flushing, Past and Present*, 1860.

Meier, Evelyn Rowley; *The Wading River, Pauguaconsuk*, Riverhead, New York, 1955.

North, Edgerton G.; *The First One Hundred Years, 1851-1951*, New York, 1951.

Persell, Edith M.; *Across the Years, The Story of Floral Park*, Uniondale, New York 1958.

Smith, Mildred H.; *History of Garden City*, Manhasset, New York, 1963.

Waller, Henry D.; *History of the Town of Flushing*, New York, 1899.

LOCAL PARISH SOURCES: HISTORIES

Astoria, New York: The Rev. Edmund D. Cooper, *An Historical Discourse Delivered in the Church of the Redeemer, Astoria, Long Island in the First Sunday in Advent, 1879*, printed in the Star office, 1880.

Amityville: *Seventy-fifth Anniversary of St. Mary's Church, Amityville, New York, 1886-1961*, privately printed.

Brooklyn: Drowne, T. Stafford; *A Commemorative Discourse*, New York, 1868.

Clippings, Church the Transfiguration, Brooklyn. Anschultz, J. Phillip; *The Church of the Holy Spirit, Brooklyn*, mss.

St. John's, St. John's Place: *St. John's — A Brief History*, mss.

Epiphany Church: Folder: Historical Data 1921- ; *The History of the Church of the Epiphany, Brooklyn, New York*, mss.

St. Phillips Church, Dyker Heights: *Fortieth Anniversary Issue, 1940; Sixtieth Anniversary, 1900-1960*.

St. Ann's Church: *Days Gone By*, privately printed.

All Saints: *We Have This Treasure, Ninety-Fifth Anniversary of All Saints, Brooklyn, New York*, mss.

St. Paul's, Clinton and Carroll Streets: *History of St. Paul's Church, Brooklyn, New York*, mss.

Church of the Nativity: *Twenty-Fifth Anniversary, Silver Jubilee of the Church of the Nativity, Brooklyn 1910-1935*, privately printed.

St. Mary's: "St. Mary's Church, Brooklyn, New York" *Tidings*, April 1965.

Chitteck, Richard O.; *St. Paul's Church in the Village of Flatbush, 1836-1936*, Brooklyn, 1936.

Church of the Redeemer: *1947 Directory, Church of the Redeemer, Fourth Avenue and Pacific Street, Brooklyn*, "A Romantic History" pp. 27-35, privately printed.

Christ Church, Bay Ridge: Sarah Mary Wilson Huntley, *In the City and in the Field, The History of Christ Church, Bay Ridge, New York, 1853-1953*, Lancaster, Pa., 1954.

Church of the Holy Trinity, Montague Street: Reynolds, Lewis; *Centennial of the Church of the Holy Trinity, 1847-1947*, privately printed.
Brown, Roscoe C.E.; *Church of the Holy Trinity, Brooklyn Heights in the City of New York, 1847-1922*, New York, 1922.

Grace Church, Brooklyn Heights: *Grace Church, Brooklyn Heights, Semi-centennial, 1847-1897*, Brooklyn, 1897.

Babylon: *Christ Church, Babylon, New York: A Brief Parish History*, privately printed.

Baldwin, All Saints Church: Commemorative Booklet Committee, *A Record of Devotion and a Plea for Progress*, privately printed, 1950.

Belle Harbor: Sheldon H. Graves; *The Fiftieth Anniversary of the Laying of the Cornerstone of St. Andrew's by-the-Sea, Belle Harbor, Long Island*, mss 1956.

Bellerose: "A Brief History of St. Thomas' Church, Bellerose," 1952 Church Directory, privately printed.

Brookhaven: Thomas I. Morrow, *A Look Over Our Shoulder, A Short History of St. James' Church, 1872-1962*, mimeographed.

Carle Place: William Barbour, *St. Mary's Episcopal Church, Carle Place, New York, Tenth Anniversary*, privately printed.

Center Moriches: *St. John's Episcopal Church, 1898-1962*, unpublished mss.

College Point: Benjamin Mottram, *St. Paul's Church, College Point 1858-1958*, privately printed.

Deer Park: *History of St. Patrick's Church, Deer Park*, mss.

Douglaston: Peter Mesney, *A Brief History of Zion Episcopal Church*, privately published; *The Story of Zion Episcopal Church, Douglaston, Long Island*, as told by Mrs. R. Barfort Krieg, privately printed, 1965.

Elmhurst: Minnie M. Germond, *A Brief History of St. James' Parish, Elmhurst, Long Island, New York, 1704-1954*, privately printed.

Farmingdale: Lorraine Leever, Compiler, *History of St. Thomas' Episcopal Church, Farmingdale, New York, Ninetieth Anniversary, 1875-1965*, mimeographed, 1965.

Floral Park: Historical Data Folder, St. Elizabeth's Church; "St. Elizabeth's Church, Floral Park, Miscellanea" *The Gateway*, Vol. XXI, No. 10, Nov. 21, 1946.

Forest Hills: Stanley Rayfield, *This Parish Under God*, privately printed, 1958.

Freeport: *Historical Data About Our Church, Church of the Transfiguration, Freeport*, mss.

Garden City: Very Rev. Arthur B. Kinsolving, "The History of the Cathedral of the Incarnation, Tones and Overtones," *The Long Island Forum*, Vol. II, No. 12, December, 1939; William M. Baldwin, *The Cathedral of the Incarnation in the Diocese of Long Island*, mss, 1936; Mary F. Youngs, *History of the Cathedral of the Incarnation*, unpublished mss.

Glen Cove: *A Short History of St. Paul's Church, Glen Cove, 1833-1958*, privately printed, 1958.

Greenport: *The Church of the Holy Trinity, Greenport, New York, 110th Anniversary 1863-1973*, privately printed.

Hempstead: Rev. William M. Carmichael, *The Rise and Progress of St. George's Church, Hempstead*, Flushing, N.Y. 1841; Rev. William Moore, *History of St. George's Church Hempstead*, New York 1881; Rev. John M. Haight, *Adventurers for God*, New York, 1932.

Hicksville: *A History of Holy Trinity Church, Hicksville*, mimeographed.

Hollis: *St. Gabriel's Church, Hollis, New York, Diamond Jubilee, 1887-1962*, privately printed, 1962.

Huntington: The Rev. Albert E. Greanoff, *Historical Narrative of St. John's Church, Huntington, New York, 1748-1948*, privately printed; The Rev. Charles William Turner, ed. *Annals of St. John's Church, Huntington, Long Island*, Huntington, N.Y. 1895.

Jackson Heights: *The Mark of St. Mark's Jackson Heights, Fortieth Anniversary,* Issue, Vol. II, No. 3, November 1963.

Jamaica: Horatio Oliver Ladd, *The Origin and History of Grace Church, Jamaica, New York,* New York, 1914.

Long Beach: *Silver Jubilee Historical Journal, 1926-1951, St. James Episcopal Church, Long Beach,* privately printed, 1951.

Lynbrook: *Christ Church, Lynbrook, Sixtieth Anniversary, 1903-1963,* privately printed.

Manhasset: Sesqui-centennial Committee, *Christ Church, Manhasset, The First One Hundred and Fifty Years, 1802-1952,* privately printed, 1952.

Malverne: Mrs. George Cerousso, compiler, *Silver Jubilee, St. Thomas' Episcopal Church of Malverne, New York,* privately printed, 1955.

North Bellmore: *St. Mark's Church, North Bellmore,* mss.

Oyster Bay: Mulford O. Cornell, *Two Hundred Fifty Years of Christ Episcopal Church, Oyster Bay, Long Island,* Hempstead, N.Y., undated.

Patchogue: Newspaper Clippings, *St. Paul's Church Builds for the Future,* privately printed, 1960.

Port Washington: *Briefs from St. Stephen's Church, Port Washington,* privately printed.

Queens Village: The Men's Club, St. Joseph's Church, *A History of St. Joseph's Church, Queens Village, New York, 1870-1950,* Queens Village, 1950.

Quoque: *The Seventy Fifth Anniversary, Church of the Atonement, Quoque, Long Island, New York, 1884-1959,* privately printed 1959.

Richmond Hill: *A Glance Backward and a Glimpse Forward, The Church of the Resurrection, Richmond Hill, New York,* privately printed, undated.

Riverhead: *Grace Episcopal Church in the Town of Riverhead, Long Island, New York, An Historical Sketch of Seventy-Five Years, 1870-1945,* privately printed, 1945.

Sayville: Charles G. Stevenson, Maj. Gen. Rtd., *St. Ann's Church, Sayville, A Centennial Historical Sketch, 1866-1966,* Sayville, 1967.

Sea Cliff: *A Review of Twenty-Five Years of St. Luke's Parish, Sea Cliff, New York, 1889-1914,* privately printed.

Setauket: *Caroline Church of Brookhaven Restoration of 1937,* privately printed.

Shelter Island: *St. Mary's Episcopal Church, Shelter Island, New York,* mss.

Smithtown: *We Go Forward, St. Thomas of Canterbury, Smithtown,* May, 1962.

Stony Brook: *The Centennial Anniversary Year, 1960, All Souls Church, Stony Brook, Long Island,* privately printed, 1960.

Valley Stream: *Mission Chapel and Parish, A Brief History of Trinity Church, Valley Stream,* mss.

Wantagh: *St. Jude's Church Journal, Fourth Anniversary Issue,* privately printed.

Westbury: The Rev. E. Frederic Underwood, Ph.D., *The First Fifty Years, Church of the Advent, Westbury,* privately printed, 1960.

Westhampton Beach: *St. Mark's Church, Westhampton Beach,* privately printed.

Whitestone: *Grace Episcopal Church, Whitestone, New York, Centennial Celebration, 1858-1958,* privately printed, 1958.

SPECIAL STUDIES:
Brandt, Joseph R.; *Why Black Power*, New York, 1968.

Cox, Harvey; *The Secular City*, New York, 1965.

Franklin, John Hope; *A History of Negro Americans*, 3rd ed. New York, 1968.

George, Henry; *Progress and Poverty*, New York, 1902.

Gladdens, Washington; *Applied Christianity*, New York, 1886.

Hadden, Jeffrey K.; *The Gathering Storm in the Churches, The Widening Gap Between Clergy and Laymen*, Garden City, New York, 1969.

Johnson, Douglas W.; *Punctured Preoccupation: What North American Christians Think About the Church*, New York, 1972.

Robinson, John A. T.; *Honest to God*, Philadelphia, 1963.

Sharp, John K.; *History of the Diocese of Brooklyn, 1853-1953*, 2 volumes, New York, 1954.

Van Buren, Paul M.; *The Secular Meaning of the Gospel, Based on an Analysis of Language*, New York, 1966.

BIOGRAPHICAL MATERIAL, REMINISCENCES, PERSONAL MEMOIRS
Christian, Henry M.; *Walt Whitman's New York*, New York, 1963.

Floyd-Jones, Thomas; *Backward Glances, Reminiscences of an Old New Yorker*, New York, 1914.

Harris, Charles T.; *Memories of Manhattan in the Sixties and the Seventies*, New York, 1928.

Nevins, Allan and Miller, Halsey Thomas; *The Diary of George Templeton Strong*, 4 volumes, New York, 1952.

Patten, Alexander J.; *Lives of the Clergy of Brooklyn and New York Embracing also 200 Biographies of Eminent Living Men in All Denominations*, New York, 1874.

Tredwell, Daniel M.; *Personal Reminiscences of Men and Things on Long Island, Part II*, Brooklyn, 1917.

Van Wykes, Frederic; *Recollections of an Old New Yorker*, New York, 1932.

NEWSPAPERS:
The New York Times

Brooklyn Daily Eagle

The Hempstead Sentinel

The Long Island Star

112